Seth Rogen

GW01551581

Contents

Articles

References

Article Licenses

Seth Rogen

<table>
<tr><td colspan="2" align="center">**Seth Rogen**</td></tr>
<tr><td colspan="2" align="center">
Rogen in August 2007</td></tr>
<tr><td>**Born**</td><td>April 15, 1982Vancouver, British Columbia, Canada</td></tr>
<tr><td>**Occupation**</td><td>Actor, comedian, voice artist, producer, screenwriter</td></tr>
<tr><td>**Years active**</td><td>1995–present</td></tr>
</table>

Seth Rogen (born April 15, 1982) is a Canadian actor, comedian, voice artist, screenwriter, and film producer. Rogen began his career doing stand-up comedy for four years during his teens, coming in second place in the Vancouver Amateur Comedy Contest in 1998. While still living in his native Vancouver, he landed a supporting role in *Freaks and Geeks*. Shortly after Rogen moved to Los Angeles for his role, *Freaks and Geeks* was canceled after one season due to poor ratings. He then got a part on the equally short-lived *Undeclared*, which also hired him as a staff writer.

After landing a job as a staff writer on the final season of *Da Ali G Show*, for which Rogen and the other writers received an Emmy nomination, he was guided by film producer Judd Apatow toward a film career. Rogen was cast in a major supporting role and credited as a co-producer in Apatow's directorial debut, *The 40-Year-Old Virgin*. After receiving critical praise for that performance, Universal Pictures agreed to cast him as the lead in Apatow's next directorial feature, *Knocked Up*.

Rogen has appeared in the films *Donnie Darko*, *You, Me and Dupree*, *Zack and Miri Make a Porno*, *Observe and Report*, and *The Green Hornet*, and also in the Apatow-produced comedies *The 40-Year-Old Virgin*, *Knocked Up*, *Superbad*, *Pineapple Express*, and *Funny People*. He and his comedy partner Evan Goldberg co-wrote the comedy films *Superbad* and *Pineapple Express*, for which he originally intended to headline while in high school. Rogen has provided voice talents in the animated films *Horton Hears a Who!*, *Kung Fu Panda*, and *Monsters vs. Aliens*. He also supports Crowdrise, a charitable networking site.[1]

Early life

Rogen was born in Vancouver, British Columbia, to Sandy, a social worker, and Mark Rogen, who works for non-profit organizations and as an assistant director of a Workmen's Circle.[2] [3] He has described his parents, who met at an Israeli kibbutz, as "radical Jewish socialists."[3] He has one older sister, Danya, who is a social worker. Rogen attended Vancouver Talmud Torah Elementary School and Point Grey Secondary School (although he never graduated), incorporating many of his classmates into his writing. He was also known for the stand-up comedy he performed at Camp Miriam, a Habonim Dror camp.[2] Rogen got his start in show business at age 13, after signing up for a comedy class. At the age of 14, with his friend Evan Goldberg, he co-wrote *Superbad*, reflecting pieces from their childhood and dad. With his deadpan humor, he placed second in the Vancouver Amateur Comedy Contest at 16 years old.

Career

Early career

Rogen's first exposure to the entertainment field began with commercial work in Canada at the age of 13.[4] After trying his hand as a standup comic for a few years, Rogen obtained his first starring role in the series *Freaks and Geeks* with only two auditions. He played cynical, acerbic "freak" Ken Miller. Judd Apatow, the show's co-producer, was very impressed with Rogen's improvisational skills. After the show was cancelled in the middle of its first season, Rogen was cast in a similar role in Apatow's second, also short-lived series, *Undeclared*, and went on to write several episodes. In 2001, Rogen also had a minor role in *Donnie Darko* (playing Ricky Danforth) and in 2003 on an episode of *Dawson's Creek* called "Rock Bottom" as "Bob" in their last season, that he also claims he never saw.[5] Following the cancellation of his second series in 2002, Rogen developed a soured attitude toward television, not wanting to act on another show unless Apatow was involved.

Writing career

Rogen's first major writing job was for Apatow's second short-lived television series, *Undeclared*, for which he was hired as a writer before he was offered an acting role.[6] During the show's run, Rogen wrote one episode by himself and co-wrote four others.[7]

Rogen's experience with *Undeclared* paid off when he and his writing partner, Evan Goldberg, joined the writing staff of *Da Ali G Show* for its second and ultimately final season. In 2005, the *Ali G Show* writing staff, including Rogen and Goldberg, received a Primetime Emmy Award nomination in the Writing For A Variety, Music Or Comedy Program category. Rogen's association with the show's star, Sacha Baron Cohen, who had belonged to the same Jewish youth group, Habonim Dror, was not over, however; in a recent interview with *Tokion* (#55), Rogen claimed to have made uncredited contributions to Cohen's film version of *Borat*, and he is credited with providing additional material for *Brüno*.[8]

In 2008 Rogen won the Best Writing (Film) Canadian Comedy Award for *Superbad*. He had written the script for this 2007 comedy years earlier, as a starring role for himself. The *Superbad* team then looked for "an 18-year-old version" of Rogen and chose frequent Rogen collaborator Jonah Hill (who is slightly less than two years younger).[9] Rogen also wrote the screenplay for the Owen Wilson movie *Drillbit Taylor*, which is based on a 70-page scriptment written by John Hughes.[10]

Acting roles

Rogen returned to the big screen in 2005 with a major supporting role in Apatow's directorial debut *The 40-Year-Old Virgin* alongside Steve Carell. The film was a success, grossing $109,449,237 domestically ($177,358,395 worldwide).[11] Apatow then cast Rogen as the lead in the 2007 film *Knocked Up*.[12] Upon completing *The 40-Year-Old Virgin*, Apatow had approached Rogen about potential starring roles, but the actor suggested many high-concept science fiction ideas. After Apatow insisted that Rogen would work better in real life situations, the two agreed on the accidental pregnancy concept that became *Knocked Up*,[13] for which Rogen was nominated for Best Actor at the 2008 Canadian Comedy Dundies, losing to Michael Cera for his role in *Superbad* which was co-written by Rogen.

Rogen (far right) at Comic-Con in 2010.

In *USA Today*'s recent profile of the so-called "frat pack" group of contemporary actors, they mention those actors' rising salaries makes it financially wiser to cast newcomers like Rogen as supporting characters, citing his roles in *The 40-Year-Old Virgin* and *Dupree* as successful examples.[14] When asked in an interview if he is in the group, Rogen has stated that he is not sure.[5] [15]

Rogen and Apatow were behind the 2007 teen comedy *Superbad* at Sony Pictures. Rogen and Goldberg wrote the film, with Apatow as one of the producers. While Rogen did pen Owen Wilson's *Drillbit Taylor*, he did not appear in it since the script mostly involved high school students. *Freaks and Geeks* co-star James Franco reunited with Rogen for the Rogen/Goldberg-written comedy, *Pineapple Express*.[16] Rogen hosted *Saturday Night Live* on October 6, 2007 and again on April 4, 2009.[17] Rogen's next release was Kevin Smith's *Zack and Miri Make a Porno*, in which he co-starred with Elizabeth Banks.[18] It was the first film Rogen has co-headlined in that grossed under $100 million at the domestic box-office. Rogen also appeared along-side Kevin Smith on the October 18th, 2008 episode of the movie review podcast Scene Unseen.[19]

He starred in the Jody Hill-directed mall cop comedy *Observe and Report*,[20] which opened in theaters on April 10, 2009.[21]

Later in 2009, Rogen starred in Apatow's third directorial feature, *Funny People*, with Adam Sandler. Rogen played a young, inexperienced comic while Sandler played a mentor of sorts to Rogen's character; the film had more dramatic elements in it than Apatow's previous directorial efforts.[22] Other co-stars included Eric Bana and Apatow's wife Leslie Mann.

In April 2008, *Empire* reported that Rogen and Evan Goldberg would write an episode for the animated television series *The Simpsons*.[23] He also voiced a character in the episode.[24] The episode was titled Homer the Whopper and was the season premiere.[25]

After years of speculation, a feature film adaptation of *The Green Hornet* will be handled by Rogen and Evan Goldberg with a theatrical release of January 2011. To prepare for his role, Rogen's physical appearance has been changed through fitness routines. In 2007, in a strategy to garner interest and funding, Rogen created a pre-pre-production trailer for *Jay and Seth vs. The Apocalypse*, a film he is now working on with Goldberg,[26] and is set to produce and take a supporting role in the film *Live With It*, from Mandate Pictures. The film is based on an autobiographical comedy script by screenwriter Will Reiser.[27]

In June 2010, Executive Producer of *Entourage*, Doug Ellin, admitted that he once considered casting Rogen for the program.[28]

Improvisation

Though Rogen has penned scripts for both film and television, his comedic stylings tend to rely heavily on improvisational dialogue. Apatow noticed this improvisation talent on the set of *Freaks and Geeks*, which influenced his decision to have Rogen write for *Undeclared* and pitch jokes for *The 40-Year-Old Virgin*. As with most Apatow projects, the dialogue in Rogen's films is usually not what it was on paper.[13] Rogen says he prefers improvised dialogue because it captures the essence of real friends spouting jokes.[29] Because Apatow never stops rolling after takes, allowing his actors to improvise differently each time, Rogen's three largest film roles to date (*The 40-Year-Old Virgin*, *Knocked Up*, and *Pineapple Express*) all achieved the rare milestone of shooting over a million feet of film, almost unprecedented for comedies.[13]

Influences

Rogen has described the shock of being thrust into an industry where he is now working alongside the comedic icons he grew up watching, such as Adam Sandler, Owen Wilson, and Jim Carrey. Rogen cites the Sandler album *They're All Gonna Laugh at You!* (which features Apatow at certain points) as the funniest thing he has ever heard, stating that the track "At A Medium Pace" was the seed for what became his comedic persona. Rogen was also a huge fan of the *Da Ali G Show*'s first season, so it was a shock to suddenly work for Sacha Baron Cohen. Rogen cites the films *Porky's* and *Bachelor Party*, in addition to films by Kevin Smith, as inspirations for writing sex comedies.[30] In an interview with MTV, he said of Smith "I feel like my strengths were always kind of ripping off a Kevin Smith movie anyway. It's not a far departure."[31] Of Smith and his films, Rogen has gone as far as to say (to Smith) "I wouldn't be a writer if it wasn't for you and your movies."[32]

Personal life

Rogen moved to Los Angeles at the age of 16, after Apatow discovered him in Vancouver. During his late teens, Rogen's parents moved from Canada with him, but by the time he landed his second television series, his parents would live in both Canada and the United States.[7] Rogen still resides in Los Angeles with his fiance, Lauren Miller, whom he met in 2004. She has had minor on-screen roles in a few of Rogen's films. She has also produced, written, and directed for unrelated films.[33] Rogen and Miller became engaged in September 2010.[34]

He is a big fan of *The Simpsons* and has always wanted to work with Matt Groening on a movie. According to "Rotten Tomatoes", his five favorite films are: The Big Lebowski (1998), Ghost Busters (1984), The Last Detail (1973), Total Recall (1990) and Goodfellas (1990).

Filmography

Year	Title	Role	Notes
1999	*Freaks and Geeks*	Ken Miller	TV Series: 18 Episodes
2001	*Undeclared*	Ron Garner	TV Series: 17 Episodes Writer
	Donnie Darko	Ricky Danforth	
2003	*Dawson's Creek*	Bob	TV Series: 1 Episode
2004	*Anchorman: The Legend of Ron Burgundy*	Scottie	
2005	*The 40-Year-Old Virgin*	Cal	Co-Producer
2006	*You, Me and Dupree*	Neil	
2007	*Knocked Up*	Benjamin Stone	Executive Producer
	Jay and Seth vs. The Apocalypse	Seth	Writer
	Superbad	Officer Michaels	Writer/Executive Producer
2008	*The Spiderwick Chronicles*	Hogsqueal	Voice only
	Horton Hears a Who!	Morton the Mouse	Voice Only
	Strange Wilderness	Ranger In The Helicopter	Voice Only
	Drillbit Taylor		Writer Only
	Kung Fu Panda	Master Mantis	Voice only
	Step Brothers	Sporting Goods Manager	
	Pineapple Express	Dale Denton	Writer/Executive Producer
	Zack and Miri Make a Porno	Zack Brown	
2009	*Fanboys*	Admiral Seasholtz Mr Roach "The Pimp" *Star trek* alien	
	Monsters vs. Aliens	B.O.B.	Voice Only
	Observe and Report	Ronnie Barnhardt	
	Funny People	Ira Wright	Executive Producer
	Paper Heart	Himself	Interview
	Family Guy	Himself	TV Series: 2 Episodes Voice Only
	The Simpsons	Lyle McCarthy	TV Series:One episode Voice Only Writer
2011	*The Green Hornet*	Britt Reid/The Green Hornet	Writer/Executive Producer
	Paul	Paul	Voice Only *Post-Production*[35]
	Kung Fu Panda 2: The Kaboom of Doom	Master Mantis	Voice Only *Post-production*
	Live With It	Kyle	Producer *Post-Production*
	Take This Waltz	Lou	*Post-Production*[36]

Awards

Year	Award	Category	Film	Result	Notes
2000	Young Artist Award	Best Performance in a TV Series - Young Ensemble	*Freaks and Geeks*	Nominated	Shared with cast
2005	Primetime Emmy Award	Outstanding Writing for a Variety, Music or Comedy Program	*Da Ali G Show*	Nominated	Shared with writing staff
2006	MTV Movie Award	Best On-Screen Team	*The 40-Year-Old Virgin*	Nominated	Shared with Steve Carell, Paul Rudd, and Romany Malco
2008	High Times Stony Award	2008 Stoner of the year	*Pineapple Express*	Won	
	Canadian Comedy Award	Best Writing (Film)	*Superbad*	Won	
	Canadian Comedy Award	Best Actor (Film)	*Knocked Up*	Nominated	
	MTV Movie Award	Best Comedic Performance, Breakthrough Performance	*Knocked Up*	Nominated	
2009	MTV Movie Award	Best Fight	*Pineapple Express*	Nominated	Shared with James Franco, and Danny McBride
	Teen Choice Award	Choice Movie Actor: Comedy	*Observe and Report, Pineapple Express*	Nominated	
2010	Kids Choice Awards	Best Voice From an Animated Movie	*Monsters vs. Aliens*	Nominated	

References

[1] "Seth Rogen's Charitable Life on Crowdrise" (http://www.crowdrise.com/sethrogen). Crowdrise.com. 2010-05-10. . Retrieved 2010-09-18.

[2] Pfefferman, Naomi. "JewishJournal.com" (http://www.jewishjournal.com/home/preview.php?id=7579). JewishJournal.com. . Retrieved 2010-09-18.

[3] Patterson, John (2007-09-14). "Comedy's new centre of gravity" (http://arts.guardian.co.uk/filmandmusic/story/0,,2168095,00.html). Guardian Unlimited. . Retrieved 2007-09-14.

[4] "Seth Rogen Biography" (http://movies.yahoo.com/movie/contributor/1804494942/bio); Retrieved October 27, 2006; Yahoo! Movies (http://movies.yahoo.com/)

[5] "Interview with Seth Rogen" (http://www.bullz-eye.com/mguide/interviews/2005/seth_rogen.htm); Harris, Will; July 13, 2006; Bullz-Eye.com - Guys' Portal to the Web (http://www.bullzeye.com/)

[6] "Rogen & Rudd From the Knocked Up Set " (http://comingsoon.net/news/movienews.php?id=16031); Newgen, Heather; August 16, 2006; ComingSoon.net (http://www.comingsoon.net/)

[7] "The Seth Rogen Interview" (http://www.televisionwithoutpity.com/articles/content/a5644/); Ariano, Tara (credited as Wing Chung); 2002; Television Without Pity (http://www.televisionwithoutpity.com/)

[8] "The Dynamite Issue!" (http://web.archive.org/web/20070827022057/http://www.tokion.com/html/frontlog/?cat=3). *Tokion Magazine* (55). Archived from the original (http://www.tokion.com/html/frontlog/?cat=3) on 2007-08-27. . Retrieved 2007-08-18.

[9] "SET VISIT: KNOCKED UP" (http://www.chud.com/index.php?type=news&id=7359); Dellamorte, Andre; August 10, 2006; Cinematic Happenings Under Development (http://www.chud.com/)

[10] "Par twists into 'Drillbit' with Wilson" (http://www.hollywoodreporter.com/thr/film/article_display.jsp?vnu_content_id=1002690738); Siegel, Tatiana; June 20, 2006; The Hollywood Reporter (http://www.hollywoodreporter.com/)

[11] "Box Office Mojo - The 40-Year-Old Virgin" (http://boxofficemojo.com/movies/?id=40yearoldvirgin.htm) Retrieved October 27, 2006; BoxOfficeMojo.com (http://www.boxofficemojo.com/)

[12] "'Virgin' director to team with Seth Rogen" (http://www.usatoday.com/life/movies/news/2005-09-02-rogen-movie_x.htm?csp=34) The Associated Press (NY); September 2, 2005; USAToday.com (http://www.usatoday.com/)

[13] "A (Kind of) New Star is Born" (http://www.mtv.com/shared/movies/flickd/k/knocked_up_set_visit_060928/); Carrol, Larry; September 28, 2006; MTV Movies - Flick'd (http://www.mtv.com/shared/movies/flickd/)

[14] "'Frat Pack' splits" (http://www.usatoday.com/life/movies/news/2006-07-12-frat-pack-main_x.htm); Wloszczyna, Susan; December 6, 2005; USA Today.com (http://www.usatoday.com/)

[15] "Movie File: Nicolas Cage, 50 Cent, 'Harry Potter,' Elisha Cuthbert & More" (http://www.mtv.com/movies/news/articles/1537770/08022006/story.jhtml); Carroll, Larry; August 8, 2006; MTV.com - Movies - News (http://www.mtv.com/movies/news/)

[16] Franco to reunite with 'Freaks' pals (http://www.upi.com/NewsTrack/view.php?StoryID=20060923-111422-3997r); United Press International; September 23, 2006; United Press International (http://www.upi.com/)

[17] "Blog Archive » Seth Rogen to host SNL" (http://billhaderonline.com/main/2007/08/06/seth-rogen-to-host-snl/). Bill Hader Online. 2007-08-06. . Retrieved 2010-09-18.

[18] Gundersen, Edna (2007-11-16). "Kevin Smith & Co. make 'Porno'" (http://www.usatoday.com/life/2007-11-15-coming-attractions_N.htm). Usatoday.com. . Retrieved 2010-09-18.

[19] scene unseen (http://www.sceneunseenpodcast.com/html/archive.html)

[20] "Seth Rogen Will Observe and Report" (http://www.comingsoon.net/news/movienews.php?id=42660). ComingSoon.net. 2008-03-06. . Retrieved 2010-09-18.

[21] "Seth Rogen's New Movie Observe and Report" (http://www.ObserveAndReport.org). Observeandreport.org. 2007-07-28. . Retrieved 2010-09-18.

[22] "In the Future with Seth Rogen" (http://www.comingsoon.net/news/movienews.php?id=45672). ComingSoon.net. . Retrieved 2010-09-18.

[23] Liam Burke (2008-04-30). "From Superbad To Superheroes - Evan Goldberg on Hornet and The Boys" (http://www.empireonline.com/news/story.asp?NID=22486). *Empire*. . Retrieved 2008-04-30.

[24] Cindy White (2008-06-04). "Rogen and Goldberg Writing Simpsons Episode" (http://uk.tv.ign.com/articles/879/879150p1.html). IGN. . Retrieved 2008-06-04.

[25] "Breaking News - SETH ROGEN, JONAH HILL, ANNE HATHAWAY, CHRIS MARTIN, SARAH SILVERMAN, ANGELA BASSETT, CHUCK LIDDELL, JACKIE MASON, NEVE CAMPBELL, ELI MANNING, PEYTON MANNING, BOB COSTAS AND THE LATE EARTHA KITT AMONG GUEST VOICES ON 21ST SEASON OF "THE SIMPSONS"" (http://www.thefutoncritic.com/news.aspx?id=20090806fox02). TheFutonCritic.com. 2009-01-14. . Retrieved 2009-10-12.

[26] By (2008-11-17). "November 17, 2008 Rogen, Showtime team on comedy - Network greenlights series for 2009" (http://www.variety.com/article/VR1117996040.html?categoryid=14&cs=1). Variety.com. . Retrieved 2010-09-18.

[27] Seth Rogen Will Try to Bring the Funny to *Cancer* (http://movies.tvguide.com/Movie-News/Seth-Rogen-Try-20190.aspx)" *TV Guide*. October 8, 2008. Retrieved on October 8, 2008.

[28] "Exclusive: Before Their Feud, Entourage Creator Considered Seth Rogen for the Show" (http://www.tvguide.com/News/Ellin-Rogen-Feud-1019859.aspx). TVGuide.com. .

[29] "Seth Rogen" (http://suicidegirls.com/interviews/Seth+Rogen/) Epstein, Daniel Robert; December 13, 2005; Suicide Girls - Interviews (http://suicidegirls.com/interviews/)

[30] "Seth Rogen Interview, Knocked Up" (http://www.moviesonline.ca/movienews_12043.html); Roberts, Sheila; MoviesOnline (http://www.moviesonline.ca/); Retrieved on 2007-19-5

[31] "Seth Rogen, Elizabeth Banks Are Ideal 'Porno' Stars, Says Kevin Smith" (http://www.mtv.com/movies/news/articles/1575636/20071203/story.jhtml); Adler, Shawn

[32] silentbobspeaks The Man Who Would Be Zack (http://silentbobspeaks.com/?p=365)

[33] Lauren Miller (I) (http://www.imdb.com/name/nm1601643/)

[34] "Life & Style Exclusive: Seth Rogen is engaged!" (http://www.lifeandstylemag.com/2010/09/seth-rogan-9-28-2010.html). Life & Style. 2010-09-28. . Retrieved 2010-09-28.

[35] "Principal photography wraps!" (http://www.whatispaul.com/2009/09/09/principal-photography-wraps/), *Paul* official website, 2009-09-09. Retrieved on 2010-02-18.

[36] "Sarah Polley Asks Seth Rogen and Michelle Williams to TAKE THIS WALTZ" (http://www.collider.com/2010/01/28/sarah-polley-asks-seth-rogen-and-michelle-williams-to-take-this-waltz/), *Collider*, 2010-01-28. Retrieved on 2010-02-18.

Further reading

- Patterson, J (2007-09-14). "Comedy's new centre of gravity" (http://film.guardian.co.uk/interview/ interviewpages/0,,2168261,00.html). *Film* (The Guardian). Retrieved 2007-09-23.

External links

- Seth Rogen (http://www.imdb.com/name/nm0736622/) at the Internet Movie Database
- The Education of A Comic Prodigy (http://www.time.com/time/magazine/article/0,9171,1622581-1,00. html) on Time.com (a division of Time Magazine)
- The Onion A.V. Club interview (http://www.avclub.com/content/interview/seth_rogen)
- Seth Rogen Interview (http://www.complex.com/CELEBRITIES/Cover-Story/Seth-Rogen-RZA) in Complex Magazine
- Telegraph.co.uk (http://www.telegraph.co.uk/arts/main.jhtml?xml=/arts/2008/08/15/bfseth115.xml) Interview with Seth Rogen (http://www.telegraph.co.uk/arts/main.jhtml?xml=/arts/2008/08/15/bfseth115. xml)
- "Irony Man" (http://www.elle.com/Entertainment/Movies-TV/Seth-Rogen) ELLE magazine

Freaks and Geeks

Freaks and Geeks	
Genre	Period teen dramedy
Created by	Paul Feig
Starring	Linda Cardellini John Francis Daley James Franco Samm Levine Seth Rogen Jason Segel Martin Starr Busy Philipps Becky Ann Baker Joe Flaherty
Opening theme	"Bad Reputation" by Joan Jett
Country of origin	United States
Language(s)	English
No. of seasons	1
No. of episodes	18 (List of episodes)
Production	
Executive producer(s)	Judd Apatow Paul Feig
Running time	44 minutes
Production company(s)	Apatow Productions DreamWorks Television
Broadcast	
Original channel	NBC
Original run	September 25, 1999 – July 8, 2000

Freaks and Geeks is an American comedy-drama television series, created by Paul Feig and executive produced by Judd Apatow, that aired on NBC during the 1999–2000 television season. Eighteen episodes were completed, but the series was canceled after only twelve had aired.

A fan-led campaign persuaded NBC to broadcast three more episodes in July 2000;[1] the three remaining unaired episodes were not seen until September of that year, when the cable network Fox Family Channel aired them in syndication.[2] The complete series was later released on DVD.

Despite a quick cancellation and only one season with 18 episodes, *Freaks and Geeks* developed a devoted cult following. The series appeared on *Time* magazine's 2007 "100 Greatest Shows of All Time" list,[3] and in 2008 *Entertainment Weekly* ranked it the 13th-best series of the past 25 years.[4]

Plot

The show centers on a teenage girl, Lindsay Weir (Linda Cardellini), and her brother, Sam (John Francis Daley), who attend William McKinley High School during the 1980–1981 school year in the town of Chippewa, Michigan, a fictional suburb of Detroit.

Lindsay's friends constitute the "freaks" — Daniel Desario (James Franco), Ken Miller (Seth Rogen), Nick Andopolis (Jason Segel), Kim Kelly (Busy Philipps) — and Sam's friends constitute the "geeks" — Neal Schweiber (Samm Levine) and Bill Haverchuck (Martin Starr) — of the title. The Weirs' parents, Harold (Joe Flaherty) and Jean (Becky Ann Baker), are featured in every episode. Millie Kentner (Sarah Hagan), Lindsay's nerdy, highly religious former best friend, is a recurring character, as is Cindy Sanders (Natasha Melnick), the pretty, popular cheerleader on whom Sam has a crush.

The show's starting point is Lindsay's transition from her life as an academically proficient student, star mathlete, and proper young girl, with Millie as her like-minded best friend, to an Army-jacket-wearing teenager who hangs out with troubled slackers. Her relationships with her new friends, and the friction they cause with her parents and with her own self-image, form one central strand of the show; the other follows Sam and his group of geeky friends as they navigate a very different part of the social universe trying to fit in.

Cast and characters

Weir family

- Linda Cardellini as Lindsay Weir
- John Francis Daley as Sam Weir
- Joe Flaherty as Harold Weir
- Becky Ann Baker as Jean Weir

Geeks

- Samm Levine as Neal Schweiber
- Martin Starr as Bill Haverchuck

Freaks

- James Franco as Daniel Desario
- Busy Philipps as Kim Kelly
- Jason Segel as Nick Andopolis
- Seth Rogen as Ken Miller

Other students

- Sarah Hagan as Millie Kentner
- Jerry Messing as Gordon Crisp
- Stephen Lea Sheppard as Harris Trinsky
- Natasha Melnick as Cindy Sanders

Faculty

- Dave "Gruber" Allen as Mr. Rosso
- Steve Bannos as Mr. Kowchevski
- Trace Beaulieu as Mr. Lacovara
- Steve Higgins as Mr. Fleck
- Leslie Mann as Ms. Foote
- Thomas F. Wilson as Coach Fredricks

Guest stars and cameo appearances

Early on, the creators of the show were not open to the idea of having guest stars on the show. A denied suggestion from NBC was to have a pop icon like Britney Spears appear as a waitress in one episode. Many of the program's crew, including producer Judd Apatow, thought that such guest-star appearances would greatly detract from the show's quality and realism. However, lesser-known "guest stars" would make occasional unhyped appearances on the show. As the producers began to fear an imminent cancellation, Apatow's old friend Ben Stiller made an appearance as a Secret Service agent in the second-to-last episode of the program, but the appearance only aired after the series had been cancelled.

Other notable guest appearances were made by Thomas F. Wilson (in the recurring role of Coach Fredricks), Chauncey Leopardi (in the recurring role of bully Alan White), Shaun Weiss (in the recurring role of student Sean and the bass player in Nick's band), Joel Hodgson (in the recurring role of a salesman who loves disco), Joanna García (in the recurring role of head cheerleader Vicki Appleby), Kayla Ewell (in the recurring role of pretty new transfer student Maureen Sampson), David Koechner (as a waiter), Kevin Corrigan (as Millie's delinquent cousin), Jason Schwartzman (as a student dealing in fake IDs), Allen Covert (as the liquor store clerk), Matt Czuchry (as a student from rival Lincoln High), Claudia Christian (as Bill's mother), Shia LaBeouf (as the school mascot that gets hurt), Samaire Armstrong (as "Deadhead" Laurie), Ben Foster (who appeared as the mentally handicapped student Eli, and often hyped the show while promoting the film *Liberty Heights*), and Alexander Gould (as Ronnie, the boy Lindsay babysits while high). Veteran character actor Kevin Tighe also appeared in two episodes as Nick's father.

Many of the writers appeared on the show at one point or another. Mike White, for instance, played Kim Kelly's oft-discussed injured brother, first appearing in the fourth episode "Kim Kelly is My Friend". Paul Feig and Gabe Sachs appear uncredited as members of the fictional band "Dimension" in "I'm With the Band". Michael Andrews, the original score composer for the series, plays the role of Dimension's lead singer. Steve Bannos played the recurring role of the math teacher Mr. Kowchevski.

Other notable guest stars include David Krumholtz as Neal's brother Barry, Lizzy Caplan as Sara, and Rashida Jones as Karen Scarfoli, first appearing in the fourth episode, "Kim Kelly is My Friend".

Opening sequence

The series' opening sequence depicts each of the main characters, with the exception of Kim Kelly (Busy Philipps), having their high school yearbook photo taken as the song "Bad Reputation" by Joan Jett and the Blackhearts plays.

Episodes

The show ran for eighteen episodes, three of which were unaired by NBC and not seen until Fox Family began running the show in 2000, and the final three episodes were premiered at the Museum of Television and Radio prior to being broadcast on television.

Ratings

The show averaged 6.77 million viewers and was #93 in the rankings during its only season.[5]

Media releases

DVDs

On April 6, 2004, a six-DVD *Freaks and Geeks* box set was released through Shout! Factory. A limited "yearbook edition" set including two additional discs was also available through the official website for the show. Fans who had signed an online petition to get the show on DVD got priority in purchasing the special set.[6]

On November 25, 2008, the deluxe "Yearbook Edition" boxed set was re-released. The set features all of the episodes, commentaries, and special features of the "Complete Series" six-DVD set, plus two extra discs and deluxe packaging. It is packaged as an 80-page color yearbook with essays, pictures, and episode synopses.[7]

Freaks and Geeks: The Complete Series	
Set details	**Special features**
• Studio: **Shout! Factory** • 18 episodes • 1.33:1 aspect ratio • English (Dolby Digital 5.1 Surround) • Subtitles: None	• 29 audio commentaries by the actors, writers, directors, network executives, parents of cast members, teachers in character and dedicated fans of the show • Over 60 deleted scenes and outtakes with commentary • 28-page booklet with an essay by series creator Paul Feig, and a Q&A with producer/writer Judd Apatow. • Cast auditions
Release date	
North America — April 6, 2004	

Books

In October 2004, two *Freaks and Geeks* books were released, titled *Freaks and Geeks: The Complete Scripts, Volume 1* and *Freaks and Geeks: The Complete Scripts, Volume 2*. Both published by Newmarket Press, each book covers nine scripts from the series as compiled by Paul Feig and Judd Apatow themselves. Extra content includes behind-the-scenes memos and notes, photos, additional plotlines and excerpts from the *Freaks and Geeks* series bibles.[8] [9]

Soundtrack

One of the distinguishing characteristics that separated *Freaks and Geeks* from similar television series at the time was its authentic soundtrack. The creators made it a priority to feature genuine, period-specific music that would help to create the tone of the show. Clearing such names as The Who, Van Halen, Rush, Styx, the Grateful Dead, The Moody Blues, and Billy Joel would prove to require much of the show's budget. Eventually, this would become an obstacle in releasing the show on DVD due to the difficulty and expense of clearing all of the music rights for the series. Many television shows (such as *Dawson's Creek* and *WKRP in Cincinnati*) had music cues changed or removed in order to facilitate relatively inexpensive DVD releases, as was done for *Freaks and Geeks* when it was seen in reruns on Fox Family. However, the creators chose to wait to release the DVD until they could find a company up to the challenge of gaining clearance for the music, as not to upset the fans of the show. Shout! Factory, a music and video company specializing in comprehensive reissues and compilations of classic and sometimes obscure pop culture eventually brought *Freaks and Geeks* to DVD with all of its music intact.[6]

Awards and nominations

The series received three Emmy Award nominations, creator Paul Feig was nominated twice for Outstanding Writing for a Comedy Series, for "Pilot" and "Discos and Dragons". It won for Outstanding Casting for a Comedy Series (Allison Jones, Coreen Mayrs and Jill Greenberg). It was nominated for two Television Critics Association Awards, for New Program of the Year and Outstanding Achievement in Drama. For acting, the series won for Best Family TV Series – Comedy and was nominated for Best Performance in a TV Series – Young Ensemble at the Young Artist Awards. For the YoungStar Awards, John Francis Daley and Sarah Hagan were nominated for Best Young Actor/Performance in a Comedy TV Series and the ensemble was nominated for Best Young Ensemble Cast – Television. The series also received several other nominations in other categories.[10]

Undeclared and beyond

In 2001, several of the actors featured in *Freaks and Geeks* appeared in a new Judd Apatow college half-hour comedy called *Undeclared*, which aired on Fox Network. Apatow fought with the network to include *Freaks and Geeks* actors, but only picked up Seth Rogen (who was already committed to the show as a writer) as a regular cast member. However, Jason Segel became a recurring character, and Samm Levine, Busy Philipps, and Natasha Melnick guest-starred in multi-episode arcs, as did prominent *Freaks and Geeks* guest stars Steve Bannos and David Krumholtz. Martin Starr was prominent in another episode, and a scene with Sarah Hagan was shot, although it was cut for television broadcast. The show was also canceled during its first season.

Six years later, actors from the two shows comprised the bulk of the starring cast of Apatow's film, *Knocked Up*, with James Franco making a brief cameo appearance as himself. In addition, many of the extras starred as teachers and principal tertiary characters from both shows. Martin Starr, Steve Bannos, and David Krumholtz all appeared as extras in *Superbad*, which was produced by Apatow and co-written by Rogen (who also has a supporting role in the film). *Walk Hard* featured Bannos, Krumholtz, and Starr in minor or cameo roles and recurring *Undeclared* guest Jenna Fischer in a lead role.

In 2008, Rogen and Franco co-starred in the Judd Apatow-produced comedy film *Pineapple Express*.

In June 2010, it was announced that IFC had acquired the rights to air both *Freaks and Geeks* and *Undeclared*.[11] *Freaks and Geeks*'s 18-episode run on IFC finished with all episodes having aired as of October 29, 2010. *Undeclared*'s IFC run began on November 5, 2010.

References

[1] "Geek Love" (http://www.salon.com/entertainment/log/2000/04/20/geeks/index.html). *Salon.com*. April 20, 2000. . Retrieved December 9, 2010.

[2] "RetroWeb Classic Television: Freaks and Geeks" (http://www.retroweb.com/freaksandgeeks.html#episodes). *RetroWeb.com*. . Retrieved December 9, 2010.

[3] "Freaks and Geeks - The 100 Best TV Shows of All" (http://www.time.com/time/specials/2007/article/0,28804,1651341_1659188_1652518,00.html). *TIME*. September 6, 2007. . Retrieved June 16, 2010.

[4] "The New Classics" (http://www.ew.com/ew/article/0,,20207076_20207387_20207339,00.html). *Entertainment Weekly*. June 17, 2008. . Retrieved June 16, 2010.

[5] "Charts and Data" (http://www.variety.com/index.asp?layout=chart_pass&charttype=chart_topshows99&dept=TV). *Variety*. August 6, 2000. . Retrieved June 16, 2010.

[6] "Freaks and Geeks - Official Press Release: April 6 is the day!" (http://www.tvshowsondvd.com/news/Freaks-Geeks/976). *TVShowsOnDVD*. January 15, 2004. . Retrieved August 12, 2010.

[7] "Freaks and Geeks - Shout Sends Over a New Fact Sheet for their Retailer Release of the Yearbook Edition" (http://www.tvshowsondvd.com/news/Freaks-Geeks-Yearbook-Edition/10730). *TVShowsOnDVD.com*. October 20, 2008. . Retrieved December 9, 2010.

[8] "Freaks and Geeks: The Complete Scripts, Volume 1 (Newmarket Shooting Script)" (http://www.amazon.com/dp/155704645X). *Amazon.com*. . Retrieved December 9, 2010.

[9] "Freaks And Geeks: The Complete Scripts" (http://www.amazon.ca/dp/1557046468). *Amazon.ca*. . Retrieved December 9, 2010.

[10] ""Freaks and Geeks" (1999) - Awards" (http://www.imdb.com/title/tt0193676/awards). *Internet Movie Database*. . Retrieved December 9, 2010.

[11] "Freaks and Geeks, Undeclared Return to TV" (http://www.tvguide.com/News/Freaks-Geeks-Undeclared-1020096.aspx). *TV Guide*.
June 30, 2010. . Retrieved August 12, 2010.

External links

- *Freaks and Geeks* (http://www.imdb.com/title/tt0193676/) at the Internet Movie Database
- *Freaks and Geeks* (http://www.tv.com/show/392/summary.html) at TV.com
- Freaks and Geeks (http://www.myspace.com/freaksandgeeksonline) on Myspace
- *Freaks and Geeks* (http://www.shoutfactory.com/browse/31/freaks_and_geeks.aspx) at Shout! Factory

Undeclared

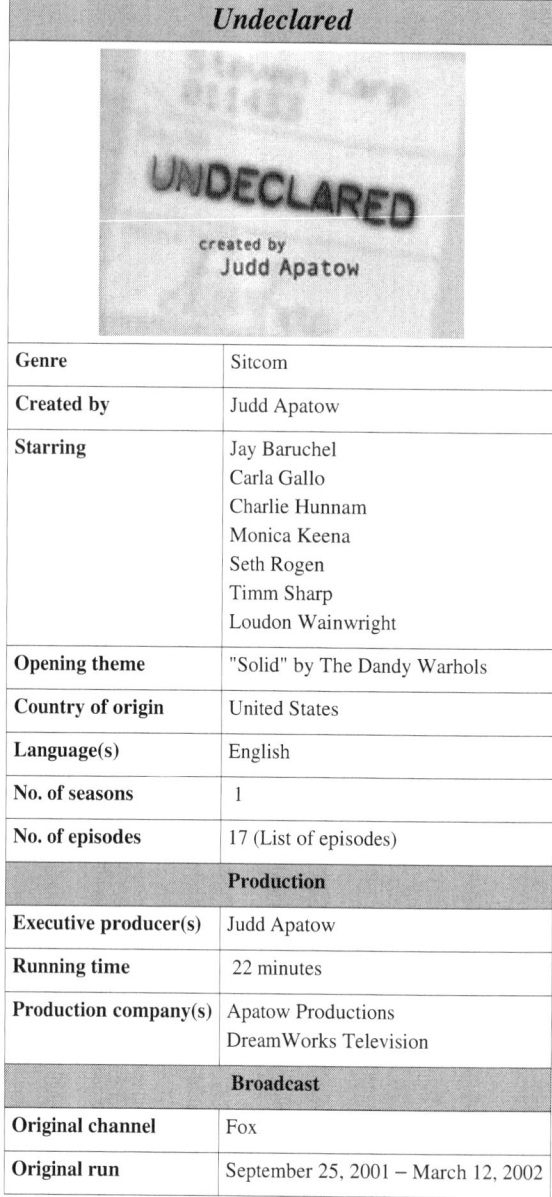

Undeclared	
Genre	Sitcom
Created by	Judd Apatow
Starring	Jay Baruchel Carla Gallo Charlie Hunnam Monica Keena Seth Rogen Timm Sharp Loudon Wainwright
Opening theme	"Solid" by The Dandy Warhols
Country of origin	United States
Language(s)	English
No. of seasons	1
No. of episodes	17 (List of episodes)
Production	
Executive producer(s)	Judd Apatow
Running time	22 minutes
Production company(s)	Apatow Productions DreamWorks Television
Broadcast	
Original channel	Fox
Original run	September 25, 2001 – March 12, 2002

Undeclared is an American television series that aired on The Fox Network during the 2001–2002 season.

Premise

The half-hour situation comedy was Judd Apatow's follow-up to his earlier television series *Freaks and Geeks*, which also lasted for one season. *Undeclared* centered on a group of college freshmen at the fictional University of North Eastern California. Unlike *Freaks*, it was set in the current time of the early 2000s rather than the 1980s. It gave a humorous look at the highs and lows of college life, from young adult relationships to the dreaded freshman fifteen. It takes its name from the status of undergraduates who have not yet decided, or "declared," a specific major of study.

Critique

College is "the reward for surviving high school. Most people have great fun stories from college and nightmare stories from high school," Judd Apatow told the *Los Angeles Times* in 2006.[1] He also speculated on why college shows find it hard to gain a foothold on network schedules: "One reason for the death of college shows is that it's difficult to be honest about campus life on network or basic cable. It's hard to portray truthfully. The truth is, kids are high, drunk and having sex. No matter what you do, you're fudging it."[2]

Media outlets such as *Entertainment Weekly* gave the show generally glowing reviews, though the general audience did not seem to share the same opinion of the show, as Fox canceled the show in March 2002 after poor ratings. In total, 16 episodes were shown on Fox, while one unaired episode was included in the DVD set released in Region 1 on August 16, 2005.

Characters

Main characters

Name	Actor	Major	Description
Steven Karp	Jay Baruchel	Undeclared	Steven was a celibate geek in high school. He has a particular affinity for *The Matrix* and *The X-Files*. He grew up only ten minutes away from the UNEC campus. In college, Steven is fairly popular among the students, but he is still somewhat nerdy.
Lizzie Exley	Carla Gallo	Psychology	Steven's neurotic, highly enthusiastic floor mate and eventual girlfriend. Used to date Eric (Jason Segel) but broke up with him after he found out that she had a one-night stand with Steven during their first day at UNEC.
Lloyd Haythe	Charlie Hunnam	Theater	Steven's British roommate. He often makes Steven leave their room so that he can have sex. Despite constantly picking on Steven, he's also very protective of his roommate and usually tries to look out for his best interests. Due to his popularity with women, Lloyd often serves as an adviser in romantic affairs to all his suitemates. Despite often playing up his Britishness and "manners", Lloyd is often the most aggressive of the group, and very quick to anger.
Rachel Lindquist	Monica Keena	Undeclared	Lizzie's roommate. Is initially nervous at the prospect of living away from her family, but eventually breaks free of her anxiety and embraces a party girl mentality.
Ron Garner	Seth Rogen	Business	Steven's wise-cracking, glasses-wearing, beer-guzzling, chubby Canadian suitemate who comes to U.N.E.C. from Vancouver. With his dry sense of humor, Ron is the brains of the group. Briefly dates Kelly (Busy Philipps), a campus tour guide.
Marshall Nesbitt	Timm Sharp	Music	Steven's suitemate who came to U.N.E.C. from Sioux City, Iowa. His parents still believe that he is a business major, although he switched courses at the last minute. Despite his less-than-stellar work ethic, he is Mr. Burundi's (Gerry Bednob) favorite worker at the cafeteria. Has a crush on Rachel.
Hal Karp	Loudon Wainwright III	(N/A)	Steven's father, who experiences a mid-life crisis after being divorced by Steven's mother. Hal sometimes spends time socially with the gang, which often results in Steven's embarrassment.

Recurring characters

- **Perry Madison** (Jarrett Grode), bland, sarcastic dorm-mate who can DJ and free-style rap. (12 episodes)
- **Tina Ellroy** (Christina Payano), Lizzie and Rachel's suitemate introduced mid-season. Moves into the vacated room in Lizzie and Rachel's suite during the unaired episode "God Visits". (11 episodes)
- **Eric** (Jason Segel), Lizzie's obsessive ex-boyfriend who she breaks up with after sleeping with Steven. Eric had been dating Lizzie since she was in high school, and he is several years older than her. Eric works as the manager of a copy shop. (7 episodes)
- **Adam** (Leroy Adams), student who lives on the gang's floor. (8 episodes)
- **P.B.** (P.B. Smiley), student who lives on the gang's floor. (6 episodes)
- **Trent** (Jim Brooks), student who lives on the gang's floor. (4 episodes)
- **Lucien** (Kevin Rankin), nerdy RA on the gang's floor who has an obsession with Hillary the RA. (4 episodes)
- **Hillary** (Amy Poehler), the head RA who hits on Lloyd; and at one point, dates Hal. (2 episodes)
- **Luke** (Kevin Hart), a religious African-American student on campus who converts Steven to Christianity. (3 episodes)
- **Greg** (David Krumholtz), Eric's close friend and co-worker at the copy shop. (2 episodes)
- **Eugene** (Kyle Gass), Eric's other close friend and co-worker at the copy shop. (2 episodes)
- **Mr. Burundi** (Gerry Bednob), Indian boss at the school cafeteria where Steven and Marshall work. (2 episodes)
- **Kelly** (Busy Philipps), an attractive tour guide on campus who Ron develops a crush on and later begins dating. (2 episodes)
- **Susuki** (Joanne Cho), Tina's roommate, whose constant violin practice annoys Tina. (2 episodes)

Guests and cameos

- Jenna Fischer (as Sorority Girl, "Prototype" and Betty, "Sick in the Head")
- Simon Helberg (as Jack, "Prototype")
- Tom Welling (as Tom, "Prototype")
- Fred Willard (as Professor Duggan, "Oh, So You Have a Boyfriend?")
- Ted Nugent (as himself, "Full Bluntal Nugety")
- Mike White (as Pet Store Employee, "Eric Visits")
- Allen Covert (as himself, "The Assistant")
- Jonathan Loughran (as himself, "The Assistant")
- Adam Sandler (as himself, "The Assistant")
- Jordan Black (as Card Guy, "Addicts")
- Will Ferrell (as Dave, "Addicts")
- Felicia Day (as Sheila, "God Visits")
- Mary Kay Place (as Mrs. Lindquist, "Parent's Weekend")
- Kimberly Stewart (as Amanda, "Parent's Weekend")
- Sarah Hagan (as Jordanna, "Eric Visits Again")
- Steve Bannos (as Dingleberry, "Rush and Pledge")
- Samm Levine (as Books, "Rush and Pledge"/"Hell Week")
- Natasha Melnick (as Jenni, "Rush and Pledge"/"Hell Week")
- Martin Starr (as Theo, "The Perfect Date")
- Youki Kudoh (as Kikuki, "Hal and Hilary")
- Ben Stiller (as Rex, "Eric's POV")

Episodes

Episode order

On the DVD, the episodes are ordered by their original broadcast order, not their production numbers. This is a mistake, according to Judd Apatow. The correct viewing order (with the story in chronological order) is as follows:[3]

1. "Prototype"
2. "Oh, So You Have a Boyfriend?" / "Full Bluntal Nugety"
3. "Eric Visits"
4. "Jobs, Jobs, Jobs"
5. "Sick in the Head"
6. "The Assistant"
7. "Addicts"
8. "God Visits"
9. "Parent's Weekend"
10. "Eric Visits Again"
11. "Rush and Pledge"
12. "Hell Week"
13. "Truth or Dare"
14. "The Day After"
15. "The Perfect Date"
16. "Hal and Hillary"
17. "Eric's POV"

Undeclared DVD cover art

Ratings

The show averaged 7.3 million viewers and was #93 in the rankings during its only season.[4]

Planned storylines

The DVD contains the script to an unproduced episode, "Lloyd's Rampage" (written by Lewis Morton), which was written for the show's second season. It revolves around Lloyd getting into a fight with Kieran, the star student of his acting class, and deciding that he wants to experience real life. So, Steven and Lloyd go to a bar and end up in a fight with some working class men, which impresses Kieran when Lloyd tells him about it. A subplot in the episode revolves around Marshall getting extremely drunk and throwing up in a bar. When he is throwing up, Perry takes a picture and video, and makes T-shirts and posters and puts them around campus. Marshall is embarrassed at first, but he is glad when he finds out about all of the attention that he gets as "Puke Dude". Unfortunately for him, this doesn't last long when everyone forgets about him after another student shits his pants in the library. Perry's last name is revealed to be Madison in this episode. The role of Kieran was written for *That '70s Show* star Topher Grace, but he never appeared in the episode because of a dispute between Judd Apatow and *That 70's Show* co-creator Mark Brazill.[5]

During a question-and-answer session, Judd Apatow stated that if the series had been picked up for a second season, there would have been an episode titled "Eric's Birthday" in which Lizzie and Steven would go to the birthday party mentioned in episode "Eric's POV". Linda Cardellini of *Freaks and Geeks* would have played his new girlfriend. In the episode, Eric would have had a cake with a picture of him and his new girlfriend printed on it. Lizzie would have been given the piece with Eric's new girlfriend's face. At the time Jason Segel was dating Linda Cardellini.

Syndication

In June 2010, it was announced that IFC had acquired the rights to air both *Undeclared* and *Freaks and Geeks*.[6] *Undeclared* premiered on IFC on November 5, 2010.[7]

DVD release

On August 16, 2005, Shout! Factory released the complete series of *Undeclared* on DVD in Region 1. The four-disc boxed set contains all 17 episodes, including an unaired episode and a bonus director's cut.

According to Apatow, the producers were unable to get clearance for all the music in the series (not being able to use about 10 songs). Since the uncleared songs were considered to not play a significant role in the series, they were switched with a suitable substitute.[3]

Undeclared: The Complete Series	
Set details	**Special features**
• Studio: **Shout! Factory** • 17 episodes • 1.33:1 aspect ratio • English (Dolby Digital 5.1 Surround) • Subtitles: None	• A never-before-seen episode ("God Visits") • Director's cut of the second episode featuring Ted Nugent ("Full Bluntal Nugety") • 18 commentaries with directors, writers and the entire cast • Deleted scenes, auditions, outtakes, rehearsals and extended takes • Loudon Wainwright live concert footage • Museum of Television & Radio Q&A • 28-page booklet • Script for unproduced episode
Release date	
Region 1 August 16, 2005	

References

[1] Smith, Lynn (February 5, 2006). "TV graduates to higher ed" (http://articles.latimes.com/2006/feb/05/entertainment/ca-college5). *The Los Angeles Times*. . Retrieved August 14, 2010.

[2] Lynn Smith (February 15, 2006). "TV dramas explore college years" (http://www.thefalcononline.com/story/article.php?id=4856). *The Falcon*. . Retrieved October 11, 2009.

[3] Scott Weinberg (June 27, 2005). "Undeclared - The Complete Series" (http://www.dvdtalk.com/reviews/16552/undeclared-the-complete-series/). *DVD Talk*. . Retrieved July 6, 2010.

[4] "How did your favorite show rate?" (http://www.usatoday.com/life/television/2002/2002-05-28-year-end-chart.htm). *USA Today*. May 28, 2002. .

[5] ""Don't have a cow, man"" (http://www.harpers.org/archive/2002/03/0079095). *Harpers Magazine*. March 2002. . Retrieved October 11, 2009.

[6] Natalie Abrams (June 30, 2010). "Freaks and Geeks, Undeclared Return to TV" (http://www.tvguide.com/News/Freaks-Geeks-Undeclared-1020096.aspx). *TV Guide*. . Retrieved July 6, 2010.

[7] "Undeclared - Series - On Air" (http://www.ifc.com/undeclared/). *IFC.com*. . Retrieved October 30, 2010.

External links

- *Undeclared* (http://www.imdb.com/title/tt0273028/) at the Internet Movie Database
- *Undeclared* (http://www.tv.com/show/2359/summary.html) at TV.com

Donnie Darko

Donnie Darko	
Theatrical release poster	
Directed by	Richard Kelly
Produced by	Adam Fields Nancy Juvonen Sean McKittrick Drew Barrymore
Written by	Richard Kelly
Starring	Jake Gyllenhaal Jena Malone Mary McDonnell Holmes Osborne Katharine Ross James Duval Maggie Gyllenhaal Drew Barrymore Patrick Swayze Noah Wyle
Music by	Michael Andrews
Cinematography	Steven B. Poster
Editing by	Sam Bauer Eric Strand
Studio	Flower Films
Distributed by	Pandora Newmarket Films
Release date(s)	October 26, 2001
Running time	113 minutes
Country	United States
Language	English

Budget	$4.5 million[1]
Gross revenue	$4,116,307[2]
Followed by	*S. Darko*

Donnie Darko is a 2001 American Surrealist thriller film directed and written by Richard Kelly and starring Jake Gyllenhaal, Drew Barrymore, Patrick Swayze, Maggie Gyllenhaal, Noah Wyle, Jena Malone, and Mary McDonnell. The film depicts the reality-bending adventures of the title character as he seeks the meaning and significance behind his troubling Doomsday-related visions.

The film was initially slated for a direct-to-video release before being picked up by Newmarket Films. Budgeted with $4.5 million[1] and filmed over the course of 28 days, the film missed breaking even at the box office, grossing just over $4.1 million worldwide.[2] Since then, the film has received favorable reviews from critics and developed a large cult following,[3] resulting in the director's cut receiving a two-disc, special edition release in 2004.[4]

Plot

In October 1988, teenager Donnie Darko (Jake Gyllenhaal) has been seeing a psychiatrist because of his troubled history. Donnie sleepwalks, and he has visions of Frank (James Duval), a menacing, demonic-looking rabbit. On October 2, Frank draws Donnie out of his room to tell him that, in 28 days, 6 hours, 42 minutes and 12 seconds, the world will end. While Donnie is outside, a jet engine crashes through his bedroom. The next morning, Jim Cunningham (Patrick Swayze), a motivational speaker, finds Donnie sleeping on the golf course and wakes him. Donnie returns home to find police and firemen at his home. After an initial investigation, no one knows where the jet engine has come from. The following day, Donnie meets Gretchen Ross (Jena Malone), a new student, who becomes one of the few people with whom Donnie can share his visions.

Donnie's father, Eddie (Holmes Osborne), takes Donnie to his therapist, Dr. Lillian Thurman (Katharine Ross), and nearly runs over Roberta Sparrow (Patience Cleveland), a seemingly senile old woman known as "Grandma Death". Afterward, Dr. Thurman increases Donnie's medication and begins hypnotherapy. Frank continues to appear to Donnie and manipulates him to commit a series of crimes and, also, tells Donnie about time travel. Donnie floods the school, steals his father's gun, and burns the home of Jim Cunningham, where firemen uncover a "kiddie porn dungeon".

Donnie, along with his older sister, Elizabeth (Maggie Gyllenhaal), decide to throw a Halloween party while their mother, Rose (Mary McDonnell), and younger sister, Sam, (Daveigh Chase), are away at a dance competition. Gretchen comes to Donnie's house for safety because her mother has suddenly disappeared, likely because of her threatening stepfather, and she and Donnie have sex for the first time at the party. At midnight, Donnie realizes that the 28 days have passed and that only 6 hours remain until the end of the world. Donnie leaves to visit "Grandma Death" along with Gretchen and two friends. While there, they are assaulted by the high school bullies (Alex Greenwald and Seth Rogen). Gretchen is knocked unconscious and thrown into the street. An approaching car swerves to avoid "Grandma Death", standing in the road, but runs over Gretchen, killing her. As the bullies run off, a man wearing a rabbit costume emerges from the car, and it's Elizabeth's boyfriend, Frank. Frank starts yelling at Donnie, who shoots Frank with his father's stolen pistol.

Donnie carries Gretchen's lifeless body to his home, places her in the family car, and speeds away, watching from nearby as a tornado forms over the city. For once, Donnie seems at peace as a vortex engulfs the jet his mother and sister are returning home in. The storm damages the plane causing an engine to fall off before Donnie transports it back in time to 28 days earlier using a wormhole. This time, though, Donnie chooses to stay in bed. He laughs and turns over as if to sleep just as the jet engine crashes through his bedroom, causing a plank to impale him (on the DVD's outtakes). As his body is taken away the next morning, Gretchen passes by on her bike and is informed by a neighborhood boy about what has happened. Gretchen tells the boy that she didn't know Donnie, and she gives a sympathetic wave to Rose.

Cast

- Jake Gyllenhaal as Donald "Donnie" Darko
- Jena Malone as Gretchen Ross
- Mary McDonnell as Rose Darko
- Holmes Osborne as Edward "Eddie" Darko
- Katharine Ross as Dr. Lilian Thurman
- James Duval as Frank
- Maggie Gyllenhaal as Elizabeth Darko
- Drew Barrymore as Karen Pomeroy
- Patrick Swayze as Jim Cunningham
- Noah Wyle as Dr. Kenneth Monnitoff
- Daveigh Chase as Samantha "Sam" Darko
- Beth Grant as Kitty Farmer
- Stuart Stone as Ronald Fisher
- Alex Greenwald as Seth Devlin
- Seth Rogen as Ricky Danforth
- Patience Cleveland as Roberta Sparrow ("Grandma Death")
- Jolene Purdy as Cherita Chen
- Ashley Tisdale as Kim
- Jerry Trainor as Lanky Kid
- David St. James as Bob Garland

Production

Filming

Donnie Darko was filmed in 28 days on a budget of $4.5 million.[1] It almost went straight to home video release but was publicly released by Drew Barrymore's production company, Flower Films.[5]

The film was shot in California. The "Carpathian ridge" scenes were shot on the Angeles Crest Highway.[6]

Music

In 2003, composer Michael Andrews and singer Gary Jules found their piano-driven cover of the Tears for Fears' "Mad World", featured in the film as part of the end sequence, a hit and the UK Christmas Number One.[7]

One continuous sequence involving an introduction of Donnie's high school prominently features the song "Head over Heels" by Tears for Fears, Samantha's dance group, "Sparkle Motion", performs with the song "Notorious" by Duran Duran, and "Under the Milky Way" by The Church is played after Donnie and Gretchen emerge from his room during the party. "Love Will Tear Us Apart" by Joy Division also appears in the film diegetically during the party and shots of Donnie and Gretchen upstairs. However, the version included was released in 1995, although the film is set in 1988. The opening sequence is set to "The Killing Moon" by Echo & the Bunnymen. In the theatrical cut, the song playing during the Halloween party is "Proud to be Loud" by Pantera, a track released on their 1988 album, which would coincide with the time setting of the film. However, the band is credited as "The Dead Green Mummies".

In the re-released Director's Cut version of the film, the music in the opening sequence is replaced by "Never Tear Us Apart" by INXS; "Under the Milky Way" is moved to the scene of Donnie and his father driving home from

Donnie's meeting with his therapist; and "The Killing Moon" is played as Gretchen and Donnie return to the party from Donnie's parents' room.

Release

The limited release of the film occurred during the month after the September 11 attacks. It was subsequently held back for almost a year for international release, where it garnered more favorable reviews. From this point, a large cult following for the movie began. Its DVD release gained an increased American audience for the film.

Marketing

- *The Donnie Darko Book*, written by Richard Kelly, is a 2003 book about the film. It includes an introduction by Jake Gyllenhaal, the screenplay of the Donnie Darko Director's Cut, an in-depth interview with Kelly, facsimile pages from the *Philosophy of Time Travel*, photos and drawings from the film, and artwork it inspired.
- NECA released first a six-inch (15 cm) figure of Frank the Bunny and later a foot-tall (30cm) 'talking' version of the same figure.

Home media

The film was originally released on VHS and DVD in March 2002. Strong DVD sales led Newmarket Films to release a "Director's Cut" on DVD in 2004. Bob Berney, President of Newmarket Films, described the film as "a runaway hit on DVD," citing United States sales of more than $10 million.

The film was released in the US on Blu-ray on February 10, 2009.

The film was released as a 2-disc Blu-ray special edition in the UK on July 19, 2010 by Metrodome Distribution and featuring both Original and Director's Cut. Also including commentaries from Director Richard Kelly and Jake Gyllenhaal, Richard Kelly and Kevin Smith and Cast and Crew including Drew Barrymore.

Director's cut

The Director's cut of the film was released on May 29, 2004, in Seattle, Washington, at the Seattle International Film Festival and later in New York City and Los Angeles on July 23, 2004. This cut includes twenty minutes of extra footage, an altered soundtrack, and visual excerpts from the (nonexistent) book *The Philosophy of Time Travel*.

The director's cut DVD, released on February 15, 2005, includes the new footage and more soundtrack changes, as well as some additional features exclusive to the two-DVD set: the director's commentary assisted by Kevin Smith, excerpts from the storyboard, a 52-minute production diary, "#1 fan video", a "cult following" video interviewing British fans, and the new director's cut trailer. The director's cut DVD was released as a giveaway with copies of the British *Sunday Times* newspaper on February 19, 2006.

Reception

Box office performance

Donnie Darko had its first screening at the Sundance Film Festival on January 19, 2001, and debuted in United States theaters in October 2001 to a tepid response. Shown on only 58 screens nationwide, the film grossed $110,494 in its opening weekend.[8] By the time the film closed in United States theaters on April 11, 2002, it had earned just $517,375.[2][8] It ultimately grossed $4.1 million worldwide.[2]

Despite its poor box office showing, the film began to attract a devoted fan base. It was originally released on DVD and VHS in March 2002. During this time, the Pioneer Theatre in New York City's East Village began midnight screenings of *Donnie Darko* that continued for 28 consecutive months.[7]

Critical reception

The film received widespread critical acclaim—Rotten Tomatoes gave the film an 84% rating (the Director's Cut received 91%),[4] while Metacritic gave it a 71 out of 100 (the Director's Cut received 88 out of 100). Critic Andy Bailey billed *Donnie Darko* as a "Sundance surprise" that "isn't spoiled by the Hollywood forces that helped birth it." Jean Oppenheimer of *New Times (LA)* praised the film, saying, "Like gathering storm clouds, Donnie Darko creates an atmosphere of eerie calm and mounting menace -- stands as one of the most exceptional movies of 2001."[9] Writing for ABC Australia, Megan Spencer called the movie, "menacing, dreamy, [and] exciting" and noted that "it could take you to a deeply emotional place lying dormant in your soul."[10] At first when the movie was released, Roger Ebert gave the film a less than positive review but later gave a positive review of the director's cut.[11]

Awards and nominations

2001 — Richard Kelly won with *Donnie Darko* for "Best Screenplay" at the Catalonian International Film Festival and at the San Diego Film Critics Society. Donnie Darko also won the "Audience Award" for Best Feature at the Sweden Fantastic Film Festival. The film was nominated for "Best Film" at the Catalonian International Film Festival and for the "Grand Jury Prize" at the Sundance Film Festival.

2002 — Donnie Darko won the "Special Award" at the Young Filmmakers Showcase at the Academy of Science Fiction, Fantasy and Horror Films. The movie also won the "Silver Scream Award" at the Amsterdam Fantastic Film Festival. Kelly was nominated for "Best First Feature" and "Best First Screenplay" with *Donnie Darko*, as well as Jake Gyllenhaal being nominated for "Best Male Lead," at the Independent Spirit Awards. The film was also nominated for the "Best Breakthrough Film" at the Online Film Critics Society Awards.

2003 — Jake Gyllenhaal won "Best Actor" and Richard Kelly "Best Original Screenplay" for *Donnie Darko* at the Chlotrudis Awards, where Kelly was also nominated for "Best Director" and "Best Movie."

2005 — *Donnie Darko* ranked in the top five on My Favourite Film, an Australian poll conducted by the ABC.[12]

2006 — *Donnie Darko* ranks ninth in FilmFour's 50 Films to See Before You Die.[13]

It also came in at #14 on Entertainment Weekly's list of the 50 Best High School Movies [14] and landed at #2 in *Empire*'s "Greatest Independent Films of All Time" [15] list.

Sequel

A 2009 sequel, *S. Darko*, centers on Sam Darko, Donnie's younger sister. Again played by Daveigh Chase, Sam begins to have strange dreams that hint at a major catastrophe. *Donnie Darko* creator Richard Kelly has stated that he has no involvement in this sequel, as he does not own the rights to the original.[16] Chase and producer Adam Fields are the only creative links between it and the original film. The sequel received extremely negative reviews.[17] [18]

Adaptations

Marcus Stern, associate director of the American Repertory Theater, directed a staged adaptation of *Donnie Darko* at the Zero Arrow Theatre in Cambridge, Massachusetts, in the fall of 2007. It ran from October 27 to November 18, 2007, with opening night fittingly scheduled on Halloween.

An article written by the production drama team stated that the director and production team planned to "embrace the challenge to make the fantastical elements come alive on stage."[19] In 2004, Stern adapted and directed Kelly's screenplay for a graduate student production at the American Repertory Theatre's Institute for Advanced Theatre Training (I.A.T.T./M.X.A.T.).

A 60 second version was created for the Empire Film Awards by Tea Fuelled Art.[20]

References

[1] Richard Kelly (director). (2004). *Donnie Darko: The Director's Cut*. [DVD].

[2] "Donnie Darko" (http://www.the-numbers.com/movies/2001/DARKO.php). The Numbers: Box Office Data, Movie Stars, Idle Speculation. . Retrieved 26 August 2009.

[3] The AV Club - "The New Cult Canon: Donnie Darko" (http://www.avclub.com/articles/the-new-cult-canon-donnie-darko,2179/)

[4] "*Donnie Darko* film review" (http://www.rottentomatoes.com/m/donnie_darko/). *Rotten Tomatoes*. IGN.com. 2001. . Retrieved 2008-09-11.

[5] Snider, Mike (2005-02-14). "'Darko' takes a long, strange trip" (http://www.usatoday.com/life/movies/news/2005-02-14-dvd-donnie-darko_x.htm). USA Today. . Retrieved 2005-02-14.

[6] Poster, Steven (Cinematographer). (2004). *Donnie Darko Production Diary*. [DVD]. 20th Century Fox.

[7] "Donnie Darko" (http://web.archive.org/web/20060512113236/http://www.indiewire.com/movies/movies_040722darko.html). Indie Wire. Archived from the original (http://www.indiewire.com/movies/movies_040722darko.html) on 2006-05-12. . Retrieved 2006-05-17.

[8] "Donnie Darko (2001)" (http://boxofficemojo.com/movies/?id=donniedarko.htm). Box Office Mojo. . Retrieved 2009-08-25.

[9] "Donnie Darko" (http://web.archive.org/web/20051214020504/http://www.indiewire.com/movies/rev_01Sund_010121_Darco.html). Indie Wire. Archived from the original (http://www.indiewire.com/movies/rev_01Sund_010121_Darco.html) on 2005-12-14. . Retrieved 2006-05-17.

[10] Review of *Donnie Darko* (http://www.abc.net.au/triplej/review/film/s702145.htm), by Megan Spencer, for ABC Australia.

[11] "Donnie Darko: The Director's Cut" (http://rogerebert.suntimes.com/apps/pbcs.dll/article?AID=/20040820/REVIEWS/408200303/1023). Rogerebert.com. . Retrieved 2009-04-20.

[12] "My Favourite Film" (http://www.abc.net.au/myfavouritefilm/). ABC. . Retrieved 2006-07-11.

[13] "C4 relaunches Film4 with '50 films to see before you die' list countdown" (http://www.brandrepublic.com/bulletins/br/article/567497/c4-relaunches-film4-50-films-die-countdown/). Brand Republic. . Retrieved 2006-09-16.

[14] http://www.ew.com/ew/gallery/0,,1532588,00.html

[15] http://www.empireonline.com/features/50greatestindependent/2.asp#50independent

[16] "IGN Article" (http://movies.ign.com/articles/873/873472p1.html). IGN. . Retrieved 2009-01-28.

[17] "*S. Darko* review" (http://www.avclub.com/articles/s-darko,27924/). A.V. Club. 2009-05-13. . Retrieved 2009-05-13.

[18] "rottentomatoes.com" (http://www.rottentomatoes.com/m/s_darko_a_donnie_darko_tale/). . Retrieved 2010-02-03.

[19] Sarah Wallace (2007-08-07). "Bringing the End of the World to Life". American Repertory Theatre. Archive copy (http://web.archive.org/web/*/http://web.archive.org/web/20071011151719/http://amrep.org/articles/6_1c/bringing.html) at the Wayback Machine.

[20] "Done in 60 seconds competition" (http://www.empireonline.com/awards2010/donein60seconds/videos/shortlist17.asp). *empireonline.com*. . Retrieved 14 February 2010.

• Commentary with Kevin Smith (2003). *Donnie Darko Directors Cut*. Faber and Faber. ISBN 0571221246

External links

- Official website (http://http://www.donniedarkofilm.com)
- *Donnie Darko* (http://www.imdb.com/title/tt0246578/) at the Internet Movie Database
- *Donnie Darko* (http://www.allmovie.com/work/237115) at Allmovie
- *Donnie Darko* (http://www.boxofficemojo.com/movies/?id=donniedarko.htm) at Box Office Mojo
- *Donnie Darko* (http://www.rottentomatoes.com/m/donnie_darko/) at Rotten Tomatoes
- *Donnie Darko: The Director's Cut* (http://www.rottentomatoes.com/m/donnie_darko_directors_cut/) at Rotten Tomatoes

Dawson's Creek

Dawson's Creek	
	Dawson's Creek intertitle
Format	Serial-Drama
Created by	Kevin Williamson
Starring	James Van Der Beek Katie Holmes Joshua Jackson Michelle Williams Kerr Smith Meredith Monroe Mary Beth Peil Busy Philipps
Opening theme	"I Don't Want to Wait" by Paula Cole (seasons 1–6); "Run Like Mad" by Jann Arden (international airings of season 1 and DVD versions of seasons 3–6 in English language only)
Country of origin	United States
No. of seasons	6
No. of episodes	128 (List of episodes)
Production	
Executive producer(s)	Tom Kapinos Greg Prange Paul Stupin Kevin Williamson
Location(s)	North Carolina, various towns
Camera setup	Single-camera
Running time	45 minutes
Broadcast	
Original channel	The WB
Original run	January 20, 1998 – May 14, 2003
External links	
Website [1]	

Dawson's Creek is an American primetime television drama which debuted on January 20, 1998, on The WB Television Network and was produced by Sony Pictures Television. The show was set in the fictional town of Capeside, Massachusetts and in Boston, Massachusetts during the later seasons. Reruns of the show are often seen in Australia on TV1, in Canada on TVtropolis, in Norway on TV3, in Denmark on TV2 Zulu, in the UK on Fiver, in France on TMC, in Greece on Macedonia TV, in India on Zee Café, in Indonesia on TPI and Global TV, in Italy on Italia 1, in Spain on LaOtra, in Lithuania on TV3, in Latin America on Liv, and in the Middle East on MBC4 and on the Orbit - Showtime Network (OSN).

Premise

Aimed at a teenage audience, the semi-autobiographical show is based on the small-town childhood of its creator Kevin Williamson (who also wrote the slasher film *Scream*). The lead character, Dawson Leery, mirrors Williamson's interests and background. Filmed in Wilmington and Durham, North Carolina, Southport, North Carolina, the show was set in a small fictional seaside town called Capeside, Massachusetts. It focused on four friends who were in the early part of their sophomore and first year of high school when the series began. The program, part of a new craze for teen-themed movies and television shows in America in the late 1990s, catapulted its leads to stardom and became a defining show for The WB.

Dawson's Creek generated a high amount of publicity before its debut, with several television critics and consumer watchdog groups expressing concerns about its anticipated "racy" plots and dialogue. The controversy even drove one of the original production companies away from the project, but numerous critics praised it for its realism and intelligent dialogue that included allusions to American television icons such as *The Dick Van Dyke Show* and *The Mary Tyler Moore Show*. By the end of its run, the show, its crew, and its young cast had been nominated for numerous awards, winning four of them. The series is known for the verbosity and complexity of the dialogue between its teenage characters—who commonly demonstrate vocabulary and cultural awareness that went beyond the scope of the average high school student, yet that is combined with an emotional immaturity and self-absorption reflecting actual teens. This precociousness has been a staple of a number of teenage-themed shows since, notably including *One Tree Hill* (also filmed in Wilmington, North Carolina), *The O.C.* and *Gossip Girl*.

Origins and reaction

Kevin Williamson, a native of the small coastal town of Oriental, North Carolina, was approached in 1995 by producer Paul Stupin to write a pilot for a television series. Stupin, who as a Fox Network executive had brought *Beverly Hills, 90210* to the air, sought out Williamson after having read his script for the slasher film *Scream*—a knowing, witty work about high school students. Initially offered to Fox, the network turned it down. The WB, however, was eagerly looking for programming to fill its new Tuesday night lineup. Williamson said "I pitched it as *Some Kind of Wonderful*, meets *Pump Up the Volume*, meets *James at 15*, meets *My So-Called Life*, meets *Little House on the Prairie*". The show's lead character and main protagonist, Dawson Leery, was based on Williamson himself: obsessed with movies and platonically sharing his bed with the girl down the creek.

Joey Potter (Katie Holmes) and Dawson Leery (James Van Der Beek) in the "Pilot" episode (c. 1998).

Procter & Gamble Productions (the company behind such daytime dramas as *Guiding Light* and *As the World Turns*) was an original co-producer of the series. The company, however, sold its interest in the show three months before the premiere when printed stories surfaced about the racy dialogue and risqué plot lines. John Kiesewetter, television columnist for *The Cincinnati Enquirer* wrote: *"As much as I want to love the show—the cool kids, charming New England setting, and stunning cinematography—I can't get past the consuming preoccupation with sex, sex, sex"*. Syndicated columnist John Leo said the show should be called "When Parents Cringe," and went on to write "The first episode contains a good deal of chatter about breasts, genitalia, masturbation, and penis size. Then the title and credits come on and the story begins." Tom Shales, of *The Washington Post* commented that creator Kevin Williamson was "the most overrated wunderkind in Hollywood" and "what he's brilliant at is pandering." In his defense, Williamson denied this was his intention, stating that "I never set out to make something provocative and racy".

The Parents Television Council proclaimed the show the single worst program of the 1997–1998 season, a title the Council would also award it for the 1998–1999 season. The Council also cited it the fourth worst show in 2000–2001. However, on the opposite end of the ideological spectrum, the National Organization for Women offered an endorsement, deeming it one of the least sexually exploitive shows on the air. For every scathing review there was a glowing one: *Variety* wrote that it was "an addictive drama with considerable heart...the teenage equivalent of a Woody Allen movie—a kind of 'Deconstructing Puberty'". *The Atlanta Journal-Constitution* called it "a teen's dream". *The Dayton Daily News* listed Capeside as a television town they'd most like to live in. *The Seattle Times* declared it the best show of the 1997–1998 season. *The New York Times* had perhaps the best headline on its review: "Young, Handsome, and Clueless in *Peyton Place*". That was precisely the sort of allusion real teenagers weren't likely to get, let alone make, but the show's punchy dialogue was full of them. Dawson calls his mother's co-anchor "Ted Baxter" and refers to his parents as "Rob and Laura Petrie". He responds to his principal's request for a film glorifying the football team as belonging to "the Leni Riefenstahl approach to filmmaking." Jen says her parents followed "the Ho Chi Minh school of parenting." The verbiage was high-flying too: star Michelle Williams confessed in interviews she had to consult her dictionary when she read the scripts.

While never a huge ratings success among the general television population, *Dawson's Creek* did very well with the younger demographic it targeted and became a defining show for the WB Network. (The first season's highest ranked episode was the finale, which was fifty-ninth, while the second highest rated was the second episode, scoring so well only because there was no programming on the other networks, which were carrying President Clinton's State of the Union address in the midst of the Lewinsky scandal.)

The show endured phenomenal success in Australia where it rated number one in its timeslot for every episode covering seasons one to four. Its incredible support extended out into the music industry too when "Songs From Dawson's Creek", released in 1999 on Sony Music, reached #1 on the Australian Album Chart. It remained in the top spot for six weeks and was certified 3x Platinum; inevitably, it was the fifth highest selling album of the year. This was followed in 2001 when "Songs From Dawson's Creek — Volume 2" was released. Debuting at #1, the show's second soundtrack went on to achieve platinum status and was praised by critics and fans alike.

Season overview

Cast and characters

Regular cast

Actor	Character	Regular Seasons	Recurring Seasons
James Van Der Beek	Dawson Leery	1–6	–
Katie Holmes	Josephine "Joey" Potter	1–6	–
Michelle Williams	Jen Lindley	1–6	–
Joshua Jackson	Pacey Witter	1–6	–
Kerr Smith	Jack McPhee	3–6	2
Meredith Monroe	Andie McPhee	3–4	2, 6 (guest appearance)
Busy Philipps	Audrey Liddell	6	5
Mary-Margaret Humes	Gail Leery	1–4	5 – 6
John Wesley Shipp	Mitch Leery	1–4	5

| Mary Beth Peil | Evelyn "Grams" Ryan | 1—6 | – |
| Nina Repeta | Bessie Potter | 1—4 | 5 – 6 |

- Despite the title being named after James Van Der Beek's character, Katie Holmes is the only cast member who appeared in all 128 episodes. Van Der Beek's character, along with Joshua Jackson and Michelle Williams, did not appear in a handful of episodes during the show's final two seasons.

- Kerr Smith and Meredith Monroe were added to the cast during the show's second season in recurring capacities until they were promoted to full-time series regulars during the show's third season. Monroe later left the series mid-way through the fourth season while Smith remained with the series for the remainder of its run. Monroe made a guest appearance in the series finale.

- At the beginning of the show's fifth season, only Mary Beth Peil remained a regular character out of the show's four "adult" characters whereas Mary-Margaret Humes, John Wesley Shipp and Nina Repeta were scaled back to recurring roles.

- Busy Philipps joined the show's cast during the fifth season as a recurring role and was a series regular character during the show's sixth and final season on the air.

Supporting cast (in alphabetical order)

Actor	Character (season which they appeared)
Jensen Ackles	C.J. (Season 6)
Sasha Alexander	Gretchen Witter (Season 4)
Mädchen Amick	Nicole Kennedy (Season 2)
Dana Ashbrook	Rich Rinaldi (Season 6)
Eion Bailey	Billy Conrad (Season 1)
Obba Babatundé	Principal Howard Green (Season 3)
Jason Behr	Chris Wolfe (Season 2)
Lourdes Benedicto	Karen Torres (Season 5)
Jaime Bergman	Denise (Season 6)
Nicole Bilderback	Heather Tracy (Season 6)
Ryan Bittle	Eric (Season 5)
Mika Boorem	Harley Hetson (Season 6)
Jordan Bridges	Oliver Chirckirk (Seasons 5 & 6)
Hilarie Burton	Herself
Adam Carolla	Himself (Season 6)
Brittany Daniel	Eve Whitman (Season 3)
Dr. Drew	Himself (Season 6)
David Dukes	Will/Joseph McPhee (Seasons 2—4)
Sherilyn Fenn	Alex Pearl (Season 5)
John Finn	John Witter (Seasons 2, 4, & 6)
Scott Foley	Cliff Elliot (Season 1)
Megan Gray	Emma Jones (Season 6)
Marla Gibbs	Mrs. Fran Boyd (Season 1)

Andy Griffith	Mr. Brooks' Friend (Season 4)
Paul Gleason	Larry Newman (Season 6)
Tony Hale	Dr. Bronin (Season 3)
Mel Harris	Helen Lindley (Season 2)
Carolyn Hennesy	Mrs. Valentine (Season 4)
Roger Howarth	Professor Greg Hetson (Season 6)
Oliver Hudson	Eddie Doling (Season 6)
Leann Hunley	Tamara Jacobs (Seasons 1 & 2)
Ian Kahn	Danny Brecher (Season 5)
Bianca Kajlich	Natasha Kelly (Season 6)
Edmund J. Kearney	Mr. Peterson (Seasons 1 & 2)
Monica Keena	Abby Morgan (Seasons 1 & 2)
Ali Larter	Kristy Livingstone (Season 2)
Bianca Lawson	Nikki Green (Season 3)
Rachael Leigh Cook	Devon (Season 2)
Jonathan Lipnicki	Buzz (Season 3)
Virginia Madsen	Maddy (Season 6)
Ken Marino	Professor David Wilder (Season 5)
Mark Matkevich	Drue Valentine (Season 4)
Mercedes McNab	Grace (Season 5)
David Monahan	Tobey Barret (Season 4 & 5)
Jennifer Morrison	Melanie Shea Thompson (Season 5)
Chad Michael Murray	Charlie Todd (Season 5)
Obi Ndefo	Bodie Wells (Seasons 1, 3, 4, & 6)
Dylan Neal	Doug Witter (Seasons 1, 3-6)
Jack Osbourne	Himself (Season 6)
Hal Ozsan	Todd Carr (Season 5-6)
Michael Pitt	Henry Parker (Season 3)
Harve Presnell	Arthur "A.I." Brooks (Season 4)
Danny Roberts	French Exchange Student (Season 4)
Mimi Rogers	Helen Lindley (Season 6)
Seth Rogen	Bob (Season 6)
Sarah Shahi	Sadia Shaw (Season 6)
Harry Shearer	Principal Peskin (Season 4)
Rodney Scott	Will Krudski (Season 3)
Gareth Williams	Mike Potter (Seasons 1, 2, & 6)

Main crew

Dawson's Creek was, mostly and in part, run by Kevin Williamson, Deborah Joy Levine, Paul Stupin, Alex Gansa, Jeffrey Stepakoff and Tammy Ader.

Filming locations

Filmed in Wilmington, North Carolina, at EUE/Screen Gems studios and on location around Wilmington, Southport and Wrightsville Beach, North Carolina. College scenes in the fifth and sixth seasons shot at Duke University, Durham, North Carolina, and additional shooting was done in Raleigh, North Carolina. In 1999 some scenes were shot on the University of Richmond campus. The fourth season episode "Eastern Standard Time" also did location shooting in New York City, including at Grand Central Terminal.

The Wilmington area benefited greatly from the show. While a number of films, commercials and music videos had been shot at the studios, the show was the first to occupy numerous soundstages for many years. One Tree Hill later occupied some of those same soundstages for several years and uses some of the same locations in Wilmington.

In addition to business brought into the community by the project, it attracted attention to the city as a filming location and boosted tourism. The visitors' bureau distributed a special guide to filming locations used in the show. When the program was cancelled in 2003, the news was reported on the front-page of Wilmington's daily newspaper, the *DailyStar*.

Dawson's Creek and home

Sunset shots of Dawson standing on his dock among the marsh grass were filmed along Hewlett's Creek on Pine Grove Road between Masonboro Loop Road and Holly Tree Drive in Masonboro, North Carolina.[2] [3] The private residences used as homes for Dawson, Jen and Joey are all located along the shores of Hewlett's Creek.

Capeside

Capeside is a fictional town in Massachusetts where *Dawson's Creek* takes place. It is located on Cape Cod, possibly somewhere mid-Cape between Falmouth and Yarmouth, as an early episodes includes these real towns in a "snow day" announcement. Incorporated in 1815, the town has a population of 35,000 and is located between the cities of Providence, Rhode Island and Boston, Massachusetts. Capeside exteriors were shot in and around Wilmington, North Carolina. Its bays and coastlines are similar to those found along the coast of Massachusetts.

A Dawson Creek actually exists in the Canadian province of British Columbia. It is named for the river of the same name that runs through it. Another exists in Oriental, NC, which flows into the Neuse River. This served as the inspiration for the show's name.

Capeside High School

Capeside High School is the high school in Capeside, Massachusetts attended by several characters during the first four seasons of the show. Exteriors were filmed at the University of North Carolina at Wilmington.

Worthington University

Worthington University is a fictional university from *Dawson's Creek*. Joey (played by Katie Holmes) and Audrey (played by Busy Philipps), characters from the series, attended this school. It is supposed to be located in Boston, Massachusetts and to have been founded in 1787 by Josiah Worthington. It is sometimes said to be an "Ivy League college".

Producers had not planned for the show to extend beyond the characters' high school years. The architectural uniformity of UNC Wilmington prevented it from being used for Worthington University exteriors. The scenes at Worthington were filmed over two hours away at Duke University,[4] and a number of its students served as extras.[4]

Some filming was also done on Franklin Street adjacent to nearby University of North Carolina at Chapel Hill.

Restaurants and bars in the show

Interiors for The Icehouse were filmed at The Icehouse bar in downtown Wilmington several blocks from less picturesque water so exteriors were filmed at the Dockside Restaurant at 1308 Airlie Road in Wrightsville Beach, NC. Nearby constructions at the real IceHouse forced producers to eliminate the bar from the storyline by burning it down.[2]

The Hells Kitchen bar featured in the show was a natural food store at 118 Princess Street in Wilmington which was purchased by producers, dressed as a seedy college bar and used for production during the show's last season. When production completed, the building was purchased by a local restaurateur, along with much of the set and decorations, and converted it into a real restaurant and bar. It retains the name as well.[2]

Leery's Fresh Fish, exteriors were filmed at Water Street Restaurant at 5 South Water Street in Wilmington.[2]

Style

Dawson's Creek was shot like a motion picture using a single camera and often filmed on location, rather than being largely studio bound. The series used soothing colors, similar to *Party of Five*, rather than the cold, harsh look of shows such as *The Practice*. While most of the episodes were conventional, there were two *Rashomon*-like episodes exploring a story from differing perspectives, and the somber fifth season episode "Downtown Crossing" featured only one regular, Joey, and her interaction with a mugger. The fourth season episode "The Unusual Suspects," was filmed as a film noir detective story—complete with camera work and music appropriate to the genre. At times, *Dawson's Creek* was deliberately self-conscious, as when Eve tells Dawson he is Felicity, beginning a discussion of why Dawson doesn't like television shows, which concludes with his observation that they cut away when the best part comes—immediately demonstrated when Eve, about to kiss him, is interrupted by the main titles. It also made fun of itself on other episodes besides that one, especially the finale, when Dawson is the creator of a TV show called "the Creek."

Awards

Dawson's Creek was nominated for fourteen awards, including ALMA Awards, Casting Society of America Awards, Golden Satellite Awards, TV Guide Awards, and YoungStar Awards. Joshua Jackson won the Teen Choice Award for Choice Actor three times and the show won the Teen Choice Award for Choice Drama once. The series also won the GLAAD Media Award for Outstanding TV Drama Series.

Spinoff

The show had, in the words of television experts Tim Brooks and Earle Marsh, a "semi-spinoff", *Young Americans*. The protagonist of *Young Americans*, Will Krudski (Rodney Scott), was introduced in three episodes at the end of the show's third season, as a former classmate of Dawson, Joey, and Pacey, who had moved away some years before and had returned for a visit. He was never referred to or seen before or since. *Young Americans* was made by the same company as *Dawson's Creek*, Columbia TriStar Television, and appeared in *Dawson's Creek's* timeslot when it went on hiatus during the summer of 2000. The show had 8 episodes. The reason the show is considered a semi-spinoff instead of a true spinoff is that Will was not originally created for *Dawson's Creek*. He was added to *Dawson's* solely to set up and promote the series *Young Americans*.

Simon & Schuster published a series of fifteen mass-market paperback novelizations of the series.

Broadcast history

International

The show also aired in numerous international markets, listed here with the premiere dates:

Country	Premiere	Channel
Albania		Vizion +
Australia	June 9, 1998	Network Ten (Original Broadcast – 1998–2003) Eleven (Rerun – Early 2011) TV1 (Syndication – 2001–Current)
Austria		ORF 1, Reruns on Puls 4
Belgium	1999	VT4, Reruns on 2Be (2008), vtm (as of 30/08/2010) and La Deux
Brazil	March 3, 1998	Rede Globo
Bulgaria	2000	Nova Television
Canada	January 20, 1998	Global
Chile	2000	MEGA
Croatia	2001, September	
Cuba	2005, January	Cubavision
Czech Republic	September 9, 2000	TV Nova
Denmark		DR1, TV 2 and currently TV 2 Zulu
France	January 10, 1999	TF1 and Télé Monte Carlo
Germany	January 3, 1999	Sat.1
Greece	January 10, 1999	Mega
Hungary	September 11, 1999	TV2 S1-S3, RTL Klub S4-S5, Cool TV S6
India	April 2008	Zee Cafe
Indonesia	1999, rerun 2007	TPI, rerun by Global TV
Ireland	May 1998	RTE TWO reruns on Channel6
Israel	September 1, 1998	Channel 3
Italy	January 3, 1999/ January 13, 2000	Tele+ (pay tv)/ Italia Uno (free to air)
Lithuania		TV3 later moved to TangoTV (TV6)
Malaysia	2000	Radio Televisyen Malaysia Channel 2 (TV2)
Malta	July 2008	Net Television
Mexico		Canal 5
Netherlands		Net5
New Zealand	June 25, 1999	TV2 (New Zealand)
Norway	September 1, 1998	TV3
Panama	1998	Channel 4 RPC
Peru		Sony Entertainment Television (Latin America)
Philippines		Studio 23
Poland	September 6, 1998	Polsat
Portugal	April 8, 2001	TVI

	Country	Date	Channel
	Romania	February 28, 1999	Pro TV
	Saudi Arabia	December 2007	MBC 4
	Serbia	September 2002	B92
	South Korea		SBS
	Spain	2000	La 2 de RTVE
	Sri Lanka	2000	ARTv
	Switzerland	December 27, 1998	TSR 2
	Thailand	May 15, 1999	True Series
	Turkey	1999	CNBC-E,2002 DiziMax,2009 Kanal 1
	Ukraine	2008	1+1
	United Kingdom	May 2, 1998	Channel 4
	Venezuela	1998	Televen

- The show originally aired in the UK on Channel 4 but later moved to Five for the last two seasons. In 2007 Five's sister channel FiveLife began airing reruns on weekdays at 7pm. In early 2008 with its evening showings having reached the final season it restarted the show in an early morning slot.

Ratings

American ratings

#	Season	U.S. ratings (millions of viewers)	Network	Rank
1	1998	6.6	The WB	#125
2	1998–1999	5.4	The WB	#118
3	1999–2000	6.5	The WB	#122
4	2000–2001	4.1	The WB	#120
5	2001–2002	3.9	The WB	#134
6	2002–2003	4.0	The WB	#134

The show was rated PG-13 according to the contents of the show.

Credits

Production credits

Created by Kevin Williamson.

Production companies

Produced by Columbia TriStar Television/Sony Pictures Television and Outerbanks Entertainment. Originally, Granville Productions and Procter & Gamble Productions were producers, but left the show before it aired.

Executive producers

Executive-produced by Kevin Williamson, Paul Stupin, Charles Rosin, Deborah Joy LeVine, Jon Harmon Feldman, Alex Gansa, Greg Berlanti, Tom Kapinos, Gina Fattore, Jeffrey Stepakoff.

Producers

Episodes were produced by Dana Baratta, Greg Berlanti, Janice Cooke-Leonard, Alan Cross, Zack Estrin, Gina Fattore, Jon Harmon Feldman, Maggie Friedman, Darin Goldberg, David Blake Hartley, Tom Kapinos, Drew Matich, Chris Levinson, Paul Marks, Drew Matich, Shelley Meals, Rina Mimoun, Steve Miner, Gregory Prange, Jed Seidel, David Semel, Cynthia Stegner, Jeffrey Stepakoff, Dale Williams, Mike White

Writers

Episodes were written by Dana Baratta, Rob Thomas, Greg Berlanti, Hadley Davis, Gina Fattore, Anna Fricke, Maggie Friedman, Alex Gansa, Diego García Gutiérrez, Liz Garcia, Laura Glasser, Holly Henderson, Tom Kapinos, Rina Mimoun, Jason M. Palmer, Jed Seidel, Jeffrey Stepakoff, Liz Tigelaar, Mike White, and Kevin Williamson

Directors

Episodes were directed by Lou Antonio, Allan Arkush, John Behring, Sanford Bookstaver, Arvin Brown, Jan Eliasberg, Michael Fields, Rodman Flender, Morgan J. Freeman, Dennie Gordon, Bruce Seth Green, Joshua Jackson, Joanna Kerns, Peter B. Kowalski, Perry Lang, Michael Lange, Nick Marck, Melanie Mayron, Robert Duncan McNeill, Steve Miner, Jason Moore, Joe Napolitano, Patrick R. Norris, Scott Paulin, David Petrarca, Gregory Prange, Krishna Rao, Steven Robman, Bethany Rooney, Arlene Sanford, David Semel, Kerr Smith, Sandy Smolan, Lev L. Spiro, David Straiton, Jay Tobias, Jesús Salvador Treviño, Michael Toshiyuki Uno, and James Whitmore, Jr.

Series regulars

James Van Der Beek, Katie Holmes, Michelle Williams, Joshua Jackson, and Mary Beth Peil were the only cast members who remained series regulars from beginning to end of the series. Katie Holmes was the only cast member to appear in every episode of the show.

Mary-Margaret Humes, John Wesley Shipp, and Nina Repeta were all regular cast members throughout the show's first four seasons until the fifth season, in which the younger characters moved on to college and only Mary Beth Peil remained the regular "adult" presence in their lives. Instead of simply vanishing from the show completely though, all three of them occasionally reprised their roles in guest starring capacities.

Kerr Smith and Meredith Monroe joined the series in the show's second season but were not billed as regulars until the third season. Though Kerr Smith remained with the show throughout the rest of its run, Meredith Monroe eventually left the show in the middle of the fourth season, but continued to be billed as a regular until the end of that year as her character returned for the season finale. She also made a guest apperence in the series finale. Her scenes in the series finale were cut from the original broadcast version, but remain intact on the show's DVD releases.

Busy Philipps joined the regular cast in the show's fifth season and remained with the show for its final two years on the air.

Bibliography and references

Darren Crosdale's *Dawson's Creek: The Official Companion* (Kansas City, Missouri: Andrews McMeel, 1999) (ISBN 0-7407-0725-6), thoroughly chronicles the show, but only covers events through to the end of the second season. Scott Andrews' *Troubled Waters: An Unauthorised and Unofficial Guide To Dawson's Creek* (Virgin Publishing 2001 (ISBN 0-7535-0625-4)) also covers the series thoroughly but it includes all episodes up to the end of Season Four and, because it is unofficial, is freer with both criticism and praise. A less thorough book from about the same time, aimed at teens, is *Meet the Stars of Dawson's Creek* by Grace Catalano, which has more about the show than the title would imply. Andy Mangels's *From* Scream *to* Dawson's Creek: *An Unauthorized Take on the Phenomenal Career of Kevin Williamson* (Los Angeles: Renaissance Books, 2000) (ISBN 1-58063-122-3) covers the show well but omits later seasons.

Other references include:

- "The best (and worst) 1999 had to offer". *Dayton Daily News*. January 2, 2000. 5C.
- Tom Bierbaum. "Clinton tide stops long enough at Creek". *Variety*. January 29, 1998. (Ratings versus state of the union speech)
- Greg Braxton. "UPN President Knocks Rival WB Network". *Los Angeles Times*. June 11, 1997. P4. (Criticism before show aired)
- Tim Brooks and Earle Marsh. *The Complete Directory to Prime Time Network and Cable TV Shows, 1946-Present*. 8th ed. New York: Ballantine Books, 2003. (General information on the show and *Young Americans*)
- John Carman. "'Creek' Runs Hot". *San Francisco Chronicle*. January 20, 1998. E1. (Review of premiere)
- "Cheers and Jeers". *TV Guide*. Issue 2619. v. 51, n. 23. June 7, 2003. 14.
- Tamara Conniff. "Music plays an important—and profitable—role in 'Dawson's Creek'". *The Hollywood Reporter*. April 17, 2002. (The show's sound)
- Robert Crane. "Twenty Questions: Kevin Williamson". *Playboy*. v. 45, n. 9. September 1998. 138. (Interview with the show's creator)
- "Dawson's Creek's low aim". (Editorial). *The Cincinnati Post*. September 22, 1997. 8A. (Editorial denouncing Procter and Gamble's role in the show, P&G being a Cincinnati company)
- Maureen Dowd. "Puppy Love Politics". *The New York Times*. June 9, 1999. A31. (Humorous mention of politicians)
- Jeffrey Epstein. "Unbound". *The Advocate*. August 31, 1999. 34. (Kevin Williamson profiled)
- Amanda Fazzone. "Boob Tube: NOW's Strange Taste in TV". *The New Republic*. Issue 4515. v. 225, n. 5. June 8, 2001. 26–35. (NOW's endorsement of the show)
- Bruce Fretts. "The Women of the WB". *Entertainment Weekly*. Issues 464 and 465. December 25, 1998 and January 1, 1999. (Profile of Katie Holmes and others)
- Matthew Gilbert. "'Dawson's Creek': A flood of hormones". *The Boston Globe*. January 20, 1998. C1. (Review of premiere)
- Matthew Gilbert. "Dawson, pals talk out into the sunset". *The Boston Globe*. May 14, 2003. D1. (Review of finale)
- Lynn Hirschberg. "Desperate to Seem 16". *The New York Times Magazine*. September 5, 1999. 42.
- John Kieswetter. "'Dawson's Creek' overflows with sex". *The Cincinnati Enquirer*. January 20, 1998. (Review of premiere) [5]
- John Kieswetter. "P&G execs reviewing family TV". *The Cincinnati Enquirer*. August 6, 2000. A1. (P&G considering its role in producing the show)
- John Kieswetter. "Readers divided on 'Dawson's'". *The Cincinnati Enquirer*. February 24, 1998. (Cincinnati viewers' reaction to the premiere)
- Caryn James. "Young, Handsome, and Clueless in Peyton Place". *The New York Times*. January 20, 1998. E5. (Review of the premiere)
- Ted Johnson. "Dawson's Peak". *TV Guide*. Issue 2345. v. 46, n. 10. March 7, 1998. 18–24. (Cover story on show's early success)
- Ted Johnson. "His So-Called Life". *TV Guide*. Issue 2345. v. 46, n. 10. March 7, 1998. 25–29. (Profile of creator Kevin Williamson)
- "Kevin Williamson: he's a scream". *TV Guide*. Issue 2337. v. 26, n. 2. January 10, 1998. 30. (Profile of creator Kevin Williamson)
- Phil Kloer. "'Dawson's Creek': Teens get wet". *The Atlanta Journal-Constitution*. January 20, 1998. B1. (Review of premiere)
- John Leo. "TV sleaze worse than ever". *Las Vegas Review-Journal*. January 25, 1998. 4E. (Column criticizing sex on television)

- Kay McFadden. "The Kids Are Alright". *The Seattle Times*. January 19, 1998. C1. (Review of premiere)
- Gareth McGrath. "Creek's Hot Properties". *Wilmington Star-News*. June 14, 2003. (Sale of props used on the show)
- Shawna Malcolm. "Casting Off". *TV Guide*. Issue 2615. v. 51, n. 19. May 10, 2003. 40.
- Jay Mathews. "'Dawson's Creek' site mecca for teens". *The Cincinnati Enquirer*. July 18, 1999. Travel section, p. 6.
- "The Merchants of Cool". *Frontline*. PBS. February 27, 2001.
- Greg Paeth. "P&G cuts its link with steamy teen series." *The Cincinnati Post*. October 23, 1997. 1C.
- Parents Television Council website [6]. Overall review [7], Worst of 1997–98 season [8],Worst of 1999–99 season [9], Worst of 2000–01 season [10]
- Joe Queenan. "Dumb and Dumber". *TV Guide*. v. 46, n. 15. April 11, 1998. 18.
- Lynette Rice. "Interest in 'Creek' Rising". *Broadcasting and Cable*. June 16, 1997. 25.
- Ray Richmond. Review of *Dawson's Creek*. *Variety*. January 19, 1998. 71.
- Ray Richmond. "Youth ache 100 episodes". *The Hollywood Reporter*. April 17, 2002. (Part of special section commemorating 100th episode.)
- Matt Roush. Review of *Dawson's Creek*. *TV Guide*. v. 46, n. 6. February 7, 1998. 16.
- Pamela Redmond Satran. "15 Signs You're Too Old to Watch Dawson's Creek". *TV Guide*. Issue 2442. v. 28, n. January 3, 15, 2000. 17.
- Tom Shales. "Stuck in the Muck". *The Washington Post*. January 20, 1998. D1.
- Maxine Shin. "If Dawson and Buffy Are Gone, Can I Still Be Young?" *New York Post*. May 20, 2003.
- Alessandra Stanley. "A President-to-Be And His Rosebud". *The New York Times*. September 10, 2004. B1.
- Kevin D. Thompson. "'Dawson's Creek' runs its course tonight". *The Palm Beach Post*. May 14, 2003.
- Ken Tucker. "The Big Kiss-off". *Entertainment Weekly*. Issue 544. June 9, 2000. 58–59.
- Josh Walk. "Pop Goes the Teen Boom?" *Entertainment Weekly*. Issue 599. June 8, 2001. 26–35.
- Andrew Wallentsein. "'Creek' to make splash on TBS". *Daily Variety*. March 19, 2003. 3.
- Ron Weiskind, Barbara Vancheri, and Rob Owens. "If We Were In TV Land". *Dayton Daily News*. October 28, 1999. 8C.
- Jeffrey Zaslow. "Straight talk". *USA Weekend*. July 10, 1998. 22.

References

[1] http://www.dawsonscreek.com/

[2] Hidek, Jeff (January 28, 2008). "'Dawson's Creek' legacy endures" (http://www.news-record.com/node/13079). *News & Record*. .

[3] Jeff Hidek & Amy Hotz (January 20, 2008). "'Creek' revisited: The super-hot, locally filmed teen drama is, like, so 10 years ago" (http://www.starnewsonline.com/article/20080120/NEWS/285137840). *The Star-News*. .

[4] "Duke: The TV Show" (http://www.dukemagazine.duke.edu/dukemag/issues/010202/depgar.html). *Duke Magazine*. January–February 2002. . Retrieved 2007-12-04.

[5] http://www.enquirer.com/columns/kiese/1998/01/012098_jki.html

[6] http://www.parentstv.org

[7] http://www.parentstv.org/guide/shows/dawson.asp

[8] http://www.parentstv.org/PTC/publications/reports/98top/10worst.asp

[9] http://www.parentstv.org/PTC/publications/reports/99top/worst.asp

[10] http://www.parentstv.org/PTC/publications/reports/top10bestandworst/2001top/main.asp

External links

- Official website (http://http://www.dawsonscreek.com/)
- *Dawson's Creek* (http://www.imdb.com/title/tt0118300/) at the Internet Movie Database
- *Dawson's Creek* (http://www.tv.com/show/192/summary.html) at TV.com

Anchorman: The Legend of Ron Burgundy

Anchorman: The Legend of Ron Burgundy	
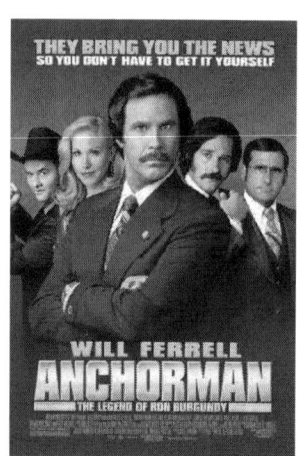 Theatrical release poster	
Directed by	Adam McKay
Produced by	Judd Apatow
Written by	Will Ferrell Adam McKay
Narrated by	Bill Kurtis
Starring	Will Ferrell Christina Applegate Paul Rudd David Koechner Steve Carell Fred Willard
Music by	Alex Wurman
Cinematography	Thomas E. Ackerman
Editing by	Brent White
Distributed by	DreamWorks
Release date(s)	July 9, 2004
Running time	94 minutes (Theatrical) 98 minutes (Unrated)
Country	United States
Language	English
Budget	$26 million
Gross revenue	$90,336,354
Followed by	*Wake Up, Ron Burgundy*

Anchorman: The Legend of Ron Burgundy is a 2004 American comedy film, directed by Adam McKay and starring Will Ferrell. The film, which was also written by Ferrell and McKay, is a tongue-in-cheek take on the culture of the 1970s, particularly the then-new Action News format. It portrays a San Diego TV station where Ferrell's title character clashes with his new female counterpart (Christina Applegate). This film is number 100 on Bravo's 100 funniest movies, and 113 on *Empire's 500 Greatest Movies of All Time*.

The film made $28.4 million in its opening weekend, and $89.3 million worldwide in its total theatrical run. A companion film assembled from outtakes and abandoned subplots, titled *Wake Up, Ron Burgundy: The Lost Movie*, was released straight-to-DVD in late 2004. In May 2008, it was confirmed that a sequel to *Anchorman* was in the planning stages,[1] but in April 2010, it was announced that the sequel was scrapped.[2]

Plot

In 1970s San Diego, Ron Burgundy (Will Ferrell) is the famous and successful anchorman for KVWN-TV Channel 4 Evening News. He works alongside his friends and news team, lead field reporter and fashion oriented Brian Fantana (Paul Rudd), sportscaster Champion "Champ" Kind (David Koechner), and extremely dimwitted chief meteorologist Brick Tamland (Steve Carell). After a successful day of work, the team is notified by their boss, Ed Harken (Fred Willard), that their station has again maintained its long-held status as the highest-rated news program in town, leading them to throw a wild party. While getting wasted, Ron sees a blond bombshell across the party and immediately tries to hit on her. After an awkward pick-up attempt, the woman denies Ron and leaves.

The next day, Ed informs the team that he has been forced by the network to hire Veronica Corningstone (Christina Applegate), a female news reporter from Asheville, North Carolina - who incidentally turns out to be the very lady Ron had tried to hit on the previous night. The team is then told that Ling-Wong, a famous panda at the San Diego Zoo, is pregnant, and that the station is going to make this its main story. The news team attempts to seduce Veronica using various inept, arrogant and even sexist flirting techniques, which all fail. Ron ends up asking her out under the guise of helping out a new co-worker, which she accepts. During their date, Ron woos Veronica by playing jazz flute in his friend Tino's (Fred Armisen) club. Veronica goes against her policy of not dating co-workers and sleeps with Ron. The next day, despite agreeing with Veronica to keep the relationship discreet, Ron shouts to the entire news office that he and Veronica are in a sexual relationship.

One day as Ron is heading to work, he throws a burrito out his car window hitting a motorcyclist (Jack Black) in the head, causing him to crash. In a fit of rage, the biker retaliates by punting Ron's dog, Baxter, off a bridge into the waters below. A horribly saddened and incoherent Ron calls Brian from a pay phone and tells him what happened. Since Ron is now late, Brian frantically tells him to come to the station because Veronica is about to take his place. Despite Ron's efforts to arrive early, Veronica goes on air. After Ron arrives, he has an argument with Veronica about the situation and they break up. The next day, Veronica is made co-anchor, much to the entire news team's disgust. The co-anchors soon become fierce rivals and argue with each other both on and off the air.

Since they want to be popular, Ron and his news team plan to go shopping and buy new suits. After misleading directions from Brick, the news team gets lost in a random alleyway. Out of nowhere, a rival channel anchorman Wes Mantooth (Vince Vaughn) and his news team ambush and taunt them, causing all of them to pull out their weapons. Before they are about to fight, Channel 2 News Team, Public News Team and Spanish Language News come over with weapons. After Ron gives one rule (Don't touch the hair or face), all of the News Teams have a big battle. The battle consists of a man on fire, horses catching Brian in a net, Brick killing one rider with a trident, the Public News anchor (Tim Robbins), chopping off the Channel 2 News anchor's (Luke Wilson) arm off with a blade and Mantooth attempting to stab Ron with his dagger. Police sirens echo in the background, thus the battle is over and everyone flees. Back at the studio, Ron tells Brick to find a safe house or a relative close by because he's possibly wanted for murder.

While in a restaurant celebrating Veronica's success, one of Veronica's co-workers tells her that Ron will read anything that's written on the teleprompter. Later, Veronica sneaks into the station and changes the words in Ron's teleprompter. The next day, instead of Ron delivering his signature, "You stay classy, San Diego," Ron closes the broadcast with, "Go fuck yourself, San Diego," Everyone in the studio, besides Ron, knows what happened and is speechless. After hearing this, an angry mob gathers outside the studio and Ed is forced to fire Ron. Veronica sees she has gone too far and attempts to apologize, but Ron angrily dismisses her while being led through the mob by security, yelling at her that she had "reduced him to rubble".

Three months later Ron is unemployed, hated by the city, has no friends and is a slovenly drunk. In this time Veronica has become very famous, but is hated by her male coworkers for sabotaging Ron. When it is announced that Ling-Wong the panda is about to give birth, all the San Diego news teams head to the zoo to cover the story. In an attempt to sabotage her, the public news anchor (Tim Robbins) pushes Veronica into the Kodiak bear habitat. When Ed can't find Veronica, he calls the bar where Ron spends most of his time and reluctantly asks him to return. Ron then summons the rest of his team by blowing the "News Horn", however, they were all standing a foot away playing pool. Baxter, who has miraculously survived, hears this call and follows the voice to find Ron. Once at the zoo, Ron jumps into the bear pen to save Veronica; this attracts everyone else in the zoo to watch. The Channel 4 news team then jumps in to help Ron. Just as the leader of the bears is about to rip Ron and Veronica apart, Baxter shows up and convinces the bear to let them live by mentioning that he is a friend of the bear's cousin, whom he met in the wild.

After Ron and Veronica reconcile, it's shown that in years to come, Brian becomes the host of a Fox reality show named *Intercourse Island*, Brick is George W. Bush's top political adviser, Champ is a commentator for the NFL before sexually harassing Terry Bradshaw, and Ron and Veronica are co-anchors for the CNN-esque *World News Center*, taking over after the narrator (real news anchor Bill Kurtis) retires.

Cast of characters

- Will Ferrell as Ron Burgundy: A five-time (local) Emmy Award-winning journalist, he is the main anchor for the KVWN Channel 4 News Team from 1964 to 1977. He is the protagonist of the film. Always confident and well-dressed, he is ignorant, egotistical, misogynistic, and narcissistic, stating that he believes "diversity" to be some type of "old, old wooden ship used in the Civil War era." It eventually is revealed that he knows almost nothing of the news or what makes it work, and is a success because he "reads the news quite very well." Despite this he remains the rock for the entire group. He develops an infatuation with newcomer Veronica Corningstone, initially having trouble wooing her with tried and true measures that allegedly won him many bimbo-type women in the past. He has a great fondness for a good glass of scotch whisky, poetry, and his good friend/pet dog Baxter, and he plays a rather mean jazz flute.

- Christina Applegate as Veronica Corningstone: From Asheville, North Carolina, she is hired to comply with newly instituted "diversity standards". In a voice-over, Corningstone implies she has previously been in this position at several other news stations. Corningstone has a strong ambition to become a network anchor and desires to be taken seriously in the male-dominated newsroom culture. Burgundy develops an infatuation for her, culminating in a love affair, which provides most of the conflict in the film. At the end of the film she becomes co-anchor with Ron for the first worldwide news network. Amy Poehler (of *Saturday Night Live* fame) was originally cast as Veronica before Applegate showed interest.

- Paul Rudd as Brian Fantana: Fantana is the stylish one of the group and is a lustful field reporter for the Channel Four News Team. He is arrogant and narcissistic and absurdly overestimates his personal qualities. He has a nickname for his penis, "the Octagon" and he also nicknamed his testes "James Westfall" and "Dr. Kenneth Noisewater". Fantana is a proud user of "Sex Panther" cologne, which emits a very strong and disgusting smell. At the end of the film, it is explained that he goes on to host the Fox Network's *Intercourse Island.'*

- David Koechner as Champion 'Champ' Kind: The sportscaster for the Channel Four News Team who seems to have hidden feelings for Ron Burgundy (despite stating that Burgundy "sounds like a gay" in a demeaning fashion when talking about Corningstone's feelings). These feelings and his homosexuality are more overt in the alternate film, *Wake Up, Ron Burgundy: The Lost Movie*. He is the most chauvinistic member of the news team. At the end of the film, it is revealed that Kind, whose signature catchphrase is "Whammy!", ends up becoming an NFL commentator, but gets fired after being accused of sexual harassment by Terry Bradshaw. John C. Reilly was originally slated to play Champ but had to drop out due to work on *The Aviator*.

- Steve Carell as Brick Tamland: The weatherman for Channel Four News. He has a habit of stating unrequested or extremely irrelevant information. Tamland is not very bright, but good hearted and loyal. Tamland says that years later, a doctor will tell him that his I.Q. is 48, technically making him mentally retarded (as he mentions this in an interview, he is seen spooning mayonnaise into a toaster). Brick is quite the innocent (though badly influenced by the others). Co-star Paul Rudd commented in rehearsals found on the DVD that the thought that Brick may be mentally retarded would "never faze them", and that the other members of the news team would never berate or become annoyed with Brick because of his stupidity, but they would merely correct him if he made a mistake. Tamland does have a darker side, however. During the battle scene, Brick starts by pulling out a hand grenade (when asked where he got it, he replies "I don't know"). Later in the skirmish, he kills a man with a trident. After the battle, Ron, who is very surprised at Brick's success with the trident, advises Brick to "lay low for a while", and to "find a safe house or a relative close by" because Brick is "probably wanted for murder". He once held a celebrity golf tournament, but when asked whether he would hold it again, he remarked "No, too many people died last year."

- Fred Willard as Ed Harken: The news director of the Channel Four News station. His youngest son, Chris, who does not appear in this film but does appear in *Wake Up, Ron Burgundy: The Lost Movie*, is apparently very ill-behaved. It is revealed that Chris (Justin Long) goes to a Catholic school and has shot a crossbow into a crowd while on LSD, was caught reading German pornography in school, and took the marching band hostage with a gun.

- Chris Parnell as Garth Holladay: Ed's assistant at the Channel Four News station. Ron Burgundy was his hero, before he used foul language during a news broadcast. He is frequently ignored by the news team, even though his main job at the station appears to be keeping them out of trouble.

- Vince Vaughn as Wes Mantooth (Uncredited): The lead anchor of the competing KQHS Channel 9 Evening News Team is Burgundy's chief rival. It is revealed early on that Mantooth is extremely sensitive about insults directed towards his mother, Dorothy Mantooth, whom he regards as a "saint." Mantooth is consistently irritated by his being second in the ratings, causing him to ultimately initiate an anchorman battle against Burgundy and three other news teams. He ultimately pulls Burgundy from a ladder out of the bear pit, explaining that while he hates him he nonetheless respects him as a journalist. The character is loosely based on the CBC news anchor Peter Mansbridge. He serves as the main antagonist of the film.

- Luke Wilson as Frank Vitchard: A competing news anchor whose station, Channel 2, is third in the ratings. During the film, he gets one arm chopped off in the anchorman battle by the lead anchor of the Public news team (Tim Robbins), and his other arm ripped off by a Kodiak Bear near the end of the film (which he deems "ri-goddamn-diculous"). During the climactic scene, he is seen (in an apparent goof) reporting for Channel 9.

- **Unknown** as Baxter, Ron's beloved dog. Burgundy's relationship with Baxter is almost one of equality, despite one party being a dog. Ron even calls him his 'little gentleman.' He has the uncanny ability to communicate with his master in English; in a scene Baxter barks at Ron, and Ron replies, "you know I don't speak Spanish, in English please." Later in the film, Baxter is punted off the towering San Diego – Coronado Bridge during an encounter between Ron and a biker (Jack Black) whom Ron hit with a burrito. Eventually, Baxter comes back at the end of the film and saves Ron and Veronica from the bears at the zoo by speaking to them about their cousin, Katow-jo, who he met in his time in the wilderness. He doesn't like Veronica, telling Ron that if she moves in he is 'not cool with that.' The name could possibly be a nod to *The Mary Tyler Moore Show* character Ted Baxter, who, like Ron, was incredibly pompous and equally, if not more, dim-witted.

Cameos

- Ben Stiller appears as Arturo Mendez (Spanish language channel news anchor)

- Tim Robbins appears as the Public News anchor (uncredited)
- Danny Trejo appears as a bartender.
- Jack Black as a motorcyclist whom Ron Burgundy hits with a burrito (uncredited)
- Neil Flynn, who plays the role of "Janitor" on the TV show *Scrubs*, also makes a cameo appearance in one of the deleted scenes as a police officer helping Ron to look for Baxter's body.
- Jerry Stiller can be seen very briefly, from a distance, sitting alone at the far end of the bar in the very beginning of the "Rocky's Bar Grill & Fine Dining" scene. (uncredited)
- Judd Apatow, who produced the film, can be seen briefly as a news station employee during the scene in which Brian is attempting to seduce Veronica with the Sex Panther cologne.
- Paul F. Tompkins is seen hosting the cat show competition.
- Jay Johnston is briefly seen as part of the Eyewitness News Team during the Anchorman gang fight.
- Robin Antin is seen only for a while when she is in the background in one of Ben Stiller's scenes.
- Fred Armisen plays Tino, the owner of the restaurant that Ron frequents.
- Adam McKay who directed the film, can be seen as one of the janitors hosing down Brian Fantana outside the TV centre and commenting on the smell of the Sex Panther cologne.
- Seth Rogen appears as Scottie, the cameraman during the cat show competition and later while the news crews are gathering to cover the panda giving birth.
- Jimmy Bennett appears as Tommy (uncredited)

Narration

The opening and closing scenes are narrated by veteran Chicago CBS (WBBM-TV) news anchor Bill Kurtis. Bill Kurtis, who currently hosts A&E's *American Justice* and *Cold Case Files*, is the winner of twenty Emmys.

Production

Although *Anchorman* is set in San Diego, the real San Diego appears only in brief aerial shots—modern shots that include many downtown buildings not yet built in the 1970s. According to the official production notes and "making of" documentary (both included on the DVD), *Anchorman* was actually filmed in Los Angeles, Glendale, and Long Beach on sets which were dressed to look like San Diego in the 1970s. Notably, Los Angeles, Glendale, and Long Beach are in the studio zone, while San Diego is not.

Reception

Critical response

Anchorman was released on July 9, 2004 in 3,091 theaters and grossed US$ $28.4 million in its opening weekend. It went on to gross $85.3 million in North America and $5.3 million in the rest of the world for a worldwide total of $89.3 million, well above its $26 million budget.[3]

The film was generally well-received by critics with a 66% rating on Rotten Tomatoes and a 63 metascore at Metacritic. Film critic Roger Ebert gave the film three out of four stars and wrote, "Most of the time... *Anchorman* works, and a lot of the time it's very funny".[4] *Rolling Stone* film critic Peter Travers also gave the film three out of four stars and wrote, "If you sense the presence of recycled jokes from *Animal House* onward, you'd be right. But you'd be wrong to discount the comic rapport Ferrell has with his cohorts, notably the priceless Fred Willard as the harried station manager".[5] In his review for *Entertainment Weekly*, Owen Gleiberman gave the film a "C+" rating and wrote, "Yet for a comedy set during the formative era of happy-talk news, *Anchorman* doesn't do enough to tweak the on-camera phoniness of dum-dum local journalism".[6] *USA Today* gave the film three out of four stars and Claudia Puig wrote, "That he can make his anchorman chauvinistic, deluded and ridiculous but still manage to give him some humanity is testimony to Ferrell's comic talents".[7] In her review for the *Los Angeles Times*, Manohla Dargis wrote, "Tightly directed by newcomer Adam McKay, a former head writer on *Saturday Night Live* who cooked up the screenplay with Ferrell, *Anchorman* never reaches the sublime heights of that modern comedy classic *There's Something About Mary*. Big deal — it's a hoot nonetheless and the scaled-down aspirations seem smart".[8]

Empire magazine ranked Ron Burgundy #26 in their "The 100 Greatest Movie Characters" poll.[9] *Empire* also ranked *Anchorman* at number 113 in their poll of the 500 Greatest Films Ever. *Entertainment Weekly* ranked Burgundy #40 in their "The 100 Greatest Characters of the Last 20 Years" poll and Ferrell said, "He is my favorite character I've played, if I have to choose one ... Looking back, that makes it the most satisfying thing I've ever done".[10]

Unrated version

In the unrated version of *Anchorman*, there are four minutes worth of additional scenes that were not shown in the theaters to secure the PG-13 rating instead of an R rating. Some of these found their way into *Wake Up, Ron Burgundy: The Lost Movie*. They are:

Ron's SportsCenter audition.

- A scene where Ron imagines that he and Veronica are married and shows them making out in front of their children.
- A scene showing Ron, on the air talking how he is proud of his mane of pubic hair.
- An alternate conversation after the party, where Champ talks about pooping out a live squirrel. Then Brick tells Champ apologetically that he ate his chocolate squirrel.
- The extended version of Ron being dragged out of the station into an angry mob after saying "Go fuck yourself, San Diego," on the news. He says "fuck" many more times in the extended version.
- Ron goes to Tino's (the restaurant where Ron took Veronica out and played jazz flute) after the incident and Tino forces him to eat cat poop before he brings him a steak. Weeping bitterly, Ron eats some of the feces, but is making such a scene that he is disturbing other restaurant patrons.

Wake Up, Ron Burgundy: The Lost Movie

The film, *Wake Up, Ron Burgundy: The Lost Movie*, was released straight to DVD in 2004, which includes alternate scenes containing much of the original plot.[11]

Sequel

In May 2008, McKay told one website he and star Will Ferrell have talked about wanting to do an *Anchorman* sequel.[1] Steve Carell told MTV he would reprise his role as Brick Tamland if the opportunity arose.[12] In an interview with ITV1's London Tonight in August 2008, Ferrell confirmed plans for a sequel but indicated it could take some time to happen.

On March 23, 2010, Ferrell said it was unlikely that a sequel would be made, telling *Zoo Magazine* that getting the cast together would be too difficult. The following month, McKay said the studio had turned down a proposal for a sequel, even after McKay had told them Ferrell, Carell and Rudd would take pay cuts.[13]

References

[1] "Is *Anchorman 2* Coming?" (http://www.collider.com/entertainment/news/article.asp/aid/7788/tcid/1). Collider. May 4, 2008. . Retrieved 2010-05-02.

[2] Davis, Erik (April 29, 2010). "Paramount Cancels 'Anchorman 2'" (http://www.cinematical.com/2010/04/29/ paramount-cancels-anchorman-2/?icid=main). Cinematical. . Retrieved 2010-05-02.

[3] "*Anchorman: The Legend of Ron Burgundy*" (http://www.boxofficemojo.com/movies/?id=anchorman.htm). *Box Office Mojo*. . Retrieved 2008-06-06.

[4] Ebert, Roger (July 9, 2004). "*Anchorman: The Legend of Ron Burgundy*" (http://rogerebert.suntimes.com/apps/pbcs.dll/article?AID=/ 20040709/REVIEWS/407090301/1023). *Chicago Sun-Times*. . Retrieved 2008-12-02.

[5] Travers, Peter (July 14, 2004). "*Anchorman: The Legend of Ron Burgundy*" (http://www.rollingstone.com/reviews/movie/6298127/ review/6298160/anchorman_the_legend_of_ron_burgundy). *Rolling Stone*. . Retrieved 2008-12-02.

[6] Gleiberman, Owen (July 7, 2004). "*Anchorman: The Legend of Ron Burgundy*" (http://www.ew.com/ew/article/0,,661411,00.html). *Entertainment Weekly*. . Retrieved 2008-12-02.

[7] Puig, Claudia (July 8, 2004). "Tune in to *Anchorman*" (http://www.usatoday.com/life/movies/reviews/2004-07-08-anchorman_x.htm). *USA Today*. . Retrieved 2010-05-04.

[8] Dargis, Manohla (July 9, 2004). "*Anchorman*" (http://www.calendarlive.com/movies/reviews/cl-et-dargis9jul09,2,588852.story). *Los Angeles Times*. . Retrieved 2010-05-04.

[9] "The 100 Greatest Movie Characters" (http://www.empireonline.com/100-greatest-movie-characters/default.asp?c=26). *Empire*. . Retrieved 2008-12-02.

[10] Ferrell, Will (June 4/11, 2010). "The 100 Greatest Characters of the Last 20 Years". *Entertainment Weekly*: pp. 64

[11] "*Find The Film* movie trivia" (http://www.findthefilm.com/movies/anchorman_the_legend_of_ron_burgundy.php). . Retrieved June 21, 2009.

[12] Carroll, Larry (June 4, 2008). "Steve Carell Says He's "Absolutely" Down For *Anchorman* Sequel" (http://moviesblog.mtv.com/2008/06/ 04/steve-carell-says-hes-absolutely-down-for-anchorman-sequel/). MTV Movies Blog. . Retrieved 2008-06-04.

[13] Fleming, Mike. "No Go On Paramount's 'Anchorman 2'?" (http://www.deadline.com/2010/04/no-go-on-anchorman-2-for-paramount/), Deadline.com, April 29, 2010

External links

- Official website (http://http://www.anchorman-themovie.com/)
- *Anchorman: The Legend of Ron Burgundy* (http://www.imdb.com/title/tt0357413/) at the Internet Movie Database
- *Anchorman: The Legend of Ron Burgundy* (http://www.allmovie.com/work/28809) at Allmovie
- *Anchorman: The Legend of Ron Burgundy* (http://www.boxofficemojo.com/movies/?id=anchorman.htm) at Box Office Mojo
- *Anchorman: The Legend of Ron Burgundy* (http://www.rottentomatoes.com/m/anchorman/) at Rotten Tomatoes
- *Anchorman: The Legend of Ron Burgundy* (http://www.metacritic.com/film/titles/anchorman) at Metacritic
- Sex Panther Cologne Web Site (http://www.sex-panther.com)

The 40-Year-Old Virgin

The 40-Year-Old Virgin	
Theatrical release poster	
Directed by	Judd Apatow
Produced by	Judd Apatow Shauna Robertson Clayton Townsend Seth Rogen Steve Carell
Written by	Judd Apatow Steve Carell
Starring	Steve Carell as **Andy Stitzer**
Music by	Lyle Workman
Cinematography	Jack N. Green
Editing by	Brent White
Studio	Apatow Productions
Distributed by	Universal Studios
Release date(s)	August 19, 2005
Running time	116 minutes
Country	United States
Language	English Spanish
Budget	$26 million
Gross revenue	$177,378,645

The 40-Year-Old Virgin is a 2005 American screwball comedy film about an involuntarily celibate man's journey to finally obtain romance and sexual intercourse. It was written and directed by Judd Apatow and co-written by the film's lead star, Steve Carell, though the film itself features a great deal of improvised dialogue.[1] The film received its general North American theatrical release on August 19, 2005 and was released on region 1 DVD on December

13, 2005.[2]

Plot

Andy Stitzer (Steve Carell) is the eponymous 40-year-old virgin. He is a well-meaning, highly neurotic, somewhat stereotypical nerd. Andy lives alone, collects action figures, plays video games, and his social life seems to consist of watching *Survivor* with his elderly neighbors. He works in the stockroom at an electronics store called SmartTech. When a friend drops out of a poker game, Andy's co-workers David (Paul Rudd), Cal (Seth Rogen), and Jay (Romany Malco) reluctantly invite Andy to join them. At the game, when conversation turns to past sexual exploits, Andy desperately makes up a story, but reveals his virginity when he compares the feel of a woman's breast to a "bag of sand". Feeling sorry for him, the group resolves to help Andy lose his virginity.

Throughout the next several days, the gang's efforts prove to be unsuccessful, partly because all three men give Andy different and sometimes contradictory advice. Later, Cal advises Andy to simply ask questions when talking to women, which makes Andy seem mysterious. His advice proves to be the most helpful, when Beth (Elizabeth Banks), a bookstore clerk, takes a liking to Andy. Andy starts to open up, and begins to form true friendships with his co-workers. David continues to obsess over his ex-girlfriend, Amy (Mindy Kaling). After meeting her unexpectedly during a speed-dating event attended by the group, he has an emotional breakdown while making a sale and is subsequently sent home by store manager Paula (Jane Lynch), who promotes Andy to fill in for him. Jay, seeing Andy's continued reluctance to approach female customers, attempts to force the issue by hiring Andy a prostitute. When Andy discovers that Jay has inadvertently hired a transvestite, he is prompted to confront his friends, and tells them that he is taking matters into his own hands. Andy lands a date with Trish Piedmont (Catherine Keener), a woman he met on the sales floor who owns a store across the street. After Andy and Trish's first date, in which they are interrupted by Trish's teenage daughter Marla (Kat Dennings) as they are about to have sex, Andy decides to tell Trish he is a virgin. Before he can tell her, Trish suggests that they postpone having sex, to which Andy enthusiastically agrees; they decide they won't have sex until their twentieth date. Meanwhile, Paula is impressed by Andy's salesmanship and promotes him to floor manager.

As Andy draws closer to his twentieth date with Trish, his friends begin to deal with the consequences of their lifestyles. David, still spiraling in his obsession with Amy, has become disillusioned with sex and has taken a vow of celibacy, prompting Cal to lure him out by hiring an attractive young woman named Bernadette (Marika Dominczyk) to work in the stockroom. After overreacting during an argument with an obnoxious customer (Kevin Hart), Jay reveals that his girlfriend Jill broke up with him after learning he has been cheating on her. Andy comforts Jay, who advises that sex can ruin a relationship. However, Jill later decides to take Jay back after learning she is pregnant. Andy and Trish's relationship grows, and Trish suggests that Andy sell his collectible action figures in order to raise enough money to open his own store. When they finally reach the twentieth date, Andy is still reluctant and resists Trish, upsetting her. An argument ensues, in which Andy accuses Trish of pushing him into changing his life against his will, and Andy leaves for the nightclub where Jay is celebrating his girlfriend's pregnancy. He quickly gets drunk, and after running into Beth, leaves for her apartment with her. Meanwhile, David finally relinquishes his celibacy and hooks up with Bernadette, and Trish's daughter Marla convinces her to go and make up with Andy.

By this time Andy has sobered up and, after witnessing Beth's disturbing methods of foreplay, he starts to have second thoughts. As Andy is leaving her bathroom, he finds his friends waiting outside, having followed to warn him about Beth and encourage him to go back to Trish. They leave together, and Andy returns to his apartment, where he finds Trish waiting for him. He attempts to apologize, but Trish, having found a myriad of suspicious belongings in his apartment, now thinks that Andy may be some sort of sexual deviant. Andy tries to convince her otherwise and declares his love for her, but she leaves in alarm and disgust. Andy chases after her on his bike but eventually runs headlong into the side of her car. Trish rushes to his side in concern, and he finally confesses to her that he is a virgin. She is surprised to learn that this is the reason behind his strange behavior, as she does not consider it to be important, and they kiss.

In the film's climax, Andy and Trish get married in a lavish ceremony with everyone in attendance, with a sidelong mention of Andy's action figures having sold for approximately half a million dollars. Afterwards, they consummate their marriage. The film ends with an over-the-top musical scene in which the cast of the film sing and dance to "Aquarius/Let the Sunshine In".

Cast

- Steve Carell as Andy Stitzer
- Catherine Keener as Trish Piedmont
- Paul Rudd as David
- Romany Malco as Jay
- Seth Rogen as Cal
- Jane Lynch as Paula
- Elizabeth Banks as Beth
- Leslie Mann as Nicky
- Kat Dennings as Marla Piedmont
- Gerry Bednob as Mooj
- Shelley Malil as Haziz
- Jonah Hill as eBay customer
- Marika Dominczyk as Bernadette
- Mindy Kaling as Amy
- Mo Collins as Gina
- Stormy Daniels as Porn star
- Loudon Wainwright as Priest
- Cedric Yarbrough as Health clinic dad #1
- David Koechner as Health clinic dad #2
- Jeff Kahn as Health clinic dad #3
- Kevin Hart as Smart Tech Customer
- Rose Abdoo as Mother at Restaurant
- Jazzmun as Prostitute Call Girl
- Nancy Carell as Health Clinic Counselor (as Nancy Walls)
- Wyatt Smith as Boy at Wedding (uncredited)
- Ann Christine as Kim (uncredited)

Reception

Critical reception

The film received largely positive reviews with 85% of 160 critics giving it a "fresh" review on Rotten Tomatoes.[3]

Ebert and Roeper gave the film a "two thumbs up" rating. Roger Ebert said, "I was surprised by how funny, how sweet, and how wise the movie really is" and "the more you think about it, the better *The 40-Year-Old Virgin* gets".[4] The pair gave minor criticisms, with Ebert describing "the way she (Catherine Keener as 'Trish') empathizes with Andy" as "almost too sweet to be funny" and Richard Roeper saying that the film was too long, and at times extremely frustrating.[4] Roeper later chose the film as the tenth best of 2005.[5] The film was criticized by Catholics for promoting the message that there is something wrong with being a virgin.[6] Conservative syndicated columnist Cal Thomas criticized *The 40-Year Old Virgin* for not being a "tribute to self-control or purity".[7]

Owen Gleiberman of *Entertainment Weekly* gave the movie an A-, saying that Carell "plays him [Andy] in the funniest and most surprising way possible: as a credible human being."

Manohla Dargis of *The New York Times* called the film a "charmingly bent comedy", noting that Carell conveys a "sheer likability" and a "range as an actor" that was "crucial to making this film work as well as it does."[8]

In December 2005, the film was chosen by the American Film Institute as one of the ten best movies of the year, the only comedy film to be so recognized (though the comedy-drama *The Squid and the Whale* was also chosen).

The film was also ranked #30 on Bravo's *100 Funniest Movies*.

Box office

In the United States, the film is rated R for "pervasive sexual content, language, and some drug use".

The film was a summer hit, and opened at #1 at the box office, grossing $21,422,815[9] on its opening weekend, and stayed at No. 1 the following weekend. The film grossed a total of $109,449,237 on the domestic market, and $67,929,408 overseas, for a total of $177,378,645. The film was 25th in global gross, and 19th in the United States that year.

Disclaimer

The AHA withheld its "no animals were harmed..." disclaimer due to the accidental deaths of several tropical fish used in the film.[10]

Milestones

The production used over a million feet of film, a milestone reached on the last day of filming and recognized with free champagne by the company providing the film stock.[11] Using the conversion of 90 feet of film per minute, this means that the shooting ratio for the film is 96:1 for the theatrical (84:1 for the unrated version).

References

[1] Commentary track for the unrated DVD version of the film.

[2] DVD details for *The 40 Year-Old Virgin* (http://imdb.com/title/tt0405422/dvd) from IMDb

[3] The 40-Year-Old Virgin (http://www.rottentomatoes.com/m/40_year_old_virgin/) from Rotten Tomatoes

[4] review on *Ebert & Roeper* (http://tvplex.go.com/buenavista/ebertandroeper/mp3/050815-40_year_old_virgin.mp3) in MP3 format

[5] Ebert & Roeper, The Best of 2005 (http://tvplex.go.com/buenavista/ebertandroeper/060102.html)

[6] Catholicnews.com (http://www.catholicnews.com/data/movies/05mv598.htm)

[7] "When gas was cheap and people were valuable" (http://townhall.com/columnists/CalThomas/2005/08/17/when_gas_was_cheap_and_people_were_valuable) by Cal Thomas

[8] Losing His Innocence, Not a Minute Too Soon (http://movies2.nytimes.com/2005/08/19/movies/19virg.html?ex=1153368000&en=ac42cc9a7086bbc9&ei=5070), an August 2005 review from *The New York Times*

[9] The 40-Year-Old Virgin (2005) (http://www.boxofficemojo.com/movies/?id=40yearoldvirgin.htm)

[10] "The 40 Year Old Virgin-Rating:Monitored, unacceptable" (http://www.ahafilm.info/movies/mr.phtml?fid=7682). American Humane Society. .

[11] Interview with Steve Carell and Paul Rudd (http://filmforce.ign.com/articles/642/642426p1.html) - from IGN

External links

- Official website (http://http://www.the40yearoldvirgin.com/)
- *The 40-Year-Old Virgin* (http://www.imdb.com/title/tt0405422/) at the Internet Movie Database
- *The 40-Year-Old Virgin* (http://www.allmovie.com/work/318215) at Allmovie
- *The 40-Year-Old Virgin* (http://www.boxofficemojo.com/movies/?id=40yearoldvirgin.htm) at Box Office Mojo
- *The 40-Year-Old Virgin* (http://www.rottentomatoes.com/m/40_year_old_virgin/) at Rotten Tomatoes

You, Me and Dupree

You, Me and Dupree	
Film poster	
Directed by	• Anthony Russo • Joe Russo
Produced by	• Mary Parent • Scott Stuber • Owen Wilson
Written by	Mike LeSieur
Starring	• Matt Dillon • Owen Wilson • Kate Hudson • Michael Douglas • Seth Rogen
Music by	Theodore Shapiro
Distributed by	Universal Pictures
Release date(s)	July 14, 2006
Running time	109 minutes
Country	United States
Language	English
Budget	$54 million
Gross revenue	$130,345,625

You, Me and Dupree is a 2006 romantic comedy film directed by Anthony Russo and Joe Russo, written by Mike LeSieur, and produced by Mary Parent, Scott Stuber, and Owen Wilson.

The film revolves around newlyweds Carl and Molly Peterson (Matt Dillon and Kate Hudson). After Carl's best man and friend Randolph Dupree (Owen Wilson), loses his job and apartment, the couple allow him to move in but Dupree inevitably overstays his welcome.

Plot

Molly (Kate Hudson) and Carl (Matt Dillon) are preparing for their wedding day in Hawaii, until Carl's friend Neil (Seth Rogen) interrupts to say that Dupree (Owen Wilson) got lost. They drive off together to pick up Dupree, who appeared to have hitched a ride with a light plane after landing on the wrong island. A day before the wedding, Molly's father (Michael Douglas), who is also CEO of the company that Carl works for, makes a toast with humorous remarks at Carl's expense, foreshadowing a conflict between the two. Later at a pre-celebration at a bar, Carl neglects Dupree to be with Molly while he is about to perform a drinking tradition. Carl and Dupree later make up on the beach, as Dupree apologizes for laughing at Molly's father's jokes, and tells Carl that he has "Carlness." Carl and Molly get married. When Carl returns to work, at Molly's father's Thompson Land Development, he is surprised to find that Mr. Thompson has promoted him to be in charge of a design he proposed, though it had been altered somewhat. Mr. Thompson makes absurd requests which proceed to get worse, starting with Thompson's drastic reimagining of Carl's new architecture project, requesting that Carl take the Thompson name instead and that Carl get a vasectomy to prevent childbearing later on.

Before returning home to celebrate his promotion with Molly, Carl stops by the bar, where he finds Neil and Dupree. After Neil leaves due to his wife's curfew, Dupree reveals that he was fired, as he apparently did not have clearance to attend the wedding, subsequently falling behind in his rent and evicted. Losing his car also, as it was the company's. Carl takes Dupree home, asking Molly if he can stay for a little while until he gets back on his feet. Molly is polite, though clearly frustrated as he is disruptive and messy.

Molly sets up Dupree with a woman at her work, a primary school, who is a Mormon librarian. Dupree agrees, though Molly is shocked to find them together when she opens her front door coming home from dinner. Romantic candles burn down the front of the living room and Dupree is evicted.

Meanwhile Carl is being continually stressed out from work, though he and Molly find time to go out for dinner. On the way back they find Dupree sitting on a bench in heavy rain with his belongings. Molly insists they take him back in. Carl makes it known that Dupree must behave this time. The next day, Dupree makes amends, refurbishing the living room, and doing Carl's thank-you letters, as well as making friends with kids from the block. Carl asks Dupree to go to career day at Molly's work as he got tied up at his work and that night Dupree cooks a large dinner for Molly, though Carl is late again, so Molly and Dupree start without him. When Carl finally shows up, he is a little jealous that they were having dinner together, and have a fight.

Carl kicks Dupree out, suspecting an affair, which shocks Dupree. The following night, Mr. Thompson is over for dinner. Dupree climbs the drain pipe and sneaks inside to get his bags back, and during dinner the guests inside hear Dupree fall off the roof. Dupree is found outside and is invited in for dinner. After Mr. Thompson takes a liking to Dupree and asks him to go fishing with him, it enrages Carl, who jumps across the table and attempts to strangle Dupree; Thompson hits Carl over the head with a candlestick shortly after. After returning from the hospital with a neck brace, Dupree and Molly confront Mr. Thompson about what he really thinks of his new son-in-law, while Carl had left. The next morning Dupree gets all the local kids to search for Carl. Dupree eventually finds Carl in the bar, and convinces him to chase after Molly. Dupree helps Carl break in to Mr. Thompson's office, as Dupree distracts Paco, the security guard, whilst Carl marches into his father-in-law's office and confronts him. The two finally reach an understanding and Thompson admits to his agenda of insulting Carl. Dupree and Carl return to the house, where Carl and Molly reunite, Carl apologizing, and agree to work it all out.

Dupree becomes an author and a motivational speaker, with Paco now at his side as his number two.

After the End Credits, Lance Armstrong is shown lying down on the grass reading Dupree's own book repeating the word "Lance-ness" to himself with different pronunciations.

Production

The film's production budget totalled $54 million.[1] Composer Rolfe Kent scored the film, and at the very last minute—a mere week before the press screenings—his score was replaced by one written by Theodore Shapiro. The scene that has Dupree arriving by plane on the wrong island was shot in the same valley as Jurassic Park. In the special features of the film, there is a different version trailer of *You, Me and Dupree* where in the trailer Dupree and Molly are married and Carl moves in. The DVD release of the film also contains a re-cut trailer horror/thriller version of the film.

Cast

- Owen Wilson as Randolph "Randy" Dupree
- Matt Dillon as Carl Peterson
- Kate Hudson as Molly Thompson Peterson
- Michael Douglas as Bob Thompson
- Seth Rogen as Neil
- Amanda Detmer as Annie
- Ralph Ting as Toshi
- Todd Stashwick as Tony
- Bill Hader as Mark
- Lance Armstrong as himself
- Billy Gardell as the bar keep

Reception

Rotten Tomatoes gives the film a rating of "rotten" based on 131 negative reviews out of a total 165.[2]

Box office

On release for 84 days in movie theaters domestically, the movie grossed $75,628,110, and in addition earned $54,717,515 in foreign markets, for a worldwide total of $130,345,625. [1]

Steely Dan response

The film's title caused a minor stir as the uncommon name, Dupree, is the same as the title character in the Steely Dan song "Cousin Dupree" from their 2000 album, *Two Against Nature*. Steely Dan founders, Donald Fagen and Walter Becker wrote a somewhat tongue-in-cheek letter to actor Owen Wilson's brother Luke Wilson about the apparent absconding of their character's name.[3] The duo invited the elder Wilson to make up for the "theft" of their character's name by coming on stage with them at one of their concerts to apologize to the band's fans. Owen Wilson gave a tongue-in-cheek response to the letter, stating in a press conference, "I have never heard the song 'Cousin Dupree' and I don't even know who this gentleman, Mr. Steely Dan, is. I hope this helps to clear things up and I can get back to concentrating on my new movie, 'HEY 19.'"[4]

References

[1] ""Box Office Mojo"" (http://boxofficemojo.com/movies/?id=youmeanddupree.htm). 2006-08-03. . Retrieved 2006-08-03.

[2] *You, Me and Dupree* (http://www.rottentomatoes.com/m/you_me_and_dupree/) at Rotten Tomatoes. Retrieved on 2009-10-03.

[3] Becker and Fagen. Open Letter to the Great Comic Actor, Luke Wilson (http://www.steelydan.com/heyluke.html) (July 17, 2006). Accessed October 3, 2006.

[4] AP Owen Wilson Says 'Dupree' Is No Rip-Off (http://www.washingtonpost.com/wp-dyn/content/article/2006/07/28/AR2006072801025.html) (July 28, 2006). Accessed October 3, 2006

External links

- Official website (http://http://www.youmeanddupree.com)
- *You, Me and Dupree* (http://www.imdb.com/title/tt0463034/) at the Internet Movie Database
- *You, Me and Dupree* (http://www.rottentomatoes.com/m/you_me_and_dupree/) at Rotten Tomatoes
- *You, Me and Dupree* (http://www.boxofficemojo.com/movies/?id=youmeanddupree.htm) at Box Office Mojo
- *You, Me and Dupree* Production Notes (http://moviegrande.com/dupree)

Knocked Up

Knocked Up	
 Theatrical release poster	
Directed by	Judd Apatow
Produced by	Judd Apatow Shauna Robertson Seth Rogen Evan Goldberg
Written by	Judd Apatow
Starring	Seth Rogen Katherine Heigl Leslie Mann Paul Rudd Jason Segel Jonah Hill Jay Baruchel Martin Starr
Music by	Loudon Wainwright III Joe Henry
Cinematography	Eric Alan Edwards
Editing by	Craig Alpert Brent White
Studio	Apatow Productions
Distributed by	Universal Pictures
Release date(s)	June 1, 2007
Running time	129 minutes (Theatrical) 133 minutes (Unrated)
Country	United States
Language	English
Budget	$33 million

Gross revenue	$219,076,518

Knocked Up is a 2007 American comedy film co-produced, written, and directed by Judd Apatow. Starring Seth Rogen, Katherine Heigl, Paul Rudd, and Leslie Mann, the film follows the repercussions of a drunken one-night stand between Rogen's slacker character and Heigl's just-promoted media personality that results in an unintended pregnancy.

Plot

Ben Stone (Seth Rogen) is a lazy, dimwitted and immature 23-year-old Jewish Canadian and claimed illegal immigrant from Vancouver, BC. He lives off funds received in compensation for an injury and sporadically works on a *Mr. Skin*-like website with his roommates (Jason Segel, Jonah Hill, Jay Baruchel, Martin Starr) in between smoking marijuana or goofing off with them at fun parks such as Knott's Berry Farm and other activities. Alison Scott (Katherine Heigl) is a career-minded woman who has just been given an on-air role with E! Entertainment Television, and is living in the pool house with her sister Debbie's (Leslie Mann) family. While celebrating her promotion, Alison meets Ben at a local night club. After a night of drinking, they end up having sex. Due to a misunderstanding as they take to her bed, they do not use protection: Alison uses the phrase "just do it already" to encourage Ben to put the condom on without obsessing over it, but he misinterprets this to mean to dispense without even using one. The following morning, they quickly learn over breakfast that they have little in common and go their separate ways, which leaves Ben visibly defeated when she walks away.

Eight weeks later, Alison experiences morning sickness during an interview with James Franco, and discovers she is pregnant. She contacts Ben for the first time since their one-night stand to tell him. Although taken aback, Ben says he will be there to support Alison having the baby. While he is still unsure about being a parent, his father (Harold Ramis) is overjoyed and tells him that he was the best thing that ever happened to him. Alison's mother (Joanna Kerns) tries to convince her daughter to have an abortion, but Alison decides to keep the child. Later, Alison and Ben decide to give their relationship a chance. The seemingly mismatched couple's efforts include Ben making an awkward marriage proposal with a empty ring box, promising to get her one someday. Alison thinks it is too early to think about marriage, because she is more concerned with hiding the pregnancy from her boss, who asked her when she first got the on-air job to be "firm" and "tight" for the cameras.

After a somewhat promising beginning, tensions surface in the relationship. Alison is increasingly anxious over Ben's lack of responsibility and commitment, and has doubts about the longevity of their relationship. These thoughts race through her mind due to her sister's unhappy marriage. Debbie's husband, Pete (Paul Rudd), works as a talent scout for rock bands, but he leaves at odd hours in the night, which makes her suspect he is having an affair. Upon investigating, she learns that he is actually part of a fantasy baseball draft, which he explains he participates in in order to have some time free from Debbie's controlling manner. This results in their estrangement, and when Ben subsequently expresses amusement at Pete's deception, it leads to a heated argument with Alison as they drive to her doctor one day. Angered, she ejects him from her car and abandons him in the middle of nowhere, leading to their own breakup.

Ben and Pete decide to go on a road trip to Las Vegas. Under the heavy influence of psychedelic mushrooms, they realize their loss and decide to take responsibility for their relationships. Simultaneously, Debbie drags a depressed Alison out partying with her, but they are refused admission to a nightclub by its apologetic bouncer (Craig Robinson) on account of Debbie's age and Alison's pregnancy, leading to Debbie's tearful laments about her life prospects and her desire to have Pete back. They subsequently reconcile at their daughter's birthday party, but when Ben tries to work things out with Alison, she is still reluctant to get back together with him, since she feels they have too little in common.

Alison's boss finds out about her pregnancy, and sees an opportunity to boost ratings with female viewers by having Alison interview pregnant celebrities. After talk with his father, Ben decides to take responsibility and goes to great effort to change his ways, including moving out of his friends' house, getting an office job as a web designer and an apartment with a baby's room. He also starts reading the pregnancy books that he had purchased early on. When Alison goes into labor and is not able to contact her doctor, she calls Ben, as Debbie and Pete are out of town on a trip. Ben discovers that the gynecologist they had been seeing (Loudon Wainwright) is out of town at a bar mitzvah in San Francisco, despite having assured them, upon their selection of him months prior, that he never took vacations.

During labor, Alison apologizes for doubting Ben's commitment and admits that she never thought the man who got her pregnant would be the right one for her. When Debbie and Pete arrive at the hospital, Ben adamantly refuses to allow her to be at Alison's side, insisting that that is his place, and relegates her to the waiting room with Pete. The couple welcomes the birth of a baby girl (a boy in the alternate ending) and settle down happily together in a new apartment in L.A.

Cast

- Seth Rogen as Ben Stone
- Katherine Heigl as Alison Scott
- Paul Rudd as Pete
- Leslie Mann as Debbie
- Jason Segel as Jason
- Jay Baruchel as Jay
- Jonah Hill as Jonah
- Martin Starr as Martin
- Charlyne Yi as Jodi
- Iris Apatow as Charlotte
- Maude Apatow as Sadie
- Ryan Seacrest as Ryan
- Joanna Kerns as Mrs. Scott
- Harold Ramis as Harris Stone
- Alan Tudyk as Jack
- Kristen Wiig as Jill
- Bill Hader as Brent
- Ken Jeong as Dr. Kuni
- J.P. Manoux as Dr. Angelo
- B. J. Novak as Doctor
- Mo Collins as Female doctor
- Loudon Wainwright as Dr. Howard
- Adam Scott as Male nurse

Production

Casting

Several of the major cast members return from previous Judd Apatow projects: Seth Rogen, Martin Starr, Jason Segel, and James Franco all starred in the short-lived, cult television series *Freaks and Geeks* which Apatow produced. From the Apatow-created *Undeclared* (which also featured Rogen, Segel and Starr) there is Jay Baruchel and Loudon Wainwright III. Paul Feig, who co-created *Freaks and Geeks* and starred in the Apatow-written movie *Heavyweights*, also makes a brief cameo as the Fantasy Baseball Guy. Steve Carell, who makes a cameo appearance as himself, co-starred alongside Rogen and Rudd in Apatow's *The 40-Year-Old Virgin*, as well as appearing in the

Apatow-produced *Anchorman*. Finally, Leslie Mann, who also appeared in *The 40-Year-Old Virgin*, is married to Apatow and their two daughters play her children in the movie.

Anne Hathaway was originally cast in the role of Alison in the film, but dropped out due to creative reasons[1] that Apatow attributed to her disagreement with plans to use real footage of a woman giving birth.[2] Jennifer Love Hewitt and Kate Bosworth auditioned for the part after Hathaway dropped out, but ended up losing to Katherine Heigl.[3]

Reception

Box office performance

The film opened at #2 at the U.S. box office, grossing $30,690,990 in its opening weekend, behind *Pirates of the Caribbean: At World's End*'s second weekend. The film has grossed $148,768,917 domestically and $70,307,601 million in foreign territories, totaling $219,076,518. The film also spent eight weeks in the box office top ten, the longest streak amongst May–June openers in 2007.[4] A company that specializes in tracking responses to advertising spanning multiple types of media attributed the film's unexpected financial success to the use of radio and television ads in combination.[5]

Critical reviews

Overall *Knocked Up* was very well received by many critics. For example, the film ended up with a 90% "certified fresh" rating on Rotten Tomatoes from 225 reviews (203 fresh, 22 rotten).[6]

The *Los Angeles Times* praised the film's humor despite its plot inconsistencies, noting that, "probably because the central story doesn't quite gel, it's the loony, incidental throwaway moments that really make an impression."[7] Chris Kaltenbach of *The Baltimore Sun* acknowledged the comic value of the film in spite of its shortcomings, saying, "Yes, the story line meanders and too many scenes drone on; *Knocked Up* is in serious need of a good editor. But the laughs are plentiful, and it's the rare movie these days where one doesn't feel guilty about finding the whole thing funny."[8]

In another such review, *Variety* magazine, while calling the film predictable, said that *Knocked Up* was "explosively funny."[9] On the television show *Ebert & Roeper*, Richard Roeper and guest critic David Edelstein gave *Knocked Up* a "two big thumbs up" rating, with Roeper calling it "likeable and real," noting that although "at times things drag a little bit.... still *Knocked Up* earns its sentimental moments."[10]

A more critical review in *Time* magazine noted that, although a typical Hollywood-style comedic farce, the unexpected short-term success of the film may be more attributable to a sociological phenomenon rather than the quality or uniqueness of the film *per se*, positing that the movie's shock value, sexual humor and historically taboo themes may have created a brief nationwide discussion in which movie-goers would see the film "so they can join the debate, if only to say it wasn't that good."[11]

Alleged copyright infringement

Canadian author Rebecca Eckler wrote in *Maclean's* magazine about the similarities between the movie and her book, *Knocked Up: Confessions of a Hip Mother-to-Be*, which was released in the U.S. in March 2005. She is pursuing legal action against Apatow and Universal Pictures on the basis of copyright infringement.[12] [13] In a public statement, Apatow said, "Anyone who reads the book and sees the movie will instantly know that they are two very different stories about a common experience."[14]

Another Canadian author, Patricia Pearson, also publicly claimed similarities between the film and her novel, *Playing House*. She declined to sue and declares Eckler's lawsuit to be frivolous.[15]

Accusations of sexism

Mike White (long time associate of Judd Apatow and screenwriter for *School of Rock*, *Freaks and Geeks*, *Orange County*, and *Nacho Libre*) is said to have been "disenchanted" by Apatow's later films, "objecting to the treatment of women and gay men in Apatow's recent movies," saying of *Knocked Up*, "'At some point it starts feeling like comedy of the bullies, rather than the bullied.'"[16]

In early reviews, both *Slate*'s Dana Stevens and the *Los Angeles Times*' Carina Chocano wrote articles noting the sexist attitudes propagated by the film, a topic which was the primary focus of a *Slate* magazine podcast in which *New York* editor Emily Nussbaum said: "Alison [Heigl's character] made basically zero sense. She was just a completely inconsistent character.... she was this pleasant, blandly hot, peculiarly tolerant, yet oddly *blank* nice girl. She seemed to have no actual needs or desires of her own...."[17] A. O. Scott of *The New York Times* explicitly compared *Knocked Up* to *Juno*, calling the latter a "feminist, girl-powered rejoinder and complement to *Knocked Up*."[18]

In a later *Vanity Fair* interview, lead actor Katherine Heigl admitted that though she enjoyed working with Apatow and Rogen, she had a hard time enjoying the film itself, calling it "a little sexist" and claiming that the film "paints the women as shrews, as humorless and uptight, and it paints the men as lovable, goofy, fun-loving guys."[19] [20] [21]

In response, Apatow did not initially deny the validity of her accusations, saying, "I'm just shocked she [Heigl] used the word *shrew*. I mean, what is this, the sixteen-hundreds?"[22]

Heigl's comments spurred widespread reaction in the media, including a *The Huffington Post* article in which she was labeled "an assertive, impatient go-getter who quickly tired of waiting for her boyfriend to propose".[23] [24] Heigl clarified her initial comments to *People* magazine, stating that, "My motive was to encourage other women like myself to not take that element of the movie too seriously and to remember that it's a broad comedy," adding that, "Although I stand behind my opinion, I'm disheartened that it has become the focus of my experience with the movie."[25]

Meghan O'Rourke of *Slate* called Heigl's comments unsurprising, noting "*Knocked Up* was, as David Denby put it in *The New Yorker*, the culminating artifact in what had become 'the dominant romantic-comedy trend of the past several years—the slovenly hipster and the female straight arrow.'"[26] *The Guardian* noted that Heigl's comments "provoked quite a backlash, and Heigl was described as ungrateful and a traitor. Some people even suggested she would never work again," remarks which were in retrospect proved incorrect and may well have propelled Heigl's career.[27]

In the wake of mounting accusations of sexism, director Judd Apatow discussed ways he might develop more authentic female characters.[28] *New York* magazine quotes Apatow as admitting, "I think the characters are sexist at times, but it's really about immature people who are afraid of women and relationships and learn to grow up." Apatow dismissed Heigl's comments, saying that they were "taken out of context," noting, "It reminds people that they need to buy *Knocked Up* on DVD and judge for themselves;" a reversal (*i.e.*, turning negative accusations of misogyny into a positive for monetary gain) which the article praised as "reverse-jujitsu marketing acumen."[29] In response to another one of Apatow's remarks regarding sexist accusations (*i.e.*, "If people say that the characters are sexist, I say, yeah, that's what I was going for in the first part of the movie, and then they change."), another article in *New York* magazine noted that Apatow was not directly responding to the nature of the accusations, which were not directed at his characters but rather the movie itself, saying, "the characters *aren't* all that sexist, but the movie kind of is," adding that, "The problems with *Knocked Up* have been pointed out by many writers...."[30]

In July 2009, while promoting their film *Funny People* Apatow and Rogen appeared on "The Howard Stern Show" and defended the work in *Knocked Up* and disagreed with the position Heigl had stated. Rogen pointed to Heigl's work in the film *The Ugly Truth* to illustrate his point. Rogen said: "I hear there's a scene where she's wearing underwear with a vibrator in it, so I'd have to see if that is uplifting for women." Apatow attempted to cut Heigl some slack for the criticisms chalking up her harsh words to exhaustion at the end of a long day of interviews, but admitted he never received an apology from Heigl. "You would think at some point I'd get a call saying she was sorry, that she was tired, and then the call never comes." [31]

Top ten lists

The film made the top-ten list of the jury for the 2007 AFI Awards as well as the top-ten lists of several well-known critics, with the AFI jury calling it the "funniest, freshest comedy of this generation." and a film that "stretches the boundaries of romantic comedies." John Newman, respected film critic for the Boston Bubble called the film "a better, raunchy, modern version of *Some Like it Hot.*"[32]

Early on the film was deemed the best reviewed wide release of 2007 by the Rotten Tomatoes' website.[33]

The film appeared on many critics' top-ten lists of the best films of 2007.[34]

- 3rd - Kyle Smith, *New York Post*
- 4th - Christy Lemire, Associated Press[35]
- 5th — Scott Tobias, *The A.V. Club*
- 6th - David Ansen, *Newsweek*
- 8th - Ella Taylor, *LA Weekly*
- 9th - *Empire*
- 9th — Scott Foundas, *LA Weekly* (tied with *Superbad*)
- 10th - A. O. Scott, *The New York Times* (tied with *Juno* and *Superbad*)
- 10th — Lisa Schwarzbaum, *Entertainment Weekly*
- 10th - Peter Travers, *Rolling Stone* (tied with *Juno*)[36]

Awards

On December 16, 2007, the film was chosen by the American Film Institute as one of the ten best movies of the year. It was one of the two pregnancy comedies on the list (*Juno* being the other). *E! News* praised the film's generally unacknowledged success, saying that, "The unplanned pregnancy comedy, shut out of the Golden Globes and passed over by the L.A. and New York critics, was one of 10 films selected Sunday for the American Film Institute's year-end honors."[37]

- The 2007 Teen Choice Awards awarded the film "Choice : Comedy". They also gave Ryan Seacrest "Best Hissy Fit", for his brief cameo, where he becomes self-obsessed and complains about rising young talents, saying that they 'fuck his day up.'
- Judd Apatow was nominated for the Writers Guild of America Award for Best Original Screenplay.
- In 2008, the film was nominated for a Canadian Comedy Award for Best Actor, for Seth Rogen. Coincidentally Rogen lost to Michael Cera for his role in *Superbad*, which Rogen had written.
- *High Times* Magazine awarded the film a Stony Award for Best Pot Comedy in 2007.[38]

Music

Strange Weirdos: Music From and Inspired by the Film Knocked Up, an original soundtrack album, was composed for the film by folk singer-songwriter Loudon Wainwright III and Joe Henry. However, the movie's lead song "Daughter" was written by Peter Blegvad.

In addition to Wainwright's tracks, there were approximately 40 songs featured in the motion picture that were not included on the official soundtrack on Concord Records.[39]

Some of the songs featured in 'Knocked Up' are:

- "We Are Nowhere and It's Now" – Bright Eyes (feat. Emmylou Harris)
- "All Night" by Damien Marley
- "Stand up tall" by Dizzee Rascal
- "Rock Lobster" by The B-52's

- "Police On My Back" by The Clash
- "The Biggest Part of Me" by Ambrosia
- "Smile" by Lily Allen
- "Girl" by Beck
- "King without a Crown" by Matisyahu
- "Toxic" by Britney Spears
- "Santeria" by Sublime
- "Tropicana" by Ratatat
- "Shimmy Shimmy Ya" by Ol' Dirty Bastard
- "Love Plus One" by Haircut 100
- "Rock You Like a Hurricane" by Scorpions
- "Reminiscing" by Little River Band
- "Ashamed" by Tommy Lee
- "Swing" by Savage (featured in the menu section of the DVD)
- "Shame on a Nigga" by Wu-Tang Clan (used in the film's trailer)
- "Grey in LA" by Loudon Wainwright III
- "End of the Line" by Traveling Wilburys (used in the film's trailer)

Home release

Several separate Region 1 DVD versions were released on September 25, 2007. There was the theatrical R-Rated version (128 minutes), an "Unrated and Unprotected" version (133 minutes) (fullscreen and widescreen available independently), a two-disc "Extended & Unrated" collector's edition, and an HD DVD "Unrated and Unprotected" version. On November 7, 2008, *Knocked Up* was released on Blu-ray following the discontinuation of HD DVD, along with other Apatow comedies *The 40-Year-Old Virgin* and *Forgetting Sarah Marshall*.

Spin-off

Variety reported in January 2011 that Paul Rudd and Leslie Mann will reprise their *Knocked Up* roles for a new film Apatow is writing and directing.[40] Apatow claims that it is not a sequel or prequel to *Knocked Up*, but a spin-off, focusing on Pete and Debbie, the couple played by Rudd and Mann.[41] The film is scheduled to begin shooting in the summer of 2011,[41] with a planned release on June 1, 2012.[40]

References

[1] 'Grey's' Star Heigl Gets 'Knocked Up' (http://www.zap2it.com/tv/news/zap-katherineheiglknockedup,0,4692586.story). Zap2it.com. April 18, 2006. Retrieved April 11, 2007.

[2] Judd Apatow's Family Values (http://www.nytimes.com/2007/05/27/magazine/27apatow-t.html?ex=1338436800& en=c446485d479ed8f6&ei=5124&partner=permalink&exprod=permalink). *The New York Times*. May 27, 2007. Retrieved June 3, 2007.

[3] Knocked Up - Shakefire.com Review (http://www.shakefire.com/articles/knockedup.html)

[4] Commentary: Hollywood turnover (http://www.hollywoodreporter.com/hr/content_display/features/columns/film_reporter/ e3icbacc817cd9e1b4ea183ece380eb12be) *THR.com.* "Among last year's May and June openers, only "Knocked Up" lasted in the top 10 for eight weeks."

[5] Radio Advertising Helps Wake Up Sleeper *Knocked Up* (http://www.marketwire.com/mw/release.do?id=756730), an August 2007 press release by Integrated Media Measurements Inc.

[6] *Knocked Up* (http://www.rottentomatoes.com/m/knocked_up/) at Rotten Tomatoes. Retrieved June 17, 2009

[7] Chocano, Carina. "'Knocked Up' is funny, but it's lacking at the core" (http://www.calendarlive.com/la-et-knocked1jun01,0,4812401. story). *Los Angeles Times*. June 1, 2007. Retrieved October 26, 2007.

[8] Kaltenbach, Chris. Baltimore Sun - Movie Review (http://www.baltimoresun.com/entertainment/movies/bal-to. knocked01jun01,0,2591933.story?coll=bal-movies-utility) June 1, 2007. Retrieved October 26, 2007.

[9] Leydon, Joe. "Knocked Up" (http://www.variety.com/review/VE1117933072.html) *Variety*. March 19, 2007. Retrieved April 11, 2007.

[10] *Knocked Up* review on *Ebert & Roeper* (http://bventertainment.go.com/tv/buenavista/ebertandroeper/index2.html?sec=6& subsec=knocked+up) May 27, 2007. Retrieved August 7, 2007.

[11] Corliss, Richard. "Not Knocked Out by 'Knocked Up'" (http://www.time.com/time/arts/article/0,8599,1630498-1,00.html). June 7, 2007. Retrieved October 26, 2007.

[12] Eckler, Rebecca: "Is That my Baby on the Screen" (http://www.macleans.ca/article.jsp?content=20070611_106143_106143), page 69-71. *Maclean's*, Volume 120 Number 22, June 11, 2007.

[13] Complaint for Copyright Infringement: Demand for Jury Trial (http://www.aolcdn.com/tmz_documents/0606_rebecca_eckler.pdf) - legal filing with United States District Court, Central District of California, January 3, 2007.

[14] Author says 'Knocked Up' ripped off (http://www.cnn.com/2007/SHOWBIZ/Movies/06/07/film.knockedup.lawsuit.ap/index.html), Associated Press, CNN, Published June 7, 2007, Retrieved June 9, 2007.

[15] Pearson, Patricia (June 10, 2007). "Knocked over by Knocked Up lawsuit" (http://www.thestar.com/article/223624). *The Star* (Toronto). . Retrieved 2007-09-01.

[16] *New York*. "Mike White Calls Out Judd Apatow" (http://nymag.com/daily/entertainment/2007/05/mike_white_calls_out_judd_apat. html). May 7, 2007.

[17] New York "'Knocked Up' Brings the Gender Wars Back!" (http://nymag.com/daily/entertainment/2007/06/ knocked_up_the_nussbaumsternbe.html)

[18] Scott, A. O. (December 5, 2007) "Seeking Mr. and Mrs. Right for a Baby on the Way" (http://movies.nytimes.com/2007/12/05/movies/ 05juno.html). *The New York Times*.

[19] Vanity Fair (December 3, 2007). "Katherine Heigl Talks About Marriage, Ratings Ploys, and Why She Thinks Knocked Up Is Sexist" (http://www.vanityfair.com/services/presscenter/pressrelease/katherine_heigl200801). Press release. . Retrieved 2007-12-27.

[20] Associated Press. Heigl having 'a really hard time' with 'Grey's' affair (http://www.cnn.com/2007/SHOWBIZ/TV/12/03/people. katherineheigl.ap/index.html) 2004. Retrieved December 14, 2007.

[21] Leslie Bennetts. "Heigl's Anatomy" (http://www.vanityfair.com/culture/features/2008/01/heigl200801). *Vanity Fair*. January 2008.

[22] "Knocked Up" Director Fires Back At Heigl (http://www.hollyscoop.com/katherine-heigl/ knocked-up-director-fires-back-at-heigl_13796.aspx)

[23] "Katherine Heigl On How "Knocked Up" Is Sexist, Ratings Ploys And Mormonism" (http://www.huffingtonpost.com/2007/12/03/ katherine-heigl-on-how-k_n_75086.html). *The Huffington Post*. . Retrieved 2007-12-30.

[24] "CALM DOWN! Katherine Heigl Did Not "Slam" Knocked Up" (http://www.themovieblog.com/2007/12/ calm-down-katherine-heigl-did-not-slam-knocked-up). The Movie Blog. . Retrieved 2007-12-30.

[25] Tim Nudd; Julie Jordan (December 7, 2007). "Katherine Heigl Clarifies *Knocked Up* Remarks". *People*.

[26] O'Rourke, Meghan. "Katherine Heigl's *Knocked Up*" (http://www.slate.com/id/2179621/). *Slate*.

[27] Saner, Emine (19 March 2008). "Joker in the Pack" (http://film.guardian.co.uk/interview/interviewpages/0,,2266494,00.html). *The Guardian* (London). . Retrieved 2008-04-09.

[28] Wloszczyna, Susan. "For Apatow, opportunity knocks" (http://www.usatoday.com/life/movies/news/2007-05-06-judd-apatow_N.htm), *USA Today*, 2007-05-06. Retrieved June 4, 2007.

[29] Youn, Soo. *New York*. "Marketing Genius Judd Apatow Turns Katherine Heigl's 'Knocked Up' Slam Into a Sales Pitch" (http://nymag. com/daily/entertainment/2007/12/marketing_genius_judd_apatow_t.html)

[30] *New York*. "Year in Review: Judd Apatow Is the Man" (http://nymag.com/daily/entertainment/2007/12/judd_apatow_comedy_scientist. html)

[31] Chernikoff, Leah (July 31, 2009). "Taste of her own Medicine?" (http://www.nydailynews.com/gossip/2009/07/31/ 2009-07-31_seth_rogen_director_judd_apatow_slam_knocked_up_costar_katherine_heigl.html). *Daily News (New York)*. . Retrieved June 8, 2010.

[32] AFI AWARDS 2007 (http://www.afi.com/tvevents/afiawards07/movies07.aspx), from the American Film Institute website

[33] http://www.rottentomatoes.com/news/comments/?entryid=424623

[34] "Metacritic: 2007 Film Critic Top Ten Lists" (http://web.archive.org/web/20080102102034/http://www.metacritic.com/film/awards/ 2007/toptens.shtml). Metacritic. Archived from the original (http://www.metacritic.com/film/awards/2007/toptens.shtml) on 2008-01-02. . Retrieved 2008-01-05.

[35] David Germain; Christy Lemire (2007-12-27). "'No Country for Old Men' earns nod from AP critics" (http://web.archive.org/web/ 20080103000750/http://www.columbiatribune.com/2007/Dec/20071227Go!013.asp). *Columbia Daily Tribune*. Archived from the original (http://www.columbiatribune.com/2007/Dec/20071227Go!013.asp) on 2008-01-03. . Retrieved 2007-12-31.

[36] Travers, Peter, (December 19, 2007) "Peter Travers' Best and Worst Movies of 2007" (http://www.rollingstone.com/news/story/ 17686508/peter_travers_best_and_worst_movies_of_2007/10) *Rolling Stone*. Retrieved 2007-12-20

[37] E! News. "AFI Boosts *Knocked Up*" (http://www.eonline.com/news/article/index.jsp?uuid=a79c004e-935f-4503-9ba9-2c7bc64913d8).

[38] "List of High Times Stony Award Winners" (http://www.museumstuff.com/learn/topics/ Stony_Awards::sub::List_Of_High_Times_Stony_Award_Winners).

[39] 'SoundtrackINFO: Knocked Up soundtrack' (http://www.soundtrackinfo.com/ost.asp?soundtrack=6215&t=yes). Soundtrackinfo.com. September, 2007. Retrieved September 29, 2007.

[40] Kroll, Justin (January 6, 2011) "Rudd, Mann reprise 'Knocked Up' roles for Apatow" (http://www.variety.com/article/VR1118029859) *Variety*. Retrieved 2011-1-7

[41] Sciretta Peter (January 7, 2011) "Judd Apatow Confirms New Film Will Not Be a 'Knocked Up' Sequel or Prequel, But A Spin-Off" (http://www.slashfilm.com/judd-apatow-confirms-film-knocked-up-sequel-prequel-spinoff/) */Film.* Retrieved 2011-01-07

External links

- Official website (http://http://www.knockedupmovie.com)
- *Knocked Up* (http://www.imdb.com/title/tt0478311/) at the Internet Movie Database
- *Knocked Up* (http://www.allmovie.com/work/347981) at Allmovie
- *Knocked Up* (http://www.boxofficemojo.com/movies/?id=knockedup.htm) at Box Office Mojo
- *Knocked Up* (http://www.rottentomatoes.com/m/knocked_up/) at Rotten Tomatoes
- *Knocked Up* (http://www.metacritic.com/film/titles/knockedup) at Metacritic
- *Knocked Up* (http://tcmdb.com/title/title.jsp?stid=647604) at the TCM Movie Database

Jay and Seth vs. The Apocalypse

Jay and Seth vs. The Apocalypse	
Directed by	Jason Stone
Produced by	Rachel Robb Kondrath Jason Stone
Written by	Seth Rogen Evan Goldberg Jason Stone
Starring	Seth Rogen Jay Baruchel
Music by	Mark Petrie
Cinematography	Jay Visit
Editing by	Neel Upadhye
Studio	Catastrophic Films
Distributed by	Mandate Films
Release date(s)	June 4, 2007
Running time	9 minutes
Country	Canada
Language	English
Budget	$3000

Jay and Seth vs. The Apocalypse is a 2007 short comedy film written by Canadian comedy writers Seth Rogen, Evan Goldberg, and Jason Stone. The film stars Canadian actors Seth Rogen and Jay Baruchel.

While most disaster films chronicle the adventures of survivors, *Jay and Seth vs. The Apocalypse* follows two of the least likely men to survive the end of the world. In the eight-and-a-half minute short film, two friends who have shut themselves in their apartment argue over potential escape plans. When the water-collection system they've built on their roof gets clogged, one of them must face whatever monsters or elements may be outside in order to fix it.[1] Their room is in shambles, which could either be the result of the apocalypse, or just a messy bachelor pad. A sardonic jibe at the room's condition is heard when one character refers to how bad everything is by saying, "it's not that much worse than our old apartment".[2]

Production

Immediately after wrapping production on *Knocked Up*, Stone and Goldberg worked to turn around the short's script in only three weeks. As a result, the haircuts and body types that Jay Baruchel and Seth Rogen sport in *The Apocalypse* are the same as those in *Knocked Up*.

Principal photography lasted for two days in September 2006, with one day of pick-ups in January 2007. An entire apartment set was built on a sound stage near downtown Los Angeles in four days with crew on a 24-hour rotation. With a total budget of $3000, the production could not afford more preparation time.

The crew shot over three hours of footage with two cameras that was pared down to the final 8.5-minute short. By the time the film was picture-locked, the property had already been optioned by Mandate Films.[3] Only one screening of the completed short was ever held, only being seen in its entirety by a handful of people. As a result, fans often mistakenly report that the trailer on YouTube was a fake, or that it was originally developed only to raise interest in a feature.

After the trailer they put up on YouTube in June 2007 got over 50,000 hits in the first two weeks, Stone and Goldberg began shopping the project around. *Variety* reports that several production companies vied for the rights for production.[4] MovieCritic reports that the interest can be attributed to Seth Rogen's "player power" in Hollywood.[5]

Joblo reports that Rogen and Baruchel are expected to star in a feature film.[6] However, /Film reports that Rogen and Baruchel have definitely signed on to star.[7] Mandate Films purchased the short from Stone and Goldberg.[8] [9] The longer script expands on the men's post-apocalyptic problems as they deal with the massive ramifications of the apocalypse. Mandate president Nathan Kahane is slated to be executive producer alongside Stone and Baruchel. The feature is projected to go into production in 2010 or 2011.[10] [11] It is reported that Mandate has given Rogen and Goldberg major control on the project and a $30 million budget.[12]

Reception

The clip on YouTube, which is the only publicly available footage from the film, bills itself as a trailer because when it was first posted, the filmmakers intended to publicly screen the short at festivals.[13] However, when the film was picked up by Mandate, the short was shelved from festival consideration. This frustrated many fans, who expected to see a feature closer to the 2007 release of the trailer online.[14] The trailer had over 200,000 views in the first 14 months since its release, and has received much more popular acclaim than the filmmakers ever imagined. Critic Novikov predicts the YouTube trailer will disappear as potential filming nears.[15]

Moviefone originally gave a countdown to a January 2009 premiere, but the date was probably based on the original 2007 trailer.[16] [17] [18]

References

[1] CinemaBlend.com: "Seth Rogen And Jay Baruchel Fight The Apocalypse", paragraphs 1 & 4 (http://www.cinemablend.com/new/ Seth-Rogen-And-Jay-Baruchel-Fight-The-Apocalypse-9128.html)

[2] EmpireMovies.com (http://www.empiremovies.com/index.php?id=23690)

[3] CinemaBlend: "Seth Rogen And Jay Baruchel Fight The Apocalypse", paragrph 2 (http://www.cinemablend.com/new.php?id=9128)

[4] Variety: "Rogen, Baruchel set for 'Apocalypse'" (http://www.variety.com/article/VR1117987205.html?categoryid=1236&cs=1& query=JAY+AND+SETH+VS.+THE+APOCALYPSE)

[5] MovieCritic.com: "Rogen has so much player power in Hollywood right now that he could wrap a hot dog in discarded newspaper and people would line up around the block for it" (http://www.moviecritic.com.au/jay-and-seth-vs-the-apocalypse-trailer/)

[6] Joblo: "Rogen's Apocalypse" by Dave Davis (http://joblo.com/rogens-apocalypse)

[7] Slashfilm: "Seth Rogen? Jay Baruchel? And The Apocalypse?! Sign Me Up!" by Drew McWeeny (http://www.slashfilm.com/2008/06/ 11/jay-and-seth-vs-the-apocalypse-trailer-to-become-feature-film/)

[8] SFF World: "Jay and Seth Vs. the Apocalypse" (http://www.sffworld.com/news/570.html)

[9] Snarkerati: "Apocalypse Now: Rogen, Baruchel to Face World's End Together" by Kirsten Anderson (http://snarkerati.com/movie-news/ apocalypse-now-rogen-baruchel-to-face-worlds-end-together/)

[10] IMBb page for Jay and Seth vs. the Apocalypse (2010) (http://www.imdb.com/title/tt1245492/)

[11] Movies.About.com: "Mandate Pictures Picks Up 'Jay and Seth vs. the Apocalypse'" by Rebecca Murray (http://movies.about.com/od/ moviesinproduction/a/jayseth061108.htm)

[12] GeeksOfDoom: "'Jay And Seth Versus The Apocalypse' Video Short To Go Full" (http://geeksofdoom.com/2008/06/12/ jay-and-seth-versus-the-apocalypse-goes-full/)

[13] Jay and Seth vs. The Apocalypse" posted to YouTube June 4, 2007 (http://www.youtube.com/watch?v=ehNFPShWTsg)

[14] Slashfilm: "The idea for the film began as an internet trailer..." (http://www.slashfilm.com/2008/06/11/ jay-and-seth-vs-the-apocalypse-trailer-to-become-feature-film/)

[15] Cinematical review paragraph one (http://www.cinematical.com/2008/06/11/jay-and-seth-vs-the-apocalypse-to-become-a-feature-film/)

[16] MovieFone.com "Jay and Seth vs. the Apocalypse Synopsis & Movie Info" (http://www.moviefone.com/movie/ jay-and-seth-vs-the-apocalypse/1399786/synopsis)

[17] interview with Jay Baruchel: Jay says *Justice League* postponed but *Jay & Seth* is still scheduled to shoot (http://www.joblo.com/jay-talks-jla-and-seth)

[18] TheMovingPicture.com: "Jay and Seth Deal with the Apocalypse " by James Cook (http://themovingpicture.net/jay-and-seth-deal-with-the-apocalypse)

External links

- *Jay & Seth vs. The Apocalypse (2012)* (http://www.imdb.com/title/tt1245492/) at the Internet Movie Database
- New York Magazine: "It's the End of the World As Seth Rogen Knows It" (http://nymag.com/daily/entertainment/2008/06/its_the_end_of_the_world_as_se.html)

Superbad (film)

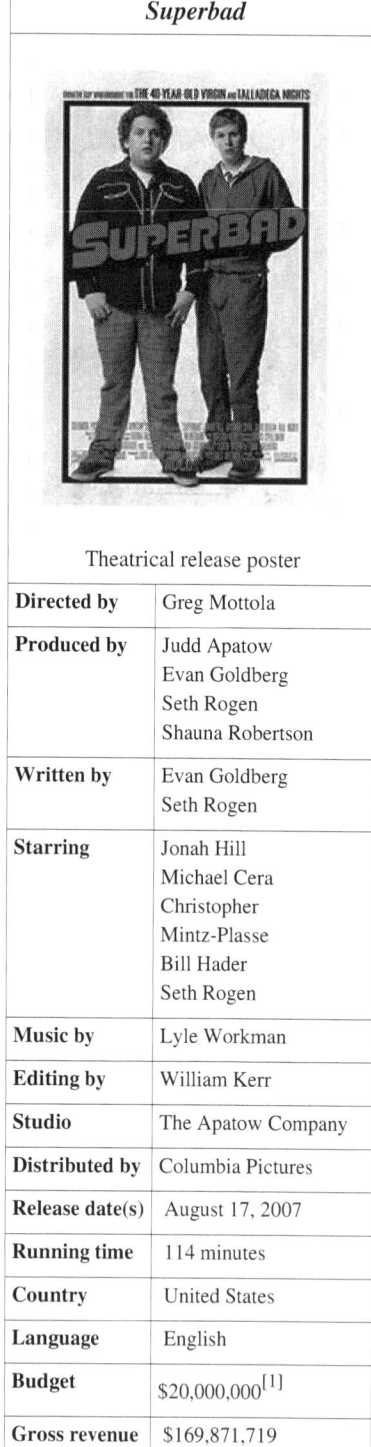

Superbad	
Theatrical release poster	
Directed by	Greg Mottola
Produced by	Judd Apatow Evan Goldberg Seth Rogen Shauna Robertson
Written by	Evan Goldberg Seth Rogen
Starring	Jonah Hill Michael Cera Christopher Mintz-Plasse Bill Hader Seth Rogen
Music by	Lyle Workman
Editing by	William Kerr
Studio	The Apatow Company
Distributed by	Columbia Pictures
Release date(s)	August 17, 2007
Running time	114 minutes
Country	United States
Language	English
Budget	$20,000,000[1]
Gross revenue	$169,871,719

Superbad is a 2007 American comedy film directed by Greg Mottola and starring Jonah Hill and Michael Cera. The film was written by Seth Rogen and Evan Goldberg, who began working on the script when they were both thirteen years old; they completed a draft by the time they were fifteen.[2] The film's main characters have the same given names as Rogen and Goldberg. The film was one of a string of hits by Judd Apatow.

Plot

It is two weeks before the end of high school. Evan (Michael Cera) and Seth (Jonah Hill) are long-time friends in their senior year of high school, about to leave for different colleges. Their mutual friend, Fogell (Christopher Mintz-Plasse), has plans to acquire a fake ID, so Seth agrees to buy alcohol for a party that his crush, Jules (Emma Stone), is hosting. Evan also offers to buy Goldslick vodka for his long-time crush Becca (Martha MacIsaac). There is some tension between Seth and Evan because Evan and Fogell will both be going to Dartmouth while Seth will be going to a state college.

While purchasing the alcohol Fogell is assaulted by a hooded robber, and the police soon arrive. The two officers, Michaels (Seth Rogen) and Slater (Bill Hader), appear to be fooled by Fogell's fake ID (which has the single name "McLovin" as his identity) and offer Fogell a lift to the party. On the way, however, they make numerous stops and display many instances of inappropriate use of police powers, including stealing beers, drinking on the job, unnecessary use of police lights, and improper use of their firearms.

While the police officers are talking to Fogell at the liquor store, Evan and Seth make the assumption that Fogell has been arrested. Seth is suddenly hit by a car, but seems uninjured. To avoid being reported, the driver, Francis (Joe Lo Truglio), agrees to take them to a party, where they reason they can steal the alcohol they need. However, Francis is not welcome at the party and is subsequently assaulted by the host, Mark (Kevin Corrigan), and Seth and Evan are forced to leave, but not before smuggling out beer in laundry detergent bottles.

Once at a safe distance the two stop to catch their breath and Seth tells Evan that he bailed on him. Evan defends himself saying that the whole thing was Seth's idea. Seth retorts saying that not only did Evan bail on him at the party but also at earlier that morning when a bully spat on Seth, and will again be bailing on him when he goes to Dartmouth that Fall. Evan then angrily confesses that he feels Seth has been holding him back for the last three years and that while he could have been out making friends and chasing girls he sat around talking "bullshit." The two then get into a shoving match. During the fight, Seth is again hit by a car, this time the police cruiser occupied by Slater, Michaels, and Fogell. Officer Slater prepares to arrest the teens but Evan runs off and the two officers chase him while the reunited Seth and Fogell make off with the rest of the alcohol. The trio eventually make it to the party.

At the party, a drunken Becca offers to give Evan a blowjob in a secluded upstairs room, but Evan declines with the excuse that she is too drunk, and a heavily intoxicated Becca ends up vomiting on the bed comforter. A drunken Seth tries to kiss Jules, who explains that she does not drink and does not want to do anything while he is intoxicated. Seth attempts to express his feelings for Jules, but passes out from the alcohol and accidentally head-butts her, giving her a black eye. Fogell successfully seduces Nicola (Aviva Farber) and gets her into bed, only to have officers Slater and Michaels break up the party after only a few seconds of sex. Officers Slater and Michaels reveal to Fogell that they were aware of his fake ID all along, and decided to ignore it since they saw a bit of themselves as teenagers in Fogell. Fogell in turn asks them a favor in return for their intrusion upon his love making: the officers pretend to haul him off to jail in front of the entire party to boost his popularity. In return, Fogell signs an affidavit to a concocted story to explain the condition of the wrecked police car which they proceed to have fun destroying. Meanwhile, Evan having passed out from intoxication is carried off by Seth to avoid arrest from the police officers who have spent the remainder of the night searching for them. At Evan's house Seth reveals his brotherly love for Evan, who then reveals the feelings are mutual.

The following morning, Evan and Seth run into Becca and Jules at the mall. After an awkward conversation about the mistakes of the previous night, Seth takes Jules to get cover up for her eye, while Evan and Becca go off to look for some comforters.

Cast

- Jonah Hill as Seth
- Michael Cera as Evan
- Christopher Mintz-Plasse as Fogell
- Seth Rogen as Officer Michaels
- Bill Hader as Officer Slater
- Emma Stone as Jules
- Martha MacIsaac as Becca
- Aviva Farber as Nicola
- Joe Lo Truglio as Francis the Driver
- Kevin Corrigan as Mark
- Danny McBride as Buddy at (5th and Paysview) Party
- Clark Duke as Teen at the Party

Reception

According to Box Office Mojo, the film opened at number one at the United States box office, grossing $33,052,411 in its opening weekend in 2,948 theaters with an average of $11,212 per theater.[3] The film stayed at #1 the second week, grossing $18,044,369.[3] The film has grossed an estimated $121,463,226 in the United States and Canada, and $48,408,493 in other territories, for a total of $170,871,719 worldwide. Compared to the relatively small budget of $20 million, the film earned a massive financial profit.[1] The film is the highest domestic grossing high school comedy of all time.[4]

Superbad received critical praise and was listed as one of the best movies of 2007 by some critics. As of January 24, 2010, the film-critics aggregate site Rotten Tomatoes listed 87% positive reviews based on 195 reviews (170 "fresh", 25 "rotten") with the consensus that it was "an authentic take on the awkwardness of the high school experience".[5] It also has an 87% "Cream Of The Crop" rating.[6] On Metacritic, the film has a score of 76% based on 36 reviews.[7]

Mick LaSalle of the *San Francisco Chronicle* called it 2007's most successful comedy. Roger Ebert of the *Chicago Sun-Times* had the headline of his review read "McLovin It," and gave the film 3 1/2 stars (out of 4) and said "The movie reminded me a little of *National Lampoon's Animal House*, except that it's more mature, as all movies are."[8] Carina Chocano of the *Los Angeles Times* said "Physically, Hill and Cera recall the classic comic duos — Laurel and Hardy, Abbott and Costello, Aykroyd and Belushi. But they are contemporary kids, sophisticated and sensitive to nuance"; she added, "I hope it's not damning the movie with the wrong kind of praise to say that for a film so deliriously smutty, *Superbad* is supercute".[9] Sean Burns of *Philadelphia Weekly* said "2007: the year Judd Apatow and Seth Rogen saved movie comedy", a reference to *Knocked Up* which was released in June.[10] Devin Gordon of *Newsweek* said "As a *Revenge of the Nerds* redux, *Superbad* isn't perfect. But it's super close."[11]

Stephen Farber of *The Hollywood Reporter*, conversely, compared the film to the similar single-day structure of *American Graffiti* and *Dazed and Confused*, but that "it doesn't have the smarts or the depths of those ensemble comedies".[12] The *Hollywood Reporter* review was referenced in the film's DVD audio commentary, particularly the review's suggestion that the two main characters have a homoerotic experience similar to the film *Y Tu Mama Tambien*.[13] Adam Graham of *The Detroit News* said, "the cops belong in a bad *Police Academy* sequel, not this movie", and also that the film "falls short of teen-classic status."[14] Roger Moore of the *Orlando Sentinel* called the film "super-derivative", "super-raunchy", and "*Freaks and Geeks: Uncensored*". Moore went on to say the film shamelessly plagiarizes from films such as *Can't Hardly Wait* and *American Graffiti*. He also said, "Like *Knocked Up*, this is a comedy they don't know how to end. The energy flags as it overstays its welcome." Wesley Morris of *The Boston Globe* said the film "has a degree more sophistication than *Revenge of the Nerds* and *American Pie*, and less than the underrated *House Party*". Morris also said, "the few smart observations could have come from an episode of one of Apatow's TV shows" and "I wanted to find this as funny as audiences did".[15]

Books

Two tie-in books to the film were published by Newmarket Press:

Superbad: The Illustrated Moviebook was published on December 4, 2007 to coincide with the release of the film on DVD. This official companion book includes: an introduction by producer Judd Apatow; the complete script by Seth Rogen and Evan Goldberg; commentaries by Apatow, Rogen and Goldberg, and journalists from *Rolling Stone, The New York Times,* and *Entertainment Weekly*; 56 film stills; "Mr. Vagtastic Guide to Buying Porn;" and 24 "phallographic" drawings by David Goldberg that viewers will recognize from the film's end credits.

Superbad: The Drawings was published on February 14, 2008. This gift hardcover art book contains 82 "phallographic" drawings created by David Goldberg (Evan Goldberg's brother) for the film.

Awards

Won

- *Canadian Comedy Awards 2008* - Seth Rogen - Best Writing. Rogen could not attend the awards ceremony but recorded a special thank you message.
- *Canadian Comedy Awards 2008* - Michael Cera - Best Male Performance
- *Chicago Film Critics Association Awards 2007* - Michael Cera - Most Promising Performer
- *Austin Film Critics Association Awards 2007* - Michael Cera - Breakthrough Artist Award
- *Young Hollywood Awards 2008* - Emma Stone - Exciting New Face

Nominated

- *2008 MTV Movie Awards* - Best Movie
- *2008 MTV Movie Awards* - Michael Cera, Jonah Hill, Christopher Mintz-Plasse - Breakthrough
- *2008 Peabody Award* - Best New Comedy Performance
- *2008 MTV Movie Awards* - Jonah Hill - Best Comedic Performance
- *Broadcast Film Critics Association Awards 2007* - Best Comedy Movie
- *Broadcast Film Critics Association Awards 2007* - Michael Cera - Best Young Actor
- *Empire Awards 2007* - Best Comedy
- *Teen Choice Awards 2007* - Choice Summer Movie - Comedy/Musical

References

[1] "Superbad (2007)" (http://www.boxofficemojo.com/movies/?id=superbad.htm). Box Office Mojo. . Retrieved 2007-09-24.

[2] Dylan Callaghan (2007-08-17). "It's Funnier With People" (http://www.wga.org/subpage.aspx?id=2446). *Writer's Guild of America.* . Retrieved 2007-11-05.

[3] "Superbad (2007) - Weekend Box Office" (http://www.boxofficemojo.com/movies/?page=weekend&id=superbad.htm). Box Office Mojo. . Retrieved 2007-09-24.

[4] Box Office Mojo: Charts - High School Comedy (http://boxofficemojo.com/genres/chart/?id=highschoolcomedy.htm)

[5] http://www.rottentomatoes.com/m/superbad/

[6] Rotten Tomatoes: *Superbad* (http://www.rottentomatoes.com/m/superbad/) Retrieved 2007-09-03

[7] Metacritic: *Superbad* (http://www.metacritic.com/film/titles/superbad) Retrieved 2007-09-03

[8] Roger Ebert (2007-08-16). ":: rogerebert.com :: Reviews :: Superbad" (http://rogerebert.suntimes.com/apps/pbcs.dll/article?AID=/20070816/REVIEWS/70817001). *Chicago Sun-Times.* . Retrieved 2007-08-19.

[9] Carina Chocano (2007-08-17). "'Superbad's' teen raunch isn't what's shocking; it's the love story" (http://web.archive.org/web/20070824051531/http://www.calendarlive.com/movies/reviews/cl-et-superbad17aug17,0,711876.story?coll=cl-mreview). *Los Angeles Times.* Archived from the original (http://www.calendarlive.com/movies/reviews/cl-et-superbad17aug17,0,711876.story?coll=cl-mreview) on 2007-08-24. . Retrieved 2007-08-19.

[10] Sean Burns. "Geek Outlook" (http://web.archive.org/web/20070930020542/http://www.philadelphiaweekly.com/articles/15259). Philadelphia Weekly. Archived from the original (http://www.philadelphiaweekly.com/articles/15259) on 2007-09-30. . Retrieved 2007-08-19.

[11] Devin Gordon (August 20-27, 2007 issue). "Revenge of the Nerds" (http://web.archive.org/web/20070828075852/http://www.msnbc. msn.com/id/20217418/site/newsweek/). Newsweek. Archived from the original (http://www.msnbc.msn.com/id/20217418/site/ newsweek/) on 2007-08-28. . Retrieved 2007-08-21.

[12] Stephen Farber (2007-08-07). "Superbad" (http://web.archive.org/web/20070930235412/http://www.hollywoodreporter.com/hr/ film/reviews/article_display.jsp?&rid=9592). *The Hollywood Reporter*. Archived from the original (http://www.hollywoodreporter.com/ hr/film/reviews/article_display.jsp?&rid=9592) on 2007-09-30. . Retrieved 2007-08-21.

[13] The DVD audio commentary on the **Superbad: Unrated Extended Edition** DVD.

[14] Adam Graham (2007-08-16). "Laughable roles" (http://www.detnews.com/apps/pbcs.dll/article?AID=/20070816/ENT02/708160419/ 1034). The Detroit News. . Retrieved 2007-08-21.

[15] Wesley Morris (2007-08-17). ""It's a nerd, he's in pain -- it's *Superbad*"" (http://www.boston.com/movies/display?display=movie& id=9508). *Boston Globe*. . Retrieved 2007-08-21.

External links

- Official website (http://http://www.areyousuperbad.com/)
- *Superbad* (http://www.imdb.com/title/tt0829482/) at the Internet Movie Database
- *Superbad* (http://tcmdb.com/title/title.jsp?stid=658794) at the TCM Movie Database
- *Superbad* (http://www.allmovie.com/work/355330) at Allmovie
- *Superbad* (http://www.boxofficemojo.com/movies/?id=superbad.htm) at Box Office Mojo
- *Superbad* (http://www.rottentomatoes.com/m/superbad/) at Rotten Tomatoes
- *Superbad* (http://www.metacritic.com/film/titles/superbad) at Metacritic

The Spiderwick Chronicles (film)

The Spiderwick Chronicles	
 Theatrical release poster	
Directed by	Mark Waters
Produced by	Mark Canton, Larry Franco Ellen Goldsmith-Vein Karey Kirkpatrick
Written by	**Screenplay:** Karey Kirkpatrick David Berenbaum John Sayles[1] **Books:** Holly Black Tony DiTerlizzi
Starring	Freddie Highmore Sarah Bolger Mary-Louise Parker Martin Short Nick Nolte David Strathairn Joan Plowright Seth Rogen Andrew McCarthy
Music by	James Horner
Cinematography	Caleb Deschanel
Editing by	Michael Kahn
Studio	Paramount Pictures Nickelodeon Movies Kennedy/Marshall
Distributed by	Paramount Pictures

Release date(s)	February 14, 2008 (USA) March 21, 2008 (UK)
Running time	97 min.
Country	United States
Language	English
Budget	$50 million
Gross revenue	$162,899,667 (worldwide)

The Spiderwick Chronicles is a 2008 fantasy film adaptation of Holly Black and Tony DiTerlizzi's bestselling series of the same name. Set in the Spiderwick Estate in New England, United States, it follows the adventures of Jared Grace and his family as they discover a field guide to faeries and battle goblins and other magical creatures. It was directed by Mark Waters and stars Freddie Highmore, Sarah Bolger, Mary-Louise Parker, Martin Short, Nick Nolte, and Seth Rogen. Produced by Nickelodeon Movies and distributed by Paramount Pictures, it was released on February 14, 2008. The film was released on DVD and Blu-ray on June 24, 2008 in the United States.[2]

Plot

Once upon a time, upon moving into the run-down Spiderwick Estate with their mother, twin brothers Jared and Simon Grace, along with their sister Mallory, find themselves pulled into an alternate world full of fairies and other creatures. Unable to explain the strange disappearances and accidents that seem to be happening on a daily basis, the family blames it all on Jared. When he, Simon and Mallory investigate what's really going on, they uncover the fantastic truth of the Spiderwick estate and of the creatures that inhabit it.

Cast

- Freddie Highmore as Jared/Simon, two brothers who find the book.
- Sarah Bolger as Mallory, sister of Jared and Simon.
- Mary-Louise Parker as Helen Grace, the mom.
- Martin Short as Thimbletack, easily angered house brownie.
- Nick Nolte as Mulgarath/Red Cap, a shapeshifting ogre and grouchy goblin general.
- David Strathairn as Arthur Spiderwick, author of the book.
- Joan Plowright as Aunt Lucinda, Spiderwick's daughter.
- Seth Rogen as Hogsqueal, unintelligent bird-eating hobgoblin.
- Andrew McCarthy as Richard Grace, divorced father.
- Tod Fennell as Helen's co-worker, brief character.
- Jeremy Lavalley as Tow Truck driver, person who runs over the mole tro

Production

A blue screen set used during filming.

In an interview, Sarah Bolger said that filming took four to five months. She said that she "was [in front of] the blue screen like 24 hours a day", and for the most part, she was "kicking and slicing and chopping things that were nowhere near". Since Bolger had many fencing scenes, she had five weeks of intense training, and three hours with the Canadian Olympic fencing coach nearly every day.[3]

Reception

The Spiderwick Chronicles received generally favorable reviews from critics; it was called "decent entertainment,"[4] "a work of both modest enchantment and enchanting modesty,"[5] and "modest and reasonably charming."[6] However, it was criticized for its reliance on special effects; a reviewer for *The New York Times* said that the movie "feels more like a sloppy, secondhand pander" and called it "frantic with incident and hectic with computer-generated effects,"[7] and another said that "the sense of wonder and magic is lost in the shuffle."[8]

Despite some negative reviews for the film overall, Freddie Highmore was generally praised for his dual role as the twins Simon and Jared. One critic said that he "skillfully portrays two distinctive personas,"[9] another said he "[had] no trouble grasping the task at hand,"[10] and a third remarked that, "the most special effect is probably Highmore".[11]

As of October 2008, the review aggregate website Rotten Tomatoes reported that 80% of critics gave the film positive reviews with an average rating of 6.6 out of 10, based on 135 reviews,[12] and Metacritic reported the film had an average score of 62 out of 100, based on 30 reviews.[13]

In its opening weekend, the film grossed an estimated $19 million in 3,847 theaters in the United States and Canada, ranking #2 behind *Jumper* at the box office.[14] With the opening day's gross on Thursday included, the film grossed an estimated $21.3 million on its opening weekend.[15] This film has grossed $162,839,667 worldwide.[16]

Video game

Sierra Entertainment enlisted Stormfront Studios to develop and produce a video game adaptation of *The Spiderwick Chronicles*, following the general storyline of the books and film.[17] It was released, shortly before the film's opening, on February 5, 2008 for Nintendo DS, Wii, PC, Xbox 360, and PlayStation 2, and rated Everyone (E10+) by the ESRB.[18]

DVD release

USA	Europe	Australia
June 24, 2008	July 14, 2008	July 31, 2008

The Spiderwick Chronicles was released on DVD and Blu-ray on June 24, 2008, in both a one-disc edition and a two-disc special edition. Both include several supplementary features, and the special edition includes several more behind-the-scenes featurettes, deleted scenes, Nickelodeon TV spots, and the theatrical trailer. The Blu-ray edition includes the identical special features of the special edition, along with a Blu-ray exclusive picture-in-picture option called "Spiderwick: It's all true!"

About 1,499,476 DVD units have been sold, bringing in $27,354,612, roughly one third of the film's budget.[19]

References

[1] Full credits at IMDB (http://www.imdb.com/title/tt0416236/fullcredits)

[2] Breaking: Paramount Unveils Blu-ray Launch Plans | High-Def Digest (http://www.highdefdigest.com/news/show/Paramount/ Disc_Announcements/Breaking:_Paramount_Unveils_Blu-ray_Launch_Plans/1696)

[3] Sarah Bolger Interview, The Spiderwick Chronicles - MoviesOnline (http://www.moviesonline.ca/movienews_14050.html)

[4] Richard Corliss (2008-02-15). "Run from Jumper, Creep Toward Spiderwick" (http://www.time.com/time/arts/article/ 0,8599,1713836,00.html). Time Magazine. . Retrieved 2008-03-05.

[5] Justin Change (2008-02-10). "The Spiderwick Chronicles" (http://www.variety.com/review/VE1117936159.html?categoryid=31&cs=1). Variety. . Retrieved 2008-03-05.

[6] Peter Sobczynski (2008-02-14). "The Spiderwick Chronicles" (http://efilmcritic.com/review.php?movie=16807&reviewer=389). eFilmCritic.com. . Retrieved 2008-03-05.

[7] A. O. Scott (2008-02-14). "A House Divided by Old Magic and New Residents" (http://movies.nytimes.com/2008/02/14/movies/14spid. html). The New York Times. . Retrieved 2008-03-05.

[8] Sean Axmaker (2008-02-13). "'Spiderwick' looks pretty but offers little" (http://seattlepi.nwsource.com/movies/351147_spider14q.html). Seattle Post-Intelligencer. . Retrieved 2008-03-05.

[9] Claudia Puig (2008-02-13). "'Spiderwick' doesn't stick, despite Highmore's performance" (http://www.usatoday.com/life/movies/reviews/ 2008-02-13-spiderwick-chronicles_N.htm). USA TODAY. . Retrieved 2008-03-05. "Freddie Highmore does a fine job in a dual role as identical twins. The talented actor skillfully portrays two distinctive personas."

[10] Elizabeth Weitzman (2008-02-14). "'Spiderwick Chronicles' fantasy can grow on you" (http://www.nydailynews.com/entertainment/ movies/2008/02/14/2008-02-14_spiderwick_chronicles_fantasy_can_grow_o.html). NY Daily News. . Retrieved 2008-03-05. "Happily, Highmore has no trouble grasping the task at hand."

[11] Ty Burr (2008-02-14). "A creepy-crawly and digitized faerie tale" (http://www.boston.com/movies/display?display=movie&id=9183). The Boston Globe. . Retrieved 2008-03-05. "The most special effect is probably Highmore, who gets to sharpen up his American accent and who makes each twin, bookish Simon and bad-boy Jared, a functioning individual."

[12] "The Spiderwick Chronicles — Movie Reviews, Trailers, Pictures — Rotten Tomatoes" (http://www.rottentomatoes.com/m/ spiderwick_chronicles/). Rotten Tomatoes. . Retrieved 2008-03-05.

[13] "Spiderwick Chronicles, The (2008): Reviews" (http://www.metacritic.com/film/titles/spiderwickchronicles). Metacritic. . Retrieved 2008-03-05.

[14] "The Spiderwick Chronicles (2008)" (http://www.boxofficemojo.com/movies/?id=spiderwickchronicles.htm). Box Office Mojo. . Retrieved 2008-02-17.

[15] "The Spiderwick Chronicles (2008) - Weekend Box Office Results" (http://www.boxofficemojo.com/movies/?page=weekend& id=spiderwickchronicles.htm). Box Office Mojo. . Retrieved 2008-02-17.

[16] "The Spiderwick Chronicles (2008) - Weekend Box Office Results" (http://www.boxofficemojo.com/movies/?id=spiderwickchronicles. htm). Box Office Mojo. . Retrieved 2008-05-05.

[17] Brendan Sinclair (2007-08-09). "Sierra snares Spiderwick Chronicles" (http://www.gamespot.com/pc/adventure/ thespiderwickchronicles/news_6176472.html). GameSpot. . Retrieved 2008-03-04.

[18] http://www.spiderwickgame.com (http://www.spiderwickgame.com/us/)

[19] http://www.the-numbers.com/movies/2008/SPDWC-DVD.php

External links

- Official site (http://www.spiderwickchronicles.com/)
- *The Spiderwick Chronicles* (http://www.imdb.com/title/tt0416236/) at the Internet Movie Database
- *The Spiderwick Chronicles* (http://www.rottentomatoes.com/m/spiderwick_chronicles/) at Rotten Tomatoes
- *The Spiderwick Chronicles* (http://www.metacritic.com/film/titles/spiderwickchronicles) at Metacritic
- *The Spiderwick Chronicles* (http://www.boxofficemojo.com/movies/?id=spiderwickchronicles.htm) at Box Office Mojo
- *The Spiderwick Chronicles* (http://www.allmovie.com/work/352256) at Allmovie
- Full production notes (http://madeinatlantis.com/movies_central/2008/ spiderwick_chronicles_production_details.htm)
- Parentalsite.com Review (http://www.parentalsite.com/movie/spiderwickchronicles2008.html)

Horton Hears a Who! (film)

Dr. Seuss' Horton Hears a Who!	
 Theatrical release poster	
Directed by	Jimmy Hayward Steve Martino
Produced by	Bob Gordon Bruce Anderson
Written by	Cinco Paul Ken Daurio Mike Reiss [uncredited]
Based on	*Horton Hears a Who!* by Dr. Seuss
Narrated by	Charles Osgood
Starring	Jim Carrey Steve Carell Carol Burnett Seth Rogen Jesse McCartney Will Arnett Dan Fogler Isla Fisher Amy Poehler Selena Gomez
Music by	John Powell
Editing by	Tim Nordquist
Studio	Blue Sky Studios
Distributed by	20th Century Fox
Release date(s)	March 14, 2008
Running time	94 minutes
Country	United States
Language	English

Budget	$85 million
Gross revenue	$297,679,954

Horton Hears a Who!, also known as ***Dr. Seuss' Horton Hears a Who!***, is a 2008 American CGI-animated feature film based on the Dr. Seuss book of the same name. It is the fourth feature film from Blue Sky Studios, and the third Dr. Seuss-based feature film, following *How the Grinch Stole Christmas* and *The Cat in the Hat*.

It is the first Dr. Seuss adaptation fully animated using CGI technology.

Plot

The film opens in the Jungle of Nool, where a drop of water falls off a leaf, eventually causing a tiny dust speck to be pushed off a flower. Meanwhile, a caring, imaginative elephant named Horton (Jim Carrey), the jungle's nature teacher, takes a dip in the pool. The dust speck floats past him in the air, and he hears a tiny yelp coming from it. Believing that an entire family of microscopic creatures are living on that speck, he places it on top of a pink clover that he holds in his trunk. Horton finds out the speck harbors the city of Who-ville and its inhabitants, led by Mayor Ned McDodd (Steve Carell). He has a wife, Sally (Amy Poehler), 96 daughters who all have names that start with the letter H, and one teenage son named JoJo (Jesse McCartney). Despite being next in line for the mayoral position, JoJo refuses to become mayor of the city.

The Mayor finds out from Dr. LaRue (Isla Fisher) that Who-ville will be destroyed if Horton does not find a "safer more stable home." Horton resolves to place the speck atop Mt. Nool, the safest place in the jungle. This outlook earns Horton nothing but ridicule from the inhabitants of Nool, especially from the leader of the jungle, the Sour Kangaroo (Carol Burnett). The Kangaroo tries to get Horton to give up the speck, so as not to put supposedly ridiculous ideas into the heads of the children. Ever faithful to his two mottos, "A person's a person, no matter how small," and "I meant what I said, and I said what I meant, an Elephant's faithful 100%" (a reference to his other story *Horton Hatches the Egg*), Horton refuses. Also taking force toward Horton are the Wickersham brothers (Frank Welker and Dan Castellaneta), a group of bullying monkeys who love making misery.

The other Whos become suspicious of the various phenomena in their world (actually caused by Horton's various mishaps), the Mayor finally reveals the truth, but at first, the Whos do not believe him any more than the animals believe Horton. The Kangaroo enlists a buzzard named Vlad Vladikoff (Will Arnett) to get rid of the speck by force. Vlad manages to steal the clover with the speck on it, flee from a chasing Horton and drop it from hundreds of feet into a valley full of nearly identical clovers. The impact destroys Who-ville. Horton picks clovers through the field and finally finds it "on the 3 millionth flower." The city's destruction, combined with hearing Horton's voice through the drain pipe, is enough to convince the rest of the Whos that the mayor is not crazy, and they all tell Horton they believe in him.

The Kangaroo finds out that Horton still has the speck, and decides to rally the jungle community into confronting Horton. The Kangaroo offers Horton to give up the speck. Unable to convince Horton, she orders the animals to rope and cage him, and that the speck be burned in a pot of boiling "beezlenut" oil.

The Mayor enlists all of his people to make noise by shouting "We are here", as well as playing a variety of instruments. In the jungle, Horton is caged, the Kangaroo takes the clover and drops it into the boiling oil. At the last minute, JoJo grabs the horn used to project Horton's voice, runs up the highest tower and yells "YOPP!", breaking through the sound barrier, just before the speck hits the oil.

Hearing the Whos' cries, Rudy (Josh Flitter), the Kangaroo's joey, grabs the clover and returns it to Horton, refusing his mother's orders to return to her pouch. The animals realize their mistake. While being praised for his integrity by his neighbors, Horton forgives the Kangaroo and she accepts his friendship. She and the animals resolve to join Horton in returning the clover to Mount Nool. Here the people of Who-ville and the animals of Nool gather in song and recite the chorus from "Can't Fight This Feeling", and begin walking the final stretch to the mountain. The film ends with the narrator revealing that the Jungle of Nool is just one speck among numerous others.

Cast

- Horton the Elephant, voiced by Jim Carrey, has an imagination since his childhood. He serves as the main protagonist of the film. It was that imagination along with his unwavering dedication that makes Horton a great teacher, unconditional friend and a force to be reckoned with.
- Ned McDodd, the Mayor of Whoville, voiced by Steve Carell, is the mayor of a microscopic world, and father of ninety-six daughters and a son named JoJo. He is the deuteragonist of the film. He is very proud and formal and cares very much for his city and its people, but when he starts hearing the voice of Horton, whom he cannot see, things begin to unravel for the Mayor. It is noted that the name of the character wasn't revealed until the theatrical release. He can be described as "The mayor of Who-ville, a man named McDodd, was devoted, fair, and a little bit odd." However as smoothly as he runs the town, at the beginning of the movie, his relationship with his son JoJo is very strained, as JoJo doesn't talk to him.
- Sour Kangaroo, voiced by Carol Burnett, is a busybody and creator of the jungle's laws who is skeptical about the existence of the Whos and Whoville on a dust speck. She serves as the main antagonist of the film. As Horton's claims begin to drive her towards darkness, she believes that once other people start listening to Horton, they'll start to come to her with questions she won't be able to answer. In order to avoid this, she begins making deals with the Wickershams and the vulture hitman Vlad Vladikoff. As the film progresses, her aims start to shift towards crushing Horton's spirit and building up her own reputation. The Kangaroo is too dismissive of the products of imagination and creativity, even to the point where she keeps her son Rudy jammed inside her pouch. She believes that outside the "comfort" her ideas provide him, non-conformity and anarchy are minutes away from turning their ordered life into chaos. Yet, in the end, Horton's convincing changes her mindset.
- JoJo McDodd is voiced by Jesse McCartney. JoJo is the Mayor's only son and the eldest of the mayor's children. He is the film's tritagonist. Since he is the oldest, JoJo is next in line to become the Mayor of Whoville, though he doesn't want to follow in his father's footsteps. He doesn't want his Dad to know because he thinks he'll let his dad down. He never speaks to his father because of this, although from the deleted scenes commentary it is implied that he does speak, but since his scenes are mostly with his father, we don't hear him speak until he shouts "YOPP!" and saves the town. After this he begins speaking to multiple characters, and even sings at the end to cap off the camera going into Whoville. He also shows a surprising talent for inventions and is somewhat of a prodigy and a musician. In fact, he turns the inside of Whoville's abandoned observatory into a giant mechanical musical instrument called the "Symphoniphone". In the deleted scenes commentary, it is revealed that at the time of the "Horton Incident," JoJo was 14.
- Rudy is voiced by Josh Flitter. Rudy is Kangaroo's young joey. He lives in his mother's pouch. Over the course of the movie, he starts to question his mother's ethics as she continually tries to demolish the clover on which Horton has caught the Whos' speck of dust. But his stifling environment can't contain his free-thinking spirit, and Rudy is ready to take the next step, even if it's his first.
- Morton the Mouse is voiced by Seth Rogen. Morton the mouse is Horton's best friend who makes up in speed what he lacks in size. He's smaller than the elephant's big toe, but when Morton speaks, Horton listens. Morton will endure Horton's whims, but when the elephant takes off on flights of fancy, Morton knows it's his job to bring him back to earth. He's successful, most of the time. Morton also acts as a messenger for Horton, bringing him news about Vlad, and says, "If you don't like the idea of his claws ripping your flesh, leave the flower and keep your eyes open!" He is not in the original book.
- Sally O'Malley McDodd is voiced by Amy Poehler. Sally is the Mayor's wife and mother of 96 daughters and one son named JoJo. With all of these children, Sally's responsibilities dwarf even those of her husband. Still, she's able to juggle them with the grace of a first lady. The last thing she needs is another problem child with an overactive imagination, but when her husband starts hearing voices, that's exactly what she gets. It's a situation even her sharp wit and pointed sarcasm can't defuse, but when the truth is revealed, she's willing to give it her all

to help her husband save Whoville. Sally deeply cares for her husband and children.

- Dr. Mary Lou LaRue is voiced by Isla Fisher. Dr. LaRue is an eccentric Whoville scientist who can be a bit scatterbrained at times. However, being the smartest of the staff at Who University, she is willing to help the Mayor find out how they can preserve the peace that holds their town together. She is one of the first Whos to believe that the Mayor was right about Whoville being a speck. She speaks with a lateral lisp.

- Vlad Vladikoff is voiced by Will Arnett He is the vulture in the scene where he tries to get the clover. There is a confusing matter about a good Vlad who is a rabbit (which bakes cookies) and a bad Vlad. Vlad is a reclusive vulture who lives in a tree stump in a swamp surrounded by thorns and snakes, feasting on a zebra carcass and shooing a jackal. The Sour Kangaroo hires him to get rid of Horton's clover. At first, he agrees to do it in exchange for her son Rudy, but he stated a brand new pair of objects never specified beforehand. After "thinking" it over, she uses reverse psychology to get him to do it for free. He speaks in a thick Russian accent and is extremely theatrical in his wickedness to the point of embarrassing himself.

- Yummo is voiced by Dan Fogler. Yummo is the rumbling leader of the Wickersham brothers who serves as a bully for Horton, as he sees him as an annoyance. He's hot-tempered, power-hungry, and just plain hungry. He helps with the capture of Horton because he agreed that Horton was poisoning the youth of the jungle, first said by Kangaroo.

- Mrs. Quilligan is voiced by Jaime Pressly. Mrs. Quilligan is a jungle bird that is a two-faced and easily influenced busybody. She sways with public opinion and everybody knows it. It's not unusual for her to be caught flip-flopping and backtracking to cover herself, keeping her firmly entrenched in the" in crowd".

- Jessica Quilligan is voiced by Laura Ortiz. Like any teenager, Jessica might be embarrassed by her mother's busybody behavior, but it's obvious to everyone else in the community that she's Mrs. Quilligan's mini-clone. She views herself as an independent thinker, but since conformity leads to acceptance, she's just another cog in the wheel. She is vain. When she and her classmates tell Horton about their clovers with worlds, Jessica states that her world is called Jessica-Land, where everyone worships her, Queen Jessica, because she is so beautiful.

- Tommy is voiced by Jonah Hill. Tommy is an orange wombat-like creature that is one of the children of the Jungle of Nool that looks up to and views Horton as a teacher. He seems to have somewhat of a frat boy/smart aleck persona, but truly believes in what Horton is trying to do, even if he is being ridiculed for it. He tends to get out of the way of trouble, such as the time when Sour Kangaroo approaches them after hearing "nonsense" about the clover worlds, he says, "Oh, um... You guys with worlds are in trouble!"

- Katie is voiced by Joey King. Katie is a small baby yak with strange mannerisms and abilities. Aside from saying "ahhh" on a few occasions, her only lines in the film are when Horton's students imagine worlds of their own on their own flowers: Katie explains that everyone in her world is a pony that eats rainbows, and excretes butterflies. She also has a frog's tongue, and the ability to float, which she demonstrates at the end of the film. Katie is one of the female pupils of Horton. On the special features, it is revealed that the character of Katie was created to be creepy, and that she thinks of herself as a huge, demonic being. In a deleted scene, she is shown as huge, and terrorizing a village and consuming villagers.

- Miss Yelp, voiced by Niecy Nash, is the Mayor's assistant. She talks in a bored voice, and does all her tasks mechanically, before she is asked. She has a MySpace profile (named Whospace in the film), which she mostly spends her time on during work.

- The Chairman, voiced by Dan Fogler, is the head of the Whoville City Council and views the Mayor as a 'blathering boob', and appears to have more power than him. It is Horton who takes him down a peg or two. He and his cronies all have blue or green hair and skin, black suits and resemble The Grinch. It is said in the DVD commentary that the last one is named Pugerson and he can't fly his box kite very well.

- The Wickersham Brothers, voiced by Frank Welker and Dan Castellaneta, are a group of vicious monkeys who serve as bullies for Horton. They have a very large family consisting of many members who help bind Horton. When Horton speaks up to all the animals of Nool about his protected speck, the Wickershams actually take pity on him, only to be forced by Sour Kangaroo to rope and cage him, but after a while, the Wickershams realize they do hear the people on the speck, and they also reject the still-resenting Sour Kangaroo. They serve as minor antagonists in the film.

• The Narrator, voiced by Charles Osgood. Osgood reads the book throughout the film.

Soundtrack

The original score for the film's soundtrack album was composed by John Powell. Near the end of the picture, the cast comes together and sings the song, "Can't Fight This Feeling" by REO Speedwagon. This version of the song was not featured on the soundtrack. The song used in the theatrical advertisements was the theme to *Beetlejuice*.

Reaction

Critical reception

The film received generally positive reviews from film critics. As of May 8, 2008, the review aggregator Rotten Tomatoes reported that 78% of critics gave the film positive reviews, based on 123 reviews, and an even better 84% rating from the top critics on the site based on 31 reviews, both classifying the film as "Certified Fresh", and making it by far the most favorably reviewed Dr. Seuss film adaptation on the site.[1] Metacritic reported the film had an average score of 71 out of 100, indicating "generally favorable reviews", based on 31 reviews, also the most favorably reviewed Dr. Seuss film on the site.[2] Brian Eggert of Deep Focus Review gave it one and a half stars out of four, criticizing its numerous pop-culture references, calling it a "mish-mash of incoherent babble" and claiming it ends up "reducing Seuss' otherwise admirable message to ordinary storytelling, when Seuss' work is anything but."

Box office

In its opening weekend, the film grossed $45,012,998 in 3,954 theaters, averaging $11,384 per theater in the United States and Canada, and ranking #1 at the box office.[3] The film previously had the 4th largest opening weekend in March, behind *Ice Age*, *Ice Age: The Meltdown* and *300*. It is now the 7th largest opening weekend in March behind *Monsters vs. Aliens* and *Alice in Wonderland*.[4] In the United States and Canada, *Horton Hears a Who* was also the #1 film its second weekend of release, grossing $24,590,596 over the Easter frame, in 3,961 theaters and averaging $6,208 per venue. It dropped to #2 in its third weekend grossing $17,740,106 in 3,826 theaters and averaging $4,637 per venue. Its fourth weekend ranked at #4 grossing $9,115,987 in 3,571 theaters and averaging $2,553 per venue. Its fifth weekend ranked at #6, grossing $5,920,566 in 3,209 theaters and averaging $1,845 per venue.

As of July 20, 2008, it has grossed a total of $295,133,433 worldwide; $154,245,889 in the United States and Canada and $140,887,544 in other territories.[5]

Home media release

Dr. Seuss' Horton Hears a Who! was released on DVD and Blu-ray on December 9, 2008. Three versions of the DVD are available: a single disc edition, a two-disc special edition, and a gift set packaged with a Horton plush.

The DVD and Blu-ray Disc were released in the UK on October 20, 2008 and in Australia on September 20, 2008.

References

[1] "Dr. Seuss' Horton Hears a Who Movie Reviews, Pictures - Rotten Tomatoes" (http://www.rottentomatoes.com/m/ horton-hears-a-who2008/). Rotten Tomatoes. . Retrieved 2008-04-14.

[2] "Horton Hears a Who! (2008): Reviews" (http://www.metacritic.com/film/titles/hortonhears). Metacritic. . Retrieved 2008-03-14.

[3] "Dr. Seuss' Horton Hears a Who! (2008) - Weekend Box Office Results" (http://www.boxofficemojo.com/movies/?page=weekend& id=hortonhearsawho.htm). Box Office Mojo. . Retrieved 2008-03-16.

[4] "Top March Opening Weekends at the Box Office" (http://boxofficemojo.com/alltime/weekends/month/?mo=03&p=.htm). Box Office Mojo. . Retrieved 2008-03-16.

[5] "Dr. Seuss' Horton Hears a Who! (2008)" (http://www.boxofficemojo.com/movies/?page=main&id=hortonhearsawho.htm). Box Office Mojo. . Retrieved 2008-03-24.

External links

- Official website (http://http://www.hortonmovie.com/)
- *Horton Hears a Who!* (http://www.bcdb.com/bcdb/cartoon.cgi?film=87576/) at the Big Cartoon DataBase
- *Horton Hears a Who!* (http://www.imdb.com/title/tt0451079/) at the Internet Movie Database
- *Horton Hears a Who!* (http://www.allmovie.com/work/361176) at Allmovie
- *Horton Hears a Who!* (http://www.boxofficemojo.com/movies/?id=hortonhearsawho.htm) at Box Office Mojo
- *Horton Hears a Who!* (http://www.rottentomatoes.com/m/horton-hears-a-who2008/) at Rotten Tomatoes
- *Horton Hears a Who!* (http://www.metacritic.com/film/titles/hortonhears) at Metacritic

Strange Wilderness

Strange Wilderness	
 Promotional movie poster for the film	
Directed by	Fred Wolf
Produced by	Adam Sandler (executive) Jack Giarraputo Allen Covert Peter Gaulke
Written by	Peter Gaulke Fred Wolf
Starring	Steve Zahn Allen Covert Jonah Hill Robert Patrick Also Starring Justin Long with Jeff Garlin and Ernest Borgnine as 'Milas'
Music by	Waddy Wachtel
Cinematography	David Hennings
Editing by	Tom Costain
Studio	Level 1 Entertainment Happy Madison Productions
Distributed by	Paramount Pictures
Release date(s)	February 1, 2008
Running time	87 min
Country	USA
Language	English
Gross revenue	6,964,734

Strange Wilderness is a 2008 comedy/adventure film produced by Adam Sandler's production company, Happy Madison Productions for Paramount Pictures, and starring Steve Zahn, Allen Covert, Justin Long, Kevin Heffernan, and Jonah Hill.

Plot

Animal enthusiast Peter Gaulke (Zahn) and his sidekick Fred Wolf (Covert) host a program about wildlife called "Strange Wilderness," which is in a steep ratings decline. Desperate to save the show, Peter hatches a Hail Mary scheme to find the one animal that could truly turn the show around and change the nature-show landscape forever—Bigfoot.[1]

Production

Jonah Hill wrote his role in the film.[2] Hill gave Cooker a given name, Lynn, because "Lynn is a strong name, and I feel like only people named Lynn can accomplish their goals — no one else, with any other name."[3]

Cast

- Steve Zahn as Peter Gaulke
- Allen Covert as Fred Wolf
- Justin Long as Junior
- Jonah Hill as Lynn Cooker
- Robert Patrick as Gus Hayden
- Ashley Scott as Cheryl
- Harry Hamlin as Sky Pierson
- Ernest Borgnine as Milas
- Jeff Garlin as Ed Lawson
- Kevin Heffernan as Whitaker
- John Farley as Mountain Doctor
- Peter Dante as Danny Guiterrez
- Oliver Hudson as TJ / Animal Handler
- Blake Clark as Dick
- Seth Rogen as Ranger In The Helicopter (Voice)

Critical reception

The film received highly negative reviews. Rotten Tomatoes gave it a 0% rating with an average reviewer rating of 2.3/10 based on 41 reviews.[4] At Metacritic, it was given a 12% (ranking 'Extreme dislike or disgust') based on 12 reviews, tying it for 30th place for the worst-reviewed films ever.

References

[1] "CanMag.Com" (http://www.canmag.com/movies.php?moviekey=strangewilderness). *Strange Wilderness Preview Page.* . Retrieved December 5, 2007.

[2] JONAH HILL IS NOT SUPERBAD FOR STRANGE WILDERNESS (http://www.youtube.com/watch?v=YEWtDQ-T8PM) at YouTube *Artisan News Service.* Uploaded February 6, 2008. Accessed October 22, 2008.

[3] Carroll, Larry. " Best Buds Justin Long, Jonah Hill Work Comedy-Duo Schtick In 'Accepted' (http://www.mtv.com/movies/news/articles/1538615/20060815/story.jhtml)." *MTV.* August 16, 2006.

[4] "Strange Wilderness at RottenTomatoes.com" (http://www.rottentomatoes.com/m/strange_wilderness/). RottenTomatoes.com. . Retrieved 2008-05-06.

External links

- *Strange Wilderness* (http://www.imdb.com/title/tt0489282/) at the Internet Movie Database
- *Strange Wilderness* (http://www.rottentomatoes.com/m/strange_wilderness/) at Rotten Tomatoes
- *Strange Wilderness* (http://www.metacritic.com/film/titles/strangewilderness) at Metacritic
- *Strange Wilderness* (http://www.boxofficemojo.com/movies/?id=strangewilderness.htm) at Box Office Mojo
- *Strange Wilderness* (http://www.allmovie.com/work/341937) at Allmovie

Drillbit Taylor

Drillbit Taylor	

Theatrical release poster	
Directed by	Steven Brill
Produced by	Judd Apatow Susan Arnold
Screenplay by	Kristofor Brown Seth Rogen
Story by	Kristofor Brown John Hughes Seth Rogen
Starring	Owen Wilson Troy Gentile Nate Hartley David Dorfman Alex Frost Josh Peck Leslie Mann
Music by	Christophe Beck
Cinematography	Fred Murphy
Studio	The Apatow Company
Distributed by	Paramount Pictures
Release date(s)	February 8, 2008 (see release history)
Running time	**Theatrical cut:** 102 minutes **Extended cut:** 109 minutes
Country	United States
Language	English
Budget	$40,000,000

Gross revenue	$49,690,625

Drillbit Taylor is a 2008 comedy film starring Owen Wilson as the title character and based on an original idea by John Hughes. The screenplay was written by Kristofor Brown and Seth Rogen. Paramount Pictures released the film on March 21, 2008.

Drillbit Taylor was John Hughes' last movie as a writer before his death on August 6, 2009. He also used his pseudonym, Edmond Dantes, for this film.

Plot

Ryan (Troy Gentile) and Wade (Nate Hartley) are two boys starting high school. On the first day of school, Ryan and Wade witness two bullies, Filkins (Alex Frost) and Ronnie (Josh Peck), attack a geek, Emmit Oosterhaus (David Dorfman) by shoving him into his locker. Wade intervenes. Filkins and Ronnie begin endlessly targeting Ryan, Wade, and Emmit.

Wade suggests hiring a bodyguard. They place an ad on the Internet, and end up selecting Drillbit Taylor (Owen Wilson). Taylor pretends to be a martial arts expert and mercenary, but is really a homeless beggar who showers at a public beach and eats out of a dumpster. His real intention of becoming their bodyguard was to rob them and use the money to buy a ticket to British Columbia.

Drillbit tells the boys to find some common interests and become friends with Filkins and Ronnie. Ryan challenges Filkins to a rap battle, but gets carried away and ends up humiliating Filkins. As an angry Filkins, alongside Ronnie ambushes Ryan, Wade and Emmit, the boys try using a tactic Drillbit taught them, but it ultimately fails.

The boys are furious with Drillbit's teachings but Drillbit defends himself. The boys decide to bring him to school as a substitute teacher, and in that capacity he is able to protect them. While there, Drillbit meets a fellow teacher, Ms. Zachey (Leslie Mann), and they start a relationship.

One morning as his mother (Lisa Lampanelli) is driving him to school, Ronnie sees Taylor taking a shower at the beach; his mother reveals that he is a homeless man. Ronnie tells Filkins. Filkins finds the boys and ends up punching Drillbit.

Later on at Wade's house, they catch Drillbit's homeless friends stealing everything in sight. Taylor confesses that his real name is Bob and he went A.W.O.L. from the U.S. Army. Enraged, the boys fire Drillbit, who later recovers all of Wade's possessions and placed them back before Wade's parents return home. Unfortunately, the boys accidentally let slip about Drillbit. Their parents take things up with the principal, who contacts the police. Filkins plays innocent and charms all the adults.

Filkins continues to ridicule the boys after Drillbit's disappearance. Tensions finally burst when Filkins interrupts Wade's attempt to ask Brooke Nguyen out. Without realizing what he was doing, Wade challenges Filkins to a fight.

Ryan and Wade arrive at Filkin's house that night, where he is hosting a party. Wade and Ryan maintain the fight for a while, but Ronnie shows up to help Filkin's fight the boys, until Emmit, who initially refused to fight comes to help, and for a while provves himself be a good figther and actually causes quite alot of pain to filkins almost defeating him even it turns out however it wasn't much use in the end as he just gets knocked unconscious by Ronnie while trying to break Filkins leg.

Drillbit then shows up and tries to talk Filkins down. Filkins punches Drillbit, who continued to take punches without a fight until it is revealed Filkins is not a minor. Drillbit quickly begins fighting and momentarily defeats Filkins. He is about to defeat Ronnie but then reveals that he is a minor. Within minutes, the police arrive and Drillbit flees for fear of prosecution. Filkins wakes up and throws a samurai sword at the boys, but Drillbit catches it. He saves them and ends up losing half of his pinky finger in the process.

Filkins is arrested and shipped off to Hong Kong where his parents are living. It is believed that Ronnie no longer ridicules the boys as his bully partner is gone.

Drillbit gets sent to prison and to the hospital for the pinky finger, but ends up being released within three weeks. Where he is reunited with Ms. Zachey and the boys.

Cast

- Owen Wilson as Bob "Drillbit" Taylor, a homeless U.S. army deserter.
- Nate Hartley as Wade, a high school freshman who along with his friend Ryan, have hopes of being popular.
- Troy Gentile as Ryan Anderson. Along with Wade, Ryan hopes of becoming popular. He loves to rap and makes brief hip hop culture references.
- David Dorfman as Emmit Oosterhaus, a kid who is first bullied by Filkins and Ronnie.
- Alex Frost as Terry Filkins, a bully with a somewhat psychopathic mind.
- Josh Peck as Ronnie Lampenelli, Filkins' friend and partner.
- Leslie Mann as Lisa Zachey, Drillbit's love interest and later girlfriend.
- Danny R. McBride as Don Armstrong, Drillbit's old friend.
- Stephen Root as Principal Neville Doppler
- Ian Roberts as Jim, Wade's stepdad
- Lisa Lampanelli as Mrs. Lampanelli
- Lisa Ann Walter as Delores Anderson (Ryan's Mother)
- Hynden Walch as Mrs. Oosterhaus, Emmit's mom
- Valerie Tian as Brooke Nguyen, Wade's first crush at school.
- David Bowe as the male teacher.
- Beth Littleford as Barbara Drennan
- Steve Bannos as Coffee Computer Guy
- Chuck Liddell as Himself
- Robert Allen Mukes as Bonecrusher
- Adam Baldwin as Ricky Linderman
- Cedric Yarbrough as Bernie Hodge
- Tichina Arnold as Photography teacher
- Kevin Hart as Pawn Shop Guy 1
- Matt Besser as Pawn Shop Guy 2
- David Koechner as Frightened Dad (unrated version)
- Shaun Weiss as the Bus Driver

Marketing

Marketing for the film included television promos and coming attractions previews, but actor Owen Wilson did not conduct any interviews to promote the film. Instead, Paramount had Wilson record introductions for Fox's Sunday night primetime shows such as *The Simpsons*, *American Dad*, *King of the Hill*, *Family Guy*, and *Unhitched*. The character of Drillbit Taylor was also featured as a "Superstar" on the Raw page of WWE.com for a period of time. Wilson's publicist said his availability was limited due to filming *Marley & Me*. John Horn and Gina Piccalo of the *Los Angeles Times* wrote that the studio was worried interviewers would bring up Wilson's hospitalization in the summer of 2007.[1]

Reception

Critical response

The film received mostly negative reviews from critics. Based on 138 reviews collected by Rotten Tomatoes, the film has an overall approval rating of 26 percent.[2] Metacritic calculated an average score of 41%.[3]

Box office

In its opening weekend, the film grossed $10.2 million in 3,056 theaters in the United States and Canada, ranking #4 at the box office.[4] As of June 11, 2008, the film has grossed $32,862,104 in the United States and $16,824,159 in foreign countries adding to a total worldwide gross of $49,686,263.

Home media

The film was released on DVD and Blu-ray Disc on July 1, 2008. About 620,927 units have been sold, bringing in $11,669,617 in revenue.[5]

Theatrical edition

- Original 102 minute version
- Line-o-Rama
- 9 deleted/extended scenes
- Gag reel
- Featurettes:
  - Directing Kids
  - The Real Don: Danny McBride

Extended Unrated Survival Edition

- Extended 109 minute version
- Commentary By: Steven Brill, Kristofor Brown, Troy Gentile, Nate Hartley, and David Dorfman
- The Writers Get A Chance To Talk: Kristofor Brown and Seth Rogen
- LINE-O-RAMA
- 13 Deleted & Extended Scenes
- Gag Reel
- Featurettes:
  - Rap Off
  - Bully
  - Sprinkler Day
  - Directing Kids
  - The Real Don: Danny McBride

References

[1] "Owen Wilson sits out 'Drillbit Taylor' promotion" (http://web.archive.org/web/20080323172749/http://www.latimes.com/entertainment/news/movies/la-et-word20mar20,1,4790174.story). *LA Times*. 2008-03-20. Archived from the original (http://www.latimes.com/entertainment/news/movies/la-et-word20mar20,1,4790174.story) on 2008-03-23. . Retrieved 2008-03-20.

[2] "Drillbit Taylor (2008)" (http://www.rottentomatoes.com/m/drillbit_taylor/). *Rotten Tomatoes*. Flixster. . Retrieved 2009-08-03.

[3] "Drillbit Taylor Reviews" (http://www.metacritic.com/film/titles/drillbittaylor). *Metacritic*. CBS. . Retrieved 2009-08-03.

[4] "Drillbit Taylor (2008) - Weekend Box Office Results" (http://www.boxofficemojo.com/movies/?page=weekend&id=drillbittaylor.htm). *Box Office Mojo*. Amazon.com. . Retrieved 2008-03-24.

[5] http://www.the-numbers.com/movies/2008/DRILB-DVD.php

External links

- Official website (http://http://www.drillbittaylor.com/)
- *Drillbit Taylor* (http://www.imdb.com/title/tt0817538/) at the Internet Movie Database
- *Drillbit Taylor* (http://www.allmovie.com/work/376144) at Allmovie
- *Drillbit Taylor* (http://www.boxofficemojo.com/movies/?id=drillbittaylor.htm) at Box Office Mojo
- *Drillbit Taylor* (http://www.rottentomatoes.com/m/drillbit_taylor/) at Rotten Tomatoes
- *Drillbit Taylor* (http://www.metacritic.com/film/titles/drillbittaylor) at Metacritic

Kung Fu Panda

Kung Fu Panda	
 Theatrical poster	
Directed by	• John Stevenson • Mark Osborne
Produced by	Melissa Cobb (producer) Bill Damaschke (executive producer) Jonathan Aibel, Glenn Berger (co-producers) Kristina Reed (associate producer) Lorne Orleans (IMAX version)
Written by	• Jonathan Aibel • Glenn Berger (screenplay) • Ethan Reiff • Cyrus Voris (story)
Starring	• Jack Black • Dustin Hoffman • Jackie Chan • Angelina Jolie • Ian McShane • Seth Rogen • Lucy Liu • David Cross • Randall Duk Kim • James Hong
Music by	• Hans Zimmer • John Powell

Cinematography	Yong Duk Jhun
Editing by	Clare de Chenu
Studio	• DreamWorks Animation • Pacific Data Images
Distributed by	Paramount Pictures
Release date(s)	June 6, 2008
Running time	92 minutes
Country	United States
Language	English
Budget	$130 million
Gross revenue	$631,744,560 [1]
Followed by	*Kung Fu Panda 2*

Kung Fu Panda is a 2008 American computer-animated film produced by DreamWorks Animation and distributed by Paramount Pictures. It was directed by John Wayne Stevenson and Mark Osborne and produced by Melissa Cobb, and stars the voice of Jack Black along with Dustin Hoffman, Angelina Jolie, Ian McShane, Seth Rogen, Lucy Liu, David Cross, Randall Duk Kim, James Hong and Jackie Chan. Set in a version of ancient China populated by anthropomorphic animals, the plot revolves around a bumbling panda named Po who aspires to be a kung fu master. When an evil kung fu warrior is foretold to escape from prison, Po is unwittingly named the chosen one destined to bring peace to the land, much to the chagrin of the resident kung fu warriors.[2]

Although the concept of a "kung fu panda" has been around since at least 1993, work on the film did not begin until 2004.[3] The idea for the film was conceived by Michael Lachance,[4] a DreamWorks Animation executive. The film was originally intended to be a parody, but director Stevenson decided instead to shoot an action comedy Wuxia film that incorporates the hero's journey narrative archetype for the lead character. The computer animation in the film was more complex than anything DreamWorks had done before. As with most DreamWorks animated films, Hans Zimmer (collaborating with John Powell this time) scored *Kung Fu Panda*. He visited China to absorb the culture and get to know the China National Symphony Orchestra as part of his preparation. A sequel, *Kung Fu Panda 2*, is in production and set for release on May 27, 2011.

Kung Fu Panda premiered in the United States on June 6, 2008, and has since received very favorable reviews from critics and most of the movie-going public, including Chinese audiences who were deeply impressed with the film's faithfulness to their culture. The film currently garners an 88% "Certified Fresh" approval rating from review aggregator Rotten Tomatoes. *Kung Fu Panda* opened in 4,114 theaters, grossing $20.3 million on its opening day and $60.2 million on its opening weekend, resulting in the number one position at the box office. The film became DreamWorks's biggest opening for a non-sequel film, highest grossing animated movie of the year, the fourth-largest weekend for a DreamWorks animated film at the American and Canadian box office, behind *Shrek the Third*, *Shrek 2*, and *Shrek Forever After*,[5] and the 49th highest-grossing film of all time.

Plot

The story is set in the Valley of Peace, a fictional land in ancient China inhabited by anthropomorphic animals. Po (Jack Black), a young, clumsy and overweight panda, is a kung fu fanatic who idolizes the Furious Five – Tigress (Angelina Jolie), Monkey (Jackie Chan), Mantis (Seth Rogen), Viper (Lucy Liu), and Crane (David Cross) – a quintet of kung fu masters trained by Master Shifu (Dustin Hoffman) to protect the valley. Because he works in his goose[6] father Ping's (James Hong) noodle restaurant, Po is unable to achieve his dream of becoming a kung fu master himself.

One day, Shifu's mentor, the elderly tortoise Master Oogway (Randall Duk Kim), has a vision that Shifu's former student and foster son, the snow leopard Tai Lung (Ian McShane), will escape from prison and return to the Valley of Peace to take revenge for being denied the Dragon Scroll, which is said to hold the secret to limitless power. Shifu holds a kung fu tournament for the Furious Five so that Oogway may identify the legendary Dragon Warrior, the one kung fu master worthy of receiving the Dragon Scroll and capable of defeating Tai Lung. Forced to take a noodle cart to the tournament, Po arrives after the doors to the tournament arena close and is unable to enter. Desperate to see the Dragon Warrior be chosen, Po straps himself to a set of fireworks and rockets into the sky. Po crashes into the middle of the arena at the moment when Oogway is to point out the Dragon Warrior. To the surprise of everyone present, Oogway chooses Po.

Unwilling to believe that a big fat panda could be the Dragon Warrior, Shifu attempts to get rid of Po by berating and ridiculing him into quitting his training with the Furious Five, who similarly despise and mock Po for his lack of skill in kung fu. After receiving helpful advice from Oogway, however, Po endures his grueling training and slowly begins to endear himself to the Five with his tenacity, culinary skill and good humor. As foreseen, Tai Lung escapes from prison, killing Chief of Security Commander Vachir (Michael Clarke Duncan) as he escapes. Sensing his death is near, Oogway makes Shifu promise to train Po and passes away. Still unable to grasp the basics of kung fu, Po despairs that he has no chance of defeating Tai Lung. Shifu, however, discovers that Po is capable of impressive physical feats when motivated by food. Using food as positive reinforcement, Shifu successfully trains Po to incorporate these feats into a makeshift yet effective kung fu style.

Meanwhile, the Furious Five set out to stop Tai Lung themselves, only to have Tai Lung paralyze and defeat them. Shifu decides Po is ready to receive the Dragon Scroll, but the scroll when opened reveals nothing but a blank, reflective surface. In despair, Shifu orders Po and the Five to evacuate the valley while he delays Tai Lung as long as possible with a fight to the death. The dejected Po finds his father who, in an attempt to console him, reveals that the long-withheld secret ingredient to his famous "secret ingredient soup" is *nothing*, explaining that things become special if people believe them to be. Realizing that this concept is the point of the Dragon Scroll, Po returns to the Jade Palace to confront Tai Lung, who has reached the Palace and nearly killed Shifu. Po proves to be a formidable challenge for Tai Lung as he tries to protect the Dragon Scroll and lure the villain away from Shifu. Eventually, the Dragon Scroll falls into Tai Lung's grasp, but he is unable to understand its symbolic meaning. Po, thanks to his large amount of body fat, is invulnerable to the nerve attacks which paralyzed the Five. He counterattacks Tai Lung and ultimately defeats him using the secret Wuxi Finger Hold. Po is praised by the Valley of Peace and earns the respect of the Furious Five, who fully acknowledge him as a true kung fu master. Shifu, exhausted but alive after his fight with Tai Lung, is finally at peace with himself now that peace has returned to the valley.

Cast

- Jack Black as Po, a Giant Panda
- Dustin Hoffman as Master Shifu, a Red Panda[8]
- Angelina Jolie as Master Tigress, a South China Tiger
- Ian McShane as Tai Lung, a Snow Leopard
- Lucy Liu as Master Viper, a Green Tree Viper
- Jackie Chan as Master Monkey, a Gee's Golden Langur
- Seth Rogen as Master Mantis, a Chinese Mantis

From left to right: Masters Viper, Monkey, Mantis (on Monkey's head), Shifu, Tigress, and Crane. The Furious Five are homages to the Crane, Snake, Monkey, Praying Mantis, and Tiger styles of Chinese martial arts.[7]

- David Cross as Master Crane, a Red-crowned Crane
- Randall Duk Kim as Master Oogway, a Galápagos Tortoise[8]
- James Hong as Mr. Ping, a Chinese Goose
- Dan Fogler as Zeng, a Chinese Goose[8]
- Michael Clarke Duncan as Commander Vachir, a Javan Rhinoceros

Production

"...we love martial arts movies. I wasn't interested in making fun of them, because I really think martial arts movies can be great films, they can be as good as any genre movie when they're done properly [...]

Let's try to make it a real martial arts movie albeit one with a comic character and let's take our action seriously. Let's not give anything up to the big summer movies. Let's really make sure that our kung fu is as cool as any kung fu ever done, so that we can take our place in that canon and make sure it's a beautiful movie, because great martial arts movies are really beautiful-looking movies and then let's see if we can imbue it with real heart and emotion."

—co-director John Stevenson on the comedic approach to the martial arts film.[9]

Publicized work on the film began before October 2004.[10] In September 2005, DreamWorks Animation announced the film alongside Jack Black, who was selected to be the main voice star.[11]

Initially, the idea for the film was to make it a spoof, but co-director John Stevenson was not particularly keen on the idea so instead chose the direction of simplistic comedy.[9] Reportedly inspired by Stephen Chow's 2004 martial arts action comedy, *Kung Fu Hustle,*[12] the co-directors wanted to make sure the film also had an authentic Chinese and kung fu feel to it. Production designer Raymond Zibach and art director Tang Heng spent years researching Chinese painting, sculpture, architecture and kung fu movies to help create the look of the film.[13] Zibach said some of the biggest influence of him are the more artful martial arts films such as *Hero, House of Flying Daggers* and *Crouching Tiger, Hidden Dragon.*[13] The aim for the film, which took four years to make, was to have a good blend of the two, as well as to give it an "epic" feel, unlike other DreamWorks animated features which resorted to "pop songs and celebrity references."[14]

In November 2005, DreamWorks Animation announced that Dustin Hoffman, Jackie Chan, Lucy Liu and Ian McShane would join Jack Black in the cast.[15]

"We've had some productions that were stressful, but this one ran very smoothly and DreamWorks is [sic] this production as a template on how they would like future productions to run. We lucked out, and there really was a sense of harmony on the animation. Even the production people. We all seemed like we were on the same page, believing in the film. That doesn't happen very often. I tell animators, you will be working on dumpers for most of your career, but every once in a while you get a gem. Kung Fu Panda was a gem."

—Dan Wagner, Head of Character Animation.[16]

The hand-drawn animation sequence at the beginning of the film was made to resemble Chinese shadow puppetry.[17] The opening, which was directed by Jennifer Yuh Nelson and produced by James Baxter, was praised by *The New York Times* reviewer Manohla Dargis as "striking" and "visually different from most mainstream American animations".[18] Other reviewers have compared the opening to the evocative style of Genndy Tartakovsky's *Samurai Jack.*[19] [20] The rest of the film is modern computer animation, which uses bright, offbeat colors to evoke the natural landscape of China.[17] The end credit sequence also features hand-drawn characters and still paintings in the background.[17]

The computer animation used throughout the film was more complex than anything DreamWorks had done before. When the head of production handed the script to VFX Supervisor Markus Manninen, she reportedly laughed and wished him "good luck". "When we started talking," said Manninen, "the movie was still a high concept. But for everyone that looked at it, it screamed complexity. We launched off saying, how can you make this movie tangible? How can you find smart ways to bring this world to life in a way that makes it a great movie and not feel like the complexity becomes the driver of the story, but the story and the emotion being the driver?"[21]

In preparation, the animators took a six hour kung fu class.[22]

Producer Melissa Cobb said that originally Po was "more of a jerk," but that the character changed after they heard Jack Black.[22] According to Jack Black, he mostly worked "in isolation", although he and Dustin Hoffman did spend a day together, which Cobb said helped with the scene where their characters face off.[22] Lucy Liu said that the film "was quite different because it was such a long process."[23] Liu said that when she was presented with the project they already had artwork of her character as well as a "short computerized video version of what she would look like when she moved."[23]

Release

The film held its worldwide premiere at the 61st Cannes Film Festival on May 15, 2008, where it received massive and sustained applause at the end of the film's screening.[24] [25] *Kung Fu Panda* later had national premieres in the United States on June 1, 2008 at Grauman's Chinese Theatre in Hollywood, Los Angeles, California,[26] and on June 26, 2008 at Leicester Square in London, for the United Kingdom.[27]

Kung Fu Panda was released on DVD and Blu-ray Disc on November 9, 2008. The special features include an animated short film starring Jack Black, Dustin Hoffman, Angelina Jolie, Jackie Chan, Seth Rogen, Lucy Liu and David Cross, a *Kung Fu Fighting* music video by Cee-Lo Green and Jack Black, a tutorial on how to use chopsticks, sound, The Tech of *Kung Fu Panda*, The Cast of *Kung Fu Panda*, deleted and alternate scenes, cast interviews and biographies with Jack Black, Dustin Hoffman, Angelina Jolie, Ian McShane, Jackie Chan, Seth Rogen, Lucy Liu and David Cross, The Premiere of Kung Fu Panda, interactive games and more. The movie can be purchased as a stand-alone DVD or as part of a two-disc pack that includes the companion story *Secrets of the Furious Five*.[28] On its first week (ending Nov. 19, 2008) it sold 2,667,861 units ($42,530,240) and 9,029,480 units in total, becoming the second highest-grossing animated film of 2008 , behind *WALL-E* (9,034,425 DVD units).[29]

Reception and box office

Kung Fu Panda has received positive reviews from critics. Rotten Tomatoes reported that 88% of 163 critics gave the film a positive review. The film has an approval rating of 76% from a select group of critics and an approval rating of 83% from users of the site.[30] Metacritic reported the film had an average score of 73 out of 100, based on 33 reviews.[31]

Richard Corliss of *Time Magazine* gave the film a positive review, stating the picture "provides a master course in cunning visual art and ultra-satisfying entertainment".[32] *The New York Times* said, "At once fuzzy-wuzzy and industrial strength, the tacky-sounding *Kung Fu Panda* is high concept with a heart," and the review called the film "consistently diverting" and "visually arresting".[18] Chris Barsanti of *Filmcritics.com* commented, "Blazing across the screen with eye-popping, sublime artwork, *Kung Fu Panda* sets itself apart from the modern domestic animation trend with its sheer beauty [...] the film enters instant classic status as some of the most gorgeous animation Hollywood has produced since the golden age of Disney."[33] The *Chicago Tribune* called the film "one of the few comedies of 2008 in any style or genre that knows what it's doing". Roger Ebert gave it three stars praising the animation, action scenes, and saying that older viewers will be forgiving.

The film topped the box office in its opening weekend, grossing $60,239,130 for a $14,642 average from 4,114 theaters and performing much better than analysts had been expecting. It also was the highest-grossing start for a DreamWorks Animation film excluding the *Shrek* films. In its' second weekend, the film retreated 44% to second place behind *The Incredible Hulk* grossing $33,612,594 for a $8,127 average from expanding to 4,136 theaters. It closed on October 9, 2008 after 125 days of release, grossing $215,434,591 domestically and $416,309,969 overseas for a worldwide total of $631,744,560. Produced on a $130 million budget, the film was a huge box office success, and was the highest-grossing non-Shrek film from DreamWorks Animation, before being surpassed by *How To*

Train Your Dragon in 2010.

Kung Fu Panda was also well-received in China.[34] It made nearly 110 million Chinese Yuan by July 2, 2008, becoming the first animated film to make more than 100 million Yuan in Chinese box offices.[35] [36] The Chinese director Lu Chuan commented, "From a production standpoint, the movie is nearly perfect. Its American creators showed a very sincere attitude about Chinese culture."[37] [38] With the film's success at the Chinese box office, some people within China have questioned the quality of China's domestic animations. The fact that such a successful film based on Chinese culture was created by the American movie industry has led to some Chinese introspection.[39] [40] [41]

The release of the film in the land where it was set was not without controversy. Zhao Bandi, a Chinese artist and fashion designer who specializes in panda-related designs, launched an online petition suggesting that the film should be boycotted.[42] [43] In his petition, Bandi stated that Hollywood was seeking to profit from Chinese culture. The film was aired soon after the 2008 Sichuan earthquake, and the petition said that the film was in poor taste to be released so soon after the disaster, given that pandas live within the area affected by the quake. Bandi also protested against the fact that the film was produced by DreamWorks, which is owned by Steven Spielberg. Spielberg withdrew from his role as an adviser to the 2008 Summer Olympics over concerns about China's role in Sudan (although Spielberg is not one of the producers of *Kung Fu Panda*). Zhao Bandi admitted that he had not actually seen the film prior to the petition.[44] However, while postings on his website both praised and criticized the film, many people said that there was no reason to boycott it. Zhao's complaints prompted an online backlash asserting that an entertaining film paying tribute to Chinese heritage would be welcome at this difficult time,[45] and some even questioned whether this was just a publicity stunt by the artist.[44]

Awards

Kung Fu Panda had been shortlisted for nomination for the Academy Award for Best Animated Feature[46] and the Golden Globe Award for Best Animated Feature Film.[47] However, both awards were won by Pixar's *WALL-E* instead. This was parodied by the film's main voice actor, Jack Black, at the 81st Academy Awards, saying "Every year I do a movie for DreamWorks, and then I take all the money and bet it all on Pixar."

By contrast, *Kung Fu Panda* won 11 Annie Awards (including Best Picture) out of 16 nominations, albeit amid controversy.[48]

Soundtrack

As with most DreamWorks animated films, composer Hans Zimmer scored the film. Zimmer visited China in order to absorb the culture and got to know the Chinese National Symphony as part of his preparation; in addition, Timbaland also contributed to the soundtrack.[49] The soundtrack also includes a partially rewritten version of the classic song, "Kung Fu Fighting", performed by Cee-Lo Green and Jack Black for the end credits. Furthermore, in some versions, the ending credit was sung by Rain. Although Zimmer was originally announced as the main composer of the film, during a test screening, CEO of DreamWorks Animation SKG Jeffrey Katzenberg announced that composer John Powell would also be contributing to the score. This marked the first collaboration in eight years for the two, who had previously worked together on Dreamworks' *The Road to El Dorado* and the action thriller *Chill Factor*. A soundtrack album was released by Interscope Records on June 3, 2008.[50]

Sequel

There will be a sequel called *Kung Fu Panda 2* which is currently in post-production and is slated for release on May 27, 2011.[51] [52] It is set to be in 3-D and will be directed by Jennifer Yuh Nelson (who directed the praised 2-D opening sequence of *Kung Fu Panda*) with the original cast returning. The story features a new villain with a mysterious weapon so powerful it threatens the very existence of kung fu, and Po must additionally confront his past.[53]

On December 3, 2010, DreamWorks Animation chief Jeffrey Katzenberg stated in an interview that there would be a total of six films in the *Kung Fu Panda* series, based on a planned story arc.[54]

Manga

A manga based on the film has been released in Japan in *Kerokero Ace* magazine's September 2008 issue.[55] It is written by Hanten Okuma and illustrated by Takafumi Adachi.[56]

Television series

A television series is in development for Nickelodeon titled *Kung Fu Panda: Legends of Awesomeness*, and is scheduled to premiere in 2011. This will be Nickelodeon's second DreamWorks deal, the first being *The Penguins of Madagascar*.[57] [58]

Holiday special

The *Kung Fu Panda Holiday Special* was aired on NBC Wednesday, November 24, 2010.[59]

Video game

A video game adaptation of the film was developed and published by Activision on June 3, 2008.[60] The game follows the same basic plot as the film, but with Tai Lung portrayed as the leader of various gangs that surround the Valley of Peace, which Po, who possesses some basic martial art skills which can be upgraded as the game progresses, must defeat. The game was released on Microsoft Windows, as well as multiple consoles. However the Windows version has been discontinued. The game received mostly positive reviews; it scored a Metacritic rating of 76% from critics[61] and a 7.5 out of 10 from IGN.[62] In 2009, it won the International Animated Film Society's Annie Award for Best Animated Video Game, "in recognition of creative excellence in the art of animation."[63]

Two web games, The Adversary [64] and The Field of Fiery Danger [65] were created for the film by Playniac [66] for Nickelodeon.

In popular culture

Baseball player Pablo Sandoval of the San Francisco Giants is nicknamed "Kung Fu Panda".[67]

References

[1] http://www.boxofficemojo.com/movies/?id=kungfupanda.htm

[2] "Kung Fu Panda sequel in pipeline" (http://news.bbc.co.uk/1/hi/entertainment/7560194.stm). *BBC*. August 14, 2008. . Retrieved September 1, 2008.

[3] Brown, Geoff (October 19, 1993). "Who framed the animator's artistry?". *The Times*.

[4] "Imagi Announces Strategic Alliance for Gatchaman and Astro Boy Toy Development" (http://www.itnews.it/news/2007/0807132403284/imagi-announces-strategic-alliance-for-gatchaman-and-astro-boy-toy-development.html). *IT News*. August 7, 2007. . Retrieved September 1, 2008.

[5] "'Shrek Forever After' roars to top of box office" (http://today.msnbc.msn.com/id/37302907/ns/today-entertainment/). *msnbc.com*. May 23, 2010. . Retrieved May 23, 2010.

[6] Stevenson, John and Mark Osborne (directors). (2008). *Kung Fu Panda*. [DVD]. Event occurs at 3.55. "...Po's father is a goose. And he is a goose, he's not a duck..."

[7] "Kung Fu Panda-production-five fighting warriors." (http://www.kungfupanda.com/). DreamWorks. . Retrieved September 1, 2008.

[8] Aibel, Jonathan; Glenn Berger. "June 3, 2008" (http://www.paramountguilds.com/movies/script/KFP_script.pdf) (PDF). .

[9] Douglas, Edward (June 2, 2008). "EXCL: *Kung Fu Panda* Co-Director John Stevenson" (http://www.comingsoon.net/news/movienews. php?id=45494). *ComingSoon.net.* . Retrieved June 5, 2008.

[10] Aggerholm, Barbara (October 5, 2004). "Giving a shark some bite; Local animator swims with the big boys" (http://www.tjgalda.com/ About/Appearances_files/record_shark_some_bite.html). *Kitchener Record.* . Retrieved September 1, 2008.

[11] "Dreamworks Animation Plans Kung Fu Panda" (http://www.empireonline.com/News/story.asp?nid=17136). Empire. September 21, 2005. . Retrieved June 5, 2008.

[12] Gaul, Lou (November 4, 2005). "1104 Film Clips" (http://news.google.com/archivesearch?q="Kung+Fu+Panda."+The+ computer-animated+picture+was+reportedly+inspired+by+Stephen+Chow's+action+comedy,+"Kung+Fu+Hustle."&btnG=Search+ Archives&hl=en&ned=us&ie=UTF-8). *Bucks County Courier Times.* . Retrieved September 1, 2008.

[13] "*Kung Fu Panda* gets cuddly" (http://www.nydailynews.com/entertainment/movies/2008/06/01/ 2008-06-01_kung_fu_panda_gets_cuddly.html). *New York Daily News.* May 31, 2008. . Retrieved June 5, 2008.

[14] Covert, Colin (June 3, 2008). "*Kung Fu Panda* pushes boundaries of cartoon art" (http://web.archive.org/web/20080609220822/http:// www.newsobserver.com/1569/story/1094727.html). *The News & Observer.* Archived from the original (http://www.newsobserver.com/ 1569/story/1094727.html) on June 9, 2008. . Retrieved June 5, 2008.

[15] "DreamWorks Announces the Cast of *Kung Fu Panda*" (http://movies.about.com/od/moviesinproduction/a/kungfu110905.htm). =UPI Entertainment News. November 9, 2005. . Retrieved September 1, 2008.

[16] Dunlop, Renne. "*Kung Fu Panda* - One For Life" (http://features.cgsociety.org/story_custom.php?story_id=4549&page=2). *CG Studios.* . Retrieved August 29, 2008.

[17] Hewitt, Chris (June 6, 2008). "*Kung Fu Panda* is fresh, surprising and beautiful" (http://www.twincities.com/movies/ ci_9488296?nclick_check=1). *TwinCities.com.* . Retrieved June 7, 2008.

[18] Dargis, Manohla (June 6, 2008). "Fuzzy Outsider, Kicking His Way Toward His Dream" (http://movies.nytimes.com/2008/06/06/ movies/06pand.html). *The New York Times.* . Retrieved June 10, 2008.

[19] "Kung Fu Cinemapoo *Kung Fu Panda* review" (http://www.kungfucinema.com/?p=2198). *Kung Fu Cinema.* . Retrieved September 1, 2008.

[20] Garrett, Stephen. "Timeout *Kung Fu Panda* review" (http://www.timeout.com/film/newyork/reviews/85508/kung-fu-panda.html). *Time Out.* . Retrieved September 1, 2008.

[21] Dunlop, Renne. "*Kung Fu Panda*" (http://features.cgsociety.org/story_custom.php?story_id=4549). *CG Studios.* . Retrieved August 29, 2008.

[22] Roberts, Sheila. "Jack Black Interview, Kung Fu Panda" (http://www.moviesonline.ca/movienews_14790.html). *MoviesOnline.* . Retrieved December 22, 2008.

[23] Roberts, Sheila. "Lucy Liu Interview, Kung Fu Panda" (http://www.moviesonline.ca/movienews_14789.html). *MoviesOnline.* . Retrieved December 22, 2008.

[24] "Cannes Film Festival on MSN Movies" (http://movies.msn.com/movies/cannes-film-festival/may16-blog). MSN. May 16, 2008. . Retrieved June 4, 2008.

[25] "*Kung Fu Panda* a martial arts masterpiece" (http://www.reuters.com/article/entertainmentNews/idUSN1631324020080516). *Reuters.* May 16, 2008. . Retrieved June 1, 2008.

[26] "Helmers talk *Kung Fu Panda*". *The Hollywood Reporter.* June 1, 2008.

[27] "Kung Fu Panda London premiere" (http://news.bbc.co.uk/newsbeat/hi/entertainment/newsid_7477000/7477138.stm). *BBC.* June 27, 2008. . Retrieved September 10, 2008.

[28] "Kung Fu Panda 2 in '11" (http://movies.ign.com/articles/915/915630p1.html). *IGN.* October 2, 2008. . Retrieved October 3, 2008.

[29] "Kung Fu Panda - DVD Sales" (http://www.the-numbers.com/movies/2008/PANDA-DVD.php). The Numbers. . Retrieved January 18, 2011.

[30] "*Kung Fu Panda* (2008)" (http://www.rottentomatoes.com/m/kung_fu_panda/). Rotten Tomatoes. . Retrieved June 5, 2008.

[31] "Kung Fu Panda (2008)" (http://www.metacritic.com/film/titles/kungfupanda). Metacritic. . Retrieved June 5, 2008.

[32] Corliss, Richard (June 5, 2008). "*Kung Fu Panda*: Wise Heart, Sweet Art" (http://www.time.com/time/arts/article/0,8599,1812145,00. html). *Time.* . Retrieved July 28, 2008.

[33] Barsanti, Chris. "*Kung Fu Panda*" (http://www.filmcritic.com/misc/emporium.nsf/reviews/Kung-Fu-Panda). *Film Critic.* . Retrieved July 28, 2008.

[34] "*Kung Fu Panda* Received with Enthusiasm in Asia" (http://news.toonzone.net/article.php?ID=24549). *Toonzone.* . Retrieved June 24, 2008.

[35] "Kung Fu Panda breaks Chinese box-office records" (http://www.telegraph.co.uk/news/worldnews/asia/china/2268139/ Kung-Fu-Panda-breaks-Chinese-box-office-records.html). *Telegraph* (London). July 8, 2008. . Retrieved August 27, 2008.

[36] ""Kung Fu Panda" Breaks Box Office Record of Animation" (http://english.cri.cn/3086/2008/07/08/1821s378282.htm). *CriEnglish.* July 8, 2008. . Retrieved August 27, 2008.

[37] "*Kung Fu Panda* reaches Chinese box office milestone" (http://www.iht.com/articles/ap/2008/07/03/arts/ AS-MOV-China-Kung-Fu-Panda.php). *International Herald Tribune*. . Retrieved July 28, 2008.

[38] Lee, Min (July 3, 2008). "*Kung Fu Panda* reaches Chinese box office milestone" (http://www.usatoday.com/life/movies/news/ 2008-07-03-kungfupanda_N.htm). *USA Today*. . Retrieved July 28, 2008.

[39] Bernstein, Richard (July 20, 2008). "The Panda That Roared" (http://www.nytimes.com/2008/07/20/weekinreview/20bernstein.html). *New York Times*. . Retrieved July 23, 2008.

[40] Fan, Maureen (July 12, 2008). "*Kung Fu Panda* Hits A Sore Spot in China" (http://www.washingtonpost.com/wp-dyn/content/article/ 2008/07/11/AR2008071103281.html). *Washington Post*. . Retrieved July 23, 2008.

[41] Watts, Jonathan (July 8, 2008). "Kung Fu Panda: "The director has really got in touch with what China is today"" (http://www.guardian. co.uk/film/audio/2008/jul/08/kungfu.panda.film). *Guardian* (London). . Retrieved August 30, 2008.

[42] "Chinese artists can't bear "Panda"" (http://www.varietyasiaonline.com/content/view/6314/1/). Variety *Asia online*. . Retrieved June 23, 2008.

[43] "Is *Kung Fu Panda* Ready for the China Challenge?" (http://blogs.wsj.com/chinajournal/2008/06/17/ is-âkung-fu-pandaâ-ready-for-the-china-challenge/?mod=googlenews_wsj). *Wall Street Journal*. June 17, 2008. . Retrieved June 22, 2008.

[44] AFP (June 20, 2008). "'Kung Fu Panda' delayed in quake-hit part of China: report" (http://afp.google.com/article/ ALeqM5hoW_bWZYYV9KojjqYyHtpZkUI0Ig?docId=080620103419.jpprv322&index=0). AFP. . Retrieved November 26, 2010.

[45] "*Panda* bounces back at China B.O." (http://www.varietyasiaonline.com/content/view/6335/1/). Variety *Asia online*. . Retrieved June 24, 2008.

[46] "14 cartoons seek 3 Oscar berths" (http://www.reuters.com/article/entertainmentNews/idUSTRE4AA0YC20081111). *Reuters*. November 11, 2008. . Retrieved NOvember 16, 2008.

[47] King, Susan (December 11, 2008). "Golden Globes nominations unveiled" (http://theenvelope.latimes.com/entertainment/ env-et-golden-globes-noms-2008dec11,0,898168.story?page=2). *Los Angeles Times*. . Retrieved December 11, 2008.

[48] O'Neil, Tom (January 31, 2009). "*Kung Fu Panda* dropkicks *Wall-E* at Annie Awards (http://goldderby.latimes.com/awards_goldderby/ 2009/01/kung-fu-panda-d.html)"]. *Los Angeles Times*. . Retrieved July 12, 2009.

[49] DuBois, Stephanie; Emily Feimster (September 18, 2007). "The Big Screen Scene" (http://www.nationalledger.com/cgi-bin/artman/ exec/view.cgi?archive=17&num=16128&printer=1). *National Ledger*. . Retrieved June 7, 2008.

[50] Cohen, Jonathan (May 12, 2008). "Jack Black, Cee-Lo cover *Kung Fu Fighting*" (http://web.archive.org/web/20080517054016/http:// www.hollywoodreporter.com/hr/content_display/film/news/e3i595b48df06c95e2eed05e9c3eb45a08c). *The Hollywood Reporter*. Archived from the original (http://www.hollywoodreporter.com/hr/content_display/film/news/e3i595b48df06c95e2eed05e9c3eb45a08c) on May 17, 2008. . Retrieved June 4, 2008.

[51] "Kung Fu Panda 2 Officially Headed to Theaters in 2011" (http://www.firstshowing.net/2008/10/01/ kung-fu-panda-2-officially-headed-to-theaters-in-2011/). *FirstShowing.net*. October 1, 2008. . Retrieved June 12, 2009.

[52] "Kung Fu Panda: The Kaboom Of Doom (2011) - QuickSilverScreen Forum" (http://ipb.quicksilverscreen.com/index. php?s=82ef41e6a1f36969dbec5a7c68650191&showtopic=214021&pid=1013851&st=0&#entry1013851). Ipb.quicksilverscreen.com. . Retrieved August 8, 2010.

[53] "*DreamWorks Animation's Slate Through 2012!*" (http://www.comingsoon.net/news/movienews.php?id=55849). *Comingsoon.net*. May 28, 2009. . Retrieved July 12, 2009.

[54] http://www.empireonline.com/news/story.asp?NID=29638

[55] "America's Kung Fu Panda Film Gets Manga in Japan (Updated)" (http://www.animenewsnetwork.com/news/2008-07-29/ america-kung-fu-panda-film-gets-manga-in-japan). *Anime News Network*. May 12, 2009. . Retrieved May 16, 2009.

[56] "Kung Fu Panda Manga Released in Japan" (http://www.animecentral.com/news/story.aspx?ID=447). Anime Central. . Retrieved May 20, 2010.

[57] "Entertainment | Kung Fu Panda series in the works" (http://news.bbc.co.uk/1/hi/entertainment/8051520.stm). *BBC News*. May 15, 2009. . Retrieved May 16, 2009.

[58] Barnes, Brooks (May 13, 2009). "'Kung Fu Panda' to Become a Series on Nickelodeon" (http://www.nytimes.com/2009/05/14/arts/ television/14drea.html?_r=1). *The New York Times*. . Retrieved May 20, 2010.

[59] NBC and DreamWorks Animation Bring One of a Kind Animated Programming to Audiences at Home For the Holidays with New Original Specials *Scared Shrekless* and *Kung Fu Panda Holiday Special* (http://www.thefutoncritic.com/news/2010/09/07/ nbc-and-dreamworks-animation-bring-one-of-a-kind-animated-programming-to-audiences-at-home-for-the-holidays-with-new-original-specials-scared-shrekless-and-kung-fu-panda-holiday-special/ 20100907nbc01/), NBC via The Futon Critic, September 9, 2010 Retrieved 26 September 26, 2010

[60] de Matos, Xav (March 12, 2008). "Are you sitting down? Kung fu Panda revealed! Impersonators and small-time actors replace the star cast of the original movie." (http://www.xbox360fanboy.com/2008/03/12/are-you-sitting-down-kung-fu-panda-revealed/). *Xbox 360 Fanboy*. . Retrieved September 1, 2008.

[61] "Kung Fu Panda" (http://www.metacritic.com/games/platforms/xbox360/kungfupanda). *Metacritic*. . Retrieved September 1, 2008.

[62] Brudvig, Erik (June 9, 2008). "Kung Fu Panda Review" (http://xbox360.ign.com/articles/880/880257p1.html). *IGN*. . Retrieved September 1, 2008.

[63] "Kung Fu Panda dominates the Annie Awards" (http://www.annieawards.org/). *The Annie Awards*. January 30, 2009. . Retrieved February 5, 2009.

[64] http://www.playniac.com/games/kung-fu-panda-the-adversary/

[65] http://www.playniac.com/games/the-field-of-fiery-danger/

[66] http://www.playniac.com/

[67] Castrovince, Anthony (February 10, 2009). "For ballplayers, what's in a (nick)name?" (http://mlb.mlb.com/news/article. jsp?ymd=20090206&content_id=3804552&vkey=news_mlb&fext=.jsp). *MLB.com*. . Retrieved 2009-05-13.

External links

- Official website (http://http://www.kungfupanda.com)
- *Kung Fu Panda* (http://www.imdb.com/title/tt0441773/) at the Internet Movie Database
- *Kung Fu Panda* (http://www.bcdb.com/bcdb/cartoon.cgi?film=65706/) at the Big Cartoon DataBase
- *Kung Fu Panda* (http://www.allmovie.com/work/354676) at Allmovie
- *Kung Fu Panda* (http://www.rottentomatoes.com/m/kung_fu_panda/) at Rotten Tomatoes
- *Kung Fu Panda* (http://www.metacritic.com/film/titles/kungfupanda) at Metacritic
- *Kung Fu Panda* (http://www.boxofficemojo.com/movies/?id=kungfupanda.htm) at Box Office Mojo

Step Brothers (film)

Step Brothers(comedy)	
Directed by	Adam McKay
Produced by	Jimmy Miller Judd Apatow Adam McKay Will Ferrell
Screenplay by	Adam McKay Will Ferrell
Story by	Adam McKay Will Ferrell John C. Reilly
Starring	Will Ferrell John C. Reilly
Music by	Jon Brion
Cinematography	Oliver Wood
Editing by	Brent White
Studio	Relativity Media The Apatow Company Mosaic Media Group Gary Sanchez Productions
Distributed by	Columbia Pictures
Release date(s)	July 25, 2008
Running time	98 minutes
Country	United States
Language	English Spanish
Budget	$65 million
Gross revenue	$128,107,642

Step Brothers is a 2008 American slapstick buddy-comedy film directed by Adam McKay, produced by Judd Apatow and Jimmy Miller, and stars Will Ferrell and John C. Reilly, who last teamed up in *Talladega Nights* (2006). The screenplay was written by Ferrell and McKay, from a story written by Ferrell, McKay and Reilly. The film was released on July 25, 2008.

Plot

Brennan Huff (Will Ferrell) and Dale Doback (John C. Reilly) are two unemployed and spoiled men who still live with and are reliant on their parents. Brennan, who lives with his divorced mother, Nancy (Mary Steenburgen), and Dale, who lives with his widower father, Robert (Richard Jenkins), have no intention of moving out or finding jobs and behave very childishly. Robert and Nancy, upon meeting during a work conference, get married and move in together, forcing Brennan and Dale to live with each other as step brothers; they are resentful and display a childish dislike towards each other. Dale warns Brennan not to touch his drum set, but Brennan does it anyway days later while Dale is not home. This ignites a huge fight and in response, Robert and Nancy warn them that they must find jobs and see their therapists within a month or else be forced out of the house. While commiserating, Brennan and

Dale discover that they share a number of common interests and gradually overcome their mutual animosity. Brennan's successful, conceited biological younger brother, Derek (Adam Scott), who is regularly cruel to Brennan out of fun comes to visit with his oddly perfect family. Brennan and Dale retreat to Dale's tree house. Derek drops by to mock them, and entices Dale to punch Derek in the face, which Dale actually does, knocking Derek out of the tree. Brennan is awed by the fact that Dale was able to stand up to Derek. Meanwhile, Derek's wife Alice (Kathryn Hahn), who is also deeply resentful of Derek, finds Dale's courage sexually arousing.

Brennan and Dale take job interviews, for which they perform very poorly, being rude to their two potential employers and pointing out too many of their flaws (such as Dale's unwillingness to work before 11 am), and offending a third (Seth Rogen) when Dale passes gas for almost a minute. In response, they decide to start their own entertainment company called "Prestige Worldwide". However, Robert and Nancy reveal that they are going to retire to sail the world in Robert's beloved boat, and allow Derek to sell the house, forcing Brennan and Dale to find other living arrangements. However, Brennan and Dale sabotage Derek's plans by masquerading as a Neo-Nazi and a Klansman, and by pretending that Brennan has died of asbestos poisoning, while Derek shows the house to potential buyers. Back at the dinner table, Brennan and Dale have trouble blending in with the others, especially Derek's rude employee, Randy (Rob Riggle). Dale excuses himself to the restroom where Alice forces him into having sex with her. Later, Brennan and Dale premiere their company's first music video, which was filmed on Robert's boat. The video ends when the boat crashes into the rocks (ruining Robert and Nancy's retirement plans), and upon arriving home, Robert brutally spanks Brennan (after Brennan insults Robert) and warns Dale that he's next.

On Christmas Eve, the boys destroy the family's tree and gifts during a spell of sleepwalking, and subsequently attack Robert and then throw him down the stairs after he tries to wake them. Angered to his limit, Robert decides to divorce Nancy causing Dale and Brennan to breakdown. Derek photographs the moment. Dale and Brennan are angered by the divorce and blame each other, reverting to their feeling of dislike towards each other. After another fight which resulted in attempts to bury each other alive, they go their separate ways and move into their own apartments. Brennan starts working for Derek's helicopter leasing firm and Dale works for a catering company. The two gradually begin acting like responsible adults. Brennan, wanting to reunite the broken family, takes the initiative to arrange Derek's sales party: The Catalina Wine Mixer, supervised by Randy. The party is a success, and Brennan wins Randy's respect and approval. However, the singer of the band that Brennan booked (played by Horatio Sanz), a (strictly 80's) Billy Joel tribute band, insults guests after being heckled to his breaking point to play non-80's Joel and is thrown off stage. Derek blames Brennan for this incident, and quickly fires him, believing that this incident will ruin his reputation. Robert then encourages Brennan and Dale to be their eccentric child-at-heart selves again, seeing as how they are now both miserable in their "adult" lives. Brennan and Dale then take the stage and perform **"Por ti Volare/(Boats n Hoes)"**. While at first they are mocked by Derek, Randy, and others (in a manner similar to how they mocked Brennan back in high school, which caused him to be afraid to sing in public in the first place), Brennan and Dale are unfazed by it, and the audience is eventually moved by the performance (which cause a montage of satirical, but artistic surreal dream sequences of each character), and tensions between the family members are alleviated, while Randy gets emotional and breaks down in tears. After the performance, Brennan and Derek make amends, giving each other a high-five (after a failed attempt to hug).

After the film's climax, Brennan and Dale form their successful company that runs karaoke bars and restaurants. Six months later, Robert and Nancy were reunited and move back into their old home, with a new tree house made from the destroyed boat just for Dale and Brennan, with some nude magazines, Chewbacca masks, and Crossbows. There are two scenes in the end credits. One of which Dale and Brennan are getting revenge on the kids that picked on them earlier in the movie, and the other is them sleepwalking getting ready to board a plane.

Cast

- Will Ferrell as Brennan Huff, Nancy's 39-year-old son.
- John C. Reilly as Dale Doback, Robert's 40-year-old son.
- Richard Jenkins as Dr. Robert Doback, Dale's widower father, a medical doctor, now married to Nancy.
- Mary Steenburgen as Nancy Huff-Doback, Brennan's divorced mother who meets Robert at a work conference.
- Adam Scott as Derek Huff, Brennan's successful younger brother, who has a Type A personality.
- Kathryn Hahn as Alice Huff, Derek's sex-crazed, emotionally crazed, negatively treated wife who has an affair with Dale.
- Andrea Savage as Denise, Brennan's therapist and inadvertent love interest.
- Rob Riggle as Randy, Derek's best friend and employee.
- Logan Manus as Chris Gardocki, an 11-year old elementary school student who, along with other kids, abuses Dale on a regular basis. He is later beaten by Dale and Brennan (who get their revenge) in the film's second climax.
- Lurie Poston as Tommy
- Elizabeth Yozamp as Tiffany
- Ken Jeong as a employment agent.
- Wayne Federman as Don, blind man.
- Abigail Wagner as Erica, store owner.
- Carli Coleman as first homebuyer wife.
- Brandon T. Webb as first homebuyer husband.
- Phil LaMarr as second homebuyer husband.
- Matt Walsh as drunk corporate guy.
- Seth Rogen as Sporting goods store manager.
- Gillian Vigman as Pam

Critical reception

The film has received mixed reviews. As of December 2010, the film has a 55% rating based on reviews from critics at the review aggregator website Rotten Tomatoes, giving the movie a "rotten" overall review. At the website Metacritic, which utilizes a normalized rating system, the film earned a mixed rating of 51/100 based on 33 reviews. Roger Ebert gave the film 1½ out of 4 stars.[1]

Location

Step Brothers was filmed in southern California. The house where Dale and Brennan live is an actual house that was rented for the purpose of filming. The address is 1987 Midwick Drive in Altadena, CA. Another filming location was the U.S. Veterans Hospital located at 16111 Plummer Street in North Hills, CA. This location served as the school where Dale and Brennan were attacked by children. Derek's birthday celebration was filmed at a restaurant known as "The Derby" and the Catalina Wine Mixer was filmed at 1 Ocean Trails Drive, Rancho Palos Verdes.

Box office performance

Step Brothers, as of January 2010, has grossed $100,468,793 domestically, and an additional $28 million internationally.[2]

DVD release

The film was released in a single-disc rated edition, a single-disc unrated edition and a 2-disc unrated edition on December 2, 2008 making $23.04m off 1,316,053 DVD units. As per the latest figures, the film has generated $60,050,590 in revenue (rental/Blu-ray not included).[3]

Sequel

Will Ferrell and John C. Reilly talked about a sequel on TheUrbanDaily.com. Reilly had the idea that they adopt children together. [4] [5]

Adam McKay was also interviewed about the possible sequel, this is how it went:

McKay: "We're kicking around the idea of Step Brothers 2. We feel like there's way more fat to be mined there. While it isn't quite the legend that Anchorman is, it has built kind of a nice following. We think it could be a pretty fun one."

SJ: What would the plot of the sequel be?

"A different kind of immature. The idea is that when we meet them, they've gotten more mature. They actually have jobs. They actually do have a semblance of a life. One of them's married and has a kid. They're still kind of goofballs but they've taken three or four steps. Then we have an idea for something happens that knocks him back to square one, and one of the brothers, John C. Reilly sort of instigates it, like 'we can't take this anymore.' And things go really bad, they're lives kind of fall apart. They have to pull it back together is sort of the basic structure. I won't say the ideas but we have a couple ideas. We had ideas in the first one that we never did that we always thought were pretty funny."

SJ: If you couldn't get Anchorman 2 greenlit, how will you be able to do so with a less popular film?

McKay: "I think any sequel you're up against it. I think the legendary comedy is worse to do a sequel to. We kind of knew going into it that it would never be as good as the first one. You just have to accept it and move ahead. I mean, Godfather II I think is the only one maybe better than the first, right? Empire better than Star Wars, I don't know about that. Terminator 2 is interesting. It's still tough though, that original idea out of the gate. Godfather II changed it up enough, that was the trick that it became a different world."

References

[1] "Step Brothers: Review" (http://rogerebert.suntimes.com/apps/pbcs.dll/article?AID=/20080723/REVIEWS/611265921/1001).
     rogerebert.com. . Retrieved 2010-10-19.
[2] the-numbers.com (http://www.the-numbers.com/movies/2008/STEPB.php)
[3] http://www.the-numbers.com/movies/2008/STEPB-DVD.php
[4] http://www.denofgeek.com/movies/114773/anchorman_and_step_brothers_sequels.html
[5] http://theurbandaily.com/movies/step-brothers-reunited-and-it-feels-so-good/

External links

- Official website (http://http://www.sonypictures.com/movies/stepbrothers)
- *Step Brothers* (http://www.imdb.com/title/tt0838283/) at the Internet Movie Database
- *Step Brothers* (http://www.allmovie.com/work/357813) at Allmovie
- *Step Brothers* (http://www.boxofficemojo.com/movies/?id=stepbrothers.htm) at Box Office Mojo
- *Step Brothers* (http://www.rottentomatoes.com/m/1193743-step_brothers/) at Rotten Tomatoes

- Scoring Session Photo Gallery (http://www.scoringsessions.com/sessions/29811) ScoringSessions.com
- Step Brothers Trailer (http://uk.player.playnetworks.net/popup.php?mid=1208&version=2.0&channel_user_id=441100018-1&width=640&height=380&bgcolor=000000) playnetworks.net

Pineapple Express (film)

Pineapple Express	
Theatrical release poster	
Directed by	David Gordon Green
Produced by	Judd Apatow Shauna Robertson
Screenplay by	• Seth Rogen • Evan Goldberg
Story by	• Judd Apatow • Seth Rogen • Evan Goldberg
Starring	Seth Rogen James Franco Gary Cole Rosie Perez Craig Robinson Amber Heard Kevin Corrigan Danny R. McBride
Music by	Graeme Revell
Cinematography	Tim Orr
Editing by	Craig Alpert
Studio	Relativity Media Apatow Productions
Distributed by	Columbia Pictures
Release date(s)	August 6, 2008

Running time	111 minutes
Country	United States
Language	English
Budget	$25 million
Gross revenue	$100,941,380

Pineapple Express is a 2008 American action stoner comedy film directed by David Gordon Green, written by Seth Rogen and Evan Goldberg and starring Rogen and James Franco. Producer Judd Apatow, who previously worked with Rogen and Goldberg on *Knocked Up* and *Superbad*, assisted in developing the story, which was partially inspired by the buddy comedy subgenre. The film was released on August 6, 2008. Franco was nominated for a Golden Globe award for his performance in the film.

Plot

The film opens in 1937 at a secret army base where marijuana is being tested for legality. After the test subject (Bill Hader) starts saying inappropriate things about his superiors and losing focus, the General in charge of the operation decides to have marijuana made illegal. It is unseen whether the test subject lives or dies, although a gunshot is heard shortly before the General declares marijuana illegal.

The film then cuts to the present, where Dale Denton (Seth Rogen) is a 25-year-old process server who, in delivering a subpoena to drug lord Ted Jones (Gary Cole), witnesses Jones and his business partner (as well as girlfriend), a corrupt police officer, Carol Brazier (Rosie Perez), commit murder. Dale panics and leaves a roach at the scene containing a rare strain of marijuana called Pineapple Express. Ted and Carol run outside but are too late to catch the witness. Ted picks up the roach and identifies it as the rare strain that he has sold to only one dealer. He sends his two henchmen, Budlofsky (Kevin Corrigan) and Matheson (Craig Robinson) to the dealer, Red (Danny McBride), who discloses that he has sold this pot only to Dale's dealer, Saul Silver (James Franco).

Dale flees to Saul's apartment in a panic because he doesn't know where else to go. After a brief conversation, Dale realizes Ted could trace the roach back to Saul. They flee Saul's apartment. Ted's henchmen persuade Saul's supplier, Red, to arrange a meeting between Red and Saul, but this fails because Dale and Saul spend the night in the woods. Matheson and Budlofsky learn Dale's identity through Red. Meanwhile, Matheson and Budlofsky hold Red hostage at his house.

Worried that the corrupt police officer could "triangulate" on their cell phones, the two men smash Dale's cell phone and throw Saul's into the woods. They then sleep 18 hours before paying a late visit to Red. They hope that talking with Red in person will help them determine whether Ted has linked them, and therefore whether he is in pursuit. Instead, Dale decides that Red will reveal their whereabouts to Ted, and the three fight. Convinced that Ted's men are pursuing them, they decide that they must leave the city. Dale goes to his girlfriend Angie's (Amber Heard) house to warn her and her parents, but Angie's father does not believe him. Instead, he threatens to shoot Dale. Matheson and Budlofsky pursue Dale and Saul to Angie's house, and her family goes into hiding.

To leave town, Dale and Saul sell some of Saul's Pineapple Express to raise bus fare. They get money after offering marijuana to a couple of middle school kids, who smoke the marijuana with Dale and Saul. A police officer catches Dale smoking a joint and arrests him. Handcuffed in the back of a squad car, Dale convinces the arresting officer that Brazier is corrupt. Saul "saves" Dale by hijacking the squad car, and drives away with Dale handcuffed in the back seat. Officer Brazier hears a police radio call of Dale's arrest for battering a police car, and pursues Dale and Saul in a high speed chase, but Dale and Saul evade her.

Dale and Saul argue about the mess they have found themselves in, resulting in Dale telling Saul that they aren't friends and never were; the two part ways, angry and upset. Saul visits his grandmother in an assisted living home and finds Budlofsky and Matheson looking for him. They kidnap Saul and take him to Ted's lair, a barn and underground pot grow house which used to be the old Army base. After ending his relationship with Angie, Dale enlists Red to help him rescue Saul from Ted, but Red backs out at the last minute and Dale is captured.

While Dale and Saul are captive, they make up and Dale admits that Saul really is his friend. Just then, a rival Asian drug gang attacks the barn to avenge a member's death at the hands of Ted and Carol. Dale and Saul free themselves and join the conflict. Dale and Ted endure a brawl that ends in Ted's death when one of the Asians sets off a bomb that destroys the barn. Matheson kills Budlofsky for refusing to kill Saul when he had the chance. When Matheson is about to kill Saul, Red bursts through the wall with his car, running over Matheson. While Saul thanks Red, Carol reaches for a gun and shoots Red. The bomb goes off, first exploding Red's car and the burning car falls on top of Carol, killing her. Dale carries an unconscious Saul out of the burning barn, and Red crawls from the wreckage.

Dale, Saul, and Red go to a diner to eat and celebrate their friendship, then Saul's grandmother picks them up and takes them to a hospital.

Cast

- Seth Rogen as Dale Denton
- James Franco as Saul Silver
- Danny McBride as Red
- Kevin Corrigan as Budlofsky
- Craig Robinson as Matheson
- Gary Cole as Ted Jones
- Rosie Perez as Officer Carol Brazier
- Ed Begley, Jr. as Robert
- Nora Dunn as Shannon
- Amber Heard as Angie Anderson
- Joe Lo Truglio as Mr. Edwards
- Arthur Napiontek as Clark
- Adam Crosby as Ack
- Cleo King as Police Liaison Officer
- Bill Hader as Private Miller
- James Remar as General Bratt
- David C. Cook as Chris Gebert
- Mae LaBorde as Mrs. Mendelson
- Jonathan Spencer as Scientist (as Jonathan Walker Spencer)
- Jeffrey Ng as Computer Programmer
- Jack Kehler as Walter
- Steve Bannos as Jared
- Ken Jeong as Ken
- Justin Long as Justin (deleted scenes)

Production

The inspiration for making *Pineapple Express*, according to producer Judd Apatow, was Brad Pitt's character in *True Romance*, a stoner named Floyd. Apatow "thought it would be funny to make a movie in which you follow that character out of his apartment and watch him get chased by bad guys".[1] According to Rogen, the ideal production budget was $40 million, but due to the subject matter "because it's a weed movie", as he described it - Sony Pictures allotted $25 million.[2]

David Gordon Green met with Apatow, Rogen and Goldberg on the set of *Knocked Up*, and later on the set of *Superbad* to discuss the project.[3] Green cited *The Blues Brothers*, *Midnight Run*, *Running Scared*, the Terrence

Malick written *The Gravy Train* and *Stir Crazy* as sources of inspiration and influence on directing the film.[3]

Rogen was originally going to play Saul, but Apatow suggested that Franco should play the role instead. After a table read, Rogen agreed, thus casting himself in the role of Dale Denton.[4]

Seth Rogen spoke with musician Huey Lewis, of Huey Lewis and the News, about writing and performing the film's theme song in November 2007.[5]

There was an exclusive sneak peek of the film attached to the *Superbad* DVD, which was released on December 4, 2007.

Release and reception

The film has received generally positive reviews from critics with a rating of 68% on the review website Rotten Tomatoes. A "red-band" trailer for the film, featuring the song "Paper Planes" by M.I.A.,[6] leaked in February 2008.[7] Sony Pictures had the video removed from YouTube within a few days of its posting.[8] Patrick Goldstein's Summer Movie Posse of the *Los Angeles Times* described its incorporation as "the most impressive use of M.I.A.'s 'Paper Planes' ever".[9] M.I.A. has said that she never authorized the use of the song.[10] *Pineapple Express* had an advance screening at the Just for Laughs Film Festival on July 19, 2008.[11] The film was released on August 6, 2008.[12] Cable network FX pre-bought exclusive rights to air the film after its theatrical run.[13] One particular aspect of the film that has been almost universally praised is the cinematography; Seth Rogen even joked on the commentary that "even people who hate the movie admit that it's shot well".

Box office

Sony released the film on Wednesday August 6, 2008 with $12,085,679 in ticket sales. Over the weekend it opened at number two behind *The Dark Knight* with $23,245,025 for a five day total of $41,318,736. The film went on to gross $87,341,380 domestically with a worldwide total of $100,941,380.[14]

Home media

The film was released on DVD and Blu-ray on January 6, 2009. Both rated and unrated versions of the film are available. It was released on DVD and Blu-ray in Australia on December 31, 2008. Both the Blu-ray and 2-disc DVD versions of the film come with a digital copy of the unrated film. As of November 1, 2009 the DVD has sold 2,510,321 and generated $43,033,863 in sales revenue.[15]

Soundtrack

The original motion picture soundtrack to the film was released on August 5, 2008.[16] Although featured in the trailer for the film,[17] the song "Paper Planes" by M.I.A. is not used in the film or on its soundtrack. Following the trailer's release, "Paper Planes" gained massive airplay, entering the Top 5 on *Billboard* Hot 100. Also featured in the film but absent from the soundtrack album are Grace Jones' Sly and Robbie produced cover of Johnny Cash's "Ring of Fire", the former of which can be found on her 1998 compilation *Private Life: The Compass Point Sessions*.

1. "Pineapple Express" by Huey Lewis and the News (4:27)
2. "Electric Avenue" by Eddy Grant (3:48)
3. "Dr. Greenthumb" by Cypress Hill (3:08)
4. "Lost at Birth" by Public Enemy (3:33)
5. "Poison" by Bell Biv DeVoe (4:20)
6. "Wanted Dread and Alive" by Peter Tosh (4:22)
7. "Don't Look Around" by Mountain (3:44)
8. "Pineapple Chase (aka The Reprise of the Phoenix)" by Graeme Revell (3:03)
9. "Bird's Lament" by Moondog & The London Saxophonic (2:02)

10. "Coconut Girl" by Brother Noland (3:36)
11. "Hi'ilawe" by Arthur Lyman (1:09)
12. "Tha Crossroads" by Bone Thugs-n-Harmony (3:45)
13. "Pineapple Fight (aka The Nemesis Proclaimed)" by Graeme Revell (3:08)
14. "I Didn't Mean to Hurt You" by Spiritualized (5:12)
15. "Woke Up Laughing" by Robert Palmer (3:35)

Possible sequel

Judd Apatow stated that there's a strong possibility for a sequel.[18] [19]

On January 6th 2011 while on The Howard Stern Show a caller asked if a sequel was in the works and Rogen replied "We talk about doing a sequel to that movie, They desperately want us to make it because of how cheap it was to make and how much money it ultimately made, we might do it"

References

[1] Svetkey, Benjamin (April 18, 2008). "'Pineapple Express': High hopes for James Franco" (http://www.ew.com/ew/article/0,,20192513,00. html). *Entertainment Weekly*. Time Inc. . Retrieved July 15, 2008.

[2] Halperin, Shirley (April 11, 2008). "Marijuana Movies: Riding High In Hollywood?" (http://www.ew.com/ew/article/0,,20190469_2,00. html). *Entertainment Weekly*. Time Inc. . Retrieved July 16, 2008.

[3] Douglas, Edward (August 4, 2008). "Exclusive: Pineapple Express' David Gordon Green" (http://www.comingsoon.net/news/movienews. php?id=47398). comingsoon.net. . Retrieved August 4, 2008.

[4] Goldman, Eric (March 18, 2008). "Judd Apatow: From Freaks and Geeks to Sarah Marshall and Beyond" (http://tv.ign.com/articles/860/ 860498p3.html). IGN. . Retrieved August 4, 2008.

[5] Halperin, Shirley (November 26, 2007). "Seth Rogen inviting Huey Lewis aboard 'Pineapple Express'?" (http://hollywoodinsider.ew.com/ 2007/11/huey-lewis-to-r.html). *Entertainment Weekly*. Time Inc. . Retrieved July 15, 2008.

[6] Foerster, Jonathan (June 12, 2008). "We've got the soundtrack to your summer" (http://www.naplesnews.com/news/2008/jun/12/ summer-mix-08-weve-got-soundtrack-your-summer/). *Naples Daily News*. . Retrieved July 15, 2008.

[7] Sperling, Nicole (February 13, 2008). "And the red-band played on... or not" (http://hollywoodinsider.ew.com/2008/02/and-the-red-ban. html). *Entertainment Weekly*. Time Inc. . Retrieved July 15, 2008.

[8] Sperling, Nicole (February 14, 2008). "Smoke up, Seth Rogen: 'Pineapple Express' red-band trailer is finally online" (http:// hollywoodinsider.ew.com/2008/02/exhale-the-pine.html). *Entertainment Weekly*. Time Inc. . Retrieved July 15, 2008.

[9] Goldstein, Patrick (April 29, 2008). "Summer Movie Posse gives its thumbs up....and down" (http://articles.latimes.com/2008/apr/29/ entertainment/et-goldstein29). *Los Angeles Times*. Tribune Company. . Retrieved July 22, 2008.

[10] "". "M.I.A. Interview About Pregnancy" (http://www.youtube.com/watch?v=kMxnvI6pdPU). YouTube. . Retrieved 2010-09-04.

[11] Kelly, Brendan; Frankel, Daniel (June 17, 2008). "'Pineapple' opens comedy festival" (http://www.variety.com/article/VR1117987609. html). *Variety*. Reed Business Information. . Retrieved July 15, 2008.

[12] Mohr, Ian (June 5, 2007). "Apatow, Rogen set 'Pineapple' date" (http://www.variety.com/article/VR1117966292.html). *Variety*. Reed Business Information. . Retrieved July 15, 2008.

[13] Dempsey, John (June 24, 2008). "FX to 'Mess With the Zohan'" (http://www.variety.com/article/VR1117988026.html). *Variety*. Reed Business Information. . Retrieved September 3, 2008.

[14] "The Pineapple Express - Box Office Data, Movie News, Cast Information" (http://www.the-numbers.com/movies/2008/PNAPL.php). *The-Numbers.com*. . Retrieved 2010-09-04.

[15] "Top Selling DVDs of 2009" (http://www.the-numbers.com/dvd/charts/annual/2009.php). *The-Numbers.com*. . Retrieved 2010-09-04.

[16] "Pineapple Express Original Soundtrack" (http://www.allmusic.com/album/r1403051). Allmusic. . Retrieved October 9, 2009.

[17] Williams, Leslie (May 14, 2008). "Leslie Williams: Selecting summer music, films" (http://web.archive.org/web/20080516233720/ http://media.www.theorion.com/media/storage/paper889/news/2008/05/14/Entertainment/Leslie.Williams.Selecting.Summer. Music.Films-3370349.shtml). The Orion Online. Archived from the original (http://media.www.theorion.com/media/storage/paper889/ news/2008/05/14/Entertainment/Leslie.Williams.Selecting.Summer.Music.Films-3370349.shtml) on May 16, 2008. . Retrieved July 22, 2008.

[18] "Judd Apatow talks possible PINEAPPLE EXPRESS sequel" (http://gordonandthewhale.com/ judd-apatow-talks-possible-pineapple-express-sequel) *GordonandtheWhale.com*. 2009-11-23. . Retrieved 2010-09-04.

[19] "Judd Apatow Says 'Pineapple Express 2' Likely, 'Superbad 2' Not So Much » MTV Movies Blog" (http://moviesblog.mtv.com/2009/ 11/20/judd-apatow-says-pineapple-express-2-likely-superbad-2-not-so-much). *MoviesBlog.MTV.com*. 2009-11-20. . Retrieved 2010-09-04.

External links

- Official website (http://http://www.sonypictures.com/homevideo/pineappleexpress)
- *Pineapple Express* (http://www.imdb.com/title/tt0910936/) at the Internet Movie Database
- *Pineapple Express* (http://www.allmovie.com/work/381510) at Allmovie
- *Pineapple Express* (http://www.rottentomatoes.com/m/pineapple_express/) at Rotten Tomatoes
- *Pineapple Express* (http://www.metacritic.com/film/titles/pineappleexpress) at Metacritic
- *Pineapple Express* (http://www.boxofficemojo.com/movies/?id=pineappleexpress.htm) at Box Office Mojo

Zack and Miri Make a Porno

<table>
<tr><td colspan="2" align="center">*Zack and Miri Make a Porno*</td></tr>
<tr><td colspan="2" align="center">
US theatrical release poster</td></tr>
<tr><td>Directed by</td><td>Kevin Smith</td></tr>
<tr><td>Produced by</td><td>Scott Mosier</td></tr>
<tr><td>Written by</td><td>Kevin Smith</td></tr>
<tr><td>Starring</td><td>• Seth Rogen
• Elizabeth Banks</td></tr>
<tr><td>Music by</td><td>James L. Venable</td></tr>
<tr><td>Cinematography</td><td>Dave Klein</td></tr>
<tr><td>Editing by</td><td>Kevin Smith</td></tr>
<tr><td>Studio</td><td>View Askew Productions</td></tr>
<tr><td>Distributed by</td><td>The Weinstein Company</td></tr>
<tr><td>Release date(s)</td><td>October 31, 2008</td></tr>
<tr><td>Running time</td><td>101 minutes</td></tr>
<tr><td>Country</td><td>United States</td></tr>
<tr><td>Language</td><td>English</td></tr>
<tr><td>Budget</td><td>$24 million[1]</td></tr>
<tr><td>Gross revenue</td><td>$42,105,111[1]</td></tr>
</table>

Zack and Miri Make a Porno is a 2008 romantic comedy film written and directed by Kevin Smith, distributed by The Weinstein Company, and starring Seth Rogen and Elizabeth Banks. It is Smith's second film (after *Jersey Girl*) not to be set within the View Askewniverse and the first not set in New Jersey. It was released on October 31, 2008.

Plot

Zack Brown (Seth Rogen) and Miriam "Miri" Linky (Elizabeth Banks) are roommates in Monroeville, Pennsylvania (a Pittsburgh suburb). They have been friends since the first grade. Despite Miri working at the local shopping mall and Zack working at a coffee shop, they have not paid their utility bills in months, with Zack devoting much of his free time to a fanatic following of the Pittsburgh Steelers and his status in the community amateur hockey team, the Monroeville Zombies. After work, their water gets turned off before they go to their high school reunion.

At the reunion, Miri attempts to seduce her attractive former classmate Bobby Long (Brandon Routh), while Zack strikes up a conversation with Brandon St. Randy (Justin Long), who reveals that he is a gay porn star, and Bobby's boyfriend. After returning home from the reunion, the apartment's electricity is turned off. Inspired by a successful viral video that was filmed by a pair of teenage boys as Miri changed in Zack's place of work for the reunion (revealing that she wore unattractive underwear, "granny panties"), and emboldened by the cultural mainstreaming of pornographic entertainment, Zack convinces Miri that they should film a pornographic movie to earn money.

Gathering a group of acquaintances and hired help as the cast and crew, they decide to film a pornographic *Star Wars* parody, entitled *Star Whores*. Delaney (Craig Robinson), the film's producer and Zack's coworker, rents film equipment and a building to use as a studio. When they return to the studio after the first night of filming, the building is being demolished, with all the equipment and costumes inside. Later at the coffee shop where Zack works, he realizes that his boss threatened to install a hidden camera, which Zack finds, and decides to use it to replace their lost film equipment. Zack retools his film to take place in the coffee shop, and the group shoots the film after hours.

Despite their insistence to one another that they would not let sex with each other affect their friendship, Zack and Miri soon develop romantic feelings for each other and their sex scene is plainly lovemaking though they do not admit it. Later that evening, Zack and Miri are at home when suddenly their apartment's electricity and water service return. The rest of the actors and crew appear at the apartment to reveal that they pooled their resources to pay one month of their bills and have come over to throw them a party. At the party, one of the other actresses, Stacey (Katie Morgan), asks Miri if it is okay for her to ask Zack to have sex as a way to prepare for her scene with him the next day. Although Miri has realized that she has developed feelings for Zack, she tells Stacey it is okay to ask him. When Stacey relates this to Zack, the two retreat to Zack's bedroom, much to Miri's dismay.

The next evening, Zack is preparing to film a scene between Stacey and another actor, Lester (Jason Mewes), that was supposed to have been with Lester and Miri. Zack is upset when Miri arrives and insists on shooting the scene as originally planned. In the back, Zack asks if she is doing this as a form of retaliation, pointing out that Stacey told him that Miri didn't mind her sleeping with Zack. Miri says that she didn't mind that Stacey merely made the *offer* to sleep with him. Perceiving this to have been some type of test, Zack admits that during their sex scene there was an emotional connection between them, and that he loves Miri. When Miri does not reciprocate, Zack storms out of the coffee shop, quitting the film and his job. When Miri returns home later, she finds Zack has moved out of the apartment.

Three months later, Delaney goes to see Zack, who has moved on to an exterior concessions job at Mellon Arena during Pittsburgh Penguins games. Delaney convinces him to come to Delaney's home to see the unfinished movie and help complete it. Zack agrees, and as Delaney and Deacon (Jeff Anderson) the cameraman explain, Zack learns that Miri never filmed her sex scene with Lester. Zack goes to Miri's apartment and reveals to her that he never slept with Stacey; instead, they talked about Miri all night. He pours his heart out to Miri, proclaiming his love for her, which she reciprocates.

In the epilogue, the audience learns that Zack and Miri are married, and with the help of Delaney and his worker's compensation settlement, they start their own video production company, *Zack and Miri Make Your Porno*, which makes amateur videos for couples.

Cast

- Seth Rogen as Zack Brown
- Elizabeth Banks as Miriam "Miri" Linky
- Craig Robinson as Delaney
- Jason Mewes as Lester
- Traci Lords as Bubbles
- Jeff Anderson as Deacon
- Katie Morgan as Stacey
- Ricky Mabe as Barry
- Justin Long as Brandon St. Randy
- Brandon Routh as Bobby Long
- Tyler Labine as Drunk Customer
- Tisha Campbell-Martin as Delaney's wife
- Tom Savini as Jenkins
- Jennifer Schwalbach as Betsy
- Gerry Bednob as Mr. Surya
- Kenny Hotz as Zack II
- Nicholas Lombardi as Teen 1
- Chris Milan as Teen 2

Production

According to *Entertainment Weekly*, The Weinstein Company greenlit the project based solely on the title.[2] Kevin Smith originally wrote the film to be set in Minnesota, where he had previously shot *Mallrats*, and where he had stated a desire to shoot again. However, for budgetary reasons, Smith opted to shoot in Pittsburgh, and re-wrote the script to take place in the Monroeville suburb.[3]

The female lead role was written for Rosario Dawson, but Dawson was unable to accept the part, as she had just signed on to film *Eagle Eye*, whose shooting schedule would have conflicted with Smith's.[4] Smith wrote the role of Zack, however, with Seth Rogen in mind, based on his performance in *The 40-Year-Old Virgin*.[5] Shooting concluded on March 12, 2008.[6]

There are numerous cultural references to Pittsburgh and the film's setting in the neighborhood of Monroeville and Pittsburgh throughout the film, including a drunken Steelers fan, a Penguins Stanley Cup flag, and the cast drinking Iron City Beer throughout the film.[7] One scene in the film was shot at the Monroeville Mall, while another scene is featured outside Mellon Arena during a hockey game. One scene contains a cameo appearance by Tom Savini. The mall was the setting of *Dawn of the Dead*, which was Savini's first film as an effects artist. About the scene Smith said, "We got to shoot at the Monroeville Mall, and for a movie buff, that's a very cool thing. We had Tom Savini [in cameo], we shot at the Monroeville Mall, it's as close to a zombie movie as I'll ever get."[7] In the film, Zack plays hockey, and his team's name is the Monroeville Zombies, which is another reference to the George A. Romero film.[8] Even one of the main cast members has Pittsburgh-area roots: porn star icon Traci Lords (who played Bubbles in the film) is a native of Steubenville, Ohio located about a half hour drive west of Pittsburgh.

Music

A song by the band Live, entitled "Hold Me Up", which Smith has said he has been trying to use for over 13 years, appears in an "emotional scene" with Zack and Miri. Smith made a statement about featuring the song in the film:

> It's an old song that I first heard in '95, when we were putting together the *Mallrats* soundtrack. It was actually in the film for the first test screening, but Live decided they wanted to hold onto it as a potential single off their next album (which would follow *Throwing Copper*). When I was editing *Jay and Silent Bob Strike Back*, the song had still never surfaced or been released, so I put in a request for it again. Again, I was denied. Third time, apparently, was the charm. Needed a song for that sequence in *Zack and Miri* and remembered the Live track. This time, the band signed off on us using the track. Took 13 years, but was worth the wait.[9]

An original song by mc chris called "Miri and Zack" was made especially for the film. An older song by mc chris, "Fett's Vette", was also used in the film, as well as "Sex and Candy" by Marcy Playground and Jermaine Stewart's 1986 hit "We Don't Have to Take Our Clothes Off."[10]

Distribution

While MGM was originally set to distribute the film, The Weinstein Company solely distributed the film after a deal between the two companies fell through.[11] With the announcement came the removal of the MGM logo from the advertising for the film, which is the first Weinstein film to be released after the deal was abruptly ended before the scheduled January 2009 date.[12]

Rating

The Motion Picture Association of America initially gave the film an NC-17 rating for "some graphic sexuality".[13] Smith submitted two additional cuts of the film with certain footage removed and was told the movie was getting much closer to an "R" rating, but that he should remove a small 14-frame shot first. Smith felt that the scene should stay in so he appealed the rating and the film was viewed by the MPAA again.[14] In an interview with MTV.com, Seth Rogen commented "It's a really filthy movie. I hear they are having some problems getting an R rating from an NC-17 rating, which is never good." He continued, complaining that "They fight against sex stuff. Isn't that weird? It's really crazy to me that *Hostel* is fine, with people gouging their eyes out and shit like that... But you can't show two people having sex — that's too much".[15] On August 5, the rating was successfully appealed to an R with no further cuts.[16] It attained the rating for "strong crude sexual content including dialogue, graphic nudity and pervasive language".[17] [18]

Promotion

On May 30, 2008, the first teaser trailer for the film was released on Smith's website, silentbobspeaks.com.[20] The teaser depicts Rogen and Banks' characters as they hold auditions. In his online diary, Kevin Smith insisted it was strictly a teaser, mentioning, "There ain't a frame of footage in this puppy that's in the actual flick, so feel free to watch it without fear of 'spoilers'. This is just a little something to give you a bit of a feel for the flick."[20] On July 21, however, the video was removed from the website following an order by the MPAA because it was designated a "teaser trailer" without passing through MPAA certification.[21] On September 2, 2008, a red band trailer of the film was released at IGN.[22]

The Canadian release poster. This poster has been banned for use in U.S. theaters by the MPAA.[19]

A poster for the film (pictured right) released in September 2008, which suggests the title characters are performing oral sex on each other, was banned for use in US theaters by the MPAA.[19] The poster used in the US lampoons the film's explicit subject matter by featuring stick figures, with the explanation in the poster's text this is the only image that can be shown.

Despite this restriction, many media outlets refused to run the poster, or any ad that includes the word "porno" in the title, including a number of newspapers, TV stations, cable channels, and city governments, some of which responded to complaints about the ads at baseball stadiums and city bus stops. Many theaters displayed the film's title on their marquee as merely *Zack and Miri*. Weinstein Company marketing head Gary Faber stated that the ad was accepted in most of the outlets that were offered it, but that the studio would consider variations of the title for outlets that rejected it, including one version of the poster without the title that bears the slogan, "Seth Rogen and Elizabeth Banks made a movie so outrageous that we can't even tell you the title."[23]

On November 10, 2008 The Weinstein Company announced that it would be re-launching the U.S. ad campaign for the film, with the main focus being a new poster that featured Rogen and Banks in a meadow with animals rendered in the style of children's animated cartoons. However, the new poster also took a jab at the controversy surrounding the image of the second poster—namely the controversy surrounding the use of the word "porno" in an image so seemingly kid-friendly—by including the statement "A poster for everyone who finds our movie title hard to swallow".[24]

DVD

Although some copies of the February 2009 "2-Disc Edition" DVD were originally released under its full intended title in the United States, the controversy continued as some DVDs continued to display the censored title used to originally promote the film (i.e. *Zack and Miri*). The cover uses neither of the previous poster images, but instead a photo montage of the principal actors in the film on a white background. The re-release includes a series of webisodes called *Money Shots*, as well as other exclusive content.[25] [26]

Reception

Box office

The film opened #2 behind *High School Musical 3: Senior Year* with $10,682,000 from 2,735 theaters with an average of $3,906.[27] Both Smith and producer Scott Mosier were disappointed by the film's poor box office performance;[28] according to Smith:

> "That was supposed to be the one that punched us through to the next level. Everyone thought it would do $60 to $70 million, and it wound up doing Kevin Smith business. I was like, 'I'm done.' If I were to write at that point in my life, it would about the poor fat kid whose movie didn't make enough money."[29]

The consistently bankable Rogen[30] also experienced his "worst box-office opening ever".[31] As of January 8, 2009, the film has grossed $31 million in North America and $5 million overseas. As of September 2009, the film had grossed almost $42 million worldwide according to Box Office Mojo.[32]

Critical

Based on 105 reviews, Rotten Tomatoes reported that the film has a "fresh" rating of 65 percent[33] and a mixed rating of 50% from "top" critics based on 34 reviews.[34] Based on 31 reviews, Metacritic gave a score of 56, which equates to a "Mixed or average reviews" rating.[35] Michael Phillips of *Chicago Tribune* said the film, "pushes its R rating pretty hard, though as with most Smith characters this side of Silent Bob, there's a lot more raunch in the talk — the sheer, voluminous, often hilarious verbosity — than in the action."[36] Roger Ebert of the *Chicago Sun-Times* gave the movie 3 stars out of a possible 4 stars and stated that, "Somehow Kevin Smith's very excesses defuse the material. He's like the guy at a party who tells dirty jokes so fast, Dangerfield-style, that you laugh more at the performance than the material."[37]

References

[1] *"Zack and Miri Make a Porno* (2008)" (http://boxofficemojo.com/movies/?id=zackandmirimakeaporno.htm). Box Office Mojo. . Retrieved 2009-09-25.

[2] Mark Rahner. "Kevin Smith, director of "Zack and Miri Make a Porno""; *[[Seattle Times* (http://seattletimes.nwsource.com/html/movies/ 2008318894_kevinsmithqampa28.html)] *October 28, 2008]*

[3] "Brian C. Gibson. "More Details for Kevin Smith's "Zach and Miri" filmschoolrejects.com February 8, 2008" (http://www. filmschoolrejects.com/news/more-details-for-kevin-smiths-zach-miri.php). Filmschoolrejects.com. 2008-02-08. . Retrieved 2010-03-22.

[4] "Peter Sciretta. "Rosario Dawson ditches Kevin Smith's Zack and Miri Make a Porno for Eagle Eye" slashfilm.com August 7, 2007" (http:// www.slashfilm.com/2007/08/07/rosario-dawson-ditches-kevin-smiths-zack-and-miri-make-a-porno-for-eagle-eye/). Slashfilm.com. 2007-08-07. . Retrieved 2010-03-22.

[5] ""The Man Who Would Be Zack" silentbobspeaks.com November 19, 2007" (http://silentbobspeaks.com/?p=365). Silentbobspeaks.com. 2007-11-19. . Retrieved 2010-03-22.

[6] ""Kevin Breaks The "Zack & Miri" Silence...Sorta!"" (http://www.newsaskew.com/2008/03/14/kevin-breaks-the-zack-miri-silencesorta). *NewsAskew.com.* 2008-03-14. .

[7] Vancheri, Barbara (2008-09-09). "Monroeville-filmed 'Zack and Miri' gets warm reception in Toronto" (http://www.post-gazette.com/pg/ 08253/910479-42.stm). *Pittsburgh Post-Gazette* (Toronto). . Retrieved 2008-10-16.

[8] Sciretta, Peter (2008-05-30). "Cool Stuff: Monroeville Zombie Hockey Jerseys" (http://www.slashfilm.com/2008/05/30/ cool-stuff-monroeville-zombie-hockey-jerseys/). Slashfilm. . Retrieved 2008-10-16.

[9] "W. Andrew Powell. "TIFF 08: Play that funky music" The Gate. September 11, 2008" (http://www.thegate.ca/front-page/02324/ tiff-08-play-that-funky-music/). Thegate.ca. 2008-09-11. . Retrieved 2010-03-22.

[10] IMDB - Zack and Miri make a Porno - Soundtrack (http://www.imdb.com/title/tt1007028/soundtrack)

[11] Pamela McClintock (September 25, 2008). Weinstein Co., MGM cut short deal (http://www.variety.com/article/VR1117992944. html?categoryid=13&cs=1) Variety. Retrieved October 16, 2008.

[12] Hilary Lewis (September 25, 2008). MGM Showing First Signs Of Weinstein Breakup (http://www.businesssheet.com/2008/9/ mgm-showing-first-signs-of-weinstein-breakup) The Business Sheet. Retrieved October 16, 2008.

[13] "Josh Tyler. "Zack And Miri Make A Porno Rated NC-17" cinemablend.com August 21, 2008" (http://www.cinemablend.com/new/ Zack-And-Miri-Make-A-Porno-Rated-NC-17-9587.html). Cinemablend.com. 2008-07-21. . Retrieved 2010-03-22.

[14] SModcast 58:Kodachrome, (released 2008-07-25) at 11 minutes, 2 seconds into the podcast

[15] Carroll, Larry; "Seth Rogen Says Kevin Smith's 'Porno' Is Having Trouble Getting An R Rating Instead Of NC-17" (http://www.mtv.com/movies/news/articles/1589686/story.jhtml) June 19, 2008.

[16] "Smith Wins Appeal for Porno's R Rating"; comingsoon.net; [[Associated Press (http://www.comingsoon.net/news/movienews.php?id=47680)]; August 5, 2008]

[17] http://www.filmratings.com

[18] ""Zack and Miri Make a Porno" at" (http://www.ropeofsilicon.com/movie/zack_and_miri_make_a_porno). Ropeofsilicon.com. . Retrieved 2010-03-22.

[19] Marc Bernardin. "Kevin Smith's Banned-in-the-US 'Porno' Poster: Exclusive first look!" (http://popwatch.ew.com/popwatch/2008/09/kevin-smith-por.html). EW.com. September 3, 2008.

[20] "Kevin Smith. "Wanna get teased?" silentbobspeaks.com May 29, 2008" (http://silentbobspeaks.com/?m=200805). Silentbobspeaks.com. 2008-05-29. . Retrieved 2010-03-22.

[21] Zack and Miri's Porno Teaser Gets Canned by the MPAA (http://www.filmschoolrejects.com/news/zack-and-miri-make-a-porno-teaser-gets-canned-by-the-mpaa.php) filmschoolrejects.com. Retrieved on March 2, 2009

[22] "Zack and Miri Make a Porno Movie Trailer - Red Band Trailer" (http://movies.ign.com/dor/objects/964901/zack-and-miri-make-a-porno/videos/zach_miri_redtrlr_082908.html). Movies.ign.com. . Retrieved 2010-03-22.

[23] David Germain. "'Porno' proves a five-letter word for movie's ads" [[Associated Press (http://www.newsvine.com/_news/2008/10/15/2001131-porno-proves-a-five-letter-word-for-movies-ads)]; October 15, 2008]

[24] "Neil Miller. "Only Kevin Smith Can Make a Porno This Cute" filmschoolrejects.com November 10, 2008" (http://www.filmschoolrejects.com/news/only-kevin-smith-can-make-a-porno-this-cute.php). Filmschoolrejects.com. 2008-11-10. . Retrieved 2010-03-22.

[25] *Zack and Miri: 2-Disc Edition*. 2008 [2009 re-rel.]. UPC 7-96019-81756-1.. This version features the censored title.

[26] "Zack and Miri Make a Porno (2-Disc Edition) (2008)" (http://www.amazon.com/dp/B001MEJYAU). *Amazon.com*. 2009. . Retrieved January 10, 2010. This version features the original title.

[27] "Weekend Box Office Results from 10/31 to 11/02" (http://www.boxofficemojo.com/weekend/chart/?view=&yr=2008&wknd=44&p=.htm). Box Office Mojo. . Retrieved 2008-11-02.

[28] "SModcast 68: The Talking Cure, Pt. 1" (http://www.podtrac.com/pts/redirect.mp3/www.smodcast.net/SModcast-68.mp3). Quick Stop Entertainment. . Retrieved 2008-12-16.

[29] Stephen Lovekin/Getty Images. "Kevin Smith, Bruce Willis, Tracy Morgan and the cast discuss 'Cop Out' | - New Jersey Entertainment | Music, Movies, TV, Events & More" (http://www.nj.com/entertainment/index.ssf/2010/02/kevin_smith_bruce_willis_tracy.html). NJ.com. . Retrieved 2010-03-22.

[30] "Seth Rogen at TSE Sports & Entertainment" (http://athletes-celebrities.tseworld.com/entertainment/actors/seth-rogen.php). Athletes-celebrities.tseworld.com. 1982-04-15. . Retrieved 2010-03-22.

[31] "John Carins. "Zack and Miri Make No Money, HSM 3 Wins Again" Film School Rejects; November 2, 2008" (http://www.filmschoolrejects.com/news/box-office-zack-and-miri-make-no-money-hsm-3-wins-again.php). Filmschoolrejects.com. 2008-11-02. . Retrieved 2010-03-22.

[32] "Zack and Miri Make a Porno (2008)" (http://www.boxofficemojo.com/movies/?id=zackandmirimakeaporno.htm). Box Office Mojo. . Retrieved May 18, 2009.

[33] "*Zack and Miri Make a Porno* (2008)" (http://web.archive.org/web/20080609085312/http://www.rottentomatoes.com/m/10008989-10008989-zack_and_miri_make_a_porno). Rotten Tomatoes. Archived from the original (http://www.rottentomatoes.com/m/10008989-10008989-zack_and_miri_make_a_porno) on 2008-06-09. . Retrieved 2008-10-31.

[34] "*Zack and Miri Make a Porno* (2008)" (http://www.rottentomatoes.com/m/1190296-zack_and_miri_make_a_porno/?critic=creamcrop). Rotten Tomatoes. . Retrieved 2010-03-12.

[35] "Zack and Miri Make a Porno (2008):Reviews" (http://www.metacritic.com/film/titles/zackandmiri?part=rss). Metacritic. . Retrieved 2008-10-31.

[36] Phillips, Michael (2008-10-31). "Zach and Miri Make a Porno - Los Angeles Times" (http://www.latimes.com/la-et-porno31-2008oct31,0,3509770.story). . Retrieved 2008-10-31.

[37] http://rogerebert.suntimes.com/apps/pbcs.dll/article?AID=/20081029/REVIEWS/810299995/1023

External links

- Official website (http://http://www.zackandmiri.com/)
- *Zack and Miri Make a Porno* (http://www.imdb.com/title/tt1007028/) at the Internet Movie Database
- *Zack and Miri Make a Porno* (http://www.allmovie.com/work/423263) at Allmovie
- *Zack and Miri Make a Porno* (http://www.boxofficemojo.com/movies/?id=zackandmirimakeaporno.htm) at Box Office Mojo
- *Zack and Miri Make a Porno* (http://www.rottentomatoes.com/m/1190296-zack_and_miri_make_a_porno/) at Rotten Tomatoes

Fanboys (2009 film)

Fanboys	
 Theatrical poster	
Directed by	Kyle Newman
Produced by	Dana Brunetti Kevin Spacey Matthew Pernicaro Evan Astrowsky Kevin Mann
Screenplay by	Ernest Cline Adam F. Goldberg
Story by	Ernest Cline Dan Pulick
Starring	Jay Baruchel Dan Fogler Sam Huntington Chris Marquette Kristen Bell
Music by	Mark Mothersbaugh
Cinematography	Lukas Ettlin
Studio	Trigger Street Productions Coalition Film Picture Machine The Weinstein Company
Distributed by	The Weinstein Company Third Rail Releasing
Release date(s)	February 6, 2009 (United States)
Running time	90 minutes
Country	United States
Language	English
Budget	$8 million

Gross revenue	$960,828[1]

Fanboys is a 2009 comedy film directed by Kyle Newman and starring Sam Huntington, Chris Marquette, Dan Fogler, Jay Baruchel and Kristen Bell. It was released in the United States on February 6, 2009, and in Canada on April 3, 2009.[2]

Plot

On Halloween night, 1998, Eric Bottler (Sam Huntington) reunites with his old high school buddies Linus (Chris Marquette), Hutch (Dan Fogler), Windows (Jay Baruchel) and Zoe (Kristen Bell) at a costume party. There is tension between Bottler and his old friends, due to Bottler being the only one that matured since high school. Bottler, now a successful car salesman, finds that his friends have not changed a bit since high school; the number one thing they still have in common is their love of Star Wars. The gang expresses their anticipation for the latest installment to the franchise, *Star Wars Episode I: The Phantom Menace*. Linus proposes an idea that Bottler and he had been plotting since they were children: to infiltrate Skywalker Ranch and steal a rough cut of the film.

The next day, Hutch and Windows meet Bottler at work and inform him that Linus has cancer. The doctors estimate that he only has roughly four months to live; *Episode I* comes out in six. To make peace with his former best friend, Bottler decides to go through with their plan and infiltrate Skywalker Ranch. They begin their trip to Texas, where they have to meet Rogue Leader, a girl Windows is having an online relationship with, for information on getting into the Ranch. While on the road, Hutch decides to take a detour to Riverside, Iowa (the future birthplace of Captain James T. Kirk) in an attempt to start a fight with some Trekkies. Hutch gets his wish after attacking a Trekkie by the name of Admiral Seasholtz (Seth Rogen) in retaliation to Seasholtz calling Han Solo a bitch, to which Hutch responds by running down their statue of Captain Kirk and Khan.

The boys' van breaks down and they stumble upon a biker bar. Once inside they ask for help and a glass of water that costs $100. Hutch, refusing to pay, tries to pass himself off as a tough guy who just got out of prison, only to discover that they are in a gay bar. In order to pay for the drink they are forced to become the "midnight entertainment" and strip to Menudo; which goes terribly wrong. "The Chief" (Danny Trejo) fixes their van after they pass out from eating guacamole laced with peyote and gives a bag of it to Linus as a parting gift.

After arriving in Texas, Windows meets Rogue Leader, who turns out to be a 10 year old girl (Allie Grant). The group encounters Harry Knowles (Ethan Suplee), who begins to beat up Windows, telling him to never talk to his niece, Rogue Leader, again. After explaining their situation Harry quizzes them to prove they are true fanboys, then gives them information on one of his contacts that knows how to successfully enter Skywalker Ranch. They are told to meet Harry's contact in Las Vegas, but before they get there they are arrested for fleeing a police vehicle and possession of peyote. Zoe arrives to bail them out of jail, and accompanies them on their journey. Once in Vegas, Hutch and Windows make an attempt to have sex with some girls while Bottler and Linus go to meet Harry's contact. They are shocked to find that his contact is none other than William Shatner. Shatner gives them the information they need and leaves. Upon his departure, Seasholtz and his Trekkie friends, who were attending a *Star Trek* convention in Vegas, attack them. Meanwhile, Hutch and Windows discover that the girls they were with are escort girls and their angry pimp (Seth Rogen) wants them to pay up.

The group escapes their adversaries but Linus was injured in the process. When taken to the hospital, the doctor (Carrie Fisher) tells them that Linus must return home for the sake of his health. When the group feels the situation has become hopeless, Eric refuses to just give up on their plan and manages to inspire the gang to continue, citing that Star Wars means very much to Linus. The group celebratingly leaves the hospital (but not without Linus kissing the doctor out of spite, much to everyone's shock) and eventually make it to Skywalker Ranch. Shortly after breaking in to the Ranch and marveling at the collection of all the original props and costumes used in the films, they are discovered by security guards and are caught after a brief chase. The Head of Security (Danny R. McBride) tells them of their impending doom when he receives a phone call from George Lucas himself. Lucas tells him that he will drop all charges if they can prove to him that they are "fanboys". After a short quiz, the Head of Security confirms that they are fanboys and Lucas drops all charges. Being aware of Linus's illness, Lucas allows him to watch the film alone. After the film ends, Bottler joins his friends around a campfire and mends his friendship with Linus.

Six months later, Bottler, Windows and Zoe emerge from their tent they used to camp out in while waiting in line for the first showing of *Episode I*. It is revealed that Bottler followed his and Linus's dream by becoming a comic book artist, Hutch has finally started his own detailing business, and Windows and Zoe are now in a relationship. Hutch arrives at the theater with beers he smuggled in, which they use to toast to Linus's memory as *Episode I* begins.

Cast

- Sam Huntington as Eric Bottler
- Chris Marquette as Linus
- Dan Fogler as Harold "Hutch" Hutchinson
- Jay Baruchel as Windows
- Kristen Bell as Zoe
- David Denman as Chaz
- Christopher McDonald as Big Chuck

There are numerous cameos related to *Star Wars* and other science-fiction/cult-hit films including Carrie Fisher, Billy Dee Williams, Seth Rogen (playing three different roles), Jason Mewes, Kevin Smith, Jaime King, Danny R. McBride, Ray Park, Craig Robinson, Ethan Suplee, Lou Taylor Pucci, Will Forte, Danny Trejo and William Shatner. In Park's role, he acts as a Skywalker Ranch security guard who says, "Time for you to get *mauled*, boy," as he pulls out two nightsticks (in response to Windows threatening him with a toy lightsaber).

Development

After George Lucas was given an advanced screening of the rough cut of the film, he enjoyed it and gave it his "stamp of approval" and even offered the original *Star Wars* sound effects for use in the film. Filmmaker and *Star Wars* fan Kevin Smith also viewed an early version of the film and asked for (and was given) a cameo in the film.[3]

The film was originally to be released on August 17, 2007. The film was pushed back once more to January 2008 because director Kyle Newman was given more funding to shoot additional scenes that the original budget did not include. Getting the cast back together would only be possible in September 2007, thus the film's release date had to be moved to 2008.[4]

The film was again pushed back because the reshoots could not take place before November/December 2007. These reshoots were directed by Steven Brill and not by Newman. On January 14, The CineManiac reported that the film was being re-edited to remove the cancer plot from and replace much of it with raunchy, vulgar humor.[5] Ain't It Cool News picked up the story and confirmed that the two different versions of the film (with and without the cancer subplot) were screened to different test audiences in Burbank, California, in January 2008 to see which one would rate higher.[6] As for a new release date, Newman stated in a Movie Geeks United! interview that the film would hopefully come out in April 2008.[7] Upon hearing about the changes being made to the film, an internet campaign was begun to protest the plot changes and demand that the original version with the cancer storyline be released in theaters.[8] [9]

Steven Brill retaliated in a derogatory manner, calling fans "losers"[10] in online correspondence which ended up in the public domain. In one exchange, Brill called a fan "dumb" and threatened to "hunt him down" in a profanity-laden emailed response[10] to a letter of complaint. In an interview[11] Newman chastised Brill's behavior saying:

> If you're going to go in and recut someone's film even though you're not even a fan of the subject matter, just because you want a paycheck, you're not passionate about it, then do that. But don't go opening your mouth and alienating the core audience of that movie. I just thought that was the most low class thing that you could do, especially considering there are so many people that worked years and years and years on this.[11]

A rough cut of the full film (that included the cancer storyline) was shown in public for the first time at *Star Wars Celebration Europe* on July 14, 2007.[12] [13]

On July 9, 2008, Newman confirmed in a TheForce.net interview that the cancer plot would be included in the final cut of the film.[14]

> The motivation was stripped [out] of the movie so it was more like, 'Hey, we're drunk. You wanna go break into Skywalker ranch?' It ultimately didn't work and that's why it, I think, came back to us, the original team to at least restore it as much as we could in the time given."[11]

Newman was given just 36 hours to reassemble his film, and edit back in the key motivational cancer plot line.

The final cut of the film was screened on July 24, 2008, in San Diego at Comic-Con.[15] It was announced there that *Fanboys* would be released to theaters on September 19, 2008,[16] but soon after, the official Weinstein Company website announced that this had changed to November 26, 2008.[17] The final release date was finally pushed to February 6, 2009.[17]

Release

Fanboys was released on February 6, 2009, in eight US markets.[18] The film expanded into 10 more cities on February 20, 2009, including a special screening in Columbus, Ohio that day, followed by a Q&A session after the film with Kyle Newman, Ernie Cline, Matt Perniciaro and Kevin Mann.[19] According to Cline's pre-show speech, he wanted to hold a special screening with fans in his home state, since he grew up in nearby Ashland, Ohio, and the story was set in a fictional town similar to Ashland. The US release poster was based on the release poster for The 40 Year Old Virgin.

The film expanded its release to seven more markets on February 27, 2009, to 13 more on March 13, 2009,[20] and an additional 9 on March 20, 2009. On April 3, 2009, it was released in Canadian theaters.[21] The film was also released on May 7, 2009 in Denmark and showed for approximately three weeks, it was released in Germany on July 30, 2009.[22]

The DVD version was released on May 19, 2009, the day of the tenth anniversary of *The Phantom Menace*. The DVD and Blu-ray was also released in Canada on June 2, 2009.[23]

The region 2 DVD was released on October 4, 2010.

Reception

Fanboys met with mostly negative reviews with critics. Roger Ebert gave it 1½ out of 4 stars, calling it "an amiable but disjointed film that identifies too closely with its heroes. Poking a little more fun at them would have been a great idea."[24] James Berardinelli gave it 2½ out of 4 stars, saying it was "mostly a middling road picture that doesn't do a lot more than any average, forgettable entry into the tired genre."[25] Ben Lyons and Ben Mankiewicz of *At the Movies* recommended to "Skip It", with Lyons saying, "It was a great premise; it just unfortunately did not come together," while Mankiewicz commenting that "it devolves into nothing more than a silly road trip movie."[26] It is currently rated at 32 percent on Rotten Tomatoes.[27]

Sequel

Dan Fogler has mentioned that the director has thought about a sequel involving *Star Wars Episode II: Attack of the Clones*.

References

[1]   "Fanboys (2009)" (http://boxofficemojo.com/movies/?id=fanboys.htm). Box Office Mojo. . Retrieved 2010-08-13.

[2]   "Fanboys Triumphant: Kevin Spacey Crashes Fan Movie Awards" (http://starwarsblog.starwars.com/index.php/2008/07/25/
      fanboys-triumphant-kevin-spacey-crashes-fan-movie-awards/). Official Star Wars Blog. 2008-07-25. . Retrieved 2010-02-08.

[3]   White, Cindy (2007-04-19). "Lucas Gives *Fanboys* F/X Help" (http://web.archive.org/web/20071023161644/http://www.scifi.com/
      scifiwire/index.php?category=0&id=41158&type=0). Scifi.com. Archived from the original (http://www.scifi.com/scifiwire/index.
      php?category=0&id=41158&type=0) on October 23, 2007. . Retrieved 2007-04-26.

[4]   Roberts, Dustin (2007-05-17). "Fanboys Pushed Back to January 2008" (http://www.theforce.net/latestnews/story/
      Fanboys_Pushed_Back_To_January_2008_105913.asp). theforce.net. . Retrieved 2007-06-08.

[5]   "Fanboys News - UPDATED!" (http://the-cinemaniac.blogspot.com/2008/01/quick-bits.html). The CineManiac. 2008-01-14. . Retrieved
      2010-02-08.

[6]   "The Skinny On Fanboys" (http://www.chris-marquette.com). 2008-01-19. . Retrieved 2010-02-08.

[7]   "FANBOYS and ZODIAC" (http://www.blogtalkradio.com/moviegeeksunited/2008/01/06/fanboys). *Movie Geeks United!*. Blog Talk
      Radio. 2008-01-06. . Retrieved 2010-02-08.

[8]   "Stop Darth Weinstein" (http://stopdarthweinstein.chris-marquette.com/). . Retrieved 2010-02-08.

[9]   Knowles, Harry (2008-01-20). "The Most Dedicated FANBOYS have Targeted The Weinstein Company for crimes against FANBOYS!"
      (http://www.aintitcool.com/talkback_display/35673?q=node/35673). Ain't It Cool News. . Retrieved 2010-02-08.

[10] "The 'Fanboys' Situation Gets Real Nasty" (http://www.cinematical.com/2008/03/26/the-fanboys-situation-gets-real-nasty//).
      Cinematical.com. March 26 2008. . Retrieved September 12, 2009.

[11] "Kyle Newman: Fanboys" (http://suicidegirls.com/interviews/Kyle+Newman:+Fanboys/). *SuicideGirls*. February 4, 2009. . Retrieved
      February 4, 2009.

[12] "Fanboys Signing at Comic-Con" (http://starwarsblog.starwars.com/index.php/2007/07/24/fanboys-signing-at-comic-con/). Official
      Star Wars Blog. 2007-07-24. . Retrieved 2010-02-08.

[13] Cline, Ernest (2008-01-21). "Standing Ovation at Fanboys Rough Cut Screening" (http://www.youtube.com/watch?v=tTqY1vHT2Bc). .
      Retrieved 2010-02-08.

[14] "Force-Cast: July 11, 2008" (http://www.theforce.net/podcast/story/ForceCast_July_11_2008_116022.asp). TheForce.net. 2008-07-11.
      . Retrieved 2010-02-08.

[15] "Trigger Street Production FANBOYS To Finally Screen And Be Released" (http://www.triggerstreet.com/gyrobase/
      TriggerDigest?oid=oid:1760218). TigerStreet.com. 2008-07-21. . Retrieved 2010-02-08.

[16] Davis, Erik (2008-07-25). "SDCC Update: Cinematical Has Seen 'Fanboys'!" (http://www.cinematical.com/2008/07/25/
      sdcc-update-cinematical-has-seen-fanboys/). Cinematical. . Retrieved 2010-02-08.

[17] Cline, Ernest (2008-11-13). "New Fanboys Poster, Trailer, and (yet another) Release Date" (http://www.ernestcline.com/blog/2008/11/
      13/new-fanboys-poster-trailer-and-release-date/). . Retrieved 2010-02-08.

[18] Roberts, Dustin (2009-01-23). "Contact Weistein Co. To See Fanboys In Your City" (http://www.theforce.net/latestnews/story/
      Contact_Weistein_Co_To_See_Fanboys_In_Your_City_120548.asp). TheForce.net. . Retrieved 2010-02-08.

[19] Barrick, Mike (2009-02-18). "Fanboys Premiere In Columbus, OH" (http://www.theforce.net/latestnews/story/
      Fanboys_Premiere_In_Columbus_OH_121213.asp). TheForce.net. . Retrieved 2010-02-08.

[20] "Fanboys Hits More Theaters: March 13" (http://starwarsblog.starwars.com/index.php/2009/03/12/
      fanboys-hits-more-theaters-march-13/). Official Star Wars Blog. 2009-03-12. . Retrieved 2010-02-08.

[21] "Fanboys in 9 New Cities: March 20" (http://starwarsblog.starwars.com/index.php/2009/03/19/fanboys-in-9-new-cities-march-20/).
      Official Star Wars Blog. 2009-03-19. . Retrieved 2010-02-08.

[22] "Fanboys" (http://www.filmstarts.de/kritiken/93105-Fanboys.html) (in German). Filmstarts.de. . Retrieved 2010-02-08.

[23] Barrick, Mike (2009-04-06). "Fanboys On DVD Details" (http://www.theforce.net/latestnews/story/
      Fanboys_On_DVD_Details_122251.asp). TheForce.net. . Retrieved 2010-02-08.

[24] Elbert, Roger (2009-02-04). "Roger Ebert - Fanboys" (http://rogerebert.suntimes.com/apps/pbcs.dll/article?AID=/20090204/
      REVIEWS/902049987). . Retrieved 2010-02-08.

[25] Berardinelli, James (2009-02-03). "Reelviews - Fanboys" (http://www.reelviews.net/php_review_template.php?identifier=1469).
      Reelviews. . Retrieved 2010-02-08.

[26] "At the Movies - Fanboys" (http://bventertainment.go.com/tv/buenavista/atm/reviews.html?scc=6&subsec=Fanboys) (Video). .
      Retrieved 2010-02-08.

[27] "Fanboys" (http://www.rottentomatoes.com/m/fanboys/). Rotten Tomatoes. . Retrieved 2010-02-08.

External links

- Official website (http://http://www.fanboys-themovie.com/)
- Weinstein Co. (http://www.weinsteinco.com/#/film/fanboys/)
- *Fanboys* (http://www.imdb.com/title/tt0489049/) at the Internet Movie Database
- *Fanboys* (http://www.allmovie.com/work/352671) at Allmovie
- *Fanboys* (http://www.rottentomatoes.com/m/fanboys/) at Rotten Tomatoes
- *Fanboys* (http://www.boxofficemojo.com/movies/?id=fanboys.htm) at Box Office Mojo

Monsters vs. Aliens

Monsters Versus Aliens	
 Theatrical Poster	
Directed by	Conrad Vernon Rob Letterman
Produced by	Lisa Stewart **Co-producers:** Jill Hopper Latifa Ouaou
Written by	Maya Forbes Wallace Wolodarsky Rob Letterman Jonathan Aibel Glenn Berger Conrad Vernon
Starring	Reese Witherspoon Seth Rogen Hugh Laurie Will Arnett Conrad Vernon Rainn Wilson Kiefer Sutherland Stephen Colbert Paul Rudd
Music by	Henry Jackman
Editing by	Joyce Arrastia Eric Dapkewicz
Studio	DreamWorks Animation
Distributed by	Paramount Pictures
Release date(s)	March 27, 2009[1]
Running time	95 minutes
Country	United States

Language	English
Budget	$175 million
Gross revenue	$383,466,116[2]

Monsters vs. Aliens is a 2009 American computer-animated 3-D feature film produced by DreamWorks Animation and distributed by Paramount Pictures. The computer-animated movie was the first to be directly produced in a stereoscopic 3-D format instead of being converted into 3-D after completion, which added $15 million to the film's budget.[3]

The film was scheduled for a May 2009 release, but the release date was moved to March 27, 2009. It was released on DVD and Blu-Ray September 29, 2009 in North America and included the easter egg to the upcoming movies and previews. *Monsters vs. Aliens* features the voices of Reese Witherspoon, Seth Rogen, Hugh Laurie, Will Arnett, Conrad Vernon, Rainn Wilson, Kiefer Sutherland, Stephen Colbert, and Paul Rudd.

Plot

Bride-to-be Susan Murphy (Reese Witherspoon) is hit by a meteorite on her wedding day, causing her to absorb a substance called quantonium and grow into a giantess. Alerted to the meteorite crash, the military arrive and capture Susan, who is labeled the monster "Ginormica" and sent to a top-secret prison facility headed by General W.R. Monger (Kiefer Sutherland) where she meets her fellow monster inmates: B.O.B. (Seth Rogen), a brainless, indestructible gelatinous blob; Dr. Cockroach, Ph.D. (Hugh Laurie), a mad scientist with the head and abilities of a cockroach; the Missing link (Will Arnett), an amphibious fish-ape hybrid; and Insectosaurus, a massive grub that is larger than Susan.

An alien named Gallaxhar (Rainn Wilson) detects the quantonium radiation emanating from Earth and deploys a gigantic robotic probe to find it. The President of the United States (Stephen Colbert) attempts to make first contact with the alien robot, which begins destroying everything in sight, impervious to any weapons. General Monger convinces the President to use the monsters to fight the robot instead. The monsters accept the mission with the promise of freedom if they succeed. Arriving in San Francisco, Susan is chased by the robot across the city to the Golden Gate Bridge, where the monsters are able to defeat the robot.

Now free, Susan returns to her hometown and introduces her family to the monsters, but they are quickly rejected after innocently causing a panic in the neighborhood. Derek, meanwhile, breaks up with Susan, claiming that he can't be married to a freak who would overshadow his career. At first devastated, Susan begins to realize that becoming a monster has improved her life, and fully embraces her new lifestyle. Suddenly, she is abducted by Gallaxhar, who kills Insectosaurus when he tries to save her. On Gallaxhar's spaceship, Susan breaks loose and chases Gallaxhar down, only to enter a machine that extracts the quantonium from her body, shrinking her to her normal size. Gallaxhar proceeds to use the quantonium to power a cloning machine which reproduces him into an army so he can invade Earth.

With assistance from General Monger, B.O.B., Dr. Cockroach, and the Missing Link infiltrate Gallaxhar's spaceship, rescue Susan, and hot-wire the spaceship's power core, activating the self-destruct sequence. During their escape, Susan is cut off from her friends, who are trapped in the power core. They tell her to save herself, but Susan instead confronts Gallaxhar, who tries to escape with the quantonium, and attempts to force him into releasing her friends. When Gallaxhar says he cannot reverse the sequence, Susan absorbs the quantonium, restoring her to her giant size and she saves her friends. The monsters leap out of the exploding spaceship and are rescued by General Monger on the back of the revived Insectosaurus, who has metamorphosed into a giant butterfly.

The monsters receive a hero's welcome home. Derek tries to get back with Susan for the sake an interview that could benefit his career. Instead, Susan rejects him by throwing him in the air where he is caught, swallowed and spit out by B.O.B. on camera. The monsters are then alerted to a giant snail attack near Paris and fly off to face the new menace.

Cast and characters

Monsters

- Reese Witherspoon as Susan/Ginormica, Susan Murphy from Modesto, California who is hit by a radioactive meteor on her wedding day, causing her to mutate and grow to a height of 49 feet 11 inches (15.21 m). Meek and unassertive, she just wants to return to her old life, but gradually warms up to her new status as a monster. In addition to her size, she is amazingly strong and has a resistance to energy attacks. She serves as the protagonist of the film. Susan is also a human.
- Seth Rogen as B.O.B. (Benzoate Ostylezene Bicarbonate), an indestructible gelatinous mass created when a genetically-altered tomato (which he referred to in the Halloween special as his mother) was injected with a chemically-altered ranch dessert topping. His greatest strength lies in his ability to digest any substance as well as being indestructible. His one weakness is that his mutation didn't give him a brain ("Turns out, you don't need one!"), making him incredibly dimwitted, such as sometimes mistaking the other monsters' goals in life for his own. His main goal in life is to digest things.
- Hugh Laurie as Dr. Cockroach, Ph.D, a brilliant but mad scientist who, in an experiment to imbue himself with the abilities of a cockroach, ending up with a giant cockroach's head and some cockroach personality, but gained the ability to climb up walls and high resistance to physical damage. He is charming and sophisticated in spite of his tendencies to eat garbage and laugh maniacally, working to help Susan learn more about her condition while in captivity. He is also an avid dancer, which was handy in overriding the ship security system.
- Will Arnett as The Missing Link, a 20,000-year-old fish-ape hybrid who was found frozen and thawed out, only to escape and wreak havoc at his old lagoon habitat. Usually referred to as Link, he behaves as a macho jock most of the time, but is out of shape. Despite this, he is an expert martial-artist and takes it upon himself to lead the team in attacks, even if his energetic attitude doesn't always work to their advantage.
- Conrad Vernon as Insectosaurus, formerly a 1 inch (25 mm) grub transformed by nuclear radiation into a 350 foot (110 m) monster with the ability to shoot silk out of his nose. He is unable to speak clearly, and is mesmerized by bright lights (usually used to lead him to other locations); He also has a close bond with the Missing Link, who can understand what Insectosaurus is saying. As Butterflysaurus, he has wings and is able to fly and becomes the Monsters' mode of transportation.

Aliens

- Rainn Wilson as Gallaxhar, an evil alien overlord who hopes to take over Earth. He is served by gigantic robot probes (around the same size as Insectosaurus) and possesses a giant cloning machine. He claims to have suffered several traumas in his youth, driving him to destroy his own homeworld, and plans to make a new one on Earth - although viewers never hear most of the story. He aims to collect quantonium - the substance that transformed Susan - to give his cloning machine enough power to generate an army of clones of himself to conquer Earth, and is determined to extract it from Susan. Gallaxhar serves as the main antagonist of the film.
- Amy Poehler as Gallaxhar's Computer, a user-friendly computer that follows his orders, albeit with a sarcastic tone.

Humans

- Kiefer Sutherland as General Warren R. Monger, a military leader who runs a top secret facility where monsters are kept. It is his plan to fight the invading aliens with the imprisoned monsters. In a scene during the credits, he claims to be 90 years old, in spite of his youthful appearance. His name is a pun on the word warmonger. Despite imprisoning the "monsters", he never shows them any particular disrespect, and upholds his part of the bargain to set them free when they defeat the alien probe. Later on, having helped the team infiltrate the ship, he comes back for them on Insectosaurus, just as he promised. At the end of the film, Gen. Monger is promoted to the President's senior security staff.
- Stephen Colbert as President Hathaway, the impulsive and dimwitted President of the United States. Not wanting to be remembered as "the President in office when the world came to an end," he agrees with General Monger's "monsters vs. aliens" plan. He is very tolerant of the use of weapons, firing repeatedly—and pointlessly—at the original alien probe. He even suggests using nuclear weapons to attack the aliens, only to be stopped every time by his more-reliable staff.
- Paul Rudd as Derek Dietl, a local weatherman and Susan's ex-fiancé. He jumps at whatever opportunity he has to boost his career, which causes him to place himself before his relationship with Susan (he cancels their plans to have a romantic honeymoon in Paris to land an anchorman job in Fresno, for example). After she sees him as the self-obsessed man he really is, she effectively turns him down by publicly humiliating him during his attempted interview with her.
- Jeffrey Tambor as Carl Murphy, Susan's over-emotional father.
- Julie White as Wendy Murphy, Susan's loving mother.
- Renée Zellweger as Katie, an adventurous human girl. Her date with her boyfriend Cuthbert is interrupted by the landing of Gallaxhar's robot.
- John Krasinski as Cuthbert, Katie's more timid boyfriend.
- Ed Helms as News Reporter
- David Koch as newsreader who comically notes how aliens only ever seem to appear in America.

Production

Ed Leonard, CTO of DreamWorks Animation, says it took approximately 45.6 million computing hours to make *Monsters vs. Aliens*, more than eight times as many as the original *Shrek*. Several hundred Hewlett-Packard xw8600 workstations were used, along with a large and powerful 'render farm' of HP ProLiant blade servers with over 9,000 server processor cores, to process the animation sequence. The movie demanded 120 terabytes of data to complete, with one explosion scene alone requiring 6 TB.[4]

Since *Monsters vs. Aliens*, all feature films released by DreamWorks Animation will be produced in a stereoscopic 3-D format, using Intel's InTru3D technology.[5] IMAX 3D, RealD and 2D versions were released.

Marketing

The teaser trailer had two versions that show General W.R. Monger's plan to use the monsters to defeat the aliens. The first version was seen on the *Kung Fu Panda* DVD and the other version was shown with *Madagascar: Escape 2 Africa*. A full-length trailer was launched on the Internet on December 23, 2008.

To promote the 3-D technology that is used in *Monsters vs. Aliens*, DreamWorks ran a 3-D trailer before halftime in the U.S. broadcast of Super Bowl XLIII on February 1, 2009. Due to the limitations of current television technology, ColorCode 3D glasses were distributed at SoBe stands at major national grocers. The Monsters, except Susan and Insectosaurus, also appeared in a 3-D SoBe commercial airing after the trailer. Bank of America gave away vouchers which covered the cost of an upgrade to a 3-D theatrical viewing of the film for its customers.[6]

Reception

Critical reception

Based on 202 reviews collected by Rotten Tomatoes, *Monsters vs. Aliens* has an overall approval rating from critics of 71%, with an average score of 6.4/10.[7] Among Rotten Tomatoes' Cream of the Crop, which consists of popular and notable critics from the top newspapers, websites, television, and radio programs, the film holds an overall approval rating of 58% based on 36 reviews.[8] By comparison, on Metacritic, which assigns a normalized rating out of 100 top reviews from mainstream critics, the film has received an average score of 56, based on 35 reviews.[9] Roger Ebert gave the film a mixed review, saying "I suppose kids will like this movie", but said "I didn't find the movie rich with humor."

Box office

On its opening weekend, the film opened at #1, grossing $59.3 million in 4,104 theaters.[10] Of that total, the film grossed an estimated $5.2 million in IMAX theaters, becoming the 5th highest-grossing IMAX debut, behind *Star Trek*, *Transformers: Revenge of the Fallen*, *The Dark Knight* and *Watchmen*.[11] The movie made $198,351,526 in the United States and Canada making it the second-highest grossing animated movie behind *Up*. Worldwide, it is the third-highest grossing animated film of 2009 with a total of $383,466,166 behind *Up* and *Ice Age: Dawn of the Dinosaurs*. According to Boxofficemojo.com the film cost $175 million to develop.

Awards

On 2010, the films is nominated for 4 Annie Awards, including *Voice Acting in a Feature Production* for Hugh Laurie. Reese Witherspoon and Seth Rogen were both nominated for best voice actor at the 2010 Nickelodeon Kid's Choice Awards for voicing Susan and B.O.B, but lost to Jim Carrey for *Disney's A Christmas Carol. Monsters Vs Aliens* was also nominated for Best Animated film but lost to *Up*. On June 24, 2009 the film won the Saturn Award for Best Animated Film.

Home media

Monsters vs. Aliens was released to DVD and Blu-ray in the US and Canada on September 29, 2009 and on October 26, 2009 in the UK. The home release for both the DVD and Blu-ray format only contain the 2D version of the movie. However, the release is packaged with a new short, *B.O.B.'s Big Break*, which is the more traditional 3D that required green and magenta glasses.[12] Also included are four pairs of 3D glasses.[12] As of November 29, 2009 the DVD has sold 4,431,584 million copies generating $73.79 million in sales so far.[13] On January 6, 2010, it was announced that a 3D version will be released on Blu-ray.[14] On February 24, a tentative March release date was set for the UK, where anyone who buys a Samsung 3D TV or 3D Blu-ray player will get a copy.[15] On March 8, it was reported that the 3D Blu-ray will be released in the United States, also with Samsung 3D products, on March 21.[16]

Video game

A video game was released on March 24, 2009 on Microsoft Windows, PlayStation 3, Xbox 360, Nintendo DS, PlayStation 2, and Wii. The game, developed by Beenox and Amaze Entertainment, allows users to play through scenes from the movie as Ginormica, B.O.B., and The Missing Link, and features drop-in/out co-op.[17] Players can play as Dr. Cockroach, Ph.D in multiplayer co-op, as well as Insectosaurus on the Nintendo DS version of the game. The music was composed by Jim Dooley, with live brass recorded at the Warner Brothers Eastwood Scoring Stage.[18] The Monsters Vs. Aliens Videogame has garnered a Metacritic score of 63 for the Xbox 360 version of the title.

Television series

Jeffrey Katzenberg announced that Nickelodeon has ordered a pilot for a *Monsters vs. Aliens* cartoon series. This will be Nickelodeon's third DreamWorks deal, first being *The Penguins of Madagascar* and the upcoming *Kung Fu Panda: Legends of Awesomeness.*[19]

Sequel

Despite its success in the United States market, Jeffrey Katzenberg was quoted in the *Los Angeles Times* that a sequel might not be made because of the film's weak performance in some key international markets.

❝There was enough of a consensus from our distribution and marketing folks in certain parts of the world that "doing a sequel" would be ❞ pushing a boulder up a hill"[20]

Spin-offs

B.O.B.'s Big Break

B.O.B. (Seth Rogen) and his monstrous crew are on a mission to bust out of Area 52, the government's top-secret holding cell. Led by mad-scientist Dr. Cockroach Ph.D. (Hugh Laurie) and macho amphibian the Missing Link (Will Arnett), the trio outwits grizzled General W.R. Monger (Kiefer Sutherland) to make a triumphant escape after Cockroach's latest escape attempt—by feeding B.O.B. a chemical mixture to turn him into a bomb—results in B.O.B. temporarily acquiring the ability to read minds, allowing them to find out about a secret exit from Area 52. Unfortunately, the plan fails when B.O.B. smashes the jet they were using to escape—believing it to be a piñata,—the resulting explosion apparently erasing B.O.B.'s new power.

The short premiered on Nickelodeon in 2D on September 26, 2009.

The 3D version is included on the Blu-Ray, the DVD 2-pack and the 3D Blu-Ray .

Monsters vs. Aliens: Mutant Pumpkins from Outer Space

A Halloween special entitled *Monsters vs. Aliens: Mutant Pumpkins from Outer Space* premiered on RTÉ One on October 26, 2009.[21] [22] [23] It is premiered on NBC in the USA on October 28, 2009.[24] In Australia on the Seven Network on November 14, 2009 and Hong Kong on the TVB Pearl on October 31, 2009. In Portugal it premiered on SIC, in 1 January 2010. Susan and the fellow monsters go back to Susan's home just in time for Halloween celebrations. Susan spends time with her parents, while the other monsters join in trick-or-treating and collect a large amount of candies. Later, it is revealed that the monsters came to destroy mutant pumpkins disguised as Jack-o-lanterns. When the pumpkins begin to eat children's candies to grow larger, the monsters and children defeat them by throwing excessive candies to bloat them up and explode them. But, in a twist ending, some of the pumpkin "blood" (a green goo that mutated the ordinary pumpkins) falls into a planting of carrots, causing a mutant carrot to be formed.

References

[1] "Monsters Scared Off by Avatar" (http://www.comcast.net/entertainment/index.jsp?fn=2007/09/20/233314.html). E! Entertainment. 2007-09-20. . Retrieved 2007-09-20.

[2] http://www.the-numbers.com/movies/2009/MVSA.php

[3] Wloszczyna, Susan (March 11, 2008). "First look: *Monsters vs. Aliens* is the ultimate; a 3-D 'first'" (http://www.usatoday.com/life/movies/news/2008-03-10-monsters-aliens_N.htm). *USA Today*. . Retrieved 2008-05-16.

[4] Boshoff, Theo (31 March 2009). "Monsters, aliens come alive" (http://www.itweb.co.za/sections/computing/2009/0903311157.asp). *ITWeb*. .

[5] Intel (2008-07-08). "Intel, Dreamworks Animation Form Strategic Alliance to Revolutionize 3-D Filmmaking Technology" (http://www.intel.com/pressroom/archive/releases/20080708corp.htm). Press release. . Retrieved 2008-11-05.

[6] Nikki Finke (Mar 19th, 2009). "WHAAAAAT? Bailed Out Bank Of America Paying Consumers To See Hollywood Film" (http://www.deadlinehollywooddaily.com/whaaat-bailed-out-bank-of-america-paying-for-consumers-to-see-hollywood-toon/). *Nikki Finke's Deadline Hollywood Daily*. .

[7] "Monsters vs. Aliens Movie Reviews, Pictures" (http://www.rottentomatoes.com/m/monsters_vs_aliens/). *Rotten Tomatoes*. IGN Entertainment. . Retrieved 2010-01-29.

[8] "Monsters vs. Aliens Movie Reviews, Pictures - Cream of the Crop" (http://www.rottentomatoes.com/m/monsters_vs_aliens/?critic=creamcrop). *Rotten Tomatoes*. IGN Entertainment. . Retrieved 2010-01-29.

[9] "Monsters vs. Aliens (2009):Reviews" (http://www.metacritic.com/film/titles/monstersvsaliens). Metacritic. . Retrieved 2010-01-29.

[10] "Weekend Box Office Estimates (U.S.) for March 27–29 weekend" (http://movies.yahoo.com/mv/boxoffice/). Yahoo! Movies. . Retrieved 2009-03-29.

[11] "Weekend Report: 'Monsters,' 'Haunting' Scare Up Big Business" (http://www.boxofficemojo.com/news/?id=2569&p=.htm). Box Office Mojo. . Retrieved 2009-03-29.

[12] "*Monsters vs. Aliens* Hits DVD and Blu-ray on Sept. 29" (http://www.comingsoon.net/news/movienews.php?id=56968). *ComingSoon.net*. July 8, 2009. . Retrieved August 13, 2009.

[13] http://www.the-numbers.com/dvd/charts/weekly/thisweek.php.

[14] ""Monsters Vs. Aliens" becomes first 3D Blu-Ray" (http://techland.com/2010/01/06/monsters-vs-aliens-becomes-first-3d-blu-ray/). January 6, 2010. . Retrieved February 2, 2010.

[15] "'Monsters vs. Aliens' 3D Blu-ray Hits UK in March – Only From Samsung" (http://bluray.highdefdigest.com/news/show/3D/Industry_Trends/DreamWorks/Samsung/Monsters_vs._Aliens_3D_Blu-ray_Hits_UK_in_March_â00_Only_From_Samsung/4288). February 24, 2010. . Retrieved March 9, 2010.

[16] "Samsung 3D Blu-rays don't work?" (http://hollywoodinhidef.com/2010/03/samsung-3d-blu-rays-dont-work/). March 8, 2010. . Retrieved March 21, 2010.

[17] "Monsters vs. Aliens Review" (http://gamefreaks365.com/review.php?artid=1641). . Retrieved 2009-07-11.

[18] Dan Goldwasser (2009-03-09). "Jim Dooley scores the *Monsters vs. Aliens* video game" (http://www.scoringsessions.com/news/168/). ScoringSessions.com. . Retrieved 2009-03-15.

[19] Georg Szalai (May 19, 2009). "Nick orders 'Monsters vs. Aliens' pilot" (http://www.hollywoodreporter.com/hr/content_display/television/news/e3ic8543054a8a9084d9bcb057ed0d2a6d0). *THR.com Television*. .

[20] DreamWorks Animation's profit drops; no sequel for 'Monsters vs. Aliens' (http://latimesblogs.latimes.com/entertainmentnewsbuzz/2009/10/dreamworks-animation-records-earnings-drop-does-better-than-wall-street-expects.html)

[21] "6:30pm to 6:55pm" (http://uk-tv-guide.com/programme-details/RTÉ+1/26+October+2009/18:30/Monsters+v+Aliens:+Mutant+Pumpkins+From+Outer+Space/Childrens/). *TV Guide*. . Retrieved October 26, 2009.

[22] "Bank Holiday Monday, October 26" (http://tvsales.rte.ie/programming/week43.htm#prog03). *RTÉ*. . Retrieved October 26, 2009.

[23] "Monsters vs Aliens: Mutant Pumpkins from Outer Space" (http://tvlistings.guardian.co.uk/text-only/?c=rte-one). *The Guardian* (London). . Retrieved October 26, 2009.

[24] "Nickelodeon orders pilot for Monsters vs. Aliens" (http://www.animated-news.com/2009/nickelodeon-orders-pilot-for-monsters-vs-aliens/). *Animated News*. . Retrieved June 15, 2009.

External links

- Official website (http://http://www.monstersvsaliens.com)
- *Monsters vs. Aliens* (http://www.imdb.com/title/tt0892782/) at the Internet Movie Database
- *Monsters vs. Aliens* (http://www.bcdb.com/bcdb/cartoon.cgi?film=89704/) at the Big Cartoon DataBase
- *Monsters vs. Aliens* (http://www.allmovie.com/work/379339) at Allmovie
- *Monsters vs. Aliens* (http://www.rottentomatoes.com/m/1194516/) at Rotten Tomatoes
- *Monsters vs. Aliens* (http://www.metacritic.com/film/titles/monstersvsaliens) at Metacritic
- *Monsters vs. Aliens* (http://www.boxofficemojo.com/movies/?id=monstersvsaliens.htm) at Box Office Mojo

Observe and Report

Observe and Report	
Promotional film poster	
Directed by	Jody Hill
Produced by	Donald De Line
Written by	Jody Hill
Starring	Seth Rogen Anna Faris Michael Peña Collette Wolfe Ray Liotta
Music by	Joseph Stephens
Cinematography	Tim Orr
Editing by	Zene Baker
Studio	Legendary Pictures
Distributed by	Warner Bros.
Release date(s)	April 10, 2009
Running time	86 minutes
Country	United States

Language	English
Budget	$18,000,000
Gross revenue	$24,881,177[1]

Observe and Report is a 2009 American black comedy film written and directed by Jody Hill, starring Seth Rogen, Anna Faris and Ray Liotta.[2]

Plot

An anonymous flasher exposes himself to shoppers in the Forest Ridge Mall parking lot. The head of mall security, Ronnie Barnhardt (Seth Rogen), makes it his mission to apprehend the offender. He is assisted by Charles (Jesse Plemons) and Dennis (Michael Peña), and the Yuen twins (John Yuan and Matthew Yuan), in his efforts.

Ronnie's dream girl, Brandi (Anna Faris) who works a mall make-up counter, is flashed the next day, becoming distraught over the situation. Ronnie tries to comfort her until a police officer, Detective Harrison (Ray Liotta), arrives and takes over Ronnie's palliative role. Ronnie feels threatened by this and is upset that his boss allowed an outsider to infringe on his search for the offender.

The criminal activity at the mall continues, as a masked person is seen robbing a shoe store, causing property damage. Detective Harrison is once again called in to investigate, his efforts hindered by Ronnie, who thinks that an Iraqi shopkeeper (Aziz Ansari) in the mall is the thief, based on the fact that he is Iraqi. In response, Harrison curses out Ronnie during a meeting with Ronnie's superior, and Ronnie decides to take steps to become a real police officer.

As part of his preparations, Ronnie decides to ride along with Detective Harrison. Harrison, fed up with Ronnie, tricks him into walking into the most dangerous part of town, and drives off. Ronnie then confronts and subsequently subdues several drug dealers, victoriously returning to the police station with a dealer's son and thanking the detective for the opportunity to prove himself. Emboldened, Ronnie arranges a date with Brandi. On their date, Brandi consumes a large quantity of alcohol as well as several tablets of clonazepam which she took from Ronnie. Ronnie takes her home and has sex with her while she is semi-conscious.

Ronnie fails the psychological examination for the police officer job. Nell (Collette Wolfe), a friendly food court worker, explains to him that her boss Roger (Patton Oswalt) and another female employee make fun of Nell for having her leg in a cast, leading Ronnie to threaten the two after giving Roger a beating. Depressed, he is persuaded by Dennis to spend the day doing a wide variety of drugs and assaulting skateboarding teenagers. At the end of the day, Ronnie finds out that Dennis was the shoe thief, and that he has been stealing from the mall for some time. Ronnie is stunned and, after a brief argument, is knocked unconscious from behind by Dennis, who then flees to Mexico.

Ronnie decides to go "undercover" in order to catch the flasher. At night he sees Harrison having sex with Brandi in his cruiser, and he confronts her in front of onlookers at the mall the next day, blowing his "cover" and damaging mall property in the process. Ronnie refuses to leave the mall and police are called in. Ronnie fights off many officers before losing a fist fight with Harrison.

After a brief time in jail, and once his wounds heal, Ronnie returns to the mall, although no longer a security guard. He is approached by Nell back on both legs, and she kisses him to console him. Interrupting their romantic moment, the flasher exposes himself to Nell and Ronnie and runs off, exposing himself to many other mall patrons. Ronnie, pursuing the flasher in a slow-motion sequence that includes him punching the Iraqi clerk in the face, retrieves a gun and shoots the flasher as he approaches Brandi. Though she thanks him, Ronnie rejects and humiliates her for betraying him.

Refusing the flasher an ambulance, Ronnie takes him to the police station, impressing and insulting the officers who had previously ridiculed him, including Harrison. A victorious Ronnie is then interviewed with the other security guards and he is accompanied by Nell, who is now his girlfriend, and he returns back to his job as the head of mall security.

Cast

- Seth Rogen as Ronnie
- Ray Liotta as Detective Harrison
- Michael Pena as Dennis
- Anna Faris as Brandi
- Dan Bakkedahl as Mark
- Jesse Plemons as Charles
- John Yuan as John Yuen
- Matthew Yuan as Matt Yuen
- Celia Weston as Mom
- Collette Wolfe as Nell
- Aziz Ansari as Saddamn
- Randy Gambill as Pervert
- Patton Oswalt as Roger
- Danny McBride as Caucasian Crackhead
- Alston Brown as Bruce
- Cody Midthunder as D-Rock

Production

The film was shot on location in the largely abandoned Winrock Shopping Center in Albuquerque, New Mexico.[3] Filming began around May 2008 and took place in Wilmington, NC.

At the request of the studio, during the test screening stage the filmmakers created a version that was more toned down, but that was scrapped as the scores for the new version were lower than the original.[4]

Writing

Written and directed by Jody Hill. The megalomaniac, manic-depressive security guard Ronnie has been compared to Travis Bickle in Martin Scorsese's *Taxi Driver*; Hill has mentioned it and also Scorsese's *The King of Comedy* as significant influences.[5] [6]

Similarity to *Paul Blart: Mall Cop*

The film has drawn some attention for having a similar premise and protagonist to the 2009 comedy *Paul Blart: Mall Cop*. Seth Rogen, in an interview with GQ, noted his awareness of a similar movie being made:

> We knew the whole time, actually. And we're friends with those guys, so we would literally send each other pictures of the wardrobe, just to make sure we weren't stepping on each other's toes. They're totally different movies.[7]

In comparing the two, *Observe and Report* was dubbed by some reviewers as "the dark mall cop movie".[8] [9] [10]

Reception

Critical reception

Critical reaction has been mixed. On Rotten Tomatoes, *Observe and Report* has an overall approval rating from critics of 51% with an average score of 5.4/10.[11] By comparison, on Metacritic, the film has received an average score of 54, based on 34 reviews.[12] Based on 11 reviews, Yahoo! Movies critics gave the film a B-.[13]

Peter Travers of *Rolling Stone* wrote that "Hill is fearless at pushing hot buttons: date rape, shooting up and worse," but added, "Rogen is nutso hilarious, nailing every note of mirth and malice," giving it a rating of three out of four stars.[14] Conversely, Peter Bradshaw of *The Guardian* awarded the movie one star out of five and disparaged Rogen's performance, writing "for Seth Rogen fans like me, this charmless, heavy-handed and cynical comedy is an uncomfortable experience."[15] Paul Byrnes wrote in *The Sydney Morning Herald*, "Much of the movie is just plain vicious. At best, it's sad and grotesque, rather than hilarious,"[16] while Manohla Dargis of *The New York Times* took particular exception to the film, arguing "if you thought Abu Ghraib was a laugh riot you might love *Observe and Report*." She continued, "It's far better and certainly easier... to sit back and relax and enjoy the show. That, after all, is precisely what Hollywood banks on each time it manufactures a new entertainment for a public that — as the stupid, violent characters who hold up a mirror to that public indicate — it views with contempt."[17]

The sex scene between Rogen and Faris attracted criticism from various groups.[18] Referring to the moment where Ronnie Barnhardt is having sex with Faris' intoxicated character, Rogen said in an interview that "then she says, like, the one thing that makes it all okay," to which Antonia Zerbisias responded, arguing that "retroactive consent is not consent" and "there's no okay in rape".[19] Peter Travers argued in *Rolling Stone* that while the scene does constitute date rape, "the bipolar Ronnie is acting totally in character," and that "the movie isn't condoning Ronnie's actions," just dishing out the kind of laughs "that stick in your throat." [20]

During an interview on *The Howard Stern Show*, Rogen stated he was disappointed by the film's overall reception but proud that "the only two people who liked it" were Stern and David Letterman.[21]

Box office

The film grossed $11,140,000 to open in fourth place in its first weekend of release, behind *Hannah Montana: The Movie*, *Fast & Furious*, and *Monsters vs. Aliens* (also featuring Seth Rogen). It averaged $4,085, playing in 2,727 theaters. To date it is the lowest-grossing film in which Seth Rogen plays a leading role, grossing $24,527,204 as of May 31, 2009.[22]

Home video release

The film was released on DVD and Blu-Ray on September 22, 2009.

Soundtrack

Observe and Report: Original Motion Picture Soundtrack	

Soundtrack by Various Artists	
Released	April 7, 2009
Genre	Soundtrack
Label	New Line Records

Observe and Report: Original Motion Picture Soundtrack was released on April 7, 2009 by New Line Records.

1. "When I Paint My Masterpiece" by The Band — 4:18
2. "The Man" by Patto — 6:07
3. "Lightsabre Cocksucking Blues" by McLusky — 1:51
4. "Sittin' Back Easy" by Patto — 3:35
5. "Brain" by The Action — 2:59
6. "Over Under Sideways Down" by The Yardbirds — 2:22
7. "Dwarves Must Die" by Dwarves — 1:23
8. "Help Is on Its Way" by Little River Band — 4:00
9. "Where Is My Mind?" by City Wolf — 4:27
10. "Babyteeth" by Pyramid — 4:10
11. "Observe and Report Score Suite" by Joseph Stephens — 4:04
12. "Super Freek (Remix)" by Amanda Blank, Nina Cream, and Aaron LaCrate — 2:26

The Queen songs It's Late and The Hero are featured in the film but not included on the soundtrack.

References

[1] http://boxofficemojo.com/weekend/chart/

[2] http://www.movies.com/observeandreport/movietimes/120411/

[3] (http://www.variety.com/review/VE1117939886.html?categoryid=31&cs=1) *Observe and Report Review* 18 Mar 2009. Retrieved 1 Apr 2009.

[4] Amy Longsdorf (2009-04-05). "See-sawing between naughty and nice" (http://www.thestar.com/Entertainment/article/613396). Toronto Star. .

[5] http://nymag.com/daily/entertainment/2009/04/observe_and_report_director.html

[6] http://www.avclub.com/articles/jody-hill,26484/

[7] GQ Blog. Seth Rogen and Jody Hill talk 'Observe and Report' (http://www.gq.com/blogs/the-q/2009/03/the-other-mall-cop-movie. html) 13 Mar 2009. Retrieved 3 April 2009

[8] Campbell, Christopher. Observe and Report = The Dark Mall Cop. Today in Film Bloggery 02/09/09 (http://blog.spout.com/2009/02/09/ observe-and-report-the-dark-mall-cop-today-in-film-bloggery-020909/), *Splout Blog*, 9 Feb 2009. Retrieved 14 Mar 2009.

[9] Legel, Laremy. Five Reasons Seth Rogen's Observe and Report Will Own Paul Blart (http://www.film.com/movies/observe-and-report/ story/five-reasons-seth-rogens-observe/25809249). *Flim.com*, 2 Feb 2009. Retrieved 14 Mar 2009.

[10] Ponto, Arya. "Observe and Report"—No, It's Not Another "Paul Blart" (http://www.justpressplay.net/movies/movie-news/ 4789-qobserve-and-reportqno-its-not-another-qpaul-blartq.html) *Just Press Play* 7 Feb 2009. Retrieved 14 Mar 2009.

[11] "Observe and Report Movie Reviews, Pictures" (http://www.rottentomatoes.com/m/observe_and_report/). Rotten Tomatoes. . Retrieved 2009-11-24.

[12] "Observe and Report (2009): Reviews" (http://www.metacritic.com/film/titles/observeandreport). Metacritic. . Retrieved 2009-04-12.

[13] "Observe and Report (2009)- Yahoo! Movies" (http://movies.yahoo.com/movie/1810025224/info). Yahoo! Movies. . Retrieved 2-009-04-11.

[14] "Observe and Report: Review" (http://www.rollingstone.com/reviews/movie/21376770/review/27182546/observe_and_report). Rolling Stones. . Retrieved 2010-01-29. - Peter Travers, Rolling Stone

[15] Bradshaw, Peter (April 24, 2009). "Film Review: Observe and Report" (http://www.guardian.co.uk/film/2009/apr/23/ observe-and-report-film-review). London: The Guardian. . Retrieved 2010-01-29. - Peter Bradshaw, The Guardian

[16] "Film Reviews - Observe & Report" (http://www.smh.com.au/news/entertainment/film/film-reviews/observe-and-report/2009/05/ 14/1241894087719.html?page=fullpage#contentSwap1). The Sydney Morning Herald. May 14, 2009. . Retrieved 2010-01-29.

[17] Dargis, Manohla (April 10, 2009). "Movie Reviews - Observe & Report - Mall Crisis? Call security. Then again, maybe not" (http:// movies.nytimes.com/2009/04/10/movies/10obse.html?ref=movies). The New York Times. . Retrieved 2010-01-29.

[18] Fisher, luchina (April 14, 2009). "Observe and Report's' Date Rape Scene: Funny or Offensive?" (http://abcnews.go.com/Entertainment/ Movies/story?id=7327855&page=1). abcnews. . Retrieved May 3, 2009.

[19] Antonia, Zerbisias (April 14, 2009). "If no means no, is yes `yes'?" (http://www.thestar.com/living/article/617839). *Thestar.com* (Toronto: John Cruickshank). . Retrieved May 3, 2009.

[20] Controversy: Is the Seth Rogen Sex Scene in "Observe and Report" Date Rape or Harmless Fun? (http://www.rollingstone.com/blogs/ traverstake/2009/04/controversy-is-the-seth-rogen.php) - Peter Travers, Rolling Stone

[21] http://www.howardstern.com/rundown.hs?d=1248926400

[22] "Weekend Box Office Results for April 10–12, 2009" (http://www.boxofficemojo.com/weekend/chart/?yr=2009&wknd=15&p=.htm). Box Office Mojo. . Retrieved 2009-04-12.

External links

- Official website (http://http://observe-and-report.warnerbros.com/)
- *Observe and Report* (http://www.imdb.com/title/tt1197628/) at the Internet Movie Database
- *Observe and Report* (http://www.rottentomatoes.com/m/observe_and_report/) at Rotten Tomatoes
- *Observe and Report* (http://www.boxofficemojo.com/movies/?id=observeandreport.htm) at Box Office Mojo
- *Observe and Report* (http://www.allmovie.com/work/433705) at Allmovie

Funny People

Funny People	
 Pinar Saritas	
Directed by	Judd Apatow
Produced by	Judd Apatow Clayton Townsend Barry Mendel Seth Rogen Evan Goldberg Jack Giarraputo Regan Losits
Written by	Judd Apatow
Starring	Adam Sandler Seth Rogen Leslie Mann Jonah Hill Jason Schwartzman Eric Bana
Music by	Michael Andrews Jason Schwartzman
Cinematography	Janusz Kamiński
Editing by	Craig Alpert Brent White
Studio	Relativity Media Apatow Productions Mr. Madison 23 Productions
Distributed by	Universal Pictures Columbia Pictures
Release date(s)	July 31, 2009
Running time	146 minutes
Country	United States

Language	English
Budget	$75 million[1]
Gross revenue	$71,585,235[1]

Funny People is a 2009 American comedy-drama film written, co-produced and directed by Judd Apatow, and starring Adam Sandler, Seth Rogen, and Leslie Mann. The film was released on 31 July 2009 in North America, and on 28 August 2009 in the United Kingdom. *Funny People* implements more dramatic elements than seen in Apatow's previous films. The film was co-produced by Apatow Productions and Mr. Madison 23 Productions, a subsidiary of Sandler's company Happy Madison. Universal Pictures and Columbia Pictures co-financed the film and it also served as a worldwide distributor.[2]

Plot

George Simmons (Adam Sandler) is a rich, but lonely comic movie star in his forties. He gets diagnosed with a rare and deadly form of cancer and starts planning to die. He decides to return to his roots and do stand-up comedy.

Ira Wright (Seth Rogen) is an aspiring stand-up comedian who dreams of quitting his day job. George and Ira meet by chance at a comedy club, which leads to Ira getting hired by the older, more successful comedian as a joke writer and "assistant." Their strange relationship deepens, with Ira acting as part best friend and part man-servant to George as the two travel around doing stand-up, and living together in George's mansion.

George contacts his ex-fiance, Laura (Leslie Mann), to apologize for cheating on her when they were together. Laura comes to one of George's shows. She tells George that her husband, Clarke (Eric Bana), cheats on her. She regrets leaving George, and they end up becoming reconciled.

George learns that his cancer is gone. Now he is forced to plan on living, and the biggest part of that plan is to be with Laura. George and Ira visit Laura at her large home in Marin County where the romance between George and Laura grows despite the presence of Ira as well as Laura and Clarke's two young daughters . Eventually, Laura's husband returns home and there is a confrontation. Laura chooses to keep her family in tact, rejecting George, who then lashes out at Ira and fires him.

Ira returns to his old job and normal life. George makes a surprise visit and offers Ira advice on his comedy, which suggests the possibility of a new stage in their friendship.

Cast

- Adam Sandler as George Simmons
- Seth Rogen as Ira Wright
- Leslie Mann as Laura
- Jonah Hill as Leo Koenig
- Jason Schwartzman as Mark Taylor Jackson
- Eric Bana as Clarke
- RZA as Chuck
- Aubrey Plaza as Daisy Danby
- Maude Apatow as Mable
- Iris Apatow as Ingrid
- Aziz Ansari as Randy

Leslie Mann, Adam Sandler and Judd Apatow in Berlin (2009)

- Torsten Voges as Dr. Lars

- Allan Wasserman as Dr. Stevens

Dave Attell, Sarah Silverman, Norm MacDonald, Paul Reiser, Tom Anderson, Charles Fleischer, George Wallace, and Andy Dick made cameo appearances as themselves in the roles of George's fellow comedians.[3] Rapper Eminem,[4] comedian Ray Romano, musician James Taylor,[5] *MADtv* member Nicole Parker,[6] and newcomer Bo Burnham[7] also appeared in small roles. *Undeclared* alum Carla Gallo had a cameo in the film as a character on *Yo Teach!*, the television show within the film that Mark stars in,[8] while Justin Long and Apatow regular Ken Jeong have cameos in the film as characters in movies for which George is famous.[9] Owen Wilson and Elizabeth Banks are featured on posters for fake movies in which George starred.[10] Bryan Batt makes an appearance as George's agent. Musicians Jon Brion, Sebastian Steinberg, and James Gadson appear in the film as members of George's jam band. Comedians Rod Man, Budd Friedman, Monty Hoffman, Mark Schiff, Orny Adams, Al Lubel, and Jerry Minor appear as themselves. Comedienne/producer/writer Carol Leifer appears as herself.

Production

Judd Apatow had expressed his desire to make a stand-up comedian mentor film loosely based on his own early experiences as a struggling performer. He could not come up with an interesting idea since most of his mentors were kind to him. He then thought of making a film about a mentor facing a life crisis, and decided to have his former roommate Adam Sandler play that role. They discussed making the film almost two years prior to production.[11]

Apatow had cast Sandler, Seth Rogen, and Leslie Mann as the three leads in March 2008.[12] Eric Bana, Jonah Hill, and Jason Schwartzman were cast in June 2008 when the title of the film was announced. When asked about the decision to cast Bana, Apatow said that both he and Rogen are fans of his films, Rogen additionally commented they cast him as the husband because he was someone who would be considered an intimidating presence to both Sandler and Rogen.[13] Bana mentioned that he decided to make his character an Australian so he could improvise more.[14]

Academy Award-winning cinematographer Janusz Kamiński handled the cinematography for the film. Apatow had Sandler, Rogen, and Hill, who all played stand-ups in the film, write their own material for routines. Apatow filmed them performing their routines in front of live audiences, using six cameras to capture their performances and audience reactions. Apatow filmed their entire performances, although only five to ten minutes of stand-up footage appear in the film. Hill admitted his performance was not well-received because he has never done stand-up. Additionally, Apatow filmed scenes from Sandler's character's fictional filmography, as well as scenes from Schwartzman's character's fictional television show *Yo Teach!*, for the film to add realism.[15]

Apatow used an old video of Sandler, from when the two were roommates, in which Sandler makes prank phone calls, and features a young Ben Stiller.

Marketing

The first teaser poster for the film was released November 13, 2008. On the day the teaser poster was released, Universal Pictures and MySpace partnered together to create a contest that would allow people to have a part in the film by just writing a comment explaining why. Additionally, Apatow held a stand-up comedy concert event called "A Night of Funny People" at the Orpheum Theater in Los Angeles to film a scene for the movie. The event was open to the general public and featured acts by Adam Sandler, Seth Rogen, Aziz Ansari, Sarah Silverman, David Spade, and Patton Oswalt, with Sandler, Rogen, and Ansari performing as their characters in the film. The first theatrical trailer for the film was released February 20, 2009 on the Internet, with a shortened version first appearing in theaters with *I Love You, Man*.

A website for a fictional television show-within-a-film was created on NBC.com.[16] The sitcom, *Yo Teach!*, "stars" the film's egocentric character Mark Taylor Jackson (Jason Schwartzman), who is a C-list actor portraying a young teacher with a class of failing students, and includes a cameo by internet celebrity Bo Burnham.[17]

A website for Aziz Ansari's character Randy Springs was created, along with a documentary of the character on FunnyOrDie.com. The documentary was directed by Jason Woliner.

Comedy Central aired a special, "Inside Funny People" on July 20, documenting the making of the film and showing clips of the stand-up. The channel also aired "Funny People: Live" on Friday, July 24, which is a live broadcast stand-up of Adam Sandler, Seth Rogen, and Jonah Hill as part of the film's promotion.

Release

Critical reception

Funny People received mixed to positive reviews from the critics and currently holds a 68% "Fresh" rating on Rotten Tomatoes and a 50% "Rotten" rating among Top Critics, based on the consensus that the film "features the requisite humor, as well as considerable emotional depth, resulting in Judd Apatow's most mature film to date."[18] Another review aggregator, Metacritic, gave the film a metascore of 60 out of 100 under the "Mixed or Average Reviews" category, based on 35 reviews.[19]

Jeffrey Wells from *Hollywood Elsewhere* received feedback from sources who had seen a test screening, with one source calling it "really funny, a really sweet movie, a lot of veracity...really a brilliant film", comparing it to the works of James L. Brooks.

Roger Ebert of the *Chicago Sun-Times* awarded the film 3½ stars of four, calling it "a real movie. That means carefully written dialogue and carefully placed supporting performances — and it's about something. It could have easily been a formula film...but George Simmons learns and changes during his ordeal, and we empathize."[20] Peter Travers of *Rolling Stone* also praised the film, writing, "Apatow scores by crafting the film equivalent of a stand-up routine that encompasses the joy, pain, anger, loneliness and aching doubt that go into making an audience laugh."[21] Kyle Smith of the *New York Post* wrote that the film was "one of the most absorbing films of the year."[22]

Michael Phillips of the *Chicago Tribune* gave the film one of its mixed reviews, complaining of the film's two-and-a-half-hour running time: "*Funny People* is...an attempt by Apatow to reconcile the huge success he has become with the up-and-comer he once was. The results run an increasingly exasperating 2½ hours."[23]

Box office

Funny People was commercially released on July 31, 2009 in the United States and Canada. It was distributed to 3,008 theaters, and grossed $8.63 million on its opening day.[1] At the end of its opening weekend, the film had grossed $23.44 million. *Funny People*, which cost an estimated $75 million to produce, made about $71 million worldwide in theatres.[24] In comparison, Apatow's previous directorial effort, *Knocked Up*, cost $33 million to produce and made over $219 million in gross receipts, while Sandler's last three movies had all made over 100 million dollars.[25]

Home media

Funny People was released on DVD and Blu-ray in the USA on November 24, 2009. There is a one-disc "Unrated & Theatrical" cut and a two-disc "Unrated Edition". The Unrated cut of the film runs at 153 minutes, 8 minutes longer than the original theatrical cut. It was released in the United Kingdom on January 18, 2010, again, on DVD and Blu-Ray.[26]

Soundtrack

Funny People: Original Motion Picture Soundtrack	
Soundtrack by Various Artists	
Released	July 28, 2009
Genre	Soundtrack
Label	Concord Records
Professional reviews	
• *PopMatters* ★★★★★★★★★★ Link [27]	

Funny People: Original Motion Picture Soundtrack was released on July 28, 2009.

1. "Great Day" by Paul McCartney (2:08)
2. "Wires" by Coconut Records (2:26)
3. "All the King's Horses" by Robert Plant and the Strange Sensation (4:19)
4. "Carolina In My Mind (Live)" by James Taylor (4:58)
5. "Keep Me In Your Heart" by Warren Zevon (3:27)
6. "Real Love" by Adam Sandler (4:56)
7. "We (Early Take)" by Neil Diamond (4:11)
8. "Jesus, Etc. (Live Summer '08)" by Wilco feat. Andrew Bird (4:01)
9. "George Simmons Soon Will Be Gone" by Adam Sandler (2:15)
10. "I Am Young" by Coconut Records (3:07)
11. "Memory" by Larry Goldings & Maude Apatow (3:53)
12. "Numb As A Statue" by Warren Zevon (4:07)
13. "Photograph" by Ringo Starr (3:58)
14. "Watching the Wheels (Acoustic Demo)" by John Lennon (3:06)

Bonus tracks on iTunes release

1. "Secret O' Life (Live)" by James Taylor (3:45)
2. "Photograph (Live)" by Adam Sandler (2:55)
3. "Everybody Knows This Is Nowhere" by Adam Sandler (4:02)
4. "Nighttiming" by Coconut Records (2:48)

The film also features "Joanna" by Kool & The Gang, "Three Little Birds" by Bob Marley, "Diamond Dave" by The Bird and the Bee, "Man in the Box" by Alice in Chains, "(I've Had) The Time of My Life" by Bill Medley & Jennifer Warnes, "Walk Like an Egyptian" by The Bangles, "In Private" by Paul McCartney, and "Give Me Love (Give Me Peace on Earth)" by George Harrison.

The Blu-ray and 2-Disc DVD also includes Adam Sandler performing The English Beat's "Save It for Later."

Additional songs used in the film's trailers are "We Will Become Silhouettes" by The Postal Service, "My Friend" by Dr. Dog, and "Nothing'severgonnastandinmyway (Again)" by Wilco.

References

[1] "Funny People (2009)" (http://www.boxofficemojo.com/movies/?id=funnypeople.htm). *Box Office Mojo.* . Retrieved 2009-08-30.

[2] Michael Fleming (2008-06-11). "Trio joins Judd Apatow film" (http://www.variety.com/article/VR1117987337.html). *Variety* (Reed Business Information). . Retrieved 2008-10-20.

[3] "Stand-Up Comedian Cameos in Judd Apatow's Funny People" (http://www.slashfilm.com/2008/12/17/stand-up-comedian-cameos-in-judd-apatows-funny-people/). Slashfilm.com. 2008-12-17. . Retrieved 2009-01-31.

[4] "Eminem In New Judd Apatow "Funny People" Movie" (http://www.rapbasement.com/eminem/051509-eminem-reveals-that-he-makes-a-cameo-in-the-new-judd-apatow-movie-funny-people.html). Rap Basement. 2009-05-16. . Retrieved 2009-05-16.

[5] Mark Shanahan and Paysha Rhone (2009-01-08). "Taylors turn to film" (http://www.boston.com/ae/celebrity/articles/2009/01/08/here_comes_the_bride/?page=2). *The Boston Globe* (Globe Newspaper Company). . Retrieved 2009-01-25.

[6] "MADtv's Nicole Parker Joins Wicked as Elphaba Beginning January 16" (http://www.broadwayworld.com/article/MADtvs_Nicole_Parker_Joins_Wicked_as_Elphaba_Beginning_January_16_20010101). Broadwayworld.com. 2009-01-07. . Retrieved 2009-01-31.

[7] From YouTube to Hollywood (http://www.boston.com/ae/celebrity/articles/2009/01/07/from_youtube_to_hollywood/)

[8] "Carla Gallo Exclusive Video Interview" (http://www.collider.com/entertainment/interviews/article.asp?aid=10411&tcid=1). Collider.com. 2009-01-09. . Retrieved 2009-01-31.

[9] "Dr. Kuni Speaks" (http://dvd.ign.com/articles/958/958665p1.html). IGN.com. 2009-03-04. . Retrieved 2009-03-04.

[10] "Judd Apatow Reveals Adam Sandler's 'Funny' Films With Owen Wilson, Elizabeth Banks and More" (http://moviesblog.mtv.com/2009/05/11/judd-apatow-reveals-adam-sandlers-funny-films-with-owen-wilson-elizabeth-banks-and-more/). MTV Movie Blog. 2009-05-11. . Retrieved 2009-05-11.

[11] "Funny People Set Visit: Judd Apatow" (http://www.comingsoon.net/news/interviewsnews.php?id=54255). Comingsoon.net. 2009-04-07. . Retrieved 2009-05-08.

[12] Fleming, Michael (2008-03-09). "Sandler reteams with Apatow" (http://www.variety.com/article/VR1117982103.html?categoryid=13&cs=1). *Variety.* . Retrieved 2009-05-08.

[13] "Eric Bana teaches AFL to Seth Rogan" (http://www.thewest.com.au/aapstory.aspx?StoryName=556045). *The West Australian.* 2009-03-05. . Retrieved 2009-05-08.

[14] "Australians Are Extra Insane: Bana" (http://www.empireonline.com.au/news/story.asp?nid=1000004459). Empire Online. 2009-04-08. . Retrieved 2009-05-08.

[15] "Judd Apatow Wants You To 'Enjoy The Ride' Of 'Funny People' For 2.5 Hours...Then Watch The Super-Long DVD" (http://moviesblog.mtv.com/2009/05/07/judd-apatow-wants-you-to-enjoy-the-ride-of-funny-people-for-25-hoursthen-watch-the-super-long-dvd/). MTV Movie Blog. 2009-05-07. . Retrieved 2009-05-08.

[16] http://www.hitfix.com/blogs/2008-12-6-motion-captured/posts/2009-5-3-the-morning-read-5-29-09

[17] http://newteevee.com/2009/05/29/bo-burnham-gets-schooled-in-yo-teach/

[18] "Funny People" (http://au.rottentomatoes.com/m/funny_people/). Rotten Tomatoes. 2009-08-10. .

[19] People "Funny People" (http://www.metacritic.com/film/titles/funnypeople?q=Funny). Metacritic. 2009-08-10. People.

[20] "Roger Ebert's review" (http://rogerebert.suntimes.com/apps/pbcs.dll/article?AID=/20090729/REVIEWS/907299997). Roger Ebert. 2009-07-30. .

[21] Funny People : Review : Rolling Stone (http://www.rollingstone.com/reviews/movie/25910332/review/29476887/funny_people)

[22] WIENERS & WOODY IN JUDD APATOW'S 'FUNNY PEOPLE' - New York Post (http://www.nypost.com/seven/07312009/entertainment/movies/lol__182161.htm)

[23] 'Funny People' stars Adam Sandler, Seth Rogen, Leslie Mann -- chicagotribune.com (http://movies.nytimes.com/2009/07/31/movies/
     31funny.html?ref=movies)

[24] Boxofficemojo Data (http://boxofficemojo.com/movies/?id=funnypeople.htm)

[25] http://boxofficemojo.com/people/chart/?id=adamsandler.htm

[26] Amazon Home Video details (http://www.amazon.com/dp/B002PLPQME)

[27] http://www.popmatters.com/pm/review/110311-various-artists-music-from-the-motion-picture-funny-people

External links

- Official Site (http://www.funnypeoplemovie.com/)
- *Yahoo Fun* (http://yahoofun.info/)
- *Funny People* (http://www.imdb.com/title/tt1201167/) at the Internet Movie Database
- *Funny People* (http://www.rottentomatoes.com/m/funny_people/) at Rotten Tomatoes
- *Funny People* (http://www.metacritic.com/film/titles/funnypeople) at Metacritic
- *Funny People* (http://www.allmovie.com/work/433971) at Allmovie
- *Funny People* (http://www.boxofficemojo.com/movies/?id=funnypeople.htm) at Box Office Mojo
- Funny People (http://www.myspace.com/funnypeople) on Myspace
- Interview with director/writer Judd Apatow (http://www.avclub.com/articles/judd-apatow,31045/)

Paper Heart

Paper Heart	
Promotional film poster	
Directed by	Nicholas Jasenovec
Produced by	Sandra Murillo Elise Salomon Charlyne Yi
Written by	Nicholas Jasenovec Charlyne Yi
Starring	Charlyne Yi Michael Cera Jake Johnson

Music by	Charlyne Yi Michael Cera
Cinematography	Jay Hunter
Editing by	Ryan Brown
Distributed by	Overture Films
Release date(s)	August 7, 2009
Running time	88 minutes
Country	United States
Language	English
Gross revenue	$1,286,744

Paper Heart is a 2009 American romantic comedy film starring Charlyne Yi and Michael Cera as fictionalized versions of themselves based on their rumored relationship, though Yi has said they never dated and remain friends.

The plot for the film is based on Charlyne Yi's original idea of a documentary, which Nick Jasenovec suggested would be accentuated with a fictional storyline.[1] [2]

Plot

Jake Johnson, Charlyne Yi, and Nick Jasenovec

The film follows Charlyne as she embarks on a quest across America to make a documentary about a subject she does not understand: love. As she and her good friend (and director) Nick search for answers and advice about love, Charlyne talks with friends, strangers, scientists, bikers, romance novelists, and children. They each offer diverse views on modern romance, as well as various answers to the age-old question: does true love really exist?

Shortly after filming begins, Charlyne meets a boy after her own heart: Michael Cera. As their relationship develops on camera, her pursuit to discover the nature of love takes on a fresh new urgency.

Cast

- Charlyne Yi as herself
- Michael Cera as himself
- Jake Johnson as Nicholas Jasenovec

Cameos

- Seth Rogen
- Demetri Martin
- Martin Starr
- Paul Rust
- Paul Scheer
- David Krumholtz

Release

Critical reception

Paper Heart received mixed reviews by critics and currently holds a 58% "Rotten" rating on Rotten Tomatoes.

Box office

Paper Heart received a limited release on August 7, 2009, in the United States and Canada, making $1,286,744.

Soundtrack

Paper Heart: Original Soundtrack	
Soundtrack by Various Artists	
Released	August 4, 2009
Genre	Soundtrack
Length	41:00
Label	Lakeshore
Producer	Alden Penner

The soundtrack of *Paper Heart* was released on August 4, 2009 by Lakeshore Records and contains music composed primarily by Michael Cera and Charlyne Yi. Alden Penner was the producer.

Tracklisting			
No.	Title	Writer(s)	Length
1.	"The Beginning"	Michael Cera, Michael Cassady, Alden Penner, Adam Etinson	2:56
2.	"Hope"	Michael Cera, Charlyne Yi, Alden Penner	1:29
3.	"Mike Modrak"	Michael Cera	1:51
4.	"Now They're Really Getting to Know Each Other"	Michael Cera, Alden Penner	1:29
5.	"Children Are Ridiculous"	Michael Cera, Alden Penner	1:50
6.	"Symphony"	Michael Cera, Charlyne Yi, Alden Penner	1:16
7.	"Don & Sally"	Michael Cera, Mary Forrest, Jamie Wheeler, Alden Penner	1:44
8.	"New York City Theme"	Michael Cera, Alden Penner	0:41
9.	"Magic Perfume"	Charlyne Yi, Matt Davis	2:18
10.	"Charlyne vs Charlyne"	Michael Cera, Jeremy Konner	1:18
11.	"The 11th Arrondissement"	Zach Condon, Perrin Cloutier	2:07
12.	"Sid & Mary Beth"	Michael Cera, Michael Cassady, Alden Penner	2:23
13.	"Moon Waltz"	Michael Cera, Charlyne Yi, Alden Penner	1:06
14.	"Chivalrous Galloping For Thy Love"	Michael Cera, Alden Penner	1:23
15.	"Psychic?"	Michael Cera, Alden Penner	0:51
16.	"Lois & Sully"	Michael Cera, Alden Penner, Dan Ring, Charlyne Yi	1:51
17.	"Learning"	Michael Cera, Alden Penner	2:35

18.	"Flying Away"	Michael Cera	2:00
19.	"Creepy Town"	Michael Cera	0:34
20.	"Sprinkling"	Charlyne Yi	2:00
21.	"Twin Dream Phoenix"	Alden Penner, Aiden Jeffery, Michael Speleit, Nathan Gage, Marie-Claire Saindon, Nicholas Scribner, Ben Borden	3:10
22.	"Girl With The Microphone"	Michael Cera, Charlyne Yi, Mary Forrest, Alden Penner	2:05

References

[1] *Last Call with Carson Daly* episode 1036
[2] *Late Night with Jimmy Fallon* episode 94

External links

- Official website (http://http://www.paperheart-movie.com)
- *Paper Heart* (http://www.imdb.com/title/tt1331064/) at the Internet Movie Database
- *Paper Heart* (http://www.allmovie.com/work/476004) at Allmovie
- *Paper Heart* (http://www.boxofficemojo.com/movies/?id=paperheart.htm) at Box Office Mojo
- *Paper Heart* (http://www.rottentomatoes.com/m/paper_heart/) at Rotten Tomatoes

Family Guy

Family Guy	
The Griffin family. Back: Lois, Peter, Meg, Chris, front: Brian, and Stewie	
Genre	Sitcom Animation Black comedy Blue comedy
Created by	Seth MacFarlane[1]
Developed by	• Seth MacFarlane • David Zuckerman
Voices of	• Seth MacFarlane • Alex Borstein • Seth Green • Mila Kunis • Mike Henry
Theme music composer	Walter Murphy
Composer(s)	• Walter Murphy • Ron Jones
Country of origin	United States
Language(s)	English
No. of seasons	9
No. of episodes	155 (List of episodes)
Production	
Executive producer(s)	• Seth MacFarlane • David A. Goodman • Chris Sheridan • Danny Smith • Mark Hentemann • Steve Callaghan • **Co-executive producers:** • Alec Sulkin • Wellesley Wild • Brian Scully

Producer(s)	• Patrick Meighan • Cherry Chevapravatdumrong • John Viener • Shannon Smith • Kara Vallow • **Consulting producers:** • Tom Devanney • Gary Janetti • Abraham Higginbotham
Editor(s)	• John Walts • Rick Mackenzie • Mike Elias
Running time	20–23 minutes
Production company(s)	• Fuzzy Door Productions • 20th Century Fox Television
Distributor	20th Television
Broadcast	
Original channel	Fox
Picture format	480i (SDTV) (1999–2002, 2005–present) 720p (HDTV) (2010–present)
Original run	**Original series:** • January 31, 1999 – February 14, 2002 **Revived series:** May 1, 2005 – Present
Status	Returning series
Chronology	
Preceded by	Larry and Steve
Related shows	• *American Dad!* • *The Cleveland Show*
External links	
Website [2]	

Family Guy is an American animated television series created by Seth MacFarlane for the Fox Broadcasting Company. The series centers on the Griffins, a dysfunctional family consisting of parents Peter and Lois; their children Meg, Chris, and Stewie; and their anthropomorphic pet dog Brian. The show is set in the fictional city of Quahog, Rhode Island, and bases much of its humor on parodying American pop culture.

The family was conceived by MacFarlane after developing two animated films, *The Life of Larry* and *Larry & Steve*. MacFarlane redesigned the films' protagonist Larry and his dog Steve, and renamed them Peter and Brian, respectively. MacFarlane pitched a 15 minute pilot to Fox which aired on December 20, 1998. After the pilot aired the show was given the green light and started production. Shortly after the third season of *Family Guy* aired in 2001, Fox canceled the series. However, favorable DVD sales and high ratings for syndicated reruns convinced the network to renew the show in 2004.

Family Guy has been nominated for 12 Primetime Emmy Awards and 11 Annie Awards, and has won three of each. It has garnered three Golden Reel Award nominations, winning once. In 2009, it was nominated for an Emmy for

Outstanding Comedy Series, the first time an animated series was nominated for the award since *The Flintstones* in 1961. *Family Guy* has also received criticism, including unfavorable comparisons for its similarities to *The Simpsons*.

Many tie-in media have been released, including *Stewie Griffin: The Untold Story*, a straight-to-DVD special released in 2005; *Family Guy: Live in Vegas*, a soundtrack-DVD combo released in 2005, featuring music from the show as well as original music created by MacFarlane and Walter Murphy; a video game and pinball machine, released in 2006 and 2007, respectively; since 2005, six books published by Harper Adult based on the *Family Guy* universe; and *Laugh It Up, Fuzzball: The Family Guy Trilogy*, a series of parodies of the original *Star Wars* trilogy released in 2010. In 2008, MacFarlane confirmed that the cast was interested in producing a feature film and that he was working on a story for film adaptation. A spin-off series, *The Cleveland Show*, premiered on September 27, 2009, as a part of the "Animation Domination" lineup on Fox. The eighth season of *Family Guy* premiered on the same night.

Origins

MacFarlane initially conceived *Family Guy* in 1995 while studying animation under the Rhode Island School of Design (RISD).[3] During college, he created his thesis film entitled *The Life of Larry*,[3] which was later submitted by his professor at RISD to Hanna-Barbera, which led to MacFarlane being hired by the company.[4] In 1996, MacFarlane created a sequel to *The Life of Larry* entitled *Larry and Steve*, which featured a middle-aged character named Larry and an intellectual dog, Steve; the short was broadcast in 1997 as one of Cartoon Network's *World Premiere Toons*.[3]

Larry (left) and Steve (right) as they appeared in *Larry & Steve* (1997), an animated short directed by Seth MacFarlane. Larry and Steve would form the basis for the *Family Guy* characters of Peter and Brian, respectively.

Executives at Fox saw the *Larry* shorts and contracted MacFarlane to create a series based on the characters entitled *Family Guy*.[5] Fox proposed MacFarlane complete a 15-minute short, and gave him a budget of $50,000.[6] Several aspects of *Family Guy* were inspired by the *Larry shorts*.[7] While working on the series, the characters of Larry and his dog Steve slowly evolved into Peter and Brian.[5] [8] MacFarlane stated that the difference between the first short, *The Life of Larry*, and *Family Guy*, was that "*Life of Larry* was shown primarily in my dorm room and *Family Guy* was shown after the Super Bowl."[7] After the pilot aired the series was green-lighted. MacFarlane drew inspiration from several sitcoms such as *The Simpsons* and *All in the Family*.[9] Premises were drawn from several 1980s Saturday morning cartoons he watched as a child, such as *The Fonz and the Happy Days Gang* and *Rubik, the Amazing Cube*.[10]

The Griffin family first appeared on the pilot MacFarlane pitched to Fox, which aired on the Fox Broadcasting Company on December 20, 1998, which featured a fifteen minute plot.[11] *Family Guy* was originally planned to start out as short movies for the sketch show *MADtv*, but the plan changed because of the budget as the show did not have a large enough budget to make any kind of animation. MacFarlane noted that he then wanted to pitch it to Fox as he thought it was the place to create a prime-time animation show.[9] *Family Guy* was also originally pitched to Fox in the same year as *King of the Hill*, but the show was not bought until years later when *King of the Hill* became successful.[9] Eventually, on May 15, 1998, Fox ordered 13 episodes of *Family Guy* to air in midseason.[12]

Production

Executive producers

Show creator Seth MacFarlane has served as an executive producer during the show's entire history, and also functions as a creative consultant. The first executive producers that worked on the show were David Zuckerman,[13] Lolee Aries, David Pritchard, and Mike Wolf.[14] *Family Guy* has had many executive producers in its history, including Daniel Palladino, Kara Vallow, and Danny Smith. David A. Goodman joined the show as a co-executive producer in season three, and eventually became an executive producer.[15] Alex Borstein, the voice of Lois, has also worked as both an executive and supervising producer, for the fourth and fifth seasons.[16] A more involved position on the show is the show runner, who acts as head writer and manages the show's production for an entire season.[17]

Writing

Matt Weitzman (left) is a former staff writer and Mike Barker is a former producer and writer of the show. Both would later go on to create *American Dad* with Seth MacFarlane.

The first team of writers, assembled for the show consisted of Chris Sheridan,[18] Danny Smith, Gary Janetti, Ricky Blitt, Neil Goldman, Garrett Donovan, Matt Weitzman and Mike Barker.[19] The normal writing process of *Family Guy* generally starts with 14 writers that take turns to write the different scripts, when the scripts are finished it is turned in to the rest of the writers for them to read. These scripts generally include cutaway gags. If there are not enough cutaway sequences, writers are sent to create them each with different versions then they are pitched and what MacFarlane and the rest of the staff writers deem funny is included in the episode. MacFarlane has explained that normally it takes 10-months to produce an episode because the show uses a hand-drawn style. For this reason the show rarely comments on current events.[20] The first writers that came to work for the show had never written for an animation show and most of them had come from live-action sitcoms.[9]

In interviews and on the DVD commentary of season one, MacFarlane explained that he is a fan of 1930s and 1940s radio programs, particularly the radio thriller anthology "Suspense", which led him to give early episodes ominous titles pertaining to death and murder, like "Death Has a Shadow" and "Mind Over Murder". MacFarlane later explained that the team dropped the naming convention after individual episodes became hard to identify, and the novelty wore off.[21] For the first few months of production, the writers shared one office lent to them by the *King of the Hill* production crew.[21]

Credited with 14 episodes Steve Callaghan is the most prolific writer on *Family Guy* staff. Many of the writers that have left the show have gone to create or produce various successful series. Neil Goldman and Garrett Donovan, would later go co-write thirteen episodes for the NBC sitcom *Scrubs* during their 8-year run on the show, starting as co-producers on the show and working their way up to executive producers.[22] Mike Barker and Matt Weitzman would later go on to create *American Dad* along with MacFarlane.[23] [24]

During the 2007–2008 Writers Guild of America strike, official production of the show halted for most of December 2007 and various periods afterward. Fox continued producing episodes without creator Seth MacFarlane's final approval, which he termed "a colossal dick move" in an interview with *Variety*. Though MacFarlane refused to work on the show, his contract under Fox required him to contribute to any episodes it would subsequently produce.[25] Production officially resumed after the end of the strike, with regularly airing episodes recommencing on February 17, 2008.[26]

Voice cast

Seth MacFarlane voices four of the show's main characters: Peter Griffin, Brian Griffin, Stewie Griffin and Glen Quagmire.[27] MacFarlane chose to voice these characters himself, believing it would be easier to portray the voices he already envisioned than for someone else to attempt it.[10] MacFarlane drew inspiration for the voice of Peter from a security guard he overheard talking while attending the Rhode Island School of Design.[28] Stewie's voice was based on the voice of English actor Rex Harrison,[29] especially his performance in the 1964 musical drama film *My Fair Lady*.[30] MacFarlane uses his regular speaking voice when playing Brian.[10] MacFarlane also provides the voices for various other recurring and one-time only characters, most prominently those of the Griffins' neighbor Glenn Quagmire, news anchor Tom Tucker, and Lois' father, Carter Pewterschmidt.[31] Alex Borstein voices Lois Griffin, Asian correspondent Tricia Takanawa, Loretta Brown, and Lois' mother Barbara Pewterschmidt.[32] Borstein was asked to provide a voice for the pilot while she was working on *MADtv*. She had not met MacFarlane or seen any of his artwork and said it was "really sight unseen".[33] At the time, Borstein performed in a stage show in Los Angeles, in which she played a redheaded mother whose voice she had based on one of her cousins.[32] [33] Seth Green primarily plays Chris Griffin and Neil Goldman.[31] [34] Green stated that he did an impression of the "Buffalo Bill" character from the thriller film *The Silence of the Lambs* during his audition.[35] [36] Mila Kunis and Lacey Chabert have both provided the voice of Meg Griffin.[31] Chabert left the series because of time conflicts with her role on *Party of Five* and schoolwork. Kunis auditioned for the role and then she was called back by MacFarlane, instructing her to speak slower, and then told her to come back another time and enunciate more. Once she claimed that she had it under control, MacFarlane hired her.[37] Mike Henry voices both Cleveland Brown and Herbert, as well as some minor recurring characters like Bruce the performance artist and The Greased-up Deaf Guy.[38] Henry met MacFarlane at the Rhode Island School of Design, and kept in touch with him after they graduated.[39] A few years later, MacFarlane contacted him about being part of the show; he agreed and came on as both a writer and voice actor.[39] During the show's first four seasons, he was credited as a guest star, but beginning with season five's "Prick Up Your Ears", he has been credited as a main cast member.[39]

Main cast members				
Seth MacFarlane	Alex Borstein	Seth Green	Mila Kunis	Mike Henry
Peter Griffin, Stewie Griffin, Brian Griffin, Glenn Quagmire, Tom Tucker, Carter Pewterschmidt, others	Lois Griffin, Loretta Brown, Barbara Pewterschmidt, Tricia Takanawa, others	Chris Griffin, Neil Goldman, others	Meg Griffin	Cleveland Brown, Herbert, Greased Up Deaf Guy, Bruce the performance artist, others

Other recurring cast members include: Patrick Warburton as Joe Swanson;[40] Adam West as the eponymous Mayor Adam West;[41] Jennifer Tilly as Bonnie Swanson;[42] John G. Brennan as Mort Goldman and Horace the bartender; Carlos Alazraqui as Jonathan Weed;[43] [44] Adam Carolla and Norm MacDonald as Death;[45] Lori Alan as Diane Simmons;[46] and Phil LaMarr as Ollie Williams and the judge.[47] Fellow cartoonist Butch Hartman has made guest voice appearances in many episodes as various characters.[48] Also, writer Danny Smith voices various recurring characters such as Ernie the Giant Chicken.[49]

Episodes will quite often feature guest voices from a wide range of professions, including actors, athletes, authors, bands, musicians, and scientists. Many guest voices starred as themselves. Leslie Uggams was the first to appear as herself in the fourth episode of the second season episode "Mind Over Murder".[50] The episode "Not All Dogs Go to

Heaven" guest starred the entire cast of *Star Trek: The Next Generation*, which includes Patrick Stewart, Jonathan Frakes, Brent Spiner, LeVar Burton, Gates McFadden, Michael Dorn, Wil Wheaton, Marina Sirtis and even Denise Crosby (season 1 as Tasha Yar), playing themselves; this is the episode with the most guest stars of the seventh season.[51] [52]

Early history and cancellation

Family Guy officially premiered after Fox's broadcast of Super Bowl XXXIII on January 31, 1999 with "Death Has a Shadow". The show debuted to 22 million viewers and controversy regarding the show's adult content.[53] The show returned on April 11, 1999 with "I Never Met the Dead Man" to decent ratings in Fox's 8:30 p.m. slot on Sunday, nestled between *The Simpsons* and *The X-Files*.[12] At the end of its first season run the show came in at #33 in the Nielsen Ratings with 12.8 million households tuning in.[54] The show launched its second season in a new time slot, Thursday at 9 p.m., on September 23, 1999. *Family Guy* was pitted against NBC's *Frasier*, and the series' ratings declined sharply.[12] Fox removed *Family Guy* from the network's permanent schedule, and began airing episodes irregularly. The show returned on March 7, 2000 instead at 8:30pm on Tuesdays, but is constantly beat in ratings by new breakout hit *Who Wants to Be a Millionaire*, coming in at #114 in the Nielsen Ratings with 6.320 million households tuning in.[55] Fox publicly announced that the show had been canceled in 2000, at the end of the second season.[56] However, following a last-minute reprieve, Fox announced on July 24, 2000 intentions to order 13 additional episodes of *Family Guy* to form a third season.[53]

The show returned November 8, 2001, once again in a tough time slot: Thursday nights at 8:00 p.m. ET. This slot brought it into competition with *Survivor* and *Friends*. (This situation was later referenced in *Stewie Griffin: The Untold Story*).[57] During its second and third-season runs, Fox frequently moved the show around different days and time slots with little or no notice and, consequently, the show's ratings suffered.[58] Upon Fox's annual unveiling of its 2002 fall line-up on May 15, 2002, *Family Guy* was absent.[12] Fox announced that the show had been officially canceled shortly thereafter.[59]

Cult success and revival

Fox attempted to sell the rights for reruns of the show, but it was difficult to find networks that were interested; Cartoon Network eventually bought the rights, "[...] basically for free", according to the president of 20th Century Fox Television Production.[60] *Family Guy* premiered in reruns on Adult Swim on April 20, 2003, and immediately became the block's top-rated programming, dominating late night viewing in its time period vs. cable and broadcast competition and boosting viewership by 239 percent.[12] [61] The complete first and second seasons were released on DVD the same week as the show premiered on Adult Swim, and the show became a cult phenomenon, selling 400,000 copies within one month.[12] Sales of the DVD set reached 2.2 million copies,[62] becoming the best-selling television DVD of 2003[63] and the second highest-selling television DVD ever, behind the first season of Comedy Central's *Chappelle's Show*.[64] The third season DVD release also sold more than a million copies.[61] The show's popularity in both DVD sales and reruns rekindled Fox's interest in it,[65] and, on May 20, 2004, Fox ordered 35 new episodes of *Family Guy*, marking the first revival of a television show based on DVD sales.[64] [66]

"North by North Quahog" was the first episode to be broadcast after the show's cancellation, and it premiered May 1, 2005. It was written by MacFarlane and directed by Peter Shin.[67] MacFarlane believed the show's three year hiatus was beneficial because animated shows do not normally have hiatuses, and towards the end of their seasons, "... you see a lot more sex jokes and (bodily function) jokes and signs of a fatigued staff that their brains are just fried".[68] With "North by North Quahog", the writing staff tried to keep the show "... exactly as it was" before its cancellation, and did not "... have the desire to make it any slicker" than it already was.[68] The episode was watched by 11.85 million viewers,[69] the show's highest ratings since the airing of the first season episode "Brian: Portrait of a Dog".[70]

Lawsuits

In March 2007, comedian Carol Burnett filed a $6 million lawsuit against 20th Century Fox, claiming that it was a trademark infringement for her charwoman cleaning character to be portrayed on the show without her permission, and that Fox violated her publicity rights.[71] [72] [73] On June 4, 2007, United States District Judge Dean Pregerson rejected the lawsuit, stating that the parody was protected under the First Amendment, citing *Hustler Magazine v. Falwell* as a precedent.[74]

On October 3, 2007, Bourne Co. Music Publishers filed a lawsuit accusing the show of infringing its copyright on the song "When You Wish upon a Star", through a parody song entitled "I Need a Jew" appearing in the episode "When You Wish Upon a Weinstein". Bourne Co., the sole United States copyright owner of the song, alleged the parody pairs a "thinly veiled" copy of their music with antisemitic lyrics. Named in the suit were Twentieth Century Fox Film Corp., Fox Broadcasting Co., Cartoon Network, MacFarlane, and Murphy; the suit sought to stop the program's distribution and unspecified damages.[75] Because "I Need a Jew" uses the copyrighted melody of "When You Wish Upon a Star", without commenting on that song, Bourne argued that it was not a First Amendment-protected parody per the ruling in *Campbell v. Acuff-Rose Music, Inc.*[76] [77] On March 16, 2009, United States District Judge Deborah Batts held that *Family Guy* did not infringe on Bourne's copyright when it transformed the song for comical use in an episode.[78]

In December 2007, *Family Guy* was again accused of copyright infringement when actor Art Metrano filed a lawsuit regarding a scene in *Stewie Griffin: The Untold Story*, in which Jesus performs Metrano's signature "magic" act involving absurd "faux" magical hand gestures while humming the distinctive tune "Fine and Dandy".[79] 20th Century Fox, MacFarlane, Callaghan, and Borstein were all named in the suit.[80]

Characters

The show revolves around the adventures of the family of Peter Griffin, a bumbling, but well-intentioned, blue-collar worker. Peter is an Irish American Catholic with a prominent Rhode Island and Eastern Massachusetts accent.[81] He is married to Lois, a stay-at-home mother and piano teacher, who has a distinct New England accent from being a member of the Pewterschmidt family of wealthy socialites.[82] Peter and Lois have three children: Meg, their teenage daughter, who is awkward and does not fit in at school, and is constantly ridiculed and ignored by family; Chris, their teenage son, who is overweight, unintelligent and, in many respects, a younger version of his father; and Stewie, their diabolical infant son of ambiguous sexual orientation who has adult mannerisms, and speaks fluently with stereotypical archvillain phrases.[83] Living with the family is Brian, the family dog, who is highly anthropomorphized, drinks martinis and engages in human conversation, though he is still considered a pet in many respects.[84]

Many recurring characters appear alongside the Griffin family. These include the family's neighbors: sex-crazed airline-pilot bachelor Glenn Quagmire, Cleveland Brown and his wife Loretta Brown, paraplegic police officer Joe Swanson, his wife Bonnie and their baby daughter Susie (it should be noted that Bonnie is pregnant with Susie from the show's beginning until the 7th episode of the 7th season); paranoid Jewish pharmacist Mort Goldman, his wife Muriel and their geeky and annoying son Neil; and elderly ephebophile Herbert. TV news anchors Tom Tucker and Diane Simmons, Asian reporter Tricia Takanawa, and *Blaccu-Weather* meteorologist Ollie Williams also make frequent appearances. Quahog mayor, Mayor Adam West, is in various episodes.

Setting

The skyline of Providence, as viewed from the northwest looking southeast, from left-to-right: One Financial Center, 50 Kennedy Plaza, and the Bank of America Tower.

The skyline's animated *Family Guy* counterpart.

The primary setting of *Family Guy* is Quahog, Rhode Island (pronounced /ˈkoʊhɒg/). MacFarlane resided in Providence during his time as a student at Rhode Island School of Design, and the show, as a consequence, contains distinct Rhode Island landmarks similar to real-world locations.[85] [86] MacFarlane often borrows the names of Rhode Island locations and icons such as Pawtucket and Buddy Cianci for use in the show. MacFarlane, in an interview with local WNAC Fox 64 News, stated that the town is modeled after Cranston, Rhode Island.[87]

Hallmarks

"Road to" episodes

The "Road to" episodes are a series of hallmark, travel episodes.[88] [89] [90] They are a parody of the seven *Road to...* comedy films, starring actors Bing Crosby and Bob Hope and actress Dorothy Lamour, which were released from 1940 until 1962.[89] These episodes usually involve Stewie and Brian in some foreign, supernatural, or science fiction location not familiar to the show's normal location in Quahog, Rhode Island. The first, entitled "Road to Rhode Island", aired on May 30, 2000, as a part of the second season. The episodes are known for featuring elaborate musical numbers, similar to the original films.[91] Episodes contain several trademarks, including a special version of the opening sequence, custom musical cues and musical numbers, and parodies of science fiction and fantasy films.[92]

The original idea for the "Road to" episodes came from MacFarlane as he is a fan of the original films of Crosby, Hope and Lamour. The first episode was directed by Dan Povenmire, who would go on to direct the rest of the "Road to" episodes until the episode "Road to Rupert", as he left the show to create *Phineas and Ferb*.[93] [94] As a result, series regular Greg Colton took over Povenmire's role as director of the "Road to" episodes.[95]

Humor

Family Guy generally uses the filmmaking method of cutaways, which occur in the majority of *Family Guy* episodes.[96] Emphasis is often placed on gags which make reference to current events and/or modern cultural icons.

Early episodes based much of their comedy on Stewie's "super villain" antics, such as his constant plans for total world domination, his evil experiments, plans and inventions to get rid of things he dislikes; and his constant tries to commit matricide. As the series progressed the writers and MacFarlane agreed that his personality and the jokes were starting to feel dated. So the writers started writing him with a different personality.[97] *Family Guy* also often includes self-referential humor. The most common form is jokes about Fox Broadcasting or the situations and occasions where the characters break the fourth wall by addressing the audience. For example in "North by North Quahog", the first episode that aired after the show's revival, included Peter telling the family that they had been canceled because Fox had to make room in their schedule for shows like, *Dark Angel, Titus, Undeclared, Action, That '80s Show, Wonderfalls, Fastlane, Andy Richter Controls the Universe, Skin, Girls Club, Cracking Up, The Pitts, Firefly, Get Real, Freakylinks, Wanda at Large, Costello, The Lone Gunmen, A Minute with Stan Hooper, Normal, Ohio, Pasadena, Harsh Realm, Keen Eddie, The $treet, The American Embassy, Cedric the Entertainer Presents, The Tick, Luis* and *Greg the Bunny*. Lois asks whether there is any hope, to which Peter replies that if all these shows are canceled they might have a chance; the shows were indeed canceled during *Family Guy*'s hiatus.[98] [99] [100]

The show uses catchphrases, and most of the primary and secondary characters have them. Notable expressions include Glenn Quagmire's "Giggity giggity goo", Peter's "Freakin' sweet" and Joe Swanson's "Bring it on!".[97] The use of many of these catchphrases declined in later seasons. The episode "Big Man on Hippocampus" mocks catchphrase-based humor: as Peter, who has forgotten everything about his life, is introduced to Meg, he exclaims, "D'oh!", to which Lois replies, "No, Peter, that's not your catchphrase."[101]

Reception, legacy and achievements

Success

Family Guy has received many positive reviews from critics. Catherine Seipp of the National Review Online described it as a "nasty but extremely funny" cartoon.[102] Caryn James of *The New York Times*, called it a show with an "outrageously satirical family" and "includes plenty of comic possibilities and parodies."[103] *The Sydney Morning Herald* named *Family Guy* the "Show of the Week" on April 21, 2009, hailing it a "pop culture-heavy masterpiece".[104] Frazier Moore from *The Seattle Times* called it an "endless craving for humor about bodily emissions". He also thought it was "breathtakingly smart" and said a "blend of the ingenious with the raw helps account for its much broader appeal". He finished up summarizing it as "rude, crude and deliciously wrong".[105] The series has also attracted many celebrities, including Emily Blunt, who has stated that *Family Guy* is her favorite series, and has expressed strong interest in becoming a guest star on the show.[106] The New Yorker's Nancy Franklin said that *Family Guy* is becoming one of the best animated shows there is, commenting on its ribaldry and popularity, even saying that it was better than *The Simpsons*, in terms of quality.[107] The show has also become a hit on Hulu, becoming the second highest viewed show after *Saturday Night Live*.[108] IGN called *Family Guy* a great show, and also commented that it has gotten better since it's revival. They also stated that they cannot imagine another half hour sitcom that provides as much laughs as *Family Guy*.[109] Empire praised the show and its writers for being able to create real hilarious moments with unlikely matieral. They also commented that one of the reasons they love the show is because nothing is sacred and it can make jokes and gags of almost everything.[110] Robin Pierson of *The TV Critic* praised the series as "a different kind of animated comedy which clearly sets out to do jokes which other cartoons can't do."[111] Family Guy has also proven popular in the United Kingdom regualrly obtaining between 700,000 and 1 million viewers for re-runs on BBC Three.[112]

Many celebrities have admitted that they are fans of the show. Robert Downey, Jr. telephoned the show production staff and asked if he could produce or assist in an episode creation, as his son is a fan of the show, so the producers came up with the character for Downey.[113] Lauren Conrad met MacFarlane while recording a *Laguna Beach* clip for the episode "Prick Up Your Ears", (season 5, 2006).[114] [115] She has watched *Family Guy* for years and considers Stewie her favorite character.[114] Commenting on his appearance in the episode "Big Man on Hippocampus", (season 8, 2010), actor Dwayne Johnson stated that he was a "big fan" of *Family Guy*,[116] having quickly befriended MacFarlane after he had in a minor role in Johnson's 2010 film *Tooth Fairy*.[116]

Awards

Family Guy and its cast were nominated for thirteen Emmy Awards, with four wins. MacFarlane won the Outstanding Voice-Over Performance award for his performance as Stewie,[117] Murphy and MacFarlane won the Outstanding Music and Lyrics award for the song "You Got a Lot to See" from the episode "Brian Wallows and Peter's Swallows",[117] Steven Fonti won the Outstanding Individual Achievement in Animation award for his storyboard work in the episode "No Chris Left Behind",[118] and Greg Colton won the Outstanding Individual Achievement in Animation award for his storyboard work in the episode "Road to the Multiverse".[119] The show was nominated for eleven Annies, and won three times, twice in 2006 and once in 2008.[120] [121] [122] In 2009, it was nominated for an Emmy for Outstanding Comedy Series, becoming the first animated program to be nominated in this category since *The Flintstones* in 1961.[123] though *The Simpsons* were almost nominated in the year 1993, but that changed since Emmy voters were hesitant to pit cartoons against live action programs.[124] [125] *Family Guy* has also been nominated and has won various awards from different award ceremony including the Teen Choice Awards and the People's Choice Awards.[126] [127] [128] In the 1000th issue of *Entertainment Weekly*, Brian Griffin was selected as the dog for "The Perfect TV Family".[129] *Wizard Magazine* rated Stewie the 95th greatest villain of all time.[130] British newspaper *The Times* rated *Family Guy* as the 45th best American show in 2009.[131] *Family Guy* ranked in two of IGN's list: It ranked number seven in the "Top 100 Animated Series" and it ranked number six in the "Top 25 Primetime Animated Series of All Time".[109] [132] *Empire* named it the twelfth greatest TV show of all time.[110] Furthermore, viewers of the UK television channel Channel 4 have voted *Family Guy* at number 5 of one of there polls: 2005's 100 Greatest Cartoons.[133] Brian was awarded the 2009 Stoner of the Year award by *High Times* due to this episode, marking the first time an animated character received the honor.[134]

Criticism and controversy

Family Guy has received a negative treatment from critics[135] and watchdog groups[136] due to its profanity, animated nudity, and violence. The FCC has received multiple petitions requesting that the show be blocked from broadcasting on indecency grounds.[137] [138]

Parental advocacy[139] and religious[140] organizations have voiced disapproval over the show's mockery of religious subjects. Similarly, *Family Guy* has drawn criticism from charities and public figures for its perceived offensiveness when handling sensitive issues, such as HIV/AIDS[141] and Down syndrome.[142] The show has also been derided by critics[58] and other cartoonists[143] [144] for the overuse of cut-away gags, pop culture references and similarities to other shows. Several episodes of *The Simpsons* and *South Park* have poked fun at *Family Guy*, highlighting the reliance on interchangeable gags as well as similarities with the former show. However, both MacFarlane and *Simpsons* creator Matt Groening have said that there is no serious feud between them and the rivalry of their shows is good-natured.[145] Professional cartoonists have criticized the show as well, such as *Ren & Stimpy* creator John Kricfalusi[143] and *South Park* creators Trey Parker and Matt Stone.[144]

Other media

Live performances

As promotion for the show, and to, as Newman described, "expand interest in the show beyond its diehard fans",[146] Fox organized four *Family Guy Live!* performances, which featured cast members reading old episodes aloud. In addition, the cast performed musical numbers from the *Family Guy: Live in Vegas* comedy album.[146] The stage shows were an extension of a performance by the cast during the 2004 Montreal Comedy Festival.[146] The *Family Guy Live!* performances, which took place in Los Angeles and New York, sold out and were attended by around 1,200 people each.[147]

In 2009 a special televised performance show aired titled *Family Guy Presents Seth & Alex's Almost Live Comedy Show* in which voice actors Alex Borstein and creator Seth MacFarlane performed songs from the show and a parody of Lady Gaga's worldwide hit "Poker Face" in voice of Marlee Matlin who appeared on the stage as a guest during the performance. Some new animated gags also appeared in the show.[148]

Film

On July 22, 2007, in an interview with *The Hollywood Reporter*, MacFarlane announced that he may start working on a feature film, although "nothing's official".[149] Then in *TV Week* on July 18, 2008, MacFarlane confirmed plans to produce a theatrically released *Family Guy* feature film sometime "within the next year".[150] He came up with an idea for the story, "something that you could not do on the show, which [to him] is the only reason to do a movie". He later went to say he imagines the film to be "an old-style musical with dialogue" similar to *The Sound of Music*, saying that he would "really be trying to capture, musically, that feel".[151]

Spin-off

MacFarlane co-created alongside Mike Henry and Richard Appel the *Family Guy* spin-off *The Cleveland Show*, which they began discussing in 2007 and which premiered September 27, 2009.[152] [153] Appel and Henry serve as the show's executive producers and showrunners, handling the day-to-day operations, with limited involvement from McFarlane.[154] Henry and Appel conceived the show as "more of a family show, a sweeter show" than *Family Guy*.[155] The show, which was picked up to air a first season consisting of 22 episodes,[156] was picked up by Fox for a second season, consisting of 13 episodes, bringing the total number to 35 episodes. The announcement was made on May 3, 2009 before the first season even premiered.[157] It was extended to a full second season.[158] Appel signed a new three-year, seven figure deal with Fox to continue serving as showrunner on *The Cleveland Show* in 2010. Fox chairman Gary Newman commented: "What is special about him is his incredible leadership ability."[159] The show would follow the *Family Guy* character Cleveland Brown, who is voiced by Henry, as he leaves the town of Quahog and moves with his son to start his own adventure.[152]

Video games

The *Family Guy Video Game!* is a 2006 action game released by 2K Games and developed by High Voltage Software. The game received very mixed reviews, averaging 50% favorable reviews for the PlayStation 2 version,[160] 51% for the PlayStation Portable version,[161] and 53% for the Xbox version,[162] according to review aggregator Metacritic. The game received praise for its humor,[163] but was criticized for its short playtime[164] and "uninteresting gameplay".[165] On November 2, 2009, IGN journalist Ryan Langley reported the production of a *Family Guy*-based party game for the Xbox 360, PlayStation 3, and Wii. He cited the LinkedIn profiles of former HB Studios developer Chris Kolmatycki and Invisible Entertainment co-owner Ron Doucet, which stated that the individuals had worked on the game.[166] MacFarlane recorded exclusive material of Peter's voice and other *Family Guy* characters for a 2007 pinball machine of the show by Stern Pinball.[167]

Merchandise

As of 2009, six books have been released about the *Family Guy* universe, all published by HarperCollins since 2005.[168] The first book based on *Family Guy*, *Family Guy: Stewie's Guide to World Domination* (ISBN 978-0-06-077321-2) by Steve Callahan, was released in April 26, 2005. Written in the style of a graphic novel, the plot follows Stewie's plans on ruling the world, despite him only being a child.[169] Other books include *Family Guy: It Takes a Village Idiot, and I Married One* (ISBN 978-0-7528-7593-4), which covers the entire events of the episode "It Takes a Village Idiot, and I Married One";[170] and *Family Guy and Philosophy: A Cure for the Petarded* (ISBN 978-1-4051-6316-3), a collection of 17 essays exploring the connections between the series and historical philosophers.[171]

Family Guy has been commercially successful in the home market.[172] The show was the first to be resurrected because of high DVD sales.[173] [174] The first volume, covering the show's first two seasons, sold a total of 1.67 million units, topping TV DVD sales in 2003, while the second volume sold another million unit.[173] [175] Both the volume six and seven DVDs debuted fifth in United States DVD sales;[176] [177] volume seven was the highest television DVD, selling 171,000 units by June 21, 2009.[177] *Family Guy Presents Blue Harvest*, the DVD featuring the *Star Wars* special "Blue Harvest", was released on January 15, 2008, and premiered at the top of United States DVD sales.[178] The DVD was the first *Family Guy* DVD to include a digital copy for download on the iPod.[178] In 2004, the first series of *Family Guy* toy figurines was released by Mezco Toyz; each member of the Griffin family had their own toy, with the exception of Stewie, of whom two different figures were made.[179] Over the course of two years, four more series of toy figures have been released, with various forms of Peter.[180] In 2008, the character Peter appeared in advertisements for Subway Restaurants, promoting the restaurant's massive feast sandwich.[181] [182]

References

[1] Erickson, Hal. "Family Guy Animated TV Series > Overview" (http://allmovie.com/work/family-guy-animated-tv-series-288489). *allmovie*. All Media Guide. . Retrieved June 4, 2009.

[2] http://www.fox.com/familyguy/

[3] Lenburg, Jeff (2006). *Who's who in animated cartoons: an international guide to film & television's award-winning and legendary animators* (Illustrated ed.). New York: Applause Theatre & Cinema Books. p. 221. ISBN 978-1-55783-671-7.

[4] Lenburg, Jeff. ""Family Guy" Seth MacFarlane to speak at Class Day: Creator and executive producer of 'Family Guy' will headline undergraduate celebration" (http://www.news.harvard.edu/gazette/2006/05.11/03-classday.html). *Harvard Gazette*. . Retrieved December 21, 2007.

[5] Bartlett, James (March 12, 2007). "Seth MacFarlane – he's the "Family Guy"" (http://greatreporter.com/mambo/content/view/1383/11/). *The Great Reporter*. Presswire Limited. . Retrieved December 31, 2007.

[6] Andreeva, Nellie (May 5, 2008). ""Family Guy" creator seals megadeal" (http://www.reuters.com/article/entertainmentNews/ idUSN0435504220080505). *The Hollywood Reporter*. . Retrieved May 31, 2008.

[7] Callaghan, p. 16

[8] Strike, Joe. "Cartoon Network Pilots Screened by ASIFA East at NYC's School of Visual Arts" (http://www.awn.com/news/events/ cartoon-network-pilots-screened-asifa-east-nycs-school-visual-arts). Animation World Network. . Retrieved November 18, 2009.

[9] "Interview with Seth MacFarlane" (http://movies.ign.com/articles/429/429628p10.html). *IGN*. News Corporation. . Retrieved December 9, 2009.

[10] Cruz, Gilbert (September 26, 2008). "Family Guy's Seth MacFarlane" (http://www.time.com/time/arts/article/0,8599,1844711,00. html). *Time* (Time Warner). . Retrieved August 28, 2009.

[11] MacFarlane, Seth. *Original Pitch By Seth MacFarlane. Family Guy: Volume 2*. [DVD]. 20th Century Fox.

[12] Tim Stack (April 18, 2005). "A Brief History of the *Family Guy*" (http://www.ew.com/ew/article/0,,1049746,00.html). *Entertainment Weekly*. . Retrieved January 17, 2011.

[13] Zuckerman, David. *Commentary for the episode "Death Has a Shadow". Family Guy: Volume 1*. [DVD]. 20th Century Fox.

[14] "Family Guy: Death Has a Shadow" (http://www.film.com/tv/family-guy-season-1-1998/episode-1-death-has-a-shadow/14854396). *Film.com*. RealNetworks. . Retrieved September 27, 2009.

[15] Steve, Callaghan (2005). *Family Guy: The Official Episode Guide, Seasons 1–3*. New York City: HarperCollins. p. 158. ISBN 9780060833053.

[16] "Alex Borstein from Family Guy" (http://www.film.com/celebrities/alex-borstein/14744926). *Film.com*. RealNetworks. . Retrieved August 24, 2009.

[17] Cagle, Daryl. "The David Silverman Interview" (http://web.archive.org/web/20051130094202/http://cagle.msnbc.com/hogan/ interviews/silverman.asp). *MSNBC*. NBC Universal. Archived from the original (http://cagle.msnbc.com/hogan/interviews/silverman. asp) on November 30, 2005. . Retrieved November 30, 2005.

[18] "Family Guy — I Never Met the Dead Man Cast and Crew" (http://tv.yahoo.com/episode/1544/castcrew). *Yahoo! TV*. Yahoo! Inc.. . Retrieved May 7, 2010.

[19] "Family Guy: Chitty Chitty Death Bang" (http://www.film.com/tv/family-guy-season-1-1998/episode-3-chitty-chitty-death-bang/ 14647430). *Film.com*. RealNetworks. . Retrieved December 10, 2010.

[20] "'American Dad' and 'Family Guy' Creator Seth MacFarlane Is Animated About Work and Play" (http://television.aol.com/ tv-celebrity-interviews/seth-macfarlane). *The TV Tattler*. AOL Inc.. August 5, 2007. . Retrieved August 8, 2010.

[21] "William S. Paley TV Fest: Family Guy" (http://tv.ign.com/articles/696/696615p1.html). *IGN*. News Corporation. . Retrieved October 3, 2009.

[22] "the futon's guide to who's in and who's out" (http://www.thefutoncritic.com/guide.aspx?id=in_and_out). The Futon Critic. . Retrieved September 6, 2009.

[23] Stanley, Alexandria (February 4, 2005) "Dad Is a C.I.A. Operative, the Kids Have a Weird Pet" (http://www.nytimes.com/2005/02/04/ arts/04tvwk.html?_r=1&fta=y&oref=slogin). *The New York Times* (The New York Times Company). . Retrieved December 22, 2007.

[24] Goyette, Jay (February 4, 2005). "*Family Guy*s Seth MacFarlane's Speech Rescheduled" (http://www.uvm.edu/theview/article. php?id=1561). *The View* (University of Vermont). . Retrieved December 22, 2007.

[25] Adalian, Josef (November 13, 2007). "Fox to air new *Guy* Sunday; MacFarlane hopes network changes plans" (http://www.variety.com/article/VR1117975944.html?categoryid=2821). *Variety* (Reed Business Information). . Retrieved November 13, 2007.

[26] "Stewie Is On The Lam On "Family Guy" Sunday, May 18, On Fox" (http://www.thefutoncritic.com/listings.aspx?id=20080424fox18). *The Futon Critic*. . Retrieved September 24, 2009.

[27] Graham, Jefferson. "Cartoonist MacFarlane funny guy of Fox's 'Family' Subversive voice of series is his". *USA Today*: p. E7.

[28] Smith, Andy. "A Real Family Reunion" (http://www.projo.com/tv/content/projo_20050430_macfarlan.1d6c9b8.html). *Providence Journal TV*. . Retrieved September 25, 2009.

[29] Dean, John. "Seth MacFarlane's $2 Billion Family Guy Empire" (http://www.foxbusiness.com/portal/site/fb/menuitem. 5b2f8f9bb693bd972f08aa8738d48a0c/?vgnextoid=8e1a04e62a94d110VgnVCM10000086c1a8c0RCRD&redirected=true). *Fox Business* (News Corporation). . Retrieved August 23, 2009.

[30] Franklin, Nancy (January 16, 2006). "American Idiots". *The New Yorker*.

[31] "Family Guy Cast and Details" (http://www.tvguide.com/tvshows/family-guy/cast/100148). *TV Guide*. . Retrieved August 24, 2009.

[32] Miller, Kirk. "Q&A: Alex Borstein" (http://newyork.metromix.com/events/article/q-and-a-alex/782347/content). *Metromix*. . Retrieved August 28, 2009.

[33] "Alex Borstein (Lois) Laughs at the Once-Dead *Family Guy*'s Longevity" (http://www.tvguide.com/news/Alex-Borstein-Lois-36289. aspx). *TV Guide*. . Retrieved August 23, 2009.

[34] Graham, Jefferson (April 9, 1999). "Seth Green fits right in with new *Family*". *USA Today* (Gannett Company).

[35] "Fans help 'Family Guy' return to Fox". *Observer-Reporter*: p. E5.

[36] Green, Seth. (September 27, 2005). *Stewie Griffin: The Untold Story: Audio Commentary*. [DVD].

[37] "Family Guy − Casting Mila Kunis" (http://www.youtube.com/watch?v=-OS3zGMcbrM). *The Paley Center for Media*. . Retrieved April 5, 2010.

[38] excerpt "Behind the scenes of 'Family Guy' *** Character 'voice' star to speak" (http://nl.newsbank.com/nl-search/we/Archives?p_product=AD&p_theme=ad&p_action=search&p_maxdocs=200&p_topdoc=1&p_text_direct-0=11597438A790F3B8&p_field_direct-0=document_id&p_perpage=10&p_sort=YMD_date:D&s_trackval=GooglePM). *The Advocate*. excerpt. Retrieved April 5, 2010.

[39] "Mike Henry of "Family Guy" talks voices, gags and instinct" (http://www.campustimes.org/mike-henry-of-family-guy-talks-voices-gags-and-instinct-1.743902). *Campus Times*. . Retrieved September 14, 2009.

[40] "Patrick Warburton:Credits" (http://www.tvguide.com/celebrities/patrick-warburton/credits/169214). *TV Guide*. . Retrieved October 8, 2009.

[41] "Adam West Credits" (http://www.tvguide.com/celebrities/adam-west/credits/138187). *TV Guide*. . Retrieved October 8, 2009.

[42] "Jennifer Tilly:Credits" (http://www.tvguide.com/celebrities/jennifer-tilly/credits/156658). *TV Guide*. . Retrieved October 8, 2009.

[43] "Mr. Saturday Knight". Steve Callaghan (writer). *Family Guy*. Fox Broadcasting Company. September 5, 2001. No. 9, season 3.

[44] "Carlos Alazraqui: Credits" (http://www.tvguide.com/celebrities/carlos-alazraqui/credits/189632). *TV Guide*. . Retrieved September 8, 2009.

[45] "Adam Carolla:Credits" (http://www.tvguide.com/celebrities/adam-carolla/credits/195025). *TV Guide*. . Retrieved October 13, 2009.

[46] "Lori Alan:Credits" (http://www.tvguide.com/celebrities/lori-alan/credits/216395). *TV Guide*. . Retrieved October 8, 2009.

[47] "Phil LeMarr:Credits" (http://www.tvguide.com/celebrities/phil-lamarr/credits/212839). *TV Guide*. . Retrieved October 8, 2009.

[48] "Butch Hartman:Credits" (http://www.tvguide.com/celebrities/butch-hartman/credits/195927). *TV Guide*. . Retrieved November 28, 2009.

[49] "Danny Smith:Credits" (http://www.tvguide.com/celebrities/danny-smith/credits/209563). *TV Guide*. . Retrieved October 8, 2009.

[50] "Family Guy: Mind Over Murder" (http://www.film.com/tv/family-guy/season-1-1998/episode-4-mind-over-murder/14854397). *Film.com*. RealNetworks. . Retrieved December 8, 2009.

[51] "'Trek' cast to reunite on 'Family Guy'" (http://www.thrfeed.com/2009/02/star-trek-next-generation-family-guy.html). *The Hollywood Reporter*. e5 Global Media. . Retrieved February 27, 2009.

[52] French, Dan. "'Trek' cast to reunite on 'Family Guy'" (http://www.digitalspy.co.uk/ustv/a147923/trek-cast-to-reunite-on-family-guy. html). *Digital Spy*. Hachette Filipacchi Ltd. . Retrieved February 16, 2009.

[53] Levin, Gary (November 18, 2003). "*Family Guy* may return" (http://www.usatoday.com/life/television/news/2003-11-18-family-guy_x. htm). *USAtoday*. . Retrieved December 6, 2009.

[54] "'1998-99 Ratings" (http://web.archive.org/web/20091029011819/http://geocities.com/Hollywood/4616/ew0604.html). *geocities*. March 24, 2004. Archived from the original (http://www.geocities.com/Hollywood/4616/ew0604.html) on 2009-10-29. . Retrieved September 16, 2010.

[55] "'1999-2000 Ratings" (http://fbibler.chez.com/tvstats/recent_data/1999-00.html). *fbibler*. March 24, 2004. . Retrieved September 16, 2010.

[56] Gilbert, Matthew. "*Family Guy* Returns, Just As Funny As Ever" (http://nl.newsbank.com/nl-search/we/Archives?p_product=BG&p_theme=bg&p_action=search&p_maxdocs=200&p_topdoc=1&p_text_direct-0=109DC26AF6A16776&p_field_direct-0=document_id&p_perpage=10&p_sort=YMD_date:D&s_trackval=GooglePM). *Boston.com*. . Retrieved August 23, 2009.

[57] Idato, Michael (January 23, 2006). "Family Guy Presents Stewie Griffin: The Untold Story" (http://www.theage.com.au/news/dvd-reviews/family-guy-presents-stewie-griffin-the-untold-story/2006/01/23/1137864848861.html). *The Age* (Melbourne: Fairfax Media). . Retrieved September 3, 2009.

[58] VanDerWerff, Todd. ""To Surveil With Love"/"Brotherly Love"/"Brian & Stewie"" (http://www.avclub.com/articles/ to-surveil-with-lovebrotherly-lovebrian-stewie,40698/). *The A.V. Club*. The Onion, Inc.. . Retrieved February 10, 2010.

[59] McKinley, Jesse (May 2, 2005). "Canceled and Resurrected, on the Air and Onstage" (http://query.nytimes.com/gst/fullpage. html?res=9A03E3D61E31F931A35756C0A9639C8B63). *New York Times* (New York Times Company). . Retrieved August 9, 2009.

[60] Gordon, Devin (April 4, 2005). "Family Reunion". *Newsweek*: p. 50.

[61] Levin, Gary (March 24, 2004). "'Family Guy' un-canceled, thanks to DVD sales success" (http://www.usatoday.com/life/television/ news/2004-03-24-family-guy_x.htm). *USA Today*. . Retrieved July 3, 2009.

[62] Poniewozik, James; McDowell, Jeanne (April 19, 2004). "It's Not TV. It's TV on DVD" (http://www.time.com/time/magazine/article/ 0,9171,993880,00.html?promoid=googlep). *Time*. . Retrieved July 2, 2009.

[63] Kipnis, Jill (February 7, 2004). "Successful "Guy"" (http://books.google.com/books?id=XREEAAAAMBAJ&pg=PA44&dq=Family+ Guy+cancelled). *Billboard*: p. 44. . Retrieved July 3, 2009.

[64] Goodale, Gloria (April 22, 2005). "Cult fans bring 'The Family Guy' back to TV" (http://www.csmonitor.com/2005/0422/p12s01-altv. html). *The Christian Science Monitor*: p. 12. . Retrieved July 2, 2009.

[65] Louie, Rebecca (April 28, 2005). "The 'Family' can't be killed. Fox thought it was out, but we pulled it back on. The 'Guy' who wouldn't die" (http://www.nydailynews.com/archives/entertainment/2005/04/28/2005-04-28_the__family_can_t_be_killed_.html). *New York Daily News*. . Retrieved July 3, 2009.

[66] Levin, Gary (November 18, 2003). "'Family Guy' may return" (http://www.usatoday.com/life/television/news/ 2003-11-18-family-guy_x.htm). *USA Today*. . Retrieved July 3, 2009.

[67] Lowry, Brian (April 28, 2005). "Family Guy" (http://www.variety.com/review/VE1117926915.html?categoryid=32&cs=1). *Variety*. . Retrieved June 23, 2009.

[68] Williamson, Kevin (May 1, 2005). "'Family Guy' returns" (http://jam.canoe.ca/Television/TV_Shows/F/Family_Guy/2005/05/01/ pf-1020572.html). *Calgary Sun* & Jam!. . Retrieved August 19, 2009.

[69] Aurthur, Kate (May 3, 2005). "A Sweeping Weekend" (http://query.nytimes.com/gst/fullpage. html?res=9507EED71F31F930A35756C0A9639C8B63). *The New York Times*. . Retrieved July 2, 2009.

[70] Levin, Gary (May 3, 2005). "'Guy' fares better than 'Dad'" (http://www.usatoday.com/life/television/news/ 2005-05-03-nielsen-analysis_x.htm). *USA Today*. . Retrieved July 3, 2009.

[71] "Carol Burnett sues over *Family Guy* cartoon cleaning woman" (http://www.sfgate.com/cgi-bin/article.cgi?f=/n/a/2007/03/16/ entertainment/e120846D80.DTL). *Associated Press* (San Francisco Chronicle). March 16, 2007. . Retrieved September 23, 2009.

[72] "Comedian Burnett sues Family Guy" (http://news.bbc.co.uk/2/hi/entertainment/6462525.stm). *BBC News*. March 17, 2007. . Retrieved June 14, 2009.

[73] "Carol Burnett v. "Family Guy"" (http://www.thesmokinggun.com/archive/years/2007/0316072carolburnett1.html). *The Smoking Gun*. Courtroom Television Network. March 16, 2007. . Retrieved October 19, 2007.

[74] "Carol Burnett suit thrown out". *Los Angeles Times*. June 6, 2007.

[75] *Bourne Co., vs. Twentieth Century Fox Film Corporation, Fox Broadcasting Company, Twentieth Century Fox Television, Inc., Twentieth Century Fox Home Entertainement, Inc., Fuzzy Door Productions, Inc., The Cartoon Network, Inc., Seth MacFarlane, Walter Murphy*, (http:/ /www.schwimmerlegal.com/family guy complaint.pdf) (United States District Court, Southern District of New York October 3, 2007).

[76] Hilden, Julie (October 31, 2007). ""The Family Guy" Once Again Tests Parody's Limits: The Copyright Suit Challenging the Show's Use of "When You Wish Upon a Star"" (http://writ.news.findlaw.com/hilden/20071031.html). *FindLaw's Writ*. FindLaw. . Retrieved September 28, 2007.

[77] "News Corp. Wins Suit Dismissal Over 'Family Guy' Song (Update1)" (http://www.bloomberg.com/apps/news?pid=conewsstory& refer=conews&tkr=DJ:US&sid=aQveqoR6.Pew). *bloomberg*. . Retrieved May 8, 2010.

[78] Kearney, Christine (March 16, 2009). ""Family Guy" wins court battle over song" (http://www.reuters.com/article/newsOne/ idUSTRE52F6W620090316). *Reuters*. . Retrieved May 8, 2009.

[79] "Magician sues over cartoon Jesus" (http://www.chortle.co.uk/news/2007/12/06/6128/magician_sues_over_cartoon_jesus). *Cortle*. . Retrieved September 25, 2009.

[80] *Arthur Metrano, vs. Twentieth Century Fox Film Corporation, Seth MacFarlane, Steve Callaghan and Alex Borstein*, (http://www.aolcdn. com/tmz_documents/1206_metrano_fox_wm.pdf) (United States District Court, Central District of California December 5, 2007).

[81] "Cavalcade Of Cartoons, No Joke: Animated Shows Make Up A Third Of The Midseason Replacements For Axed Fall Premieres". *The Charlotte Observer*.

[82] Hines, Michael. "*Family* funny business". *Chicago Tribune*. Tribune Company.

[83] James, Caryn (January 29, 1999). "TV Weekend; Where Matricide Is a Family Value" (http://query.nytimes.com/gst/fullpage. html?res=9402E1DD1E39F93AA15752C0A96F958260). *New York Times* (New York Times Company). . Retrieved October 3, 2008.

[84] Graham, Jefferson. "Fox revisits *Family Guy*". *USA Today* (Gannett Company).

[85] Epstein, Daniel Robert. "Interview with Seth MacFarlane, creator of The Family Guy" (http://www.ugo.com/channels/filmTv/features/ familyguy/scthmacfarlane.asp). *UGO Networks*. . Retrieved April 8, 2008.

[86] Bartlett, James. "Seth MacFarlane – he's the "Family Guy"" (http://greatreporter.com/mambo/content/view/1383/11/). *Greatreporter.com*. . Retrieved June 9, 2008.

[87] "Family Guy writer at Bryant". *The Providence Journal*.

[88] Phelps, Ben (October 16, 2009). "Relying on stereotypes, 'Family Guy' sticks to its formula, 'Cleveland' shows a softer side" (http://www. tuftsdaily.com/relying-on-stereotypes-family-guy-sticks-to-its-formula-cleveland-shows-a-softer-side-1.2001650#4). *Tufts Daily*. Tufts University. . Retrieved August 6, 2010. "The show kicked off its eighth season with another entry in the now-classic "Road to …" series, which allows for many different sight gags and opportunities for a wide range of humor."

[89] Love, Brett (January 29, 2007). "Family Guy: Road to Rupert" (http://www.tvsquad.com/2007/01/29/family-guy-road-to-rupert/). *TV Squad*. America On Line. . Retrieved August 6, 2010. "The FG team went back to familiar territory this week, bringing us another "Road to..." episode."

[90] Haque, Ahsan. "Family Guy: Stewie and Brian's Greatest Adventures" (http://tv.ign.com/articles/105/1057773p2.html). *IGN*. News Corporation. . Retrieved September 4, 2010.

[91] Iverson, Dan; Scott Lowe. "The Cleveland Show Casting Couch" (http://stars.ign.com/articles/890/890465p5.html). *IGN*. News Corporation. . Retrieved August 23, 2010.

[92] Iverson, Dan (January 29, 2007). "Family Guy: "Road to Rupert" Review" (http://tv.ign.com/articles/759/759248p1.html). *IGN*. News Corporation. . Retrieved September 1, 2010.

[93] Bond, Paul. (June 7, 2009). "Q&A: Dan Povenmire" (http://74.125.93.132/search?q=cache:h-TlYnF0OCMJ:www.hollywoodreporter. com/hr/content_display/news/e3i0bc78baf8235f8b4159fd786ff9f8736+Emmy+nominee+Dan+Povenmire&cd=1&hl=en&ct=clnk& gl=us&client=firefox-a). *The Hollywood Reporter*. e5 Global Media. Archived from the original (http://www.hollywoodreporter.com/hr/ content_display/news/e3i0bc78baf8235f8b4159fd786ff9f8736) on November 24, 2009. .

[94] "Family Guy: Road to Europe" (http://www.film.com/tv/family-guy/season-3-2001/episode-20-road-to-europe/14647450). *Film.com*. RealNetworks. . Retrieved October 21, 2009.

[95] "Family Guy: Road to Germany" (http://www.film.com/tv/family-guy/season-8-2008/episode-3-road-to-germany/23570232). *Film.com*. RealNetworks. . Retrieved August 24, 2010.

[96] "*Family Guy*'s Seth MacFarlane interviewed!" (http://www.fhm.com/reviews/tv/ seth-macfarlane--exclusive-interview-with-the-family-guy-guy-20090624). *FHM*. June 24, 2009. . Retrieved September 24, 2009.

[97] Haque, Ahsan. "Top 25 Family Guy Characters" (http://tv.ign.com/articles/987/987014p8.html). *IGN*. New Corporation. . Retrieved May 25, 2009.

[98] Bianculli, David (April 28, 2005). "'Dad' Joins MacFarlane's 'Family'" (http://www.nydailynews.com/archives/entertainment/2005/04/ 28/2005-04-28__dad__joins_macfarlane_s__fa.html). *New York Daily News*. . Retrieved September 19, 2009.

[99] "Back in the Fold". *Pittsburgh Post-Gazette*: p. W37. April 28, 2005.

[100] Rohan, Virginia (May 1, 2005). "An amazing comeback cartoon — Why Fox resurrected Family Guy". *The Record* (Bergen County, New Jersey).

[101] Jordan, Julie. "Tiffani Thiessen Is Expecting a Baby" (http://www.people.com/people/article/0,,20318518,00.html). *People Magazine*. Time Inc.. . Retrieved September 4, 2010.

[102] "Return of the Family Guy" (http://www.nationalreview.com/seipp/seipp200502040749.asp). *National Review*. . Retrieved October 3, 2009.

[103] James, Caryn (September 13, 1998). "The New Season/Television: Critic's Choice; A Little Dysfunctional Family Fun" (http://www. nytimes.com/1998/09/13/arts/the-new-season-television-critic-s-choice-a-little-dysfunctional-family-fun.html). *The New York Times* (The New York Times Comapny). . Retrieved October 3, 2009.

[104] "Show of the Week: Family Guy" (http://www.smh.com.au/news/entertainment/tv--radio/tv-reviews/show-of-the-week-family-guy/ 2009/04/20/1240079595389.html). *The Sydney Morning Herald* (Fairfax Media). April 21, 2009. . Retrieved October 3, 2009.

[105] Moore, Frazier (July 4, 2008). "Return of the Family Guy" (http://seattletimes.nwsource.com/html/television/ 2008032607_tvfamilyguy04.html). *The Seattle Times* (The Seayyle Times Company). . Retrieved October 3, 2009.

[106] "Emily Blunt wants to star in Family Guy" (http://www.nation.com.pk/pakistan-news-newspaper-daily-english-online/Entertainment/ 12-Jun-2009/Emily-Blunt-wants-to-star-in-Family-Guy). *The Nation*. June 12, 2009. . Retrieved December 11, 2009.

[107] "American Idiots" (http://www.newyorker.com/archive/2006/01/16/060116crte_television). *The New Yorker* (Condé Nast Publications). January 6, 2006. . Retrieved December 11, 2009.

[108] TVbythenumbers.com "Hulu Movers & Shakers: 2009 Recap" (http://tvbythenumbers.com/2009/12/31/ hulu-movers-shakers-2009-recap/37371). TV by the Numbers. TVbythenumbers.com. Retrieved August 25, 2010.

[109] "Top 100 Animated Series-7, Family Guy" (http://tv.ign.com/top-100-animated-tv-series/7.html). *IGN*. News Corporation. October 14, 2009. . Retrieved August 23, 2010.

[110] "The 50 Greatest TV Shows of All Time–12–Family Guy" (http://www.empireonline.com/50greatesttv/default.asp?tv=12). *Empire*. 2008. . Retrieved August 26, 2010.

[111] Pierson, Robin (August 7, 2009). "Episode 1: Death Has A Shadow" (http://thetvcritic.org/death-has-a-shadow/). *The TV Critic*. . Retrieved August 23, 2010.

[112] http://www.barb.co.uk/report/weeklyTopProgrammesOverview?

[113] Sheridan, Chris. (2005). *Family Guy season 4 DVD commentary for the episode "The Fat Guy Strangler"*. [DVD]. 20th Century Fox.

[114] Radish, Christina (April 21, 2009). "Lauren Conrad interview about Family Guy" (http://www.iesb.net/index. php?option=com_content&view=article&id=6754:family-guy-interview-with-lauren-conrad&catid=41:news&Itemid=71). Iseb.net. . Retrieved November 9, 2009.

[115] Chevapravatdumrong, Cherry. (2006). *Family Guy season 5 DVD commentary for the episode "Prick Up Your Ears"*. [DVD]. 20th Century Fox.

[116] "Interview: Dwayne Johnson for Tooth Fairy" (http://screencrave.com/2010-01-20/interview-dwayne-johnson-for-tooth-fairy/). *ScreenCrave*. January 20, 2010. . Retrieved March 16, 2010.

[117] McLean, Thomas (June 1, 2007). "Seth MacFarlane: *Family Guy, American Dad!*" (http://www.variety.com/awardcentral_article/VR1117966166.html?nav=eproducer07). *Variety*. . Retrieved December 21, 2007.

[118] "Academy of Television Arts & Sciences Announces Emmy Award Winners in Costumes for a Variety or Music Program and Individual Achievement in Animation" (http://www.emmys.tv/2009/academy-television-arts-sciences-announces-emmyÂ®-award-winners-costumes-variety-or-music-progra). Academy of Television Arts & Sciences. August 21, 2007. . Retrieved June 19, 2010.

[119] "2010 Creative Arts Emmy Winners Press Release" (http://www.emmys.com/sites/emmys.com/files/CRTV2010winners_pressrel.pdf). Academy of Motion Picture Arts and Sciences. August 22, 2010. . Retrieved August 22, 2010.

[120] "Legacy: 34th Annual Annie Award Nominees and Winners" (http://www.annieawards.org/34thwinners.html). Annie Awards. . Retrieved October 27, 2009.

[121] "Legacy: 35th Annual Annie Award Nominees and Winners" (http://annieawards.org/35thwinners.html). Annie Awards. . Retrieved October 27, 2009.

[122] "Annie Awards: For Your Consideration" (http://annieawards.org/foryourconsideration.html). Annie Awards. . Retrieved December 5, 2009.

[123] Collins, Scott (July 17, 2009). "Family Guy breaks the funny bone barrier with Emmy nod" (http://articles.latimes.com/2009/jul/17/entertainment/et-emmy-family17). *Los Angeles Times* (Tribune Company). . Retrieved August 24, 2009.

[124] Holloway, Diane (February 2, 1993). "`Simpsons' get Emmy 's respect - Academy lets series drop cartoon status to compete as sitcom". Austin American-Statesman. p. B4.

[125] Jean, Al. (2004). *The Simpsons season 4 DVD commentary for the episode "Mr. Plow"*. [DVD]. 20th Century Fox.

[126] Associated Press (February 6, 1992). "Roberts, Costner among nominees for 18th People's Choice Awards". The Pantagraph.

[127] "People's Choice Awards Past Winners: 2006" (http://web.archive.org/web/20071113104708/http://www.pcavote.com/pca/history.jsp?year=2006). CBS. Archived from the original (http://www.pcavote.com/pca/history.jsp?year=2006) on November 13, 2007. . Retrieved November 14, 2007.

[128] "Teen Choice Awards Official Website" (http://web.archive.org/web/20071011001654/http://www.fox.com/teenchoice/winners/). Fox.com. Archived from the original (http://www.fox.com/teenchoice/winners/) on October 11, 2007. . Retrieved October 23, 2007.

[129] "TV: Breaking Down the List". Entertainment Weekly (Time Warner) (#999/1000): 56. June 27, 2008 & July 4, 2008.

[130] "The 100 Greatest Villains of All Time". *Wizard* (Wizard Entertainment) (177): 86. July 2006.

[131] Bettridge, Daniel (April 15, 2009). "The 50 best US television shows" (http://entertainment.timesonline.co.uk/tol/arts_and_entertainment/tv_and_radio/article6061203.ece). *The Times* (London: News Corporation). . Retrieved October 2, 2009.

[132] "Top 25 Primetime Animated Series of All Time 10-6" (http://tv.ign.com/articles/736/736051p4.html). *IGN*. News Corporation. . Retrieved August 23, 2010.

[133] "100 Greatest Cartoons" (http://www.channel4.com/entertainment/tv/microsites/G/greatest/cartoons/results.html). Channel 4.com. . Retrieved October 8, 2009.

[134] Hager, Steven; Lewin, Natasha (December 31, 2009). "The 2009 HIGH TIMES Stony Awards" (http://hightimes.com/entertainment/ht_admin/6089). *High Times*. . Retrieved February 9, 2010.

[135] Tucker, Ken (September 4, 1999). "Family Guy" (http://www.ew.com/ew/article/0,,273010,00.html). *Entertainment Weekly*. . Retrieved February 28, 2009.

[136] "Top 10 Best and Worst Shows on Primetime Network TV 2005–2006" (http://www.parentstv.org/ptc/publications/reports/top10bestandworst/2006/main.asp). *ParentsTV.org*. Parents Television Council. . Retrieved December 21, 2006.

[137] "Content examples from NCIS, Family Guy, and The Vibe Awards." (http://www.parentstv.org/ptc/action/sweeps/content.htm). *ParentsTV.org*. Parents Television Council. . Retrieved 2007-05-20.

[138] Shields, Todd (2004-12-06). "Activists Dominate Content Complaints" (http://web.archive.org/web/20041214055118/http://www.mediaweek.com/mediaweek/headlines/article_display.jsp?vnu_content_id=1000731656). *ediaweek.com*. Archived from the original (http://mediaweek.com/mediaweek/headlines/article_display.jsp?vnu_content_id=1000731656) on 2004-12-14. .

[139] Learmonth, Michael. PTC unhappy with TV's religious stereotypes (http://www.variety.com/article/VR1117955772.html?categoryid=14&cs=1). *Variety*: December 14, 2006. Cited the PTC's 2006 *Faith in a Box* report covering treatment of religion on entertainment television.

[140] Kerby, Carl. The trouble with TV (http://www.answersingenesis.org/us/newsletters/0107lead.asp). Answers in Genesis: January 2007

[141] Adams, Bob (2005-08-22). ""Family Guy" has fun with AIDS" (http://web.archive.org/web/20050923175341/http://advocate.com/exclusive_detail_ektid19925.asp). *Advocate.com*. PlanetOut Inc.. Archived from the original (http://www.advocate.com/exclusive_detail_ektid19925.asp) on 2005-09-23. . Retrieved 2006-12-12.

[142] "Sarah Palin Responds To "Family Guy"" (http://www.huffingtonpost.com/2010/02/16/sarah-palin-responds-to-f_n_464939.html). *Huffington Post*. . Retrieved 2010-02-17.

[143] Amid Amidi (August 31, 2004). "The John Kricfalusi Interview, Part 2" (http://www.cartoonbrew.com/old-brew/the-john-kricfalusi-interview-part-2). *Cartoon Brew*. Cartoon Brew LLC.. Archived from on August 31, 2004. . Retrieved March 26, 2007.

[144] "Trey Parker and Matt Stone" (http://exclaim.ca/articles/questionaire.aspx?csid1=70). Exclaim!. June 2005. . Retrieved March 26, 2007.

[145] Nathan Rabin (April 26, 2006). "Interview: Matt Groening" (http://www.avclub.com/content/node/47771). *The A.V. Club*. Onion Inc.. . Retrieved December 12, 2006.

[146] Adalian, Josef (March 10, 2005). "Family Guy Center Stage". *Variety*: p. 1.

[147] "'Family Guy' Returns to FOX" (http://www.foxnews.com/story/0,2933,155143,00.html). Fox News. April 30, 2005. . Retrieved July 3, 2009.

[148] Family Guy Presents Seth & Alex's Almost Live Comedy Show': Almost pretty funny (http://watching-tv.ew.com/2009/11/08/seth-macfarlane-comedy-show)

[149] Szalai, Georg (July 23, 2007). ""Family Guy" movie possible, MacFarlane says" (http://www.reuters.com/article/televisionNews/idUSN2230656720070724). *Reuters*. . Retrieved August 31, 2009.

[150] "TCA Video: *Family Guy* Spoilers; Movie Plans" (http://www.tvweek.com/news/2008/07/tca_video_family_guy_spoilers.php). *TV Week*. . Retrieved August 23, 2009.

[151] Dean, Josh. "Seth MacFarlane's $2 Billion Family Guy Empire" (http://www.fastcompany.com/magazine/130/family-values.html?page=0,0). *FastCompany.com*. . Retrieved October 21, 2008.

[152] "FOX Announces Fall Premiere Dates For The 2009-2010 Season" (http://www.thefutoncritic.com/news.aspx?id=20090615fox01). *The Futon Critic*. June 15, 2009. . Retrieved April 3, 2010.

[153] "Fox Primetime - The Cleveland Show - Fact Sheet" (http://www.foxflash.com/div.php/main/page?aID=1z2z2z252z1z2). *Fox Flash*. . Retrieved April 3, 2010.

[154] Itzkoff, Dave (November 30, 2008). "Fox seeks a new hit, this time in Cleveland - Seth MacFarlane gives sneak preview of 2009's Family Guy spinoff". *The Toronto Star*: p. E12.

[155] Idato, Michael (December 17, 2009). "A sweeter family guy - comedy". *The Age*: p. 15.

[156] Lynette Rice (November 10, 2008). "Fox orders full season of 'Family Guy' spin-off" (http://hollywoodinsider.ew.com/2008/11/the-family-guy.html). *Entertainment Weekly*. . Retrieved February 14, 2010.

[157] Hughes, Jason (March 4, 2009). "The Cleveland Show renewed before it begins" (http://www.tvsquad.com/2009/05/04/the-cleveland-show-renewed-before-it-begins/). *TV Squad*. . Retrieved February 14, 2010.

[158] Fernandez, Maria Elena (October 14, 2009). "Fox orders a full second season of 'The Cleveland Show'" (http://latimesblogs.latimes.com/showtracker/2009/10/fox-orders-a-full-second-season-of-the-cleveland-show.html). *Los Angeles Times*. . Retrieved April 3, 2010.

[159] Andreeva, Nellie (February 8, 2010). "Rich Appel signs new 20th TV deal" (http://www.hollywoodreporter.com/hr/content_display/television/news/e3ib96053a9e47796d7b788123c972316d5). *The Hollywood Reporter*. . Retrieved April 3, 2010.

[160] "Family Guy (ps2) reviews" (http://www.metacritic.com/games/platforms/ps2/familyguy). *Metacritic*. . Retrieved August 29, 2009.

[161] "Family Guy (psp) reviews" (http://www.metacritic.com/games/platforms/psp/familyguy). *Metacritic*. . Retrieved August 29, 2009.

[162] "Family Guy (xbx) reviews" (http://www.metacritic.com/games/platforms/xbx/familyguy). *Metacritic*. . Retrieved August 23, 2009.

[163] Kennedy, Sam (October 23, 2006). "Family Guy Review" (http://www.1up.com/do/reviewPage?cId=3154624). *1UP.com*. . Retrieved August 29, 2009.

[164] Dutka, Ben (December 21, 2006). "Family Guy Review". *PSX Extreme*.

[165] Navarro, Alex (October 24, 2006). "Family Guy Review for Xbox" (http://www.gamespot.com/xbox/adventure/familyguy/review.html). *GameSpot*. . Retrieved August 23, 2009.

[166] Langley, Ryan (November 2, 2009). "Family Guy Party Game in Development" (http://xbox360.ign.com/articles/104/1041328p1.html). IGN. . Retrieved April 20, 2010.

[167] Finley, Adam (February 3, 2007). "Family Guy pinball is freakin' sweet" (http://www.tvsquad.com/2007/02/03/family-guy-pinball-is-freakin-sweet/#). TV Squad. . Retrieved October 19, 2009.

[168] "Search results: Family Guy" (http://www.harpercollins.com/search/index.aspx?kw=family+guy). *HarperCollins*. . Retrieved August 23, 2009.

[169] "Family Guy: Stewie's Guide to World Domination by Steve Callahan" (http://www.harpercollins.com/books/9780060773212/Family_Guy_Stewies_Guide_to_World_Domination/index.aspx). *HarperCollins*. . Retrieved August 23, 2009.

[170] "Family Guy: It Takes a Village Idiot, and I Married One" (http://www.harpercollins.com/books/9780061143328/Family_Guy_It_takes_a_Village_Idiot_and_I_Married_One/index.aspx). *HarperCollins*. . Retrieved December 26, 2008.

[171] "Philosophy Professor Jeremy Wisnewski Publishes Book on *Family Guy*" (http://www.hartwick.edu/x21175.xml). *Hartwick College*. September 18, 2007. . Retrieved August 23, 2009.

[172] Collins, Cott (November 13, 2005). "Some Television Reruns Hit Their Prime on DVD". *Los Angeles Times*: p. A1.

[173] Levin, Gary (March 24, 2004). "*Family Guy* un-canceled, thanks to DVD sales success" (http://www.usatoday.com/life/television/news/2004-03-24-family-guy_x.htm). *USA Today*. . Retrieved August 24, 2009.

[174] Levin, Gary (March 25, 2004). "*Family Guy* un-canceled, thanks to DVD sales success; Cartoon returning after 2-year hiatus". *USA Today*: p. D3.

[175] Poniewozik, James (April 11, 2004). "It's Not TV. It's TV on DVD" (http://www.time.com/time/magazine/article/0,9171,1101040419-610063,00.html). *Time*. . Retrieved August 29, 2009.

[176] "Top DVD Sales for the 11/15/2008 issue" (http://www.reuters.com/article/boxOfficeCharts/idUSN0738957420081107). *Reuters*. November 7, 2008. . Retrieved August 31, 2009.

[177] "US DVD Sales Chart for Week Ending Jun 21, 2009" (http://www.the-numbers.com/dvd/charts/weekly/2009/20090621.php). *The Numbers*. June 21, 2009. . Retrieved August 4, 2009.

[178] Arnold, Thomas K. (January 23, 2009). "Force is with "Family Guy" DVD" (http://www.reuters.com/article/televisionNews/idUSN2317366320080124). *Reuters*. . Retrieved August 31, 2009.

[179] Clodfelter, Tim (November 11, 2004). "Here's the Offbeat Stuff that true geeks are made of". *Winston-Salem Journal*: p. 33.

[180] Szadkowski, Joseph (June 3, 2006). "Undead monster doomed to wander the high seas". *The Washington Times*.

[181] Steinberg, Brian (December 30, 2007). "The year in advertising" (http://www.boston.com/business/globe/articles/2007/12/30/the_year_in_advertising/?page=2). *The Boston Globe*. . Retrieved October 19, 2009.

[182] "Subway – it's for the fat-loving guy, too". *The News Tribune*. November 30, 2007.

External links

- Official website (http://http://www.fox.com/familyguy/)
- *Family Guy* (http://www.imdb.com/title/tt0182576/) at the Internet Movie Database
- *Family Guy* (http://www.tv.com/show/348/summary.html) at TV.com
- *Family Guy* (http://tv.yahoo.com/show/30361/) at Yahoo! TV

Homer the Whopper

The Simpsons episode	
"Homer the Whopper"	
Promotional image featuring Homer as Everyman and Lyle McCarthy.	
Episode no.	442
Prod. code	LABF13
Orig. airdate	September 27, 2009[1]
Show runner(s)	Al Jean
Written by	Seth Rogen Evan Goldberg
Directed by	Lance Kramer
Chalkboard	"The class hamster isn't just sleeping."
Couch gag	The Simpsons arrive at a subway station, where the subway doors open to reveal their living room.
Guest star(s)	Seth Rogen as Lyle McCarthy Matt Groening as himself Kevin Michael Richardson as the security guard

"**Homer the Whopper**" is the season premiere of *The Simpsons'* twenty-first season. It originally aired on the Fox network in the United States on September 27, 2009.[1] In the episode, Comic Book Guy creates a new superhero called Everyman who takes powers from other superheroes. Homer is cast as the lead in the film adaptation. To get Homer into shape, the movie studio hires a celebrity fitness trainer, Lyle McCarthy, to help him. Homer gets into great shape and is really excited, but when McCarthy leaves to train another client, he starts over-eating again and ultimately this leads to the film's failure.

The episode was written by Seth Rogen and Evan Goldberg, who are "obsessed" fans of the show,[2] and directed by Lance Kramer. "Homer the Whopper" was intended to be a commentary on how Hollywood treats superhero films. Rogen also guest stars in the episode as the character Lyle McCarthy, making him the second guest star to both write an episode and appear in it; Ricky Gervais was the first. "Homer the Whopper" has received mixed reviews from television critics and acquired a Nielsen rating of 4.3 in its original broadcast.

Plot

Bart and Milhouse convince Comic Book Guy to publish a comic book he wrote titled Everyman, in which the title character can absorb superpowers from the characters of comic books he touches. The comic becomes an instant hit, and many Hollywood studios become interested in making it into a movie. Comic Book Guy agrees to let Everyman become a movie, but only if he can pick the star. When Comic Book Guy sees Homer, he considers Homer perfect for the role, as he wants Everyman to be played by a middle-aged fat man. But the studio executives realize that audiences want a physically fit actor for the role, so they hire celebrity fitness trainer Lyle McCarthy to get Homer into shape. After a month, Homer becomes fit and the movie begins production.

Soon afterward, however, McCarthy leaves Homer for another client. Without McCarthy to keep him in shape, Homer starts eating again and gains all the weight back. Homer can no longer fit into his costume or even his trailer, and the movie begins to go over budget. The studio executives and Comic Book Guy worry that the film will not be successful. The final version of the movie features scenes with the fat Homer and the physically fit Homer merged together, upsetting and confusing the audience. After the premiere of the film, McCarthy returns and offers to get Homer into shape again, which Homer accepts. The studio executives offer to let Comic Book Guy direct the sequel, on the condition that Comic Book Guy lie to the fans and say he liked the film. Comic Book Guy rejects the offer and openly criticizes the movie online, and thus it becomes a box office failure and Everyman is never adapted again.

Production

Seth Rogen co-wrote the episode and guest starred as the character Lyle McCarthy.

Seth Rogen and Evan Goldberg, writers of the film *Superbad*, are "obsessed" fans of *The Simpsons*. After learning that *The Simpsons* executive producer James L. Brooks was a fan of *Superbad*, they decided to ask the producers of the show if they could write an episode.[2] [3] In 2006, Ricky Gervais, co-creator of *The Office*, received credit for writing the season 17 episode "Homer Simpson, This Is Your Wife". Rogen and Goldberg "thought if [Gervais] got to write one, maybe [they] could try."[2] They were invited to *The Simpsons* writers room, where they pitched several episode ideas. One was accepted, and they wrote an outline with the help of some feedback from the regular writers.[4]

Rogen commented that he and Goldberg wanted to show with the episode how Hollywood generally ruins superhero films. He said that "the whole joke is that Homer is cast to play a guy who's an everyman and they try to make him into this physically fit guy."[5] Rogen also noted that the plot mirrors the situation he was in while working on the film *The Green Hornet*, when he had to lose weight and do physical training for his role.[2] Show runner Al Jean commented that the writers tried not to repeat the comic book film theme from the "Radioactive Man" episode. Instead they decided to parody the fact that almost every comic book has been turned into a film. Jean commented that that scene in the episode in which the studio executives "are trying to think up an idea that hasn't been done really is what they are doing these days [in real life]."[6]

The table read took place in August 2008, and production on the episode began soon after that.[7] Rogen later said that "we sat down for a read-through and three hours later I'm in a studio improv-ing with Homer Simpson, it was the single greatest day of my life."[8] Rogen also guest stars in the episode as the character Lyle McCarthy, making him the second guest star to both write an episode and appear in it; Gervais also appeared in the episode he wrote.[1] *The Simpsons* creator Matt Groening also makes an appearance in the episode.[9] [10]

Reception

In its original American broadcast in the United States on September 27, 2009,[1] [11] "Homer the Whopper" was watched in 8.31 million homes and acquired a 4.3 Nielsen rating/12% share.[12] [13] The rating was down seven percent from the previous season's premiere,[13] which was viewed in 9.3 million homes the night it aired.[14]

Since airing, "Homer the Whopper" has received mixed to positive reviews from television critics. Steve Fritz of Newsarama called the episode "amazing" and commented that the "overall comic book theme was perfect."[6] Reviewers for *TV Guide* cited Matt Groening's cameo, the dinner table scene, Homer trying to lose weight at the Kwik-E-Mart, and the opening scene where Bart questions Comic Book Guy about Spider-Man as the highlights of the episode.[9]

Robert Canning of IGN was positive about "Homer the Whopper", giving it a 8.6/10 rating. He commented that the first act of the episode was the strongest, while the others were weaker. Canning believed the reason for this was that the viewers have already seen Homer "struggle with his weight countless times, and Rogen's trainer, though funny much of the time, will likely never be remembered as a classic guest role." He added, however, that Rogen and Goldberg are able to find "a few new angles with the weight jokes, so it's not a complete loss." Overall, Canning thought "Homer the Whopper" was a good start to the twenty-first season, and although the plot may not be very original, the writers added "freshness to the proceedings."[15] *The A.V. Club*'s Todd VanDerWerff did not think the script was as good as Gervais', but commented that Rogen and Goldberg "managed to make a mostly amusing season premiere." He added that he thought the Hollywood satirizing featured in this episode had been overused on the show, but "the specificity of what the [episode] was making fun of—trainers who help stars slim down (in this case, helping Homer slim down)—went a long way toward making the episode palatable." VanDerWerff concluded that while the episode "didn't try anything new [...], [he] had fun with it all the same."[16]

References

[1] "Fox Primetime" (http://www.foxflash.com/div.php/main/page?aID=1z2z2z176z3z8&ID=5271). Fox Flash. . Retrieved 2009-09-26.

[2] Keveney, Bill (2009-09-23). "Rogen gets a dream gig: 'Simpsons' writer, voice" (http://www.usatoday.com/life/television/news/ 2009-09-23-rogen-simpsons_N.htm). *USA Today*. . Retrieved 2009-09-24.

[3] Wagner, Curt (2009-09-25). "Seth Rogen kicks off 21st season of 'The Simpsons'" (http://www.chicagonow.com/blogs/show-patrol/ 2009/09/seth-rogen-kicks-off-21st-season-of-the-simpsons.html). *Chicago Now*. . Retrieved 2009-09-27.

[4] Liam Burke (2008-04-30). "From Superbad To Superheroes - Evan Goldberg on Hornet and The Boys" (http://www.empireonline.com/ news/story.asp?NID=22486). *Empire*. . Retrieved 2008-04-30.

[5] The Associated Press (2009-09-28). "D'oh! Seth Rogen writes a 'Simpsons' episode" (http://www.msnbc.msn.com/id/33027622/ns/ entertainment/). MSNBC. . Retrieved 2009-10-16.

[6] Fritz, Steve (2009-09-26). "Animated Shorts: Al Jean & THE SIMPSONS 21 Years Later" (http://www.newsarama.com/tv/ 090926-simpson-al-jean.html). Newsarama. . Retrieved 2009-09-26.

[7] Jami Philbrick (2008-07-26). ""Superbad" writers Rogen and Goldberg to pen episode of "The Simpsons"" (http://live.comicbookresources. com/2008/07/26/superbad-writers-rogen-and-goldberg-to-pen-episode-of-the-simpsons/). Comic Book Resources. . Retrieved 2008-08-01.

[8] Evan Fanning (2008-09-14). "Why Seth Rogen is on a high" (http://www.independent.ie/entertainment/film-cinema/ why-seth-rogen-is-on-a-high-1475161.html). *Irish Independent*. . Retrieved 2008-09-17.

[9] "The Simpsons Episode Recap: "Homer the Whopper"" (http://www.tvguide.com/Episode-Recaps/simpsons/ Simpsons-Episode-Recap-1010254.aspx). *TV Guide*. . Retrieved October 16, 2009.

[10] "Homer the Whopper" (http://tv.nytimes.com/episode/94944/Simpsons/overview). *The New York Times*. . Retrieved 2009-10-20.

[11] Dan Snierson (2009-07-24). "'The Simpsons': Coldplay's Chris Martin, Sarah Silverman among season 21 guests" (http://hollywoodinsider. ew.com/2009/07/24/the-simpsons-coldplays-chris-martin-sarah-silverman-among-season-21-guests/). *Entertainment Weekly*. . Retrieved 2009-07-25.

[12] Kissell, Rick (2009-09-29). "Laffers rule TV's premiere week" (http://www.variety.com/article/VR1118009337.html). *Variety*. . Retrieved 2009-10-01.

[13] Adalian, Josef (2009-09-28). "Sunday Ratings: 'Cleveland' Rocks, 'Housewives' Takes a Hit" (http://www.thewrap.com/ind-column/ sunday-ratings-cleveland-rocks-housewives-takes-hit-7865). *The Wrap*. . Retrieved 2009-09-28.

[14] Mandy Bierly (2008-09-29). "Ratings: 'Desperate Housewives' returns to win Sunday night" (http://hollywoodinsider.ew.com/2008/09/ desperate-house.html). *Entertainment Weekly*. . Retrieved 2008-09-29.

[15] Canning, Robert (2009-09-25). "The Simpsons: "Homer the Whopper" Review" (http://au.tv.ign.com/articles/102/1028410p1.html). IGN. . Retrieved 2009-09-27.

[16] VanDerWerff, Todd (2009-09-28). ""Homer the Whopper"/"Pilot"/"Road to the Multiverse"/"In Country ... Club"" (http://www.avclub. com/articles/homer-the-whopperpilotroad-to-the-multiversein-cou,33389/). *The A.V. Club.* . Retrieved 2009-10-03.

External links

- "Homer the Whopper" (http://www.imdb.com/title/tt1502337/) at the Internet Movie Database
- "Homer the Whopper" (http://www.tv.com/episode/1236288/summary.html) at TV.com

The Green Hornet (2011 film)

The Green Hornet	
Teaser poster	
Directed by	Michel Gondry
Produced by	Neal H. Moritz
Written by	Seth Rogen Evan Goldberg
Based on	*The Green Hornet* by George W. Trendle Fran Striker
Starring	Seth Rogen Jay Chou Christoph Waltz Cameron Diaz
Music by	James Newton Howard
Cinematography	John Schwartzman
Editing by	Michael Tronick
Studio	Original Film
Distributed by	Columbia Pictures
Release date(s)	January 14, 2011
Running time	119 minutes
Country	United States
Language	English
Budget	$120 million[1]
Gross revenue	$78,525,295[1]

The Green Hornet is a 2011 superhero action-comedy film, based on the character of the same name that had originated in a 1930s radio program and has appeared in movie serials, a television series, comic books and other media. Directed by Michel Gondry, the film stars Seth Rogen, who co-wrote the screenplay with Evan Goldberg.

Supporting actors include Jay Chou as Kato, Christoph Waltz, Cameron Diaz, Edward James Olmos, David Harbour, and Tom Wilkinson.

The film was released in North America and Japan on January 12, 2011 and the United Kingdom and Ireland on January 14, 2011, in versions including RealD Cinema and IMAX 3D.

Plot

Britt Reid (Seth Rogen) is the 28-year-old slacker son of widower James Reid (Tom Wilkinson), publisher of the Los Angeles newspaper *The Daily Sentinel*. Britt is an irresponsible playboy, but his attitude changes when James is found dead from an allergic reaction to a bee sting. After the funeral, Britt fires the staff aside from his maid. Britt later rehires Kato (Jay Chou), James' mechanic and a skilled martial artist, upon learning Kato makes his coffee.

Britt and Kato get drunk together and, upon agreeing that they both hated James, visit the graveyard to cut the head off James' memorial statue as payback. After they succeed, they see a couple being mugged, and rescue them. Britt and Kato are themselves mistaken by police for criminals and chased through the streets, but Kato evades them and he and Britt return to the mansion.

Britt convinces Kato they should become crimefighters who pose as criminals in order to infiltrate real criminals, and also to prevent enemies from using innocents against them. Kato agrees, and develops a car outfitted with several gadgets and weapons, which they call the Black Beauty. Britt plans to capture Benjamin Chudnofsky (Christoph Waltz), a Russian mobster who is united the criminal families of Los Angeles under his command, and whom his father was trying to expose. To get Chudnofsky's attention, Britt uses the *Daily Sentinel* as a vehicle to publish articles about the "high-profile criminal" the Green Hornet.

Britt hires Lenore Case (Cameron Diaz), who has a degree in criminology, as his assistant and researcher, and uses her unwitting advice to raise the Green Hornet's profile. Britt and Kato blow up several of Chudnofsky's meth labs, leaving calling cards so Chudnofsky can contact them. Throughout all this, *Daily Sentinel* managing editor Mike Axford (Edward James Olmos) fears this single-minded coverage will endanger Britt's life, and District Attorney Frank Scanlon (David Harbour) frets over public perception that he cannot stop the Green Hornet.

Britt asks Lenore out, but she rebuffs him and instead invites Kato to dinner, making Britt jealous. Kato learns from her that mobsters often offer a peace summit to rivals in order to get close enough to kill them; Britt then tells Kato that Chudnofsky has offered them such a meeting. Kato tries dissuading him, but Britt, feeling overshadowed, follows his instincts. This nearly proves fatal when Chudnofsky tries to kill them.

Barely escaping to the mansion, Britt and Kato argue and fight, and Britt fires both Kato and Lenore, whom he believes are in a relationship. Kato receives an email from Chudnofsky on the Hornet's calling-card email address, offering $1 million dollars and half of Los Angeles if he kills Britt. Meanwhile, Britt discovers Scanlon is corrupt, learning that he tried to bribe James into downplaying the level of crime in the city to help his career.

Scanlon invites Britt to meet in a restaurant, where he reveals he murdered Britt's father. Kato arrives, and instead of killing Britt, he attacks Chudnofsky's men, allowing him and Britt, whom Chudnofsky deduces is the real Green Hornet, to escape. They head to the *Daily Sentinel*, where Britt intends to upload a recording of Scanlon's confession onto the Web — and belatedly discovers he did not manage to record it. Chudnofsky and his men follow the duo there, where a firefight ensues. Kato ultimately stabs Chudnofsky in the eyes in self-defense and Britt shoots him to death. A SWAT team appears and fires at the Green Hornet and Kato, while they use the remains of a nearly demolished, second Black Beauty to run Scanlon out the 10th-floor window, killing him. They survive by ejecting the ejector seats. The Green Hornet and Kato flee to Lenore's house, where she learns their secret identities and that she has been the accidental mastermind behind the Green Hornet's plots. Despite being furious, she helps them hide from the police and tends to Britt's shoulder gunshot wound but left the bullet in his shoulder because he was a "p-ssy".

The next morning, Britt promotes Axford to editor-in-chief and stages being shot in the shoulder by Kato, further establishing the Green Hornet as a threat (and allowing Britt to get treated by professionals in a hospital). Later, the two weld James's stolen bust back onto his memorial statue as a sign of forgiving James however the statue's head is looking down instead of up which Britt thinks it's James's true face. Now with Lenore to aid them, Britt and Kato vow to continue protecting the law by breaking it.

Cast

- Seth Rogen as Britt Reid/The Green Hornet, a wealthy newspaper publisher who is secretly the masked crimefighter The Green Hornet.
- Jay Chou as Kato, a personal mechanic who becomes the Green Hornet's valet and sidekick.
- Christoph Waltz as Benjamin Chudnofsky/Bloodnofsky, a paranoid Russian gangster who plans to join all of the crime families of Los Angeles together to organize a "super-mafia."[2]
- Cameron Diaz as Lenore "Casey" Case, the love interest of Reid and Kato.[2]
- Tom Wilkinson as James Reid, Britt's wealthy father and successful newspaper publisher
- Edward James Olmos as Mike Axford
- Edward Furlong as Tupper, the meth dealer
- Analeigh Tipton as Ana Lee
- David Harbour as D.A. Frank Scanlon
- James Franco as the rival drug dealer[3]

Development

Variety reported in October 1992 that the Green Hornet was one of the properties represented by Leisure Concepts Inc., and though trade paper said, without explanation, "rights in limbo",[4] negotiations were ongoing with Universal Pictures.[5] By September 1993, Chuck Pfarrer had finished the screenplay.[6] Rich Wilkes was hired to rewrite Pfarrer's script, which resulted in George Clooney signing a pay-or-play contract. Clooney dropped out in December 1995 to star in *Batman and Robin*, and an anonymous source at Universal told *Entertainment Weekly* the following May that Greg Kinnear was being looked at for the title role.[7] Jason Scott Lee by this time had signed on to co-star as Kato.[7] Universal hired music video director Michel Gondry in January 1997 for his feature film directional debut.[8] Gondry rewrote the Wilkes screenplay with Edward Neumeier, saying that "after one-and-a-half years, it was shelved by the studio. . . . We already had the designs for the cars, the weapons. . . ."[9] Lawrence Gordon and Lloyd Levin had been signed on to produce by January 1997.[8] Mark Wahlberg was offered the lead role,[10] but the film languished in development hell and Gondry eventually left.[9]

In April 2000, Universal entered early negotiations with Jet Li to star as Kato[11] for $5.2 million against 5% of the film's gross.[12] Dark Horse Entertainment and Charles Gordon joined Larry Gordon and Lloyd Levin as producers.[11] Christopher McQuarrie was writing a script by June 2000, [12] but with it uncompleted by October, Li moved on to work on *The One* while remaining attached to *The Green Hornet*.[13] After spending about $10 million in development since 1992, Universal put *The Green Hornet* in turnaround in November 2001, by which time Li and the producers were no longer involved. Paramount and Columbia Pictures showed interest in picking up Universal's option, but Miramax Films won the bidding that month with what *Variety* reported as "a deal approaching $3 million."[14] In May 2003 the studio was working with automobile companies on product placement opportunities for the Black Beauty. As part of the deal, Miramax would receive its "hero car" and $35 million in additional marketing. The car company that would have landed the deal would be given the chance to help develop *The Green Hornet*, since a script had yet to be written and no director was attached to the planned 2005 release. *Variety* noted this figure would have tied the record $35 million deal between Ford Motor Company and MGM that featured the company's Aston Martin Vanquish, Jaguar XKR, and Ford Thunderbird in the James Bond film *Die Another Day*.[15]

In February 2004, Miramax president Harvey Weinstein hired cult filmmaker and comic book writer Kevin Smith to write and direct the film, based on their previous four-film collaborations. "I dig the fact that he kicked off a run of billionaire playboys who decided to put on a mask and fight crime and that he was Batman before there was a Batman," Smith said. "I always said I'd never do a superhero film, based on my limited experience writing on *Superman Lives* and having to answer to the studio, Jon Peters, the comics company and eventually a director. Then there's a fandom that gets up in arms if you even try to stray from their character. Here, there is simplicity in the character and the situation."[16] Jon Gordon and Hannah Minghella were now on as producers, with Harold Berkowitz and George Trendle, son of the character's co-creator, as executive producers.[16]

Smith approached Jake Gyllenhaal for the lead role in March 2004.[17] In mid-November of that year, he said he had written about 100 pages, and estimated another 100 to come.[18] In February 2006, Smith's official website noted, "Kevin officially no longer has anything to do with the *Fletch* or *Green Hornet* projects."[19] Smith went on to write the Dynamite Entertainment comic book *Green Hornet*, which has run 11 issues as of late 2010.[20] [21]

In March 2007, producer Neal H. Moritz, who had been trying to acquire the film rights to the character for years, obtained the rights and through his Sony-based production company Original Film optioned them to Columbia Pictures.[22] In July 2007 Seth Rogen, in addition to starring in the lead role, was hired to co-write the script with frequent collaborator Evan Goldberg. Columbia also hired Rogen as an executive producer for *The Green Hornet*.[23] Rogen in July 2007 said he had not begun writing the screenplay yet, but anticipated the tone would be that of "a buddy action movie" with humor, "like *Lethal Weapon* and *48 Hrs.*.[24] In September 2008, Columbia Pictures announced A June 25, 2010, release date, and that Hong Kong star Stephen Chow had signed on to direct and to co-star as Kato. Chow, a fan of the TV show as a kid, explained, "The idea of stepping into Bruce Lee's shoes as Kato is both humbling and thrilling, and to get the chance to direct the project as my American movie debut is simply a dream come true."[25] Chow dropped out as director the following December over creative differences.[26] On February 24, 2009, Columbia Pictures announced that Michel Gondry would direct the film, on which Chow had remained as Kato,[27] after impressing Columbia production presidents Doug Belgrad and Matt Tolmach with his pitch.[28] Gondry had previously been involved with *The Green Hornet* when Universal Pictures was planning its version in 1997.[8]

Chow dropped out as Kato in July 2009 over scheduling conflicts other projects.[29] By this time the release date had been pushed to July 9, 2010.[29] In August, he was replaced with Taiwanese singer-actor Jay Chou.[30] The studio was then in early talks with Nicolas Cage to play the gangster villain, and Cameron Diaz was negotiating to play researcher and love interest Lenore Case.[30]

Production notes

Nicolas Cage had been in talks to play the role of Benjamin Chudnofsky,[30] saying in 2009, "*The Green Hornet* was something I wanted to do. I think Michel Gondry is very talented and I had hoped it would work. But I think Seth Rogen and Michel had a different direction for the character tonally than the way I wanted to go. ... I wasn't interested in just being straight-up bad guy who was killing people willy-nilly. I had to have some humanity and try to give it something where you could understand why the character was the way he was. But there wasn't enough time to develop it."[31]

The filmmakers had wanted Van Williams, who played the Green Hornet in the 1960s television series, to make a cameo appearance as a cemetery guard, but Williams was unavailable.[32]

Producer Neal H. Moritz considered filming *The Green Hornet* in Detroit, Michigan, New York City, and Louisiana, but ultimately chose Los Angeles, California, as the primary location shooting. "Ultimately, we made the decision, and thankfully the studio agreed with us, that the creative positives of shooting in Los Angeles outweighed the tax incentives offered to us elsewhere," Moritz said.[33] Principal photography began at Sony Pictures Studios in Culver City, California on September 2, 2009 for one week. Filming then moved to Chinatown, Los Angeles for scenes featuring Kato's apartment. Through November, other locations included Sun Valley, Holmby Hills, Bel-Air,

Hawthorne and various locations downtown, including City Hall and the Los Angeles Times Building, which stands in for the *Daily Sentinel* newspaper where Britt Reid works.[33]

The production modified 29 Imperial Crown sedans from model years 1964 to 1966 to portray the Green Hornet's luxurious supercar, the Black Beauty.[34]

Release

Sony replaced the film's June 26, 2010 release date with *Grown Ups*, which moved *The Green Hornet* to July 9, 2010.[35] Sony then scheduled the film for December 22, 2010, before announcing on April 23, 2010, that it was pushing to January 14, 2011, to secure more time to convert it to 3D.[36]

In July 2009, Sony presented a panel at San Diego Comic-Con International, where Seth Rogen and director Michel Gondry unveiled the first look for the Black Beauty.[37] The first trailer was released online on June 24, 2010, and was attached to screenings of *Grown Ups, Salt, The Other Guys, The Expendables, Machete, Resident Evil: Afterlife, Wall Street: Money Never Sleeps, The Town,, Red, Skyline, Love and Other Drugs, Harry Potter and the Deathly Hallows Part 1, The Chronicles of Narnia: The Voyage of the Dawn Treader,* and *Tron Legacy.* In the UK, the trailer was attached with showings of *The Social Network* and *Tron: Legacy.*

The film was released in the U.S. and some foreign markets on January 14, 2011, opening in 3,584 theaters domestically.[1]

Reception

Critical

The Green Hornet received generally mixed reviews. Review aggregate Rotten Tomatoes reports that 46% of 195 critics gave the film a positive review, with an average score of 5.2/10. The site's critical consensus is: "It's sporadically entertaining, but *The Green Hornet* never approaches the surreal heights suggested by a Michel Gondry/Seth Rogen collaboration."[38] Metacritic, in comparison, assigned the film an average score of 39/100, indicating "generally unfavorable reviews".[39]

Kenneth Turan of the *Los Angeles Times* called it "[a]n anemic, 97-pound weakling of the action comedy persuasion ... a boring bromedy that features mumblecore heroics instead of the real thing."[40] Lou Lumenick of the *New York Post* found it "an overblown, interminable and unfunny update (in badly added 3-D)", and called star Rogen "miscast".[41] UK critic Peter Bradshaw of the British newspaper *The Guardian*, said, "Almost everything about the film is disappointing. Christoph Waltz is under-par as the villain with nothing like the steely charisma of his Nazi in *Inglourious Basterds*.[42] Richard Roeper gave the film a D+, calling it "a lazy, sloppy, unfunny comedy that makes almost no use of the 3-D technology, and it just falls flat."[43] Roger Ebert gave it one star and called it "an almost unendurable demonstration of a movie with nothing to be about. Although it follows the rough storyline of previous versions of the title, it neglects the construction of a plot engine to pull us through." He also noted the poor use of 3-D and suggested it was added solely in order to charge extra.[44]

However, Elizabeth Weitzman of the New York *Daily News* gave it 3 1/2 stars out of 5, and commented that the "irreverently funny" film had "a vibe so casual you half expect star Seth Rogen to amble off screen and put his feet up on the seat next to you," and praising director Gondry's "sense of humor and acute visual skill" even while calling the movie "cheerfully unfocused".[45]

Box office

The Green Hornet had an opening weekend domestic gross of $33,700,000, topping the U.S. movie chart its first week of release. After four days, it had earned an estimated $40 million domestically and $16.1 million overseas.[1]

Merchandising

Factory Entertainment produced six-inch action figures and a die-cast Black Beauty, among other collectibles. Hollywood Collectibles has made a full-size prop gas gun replica. Mezco Toyz has made a set of 12-inch action figures, with the prototypes donated to the Museum of the Moving Image.[46]

The studio and CKE Restaurants, Inc., the parent company of Carl's Jr. and Hardee's, formed a promotional marketing partnership that included commercials featuring Seth Rogen and Jay Chou in character as the Green Hornet and Kato; a beverage promotion with Dr. Pepper; *The Green Hornet* food items, kids' meal toys, and employee uniforms; and a contest with the grand prize of a Black Beauty car from the film.[47]

A tie-in video game for iPhone and iPad was released, entitled *The Green Hornet: Wheels of Justice*.[48] The game is a 3D top-down driving game. It also featured a hidden mini-game fighting game called *The Green Hornet: Crime Fighter*, which was also released for browsers and Android phones.[49]

Promotion

The Discovery Channel television show *MythBusters* aired a "Green Hornet Special" that featured Seth Rogen joining the hosts in testing two "myths" from the movie.[50] The cable network Syfy aired a marathon of the *The Green Hornet* TV series January 11, 2011, to help promote the film.[51]

References

[1] "The Green Hornet (2011)" (http://www.boxofficemojo.com/movies/?id=greenhornet.htm). *Box Office Mojo*. . Retrieved January 22, 2011.

[2] Marc Graser (2009-09-14). "Christoph Waltz joins 'Green Hornet'" (http://www.variety.com/article/VR1118008576). *Variety*. . Retrieved 2010-10-28.

[3] Debruge, Peter. "*The Green Hornet*" (review) (http://www.variety.com/review/VE1117944278?refcatid=31), *Variety*, January 11, 2011

[4] Eller, Claudia, and John Evan Frook (1992-10-09). "NL spins slick pic for Dummies" (http://www.variety.com/article/VR101240). *Variety*. . Retrieved 2009-08-29.. (Requires subscription.)

[5] Broeski, Pat H. (1992-10-18). "From the Comics to a Screen Near You" (http://www.nytimes.com/1992/10/18/movies/film-from-the-comics-to-a-screen-near-you.html). *The New York Times*. . Retrieved 2009-08-31.

[6] Fleming, Michael (1993-09-02). "Woo Abuse" (http://www.variety.com/article/VR110212). *Variety*. . Retrieved 2009-08-29.

[7] Staff (1996-05-03). "Hornet's Best" (http://www.ew.com/ew/article/0,,292349,00.html). *Entertainment Weekly*. . Retrieved 2009-08-31.

[8] Cox, Dan (1997-01-29). "'Hornet' Flies with Gondry" (http://www.variety.com/article/VR1117432976). *Variety*. . Retrieved 2009-08-29.. WebCitation archive (http://www.webcitation.org/5vORmePsx).

[9] Hebron, Sandra (2007-02-07). "Michel Gondry" (http://www.guardian.co.uk/film/2007/feb/07/guardianinterviewsatbfisouthbank). *The Guardian*. . Retrieved 2009-09-04.. WebCitation archive (http://www.webcitation.org/5vOS7Cq3b).

[10] Petrikin, Chris (1997-10-28). "Wahlberg Eyes 'Corruptor' Pic" (http://www.variety.com/article/VR1116675317). *Variety*. . Retrieved 2009-08-29.. (Requires subscription.)

[11] McNary, Dave (2000-04-11). "U Eyes Li for 'Green Hornet'" (http://www.variety.com/article/VR1117780411). *Variety*. . Retrieved 2009-08-29.. (Requires subscription.)

[12] Fleming, Michael (2000-06-22). "Li sees green for 'Hornet'; wife boosts Stevens" (http://www.variety.com/article/VR1117782948). *Variety*. . Retrieved 2009-08-29.. (Requires subscription.)

[13] Lyons, Charles, and Michael Fleming (2000-10-04). "Li Is the 'One' for Roth pic" (http://www.variety.com/article/VR1117787296). *Variety*. . Retrieved 2009-08-29.. (Requires subscription.)

[14] Brodesser, Claude (2001-11-20). "New Buzz for 'Hornet' After U Option Expires" (http://www.variety.com/article/VR1117856141). *Variety*. . Retrieved 2009-08-29.. (Requires subscription.)

[15] Graser, Marc, and Nicole LaPorte (2003-05-27). "H'wood Hot Rods Spinning Wheels" (http://www.variety.com/article/VR1117886975). *Variety*. . Retrieved 2009-08-29.. (Requires subscription.)

[16] Rooney, David; Michael Fleming; Dave McNary (2004-02-17). "'Hornet' Buzzes Smith" (http://www.variety.com/article/VR1117900346). *Variety*. . Retrieved 2009-08-29.. (Requires subscription.)

[17] Susman, Gary (2004-03-18). "Miller Time" (http://www.ew.com/ew/article/0,,602061,00.html). *Entertainment Weekly*. . Retrieved 2009-08-31.

[18] Murray, Rebecca (2004-10-14). "Kevin Smith on "The Green Hornet" Script, "Star Wars", and Other Projects" (http://movies.about.com/od/directorinterviews/a/hornet101404.htm). About.com. . Retrieved 2009-08-30.

[19] Cryer, Jay (2006-02-17). "Wondercon: What We Learned!" (http://www.newsaskew.com/cgi-bin/coranto/iSay.cgi?Page=Comments&ID=EEupEZAZuZLZgWaazm). *News Askew*. . Retrieved 2009-09-05.

[20] Bernardin, Marc (2009-05-13). "EW Exclusive: Kevin Smith takes on Batman and the Green Hornet" (http://popwatch.ew.com/2009/05/13/kevin-smith-com/). *Entertainment Weekly*. . Retrieved 2009-08-31.

[21] *Green Hornet*, Dynamite Entertainment, 2010 Series (http://www.comics.org/series/44666/) at the Grand Comics Database

[22] McNary, Dave, and Diane Garrett (2007-03-20). "Columbia flies with 'Green Hornet'" (http://www.variety.com/article/VR1117961471). *Variety*. . Retrieved 2009-08-29.

[23] Garrett, Diane (2007-07-19). "Columbia flies with 'Green Hornet'" (http://www.variety.com/article/VR1117968873). *Variety*. . Retrieved 2009-08-29.

[24] Murray, Rebecca (2007-07-29). "Exclusive Interview with the Cast of Superbad" (http://movies.about.com/od/superbad/a/superbad072907_3.htm). About.com. . Retrieved 2010-10-27.

[25] Siegel, Tatiana (2008-09-19). "Chow to direct Columbia's 'Hornet'" (http://www.variety.com/article/VR1117992539). *Variety*. . Retrieved 2009-08-29. (Requires subscription.)

[26] Fleming, Michael (2008-12-18). "Chow No Longer to Direct "Hornet"" (http://www.variety.com/article/VR1117997630.html?categoryid=13&cs=1). Variety.com. . Retrieved 2010-12-25.. WebCitation archive (http://www.webcitation.org/5vOMa2qel).

[27] "Michel Gondry to Direct 'The Green Hornet'" (http://www.sonypictures.com/movies/thegreenhornet/pressrelease/index.html?hs317=TheGreenHornet+PressRelease). Columbia Pictures press release. February 24, 2009. . Retrieved 2010-12-25.. WebCitation archive (http://www.webcitation.org/5vOMAvzmF)

[28] Fleming, Michael (2009-02-24). "Michel Gondry set for 'Green Hornet'" (http://www.variety.com/article/VR1118000508). *Variety*. . Retrieved 2009-08-29. (Requires subscription.)

[29] Graser, Marc (2009-07-14). "Chow buzzes out of 'Hornet'" (http://www.variety.com/article/VR1118005995). *Variety*. . Retrieved 2009-08-29. (Requires subscription.)

[30] McNary, Dave (2009-08-07). "'Green Hornet' casts Kato role" (http://www.variety.com/article/VR1118007008). *Variety*. . Retrieved 2009-08-29.. WebCitation archive (http://www.webcitation.org/5vkEwRIyZ).

[31] Slotek, Jim, and Kevin Williamson. "Cage Anti Hero" (http://www.torontosun.com/entertainment/movies/2009/10/11/11369901-sun.html), *Toronto Sun*, October 11, 2009. Retrieved January 15, 2011. WebCitation archive (http://www.webcitation.org/5vkEo68wU).

[32] Marshall, Rick. "Michel Gondry Talks 'Green Hornet' Legacy, No Cameo For Van Williams" (http://splashpage.mtv.com/2010/03/22/michel-gondry-green-hornet-van-williams-cameo/), MTV News, March 22, 2010. WebCitation archive (http://www.webcitation.org/5vQ2SOuw4).

[33] Verrier, Richard (2009-09-09). "'The Green Hornet' does battle in LA" (http://latimesblogs.latimes.com/entertainmentnewsbuzz/2009/09/the-green-hornet-does-battle-in-la.html). *Los Angeles Times*. . Retrieved 2009-09-10.. WebCitation archive (http://www.webcitation.org/5vOtRdp2t)

[34] Huffman, John Pearley (2010-05-14). "Twenty-Nine Chrysler Imperials as Black Beauty in One 'Green Hornet'" (http://www.nytimes.com/2010/05/16/automobiles/16BEAUTY.html/). *The New York Times*. . Retrieved 2010-12-03.

[35] McClintock, Pamela (2009-07-01). "Sony shuffles 2010 comedies" (http://www.variety.com/article/VR1118005622). *Variety*. . Retrieved 2009-08-29.

[36] Subers, Ray. "'Green Hornet' Adds 3D, Moves to 2011" (http://www.boxofficemojo.com/news/?id=2734), BoxOfficeMojo.com, April 23, 2010

[37] Vary, Adam B. (2009-07-23). "Comic-Con video: Seth Rogen talks 'The Green Hornet'" (http://popwatch.ew.com/2009/07/23/seth-rogen-green-hornet-comiccon-2009/). *Entertainment Weekly*. . Retrieved 2009-08-31.

[38] "The Green Hornet (2011)" (http://www.rottentomatoes.com/m/green_hornet/). *Rotten Tomatoes*. Flixster. . Retrieved January 16, 2011.

[39] "The Green Hornet" (http://www.metacritic.com/movie/the-green-hornet). *Metacritic*. . Retrieved January 22, 2011.

[40] Turan, Kenneth. "Movie review: 'The Green Hornet'" (http://www.latimes.com/entertainment/news/la-et-green-hornet-20110114,0,7585005.story), *Los Angeles Times*, January 14, 2011

[41] Lumenick, Lou. "'Hornet' Stink Is Deadly" (http://www.nypost.com/p/entertainment/movies/hornet_stink_is_deadly_Mm7VB4m6uGxaFLbiMR6vKN), *New York Post*, January 14, 2011

[42] Bradshaw, Peter. "'The Green Hornet' – Review'" (http://www.guardian.co.uk/film/2011/jan/13/the-green-hornet-review), *The Guardian*, January 13, 2011.

[43] *The Green Hornet* Review (http://www.richardroeper.com/reviews/popup.aspx?ReviewId=259), Roeper, Richard, January 2011

[44] "The Green Hornet" (http://rogerebert.suntimes.com/apps/pbcs.dll/article?AID=/20110112/REVIEWS/110119995/1023). *Chicago Sun-Times*. 2011-01-12. .

[45] Weitzman, Elizabeth. "*The Green Hornet*" (review) (http://www.nydailynews.com/entertainment/2011/01/14/2011-01-14_green_hornet_review_seth_rogen_and_michel_gondry_make_it_look_easy.html), New York News (New York)Daily News, *January 14, 2011*

[46] Wright, Eddie. "Mezco Donates The Green Hornet Prototype Action Figures to Museum of the Moving Image" (http://geek-news.mtv.com/2010/12/16/mezco-donates-the-green-hornet-prototype-action-figures-to-museum-of-the-moving-image/), MTV Geek!, December 16, 2010

[47] "Carl's Jr. and 'The Green Hornet' Bring Action-Packed Excitement to the Drive-Thru with Sony Pictures Deal" (http://www.carlsjr.com/company/releases/carls-jr-and-the-green-hornet-bring-action-packed-excitement-to-the-drive-thru-with-sony-pictures-deal), Carl's Jr. press release, October 8, 2010

[48] "*The Green Hornet* by Sony Pictures" (http://itunes.apple.com/us/app/the-green-hornet/id380572877?mt=8), iTunes Preview, Apple.com, n.d.

[49] (http://www.thegreenhornetgame.com/)

[50] "Playlist: *MythBusters*: Green Hornet Special" (http://dsc.discovery.com/videos/mythbusters-green-hornet/), Discovery.com, n.d.

[51] Patrick Hester (2011-1-10). "The Green Hornet Marathon Comes to SyFy" (http://www.sfsignal.com/archives/2011/01/the-green-hornet-marathon-comes-to-syfy/). SFSignal. . Retrieved 2011-1-13.

External links

- Official website (http://http://www.greenhornetmovie.com/)
- *The Green Hornet* (http://www.allmovie.com/work/393767) at Allmovie
- *The Green Hornet* (http://www.boxofficemojo.com/movies/?id=greenhornet.htm) at Box Office Mojo
- *The Green Hornet* (http://www.imdb.com/title/tt0990407/) at the Internet Movie Database
- *The Green Hornet* (http://www.metacritic.com/movie/the-green-hornet/) at Metacritic
- *The Green Hornet* (http://www.rottentomatoes.com/m/green_hornet/) at Rotten Tomatoes

Paul (film)

Paul	
Teaser poster	
Directed by	Greg Mottola
Produced by	Nira Park Tim Bevan Eric Fellner
Written by	Simon Pegg Nick Frost
Starring	Simon Pegg Nick Frost Seth Rogen Jason Bateman Kristen Wiig
Music by	David Arnold
Cinematography	Lawrence Sher
Editing by	Chris Dickens
Studio	Relativity Media StudioCanal Working Title Films Big Talk Pictures
Distributed by	Universal Pictures
Release date(s)	March 18, 2011 [1]
Country	United Kingdom United States
Language	English

Paul is an upcoming 2011 ensemble science fiction comedy film directed by Greg Mottola and written by and starring Simon Pegg and Nick Frost.

Plot summary

Two British comic geeks (Pegg and Frost) go on a road trip through America. On the way, they discover an alien named Paul (voiced by Seth Rogen) at Area 51 and become the targets of a nationwide manhunt. [1]

Production

Principal photography wrapped on September 9, 2009,[2] with additional scenes filmed in July 2010 at the Albuquerque Convention Center, which was designed to look like the 2010 San Diego Comic-Con.[3] After obtaining permission to use the Comic-Con brand, the settings had to be changed to avoid crowds and extras were used to portray attendees.

During filming, Joe Lo Trugllio was a stand-in for the character Paul, the only character who was created by CGI. Seth Rogen did motion capture and voice work during post-production.

A teaser trailer was released on the 18th of October, 2010.[4] It was shown before certain screenings of *Vampires Suck*, *Let Me In*, *Harry Potter and the Deathly Hallows Part 1*, *Burke and Hare* and *The Social Network* in the UK.

The film's main character and namesake, "Paul" has attracted some small criticism for being too much like the *American Dad* character Roger the Alien. Due to their same apperance and some mannerisms, e.g smoking, and both their "slacker" type personalities.

The trailer featured the music "All Over The World" by the Electric Light Orchestra.

Cast

- Simon Pegg[1] as Graham Willy, 32[5]
- Nick Frost[1] as Clive Gollings, 33[5]
- Seth Rogen as the voice of Paul[1]
- Jason Bateman[1] as Special Agent Lorenzo Zoil[5]
- Kristen Wiig[1] as Ruth
- Bill Hader[1] as Agent Haggard
- Gregg Turkington as Neil Hamburger
- Jane Lynch[1] as Pat Stevenson
- Sigourney Weaver[6] as Tara
- Blythe Danner[6] as Tara Walton
- Mia Stallard as Young Tara
- Joe Lo Truglio[6] as O'Reilly
- John Carroll Lynch as Moses Buggs
- David Koechner as Gus
- Jesse Plemons as Jake
- Jeffrey Tambor as Adam Shadowchild
- Luke Jackson as Ford
- Paula LaBaredas as Princess Leia
- Chris Bentley as Highway Patrolman (*uncredited*)
- Justin Reed as Comic Con Guest
- Gilbert Gottfried

According to Robert Kirkman, he, along with *Invincible* co-creator Cory Walker and current *Invincible* artist Ryan Ottley, will have a cameo in the movie.[7]

References

[1] Michael Fleming (2011-01-06). "Paul" (http://www.comingsoon.net/films.php?id=48063). *Comingsoon.net.* . Retrieved 2011-01-8.

[2] "Principal Photography Wraps!" (http://blog.whatispaul.com/2009/09/09/principal-photography-wraps/). What Is Paul? - The *Paul* Production Blogs. September 9, 2009. . Retrieved 2010-07-25.

[3] "Paul Set Visit Report. The New Simon Pegg/Nick Frost Comedy!" (http://www.latinoreview.com/news/ paul-set-visit-report-the-new-simon-pegg-nick-frost-comedy-10495). LatinoReview.com. . Retrieved 2010-07-25.

[4] "Matt's Movie Reviews Paul trailer" (http://www.mattsmoviereviews.net/trailers-paul.html). Matt's Movie Reviews. 2010-10-18. .

[5] *Paul (2010)* (http://www.imdb.com/title/tt1092026/) at the Internet Movie Database

[6] Variety staff (2009-06-17). "Sigourney Weaver, Blythe Danner, Joe Lo Truglio" (http://www.variety.com/article/VR1118005089. html?categoryId=28&cs=1). *Variety.* . Retrieved 2009-06-18.

[7] Robert Kirkman (August 9, 2009). "Flying out tomorrow to New Mexico..." (http://twitter.com/RobertKirkman/status/3216236821). Twitter (via Echofon). . Retrieved 2010-07-25.

External links

- Official website (http://http://www.whatispaul.com/)
- *Paul* (http://www.allmovie.com/work/475294) at Allmovie
- *Paul* (http://www.boxofficemojo.com/movies/?id=paul.htm) at Box Office Mojo
- *Paul* (http://www.imdb.com/title/tt1092026/) at the Internet Movie Database
- *Paul* (http://www.metacritic.com/movie/paul) at Metacritic
- *Paul* (http://www.rottentomatoes.com/m/paul/) at Rotten Tomatoes

Kung Fu Panda 2

Kung Fu Panda 2	
 Teaser poster	
Directed by	Jennifer Yuh Nelson
Produced by	Melissa Cobb (producer) Guillermo del Toro (Executive producer) Jonathan Aibel Glenn Berger (Co-producers)
Written by	Jonathan Aibel Glenn Berger Charlie Kaufman[1]
Starring	Jack Black
Music by	Hans Zimmer John Powell
Studio	DreamWorks Animation Pacific Data Images
Distributed by	Paramount Pictures
Release date(s)	May 27, 2011
Country	United States
Language	English
Budget	$160 million
Preceded by	*Kung Fu Panda*

Kung Fu Panda 2, formerly titled ***Kung Fu Panda 2: The Kaboom of Doom***, is an upcoming animated film and the sequel to the 2008 film, *Kung Fu Panda*.[2] It is set to be in 3D, will be directed by Jennifer Yuh Nelson, and executive produced by Guillermo del Toro (*Pan's Labyrinth, Blade II*), with most of the original cast returning, along with some new characters.[2] The film is set to be released on May 27, 2011 and was originally going to be named *Kung Fu Panda 2: Pandamonium*.[3]

Jack Black, the voice of Po the Panda, announced a *Kung Fu Panda* sequel during the 2009 Nickelodeon Kid's Choice Awards. The rest of the first film's cast, including Black, Dustin Hoffman, Jackie Chan, Angelina Jolie, Lucy Liu, Seth Rogen, David Cross and James Hong, are all set to reprise their roles. New cast members include Victor Garber, Michelle Yeoh, Gary Oldman, and Jean-Claude Van Damme.[4]

Plot

Po (Jack Black), now a kung fu master, is fighting alongside with Master Shifu (Dustin Hoffman) and The Furious Five—Monkey (Jackie Chan), Crane (David Cross), Tigress (Angelina Jolie), Viper (Lucy Liu), and Mantis (Seth Rogen). They have to join forces with another group of kung fu masters— Skunkman (James Woods), Thundering Rhino (Victor Garber), Soothsayer (Michelle Yeoh) and Croc (Jean-Claude Van Damme), in order to defeat Lord Shen (Gary Oldman), an evil king peacock who emerged with a deadly new weapon.

Cast

- Jack Black as Po, a Giant Panda
- Dustin Hoffman as Master Shifu, a Red Panda
- Angelina Jolie as Master Tigress, a South China Tiger
- Lucy Liu as Master Viper, a Green Tree Viper
- Jackie Chan as Master Monkey, a Gee's Golden Langur
- Seth Rogen as Master Mantis, a Chinese Mantis
- David Cross as Master Crane, a Red-crowned Crane
- James Hong as Mr. Ping, a Chinese Goose
- Victor Garber as Master Thundering Rhino, a Rhinoceros
- Michelle Yeoh as The Soothsayer, a Goat
- Gary Oldman as Lord Shen, a Peacock
- James Woods as Master Skunkman, a Skunk (this character is currently uncredited in the Internet Movie Database page for unknown reasons)
- Jean-Claude Van Damme as Master Croc, a Crocodile

Marketing

The teaser trailer was shown with both 2D and 3D versions of the film *Megamind* and *Harry Potter and the Deathly Hallows: Part 1*. The trailer was then released on the Internet on November 7, 2010. Three posters have been released so far.

On December 30, 2010, DreamWorks released a fifteen second TV spot for the movie.

Video game

THQ will release a video game based on the movie on May 23, 2011 for the PlayStation 3, Xbox 360, Wii, and DS. A 3DS version will also be made.

References

[1] http://screenrant.com/kung-fu-panda-2-charlie-kaufman-sandy-59883/

[2] "DreamWorks Animation Sets Kung Fu Panda 2 Date" (http://www.comingsoon.net/news/movienews.php?id=49282). *ComingSoon.net.* . Retrieved 2010-05-20.

[3] " Kung Fu Panda: The Kaboom Of Doom (http://www.comingsoon.net/films.php?id=46350)". *ComingSoon.net.* April 13, 2010.

[4] "Yeoh, Van Damme and Garber Join Kung Fu Panda Sequel" (http://www.comingsoon.net/news/movienews.php?id=66350). *ComingSoon.net.* 2010-05-25. . Retrieved 2010-07-12.

External links

- Official website (http://http://www.kungfupanda.com/)
- *Kung Fu Panda 2* (http://www.allmovie.com/work/471909) at Allmovie
- *Kung Fu Panda 2* (http://www.bcdb.com/bcdb/cartoon.cgi?film=106789/) at the Big Cartoon DataBase
- *Kung Fu Panda 2* (http://www.boxofficemojo.com/movies/?id=kungfupanda2.htm) at Box Office Mojo
- *Kung Fu Panda 2* (http://www.imdb.com/title/tt1302011/) at the Internet Movie Database
- *Kung Fu Panda 2* (http://www.rottentomatoes.com/m/kung_fu_panda_the_kaboom_of_doom/) at Rotten Tomatoes

Live With It

Live with It	
Directed by	Jonathan Levine
Produced by	Evan Goldberg Ben Karlin Seth Rogen
Written by	Will Reiser
Starring	Joseph Gordon-Levitt Anna Kendrick Seth Rogen Anjelica Huston Bryce Dallas Howard
Music by	Michael Giacchino
Editing by	Zene Baker
Studio	Mandate Pictures Relativity Media
Distributed by	Lionsgate Summit Entertainment
Release date(s)	August 26, 2011
Country	Canada
Language	English

Live with It is an upcoming film directed by Jonathan Levine. The film stars Joseph Gordon-Levitt, Anna Kendrick, Seth Rogen, Bryce Dallas Howard and Anjelica Huston.

Cast

- Joseph Gordon-Levitt as Adam, a man diagnosed with cancer
- Anna Kendrick as Katie, Adam's doctor
- Seth Rogen as Kyle, Adam's comedic best friend
- Bryce Dallas Howard as Rachael, Adam's girlfriend
- Anjelica Huston as Diane
- Philip Baker Hall as Alan

Plot

A man is diagnosed with cancer but tries not to let it ruin his life.

Development

The film was originally going to be called *I'm With Cancer*, before it was announced that this was a working title. The film was later renamed as Live With It. James McAvoy was originally going to play the lead role before he left the film due to personal reasons and was replaced by Joseph Gordon-Levitt.[1] The film will be loosely based on the life of screenwriter Will Reiser. Filming occurred from 22 February 2010 - 31 March 2010.[2]

References

[1] "Joseph Gordon-Levitt Replaces James McAvoy In I'm With Cancer" (http://www.cinemablend.com/new/
   Joseph-Gordon-Levitt-Replaces-James-McAvoy-In-I-m-With-Cancer-17335.html). Cinemablend.com. 2010-03-02. . Retrieved 2010-10-20.
[2] (http://www.imdb.com/title/tt1306980/business)

External links

- *Live with It* (http://www.imdb.com/title/tt1306980/) at the Internet Movie Database

Article Sources and Contributors

Seth Rogen *Source*: http://en.wikipedia.org/w/index.php?oldid=409481846 *Contributors*: AEMoreira042281, AN(Ger), Aaron Bowen, AaronY, Abb615, Abboj, Addihockey10, Adimovk5, Aigirl, Ajhoax, Alansohn, Albyduckett, Ale jrb, All Hallow's Wraith, AmazingEric, Amniarix, Amoammo, Andy Marchbanks, Andyjsmith, Anibar E, Ankimai, Annapakman, Antiuser, Apefacethedude, Arakunem, Arctic Night, ArglebargleIV, ArielGold, Atif.t2, Austinkelley123, BTTNext, Baldbobbo, BarretBonden, Bear91602, Beeblebrox, Beetstra, BelzerBall, Bencey, Bernzsed, Bettybrown922, Billimays14, Bjskydiver, Blanchardb, Blazebowlz, Blehfu, Bobbarkerisking, Bobbyllama, Boing! said Zebedee, Bongwarrior, Bovineboy2008, Brewcrewer, Brookmonmf, Brttrx, Brunton, Bsadowski1, Bw101, Caltas, Camw, Canihaveacookie, Capricorn42, Captain Weirdo the Great, Cargoking, Catkilledbyagoat14, Cenarium, Charkle, Chitcena54, Chris j. Rodriguez, Chrisbolt, Christian75, Citrus538, Ckessler, Clarkey2008, Claydoolan, Clemenjo, Cnota, Cognistudio, CommonsDelinker, Corkdraw, Coughitstomcough, Courcelles, Courcelles is travelling, Crackandrhymes, Cranopolis, Cresix, Crumbsucker, CurtisOrr, CutOffTies, D6, DARTH SIDIOUS 2, Dann-Fonda, DarkPaladin126, Darkhawk, Darkspots, Darrenhusted, Darth Panda, Darwinek, David0811, Deanster321, Deathstar79, Deconstructhis, Deenoe, DepressedPer, Dimes11th10, Discospinster, Djbj16, DonnyD97, Download, Dp76764, Drew16149, Drunkenpeter99, Dylan620, Editationer, Eeekster, Egsan Bacon, Elemesh, Epbr123, Erck, Ericwirtanen, Erik, Error411, Estevanbm, Euryalus, Everard Proudfoot, Excirial, Exquisitecorpses, Extr3mer, FCYTravis, FastLizard4, Fatoriole, Fernandobouregard, Film Maker TKO, Finalius, Fixeditverygood, Flewis, Framedfigure2, FrankRizzo2006, FrenchIsAwesome, Furrykef, Fyyer, Fæ, GRB080, Gaelen S., Gail, Gaius Cornelius, Garion96, Gary King, Garzilly, Gialloneri, Gilliam, Gimmetoo, Gingermonkey3, GraemeL, Granpuff, Greggorygonzales, Guat6, Gunther ray, GuruAskew, Hairhorn, HalfShadow, Halmstad, Hargleflargle, Hazel77, Hillman15, Hiphopray, Homie C, Hoodro13, Horkana, Hullaballoo Wolfowitz, Hydrogen Iodide, Hypo11, IAmAnonoJoker, IW.HG, Ianblair23, Icseaturtles, Igoldste, Immunize, IndulgentReader, Info845, Iridescent, Irishguy, Iroony, Itzsilencer, J.D., J.delanoy, JAMILAHCW, JForget, JNW, JSmith9579, JYi, Jack Merridew, Jack O'Lantern, Jailane, JakeDHS07, JamesReyes, Jaybling, Jaydec, Jclemens, Jeffrey Mall, Jhsounds, Jmlk17, Jncraton, Jock Boy, Joe59108, Joebears1, JoeyDawgJAC, Joeymalone, Jonathan.s.kt, Jonathon A H, Journalist, Jschuley, Juhko, Jusdafax, Justme89, Jwein, Jyoungtime, K obrien210, Kascnef82, Katalaveno, Katharineamy, KathrynLybarger, Kevin, Kevinenax, Kidlittle, Kimbaboo, Kingpin13, Kmitseff, Koavf, Kpeatt, Kredible1, L Kensington, LCMike, Lacon432, Larsthemarble, Lateg, Lawlessurchin, Lear's Fool, LeaveSleaves, Lebonj, Leclaird, Li@m, Lickmynuggets, Little Mountain 5, Llanwar, Lloydsindo, Logan, Londo06, Londontube, Loodog, Lova Falk, Lovellama, Lumberjudge, Luvnugz420, M brar, MBK004, Madchester, Madhero88, Magetoo, Magpiecomics, Malcolmxl5, Mar bells87, Marek69, MarionFrazier, Martarius, Materialscientist, Matt Deres, Mattgirling, Max7681, Maxis ftw, Mazdapickup89, McGeddon, McSly, Mdebets, MegaSloth, Megaman en m, Meredyth, Mexamericanmutt, MichaelQSchmidt, Michaelmegadeth, Mikecraig, Mikepanhu, MikeyTheNinja, Minimac, Minimac's Clone, Minshullj, Mipadi, Miquonranger03, Misfit575, Mkubica, Mmxx, Momo san, Mr. Stradivarius, Mseyers, N5iln, NHRHS2010, NJZombie, NawlinWiki, Ncchat, Nehrams2020, NeilN, Neurolysis, Nign0g1, Nikoiswhatweaimfor, Ninetyone, Nishkid64, Niteowlneils, Noahbissell45, Nonchablunt, Norbie788, Northwest, NotAnonymous0, Nqcowboy87, NrDg, Nsaa, Nues20, NumaMandaline, Nymf, OM, ONEder Boy, OOODDD, Obamarama234, Observeandreport, Old Moonraker, Olmada111, Orayzio, Otisjimmy1, Ow1995, PJfixesit, Pablothegreat85, PamD, Paste, Patrick, Pdcook, Pedro, Peterclemenza, Pewwer42, Phbasketball6, Philip Trueman, Philipp Wetzlar, Philkon, Philmknut22, Piano non troppo, Pikasonic, Pinkville, Pirogator, Plange, Poetdancer, PranksterTurtle, Pritoolmachine2806, Proofreader77, Pseudomonas, Pskibobby, Public Menace, Pumpkinking0192, Quadell, Quentin X, Questatribecalled, RJaguar3, Radiant chains, Radon210, RainbowOfLight, RandomStringOfCharacters, Rapsterrrrr008, Ratdreams, Razorflame, Reach Out to the Truth, Readysteadystop, Recognizance, RedHillian, Redpumas018, Rhodesct, Rich Farmbrough, Rickjames515, Rito Revollto, Rjwilmsi, Robepolicorjug, RockinGOAT, Ronny corral, Ronsparkscomedy, Rrburke, Rtyq2, RyanCross, Rypcord, Ryulong, SCΛRECROW, SD5, SQGibbon, ST47, Salamurai, Saltywood, Samsamblondell002, Sanfranman59, Sceptre, Scooby7292, Scorpion0422, ScottMHoward, Seaphoto, See me let go, Shadowjams, Shak 10, Shirulashem, Shlomke, Sid325, Silent Tom, Sixedheart, Sjakkalle, SkyWalker, Skyphoenix, Sluggobeast, Smash, Snarfa, Sodowe, Someguy1221, Spellcast, Srushe, Stainedglasscurtain, Starswept, StaticGull, Steam5, Stephen's black friend, Steve, Stevenshapiro, Stoopideggs2, Stroppolo, Suffusion of Yellow, Sugarlover101, Sumahoy, SuperHamster, Suran.c, Svenji, Swellman, T24G, THEN WHO WAS PHONE?, Tbhotch, Tcncv, Telegraphonline, Tell-Tale Ghost, Tempodivalse, TerryE, ThatGuamGuy, The Editor 155, The Inedible Bulk, The Magnificent Clean-keeper, The Parting Glass, The Thing That Should Not Be, The sock that should not be, The wub, TheFireTones, TheMidnighters, TheNewPhobia, Thefro552, Themightylol, Tide rolls, Tiggytighe08, Tim bates, Timotheus Canens, Tinton5, TomCat4680, Tommy2010, Tony1, Topgun530, Tpbradbury, Trevor MacInnis, Treybien, Tubesurfer, Ukexpat, Ulric1313, Varlaam, Vianello, WCityMike, WacoJacko, WadeSimMiser, Wadems, Ward3001, Warreed, Weeliljimmy, Wiikkiiwriter, Wikifan12345, Wildhartlivie, William Avery, Wisdom89, Wolfer68, Wongm, Woopwoop123456, WordBanana, Wtmitchell, XuxiRawe22, Y2kcrazyjoker4, Yamla, Yllosubmarine, Yoitskevn, Zazaban, ZooFari, Zsero, 1358 anonymous edits

Freaks and Geeks *Source*: http://en.wikipedia.org/w/index.php?oldid=408837610 *Contributors*: ABCxyz, AKA, Aaronmcintosh, AlbertSM, AlistairMcMillan, Allwham, Amalas, Amcbride, AndrewBuck, Asdfqwe123, AshTFrankFurter2, Axem Titanium, Babbage, BabuBhatt, Bearcat, Beatlejuice1972, Billforpresident, Bobo192, BostonRed, Bovineboy2008, Branddobbe, Brodieex, Calbaer, Carbonite, Catgut, Cbuckley, Ceyockey, Chris the speller, Ckatz, CobraWiki, Commander Keane, ConradPino, Cookie90, CoolKatt number 99999, DCGeist, Danielhouse, Dansham, Danthemankhan, Darguz Parsilvan, David.rand, David0811, Dcljr, Dfelfoldi, Dlabtot, Drovethrughosts, Dylanjbyrne, Earl Andrew, Elkman, Ericwirtanen, Evenios, Everything counts, EzraZebra, FAThomssen, FMAFan1990, Fajilan, Father McKenzie, Fernandobouregard, Firehat87, Flowerkiller1692, Flypanam, FrankRizzo2006, FrenchIsAwesome, Fsamuels, Gaius Cornelius, Guidoism, Hugo999, Hungerf3, Iam4Lost, J.delanoy, JAMILAHCW, JSmith9579, JYi, Jabencarsey, Jacj, Jennica, Jeremy Butler, JulieKO, Keever1102, Keikomi, Keilana, Kelly Martin, Kidicarus222, KikiKoriko, Kingofkrunk, Koavf, Kuralyov, LOL, La Pianista, LaughingLion, Leonardo2505, Lexi Marie, Leyo, LinkToddMcLovinMontana, Lockzeis, M fic, Madchester, MakeRocketGoNow, Mark dittmer, Mdumas43073, Mike Payne, MikeMoriendi, Mlaffs, MoistTowelette, Moncrief, Mseyers, Musicpvm, NRFranklin, Ndysmth, NoCultureIcons, Nova Prime, Orodruin7, Ortvolute, Peabody80, Pele Merengue, Phragit, Phydend, Piano non troppo, Premeditated Chaos, QuasyBoy, R7, Radaar, Rbanzai, Redeagle688, Rehevkor, Ricky81682, Robwingfield, Rudjek, Ryangibsonstewart, Saltywood, Scooby7292, Shanshu, Shrff, Silent Tom, Snen, Snootch121, Sohollywood, SonicAD, Srah, Srikipedia, Strabismic, SuperDude115, Surachit, SweetNightmares, Tdogg241, Tedder, ThatGuamGuy, The wub, Thecomedian, Thekryptonitecondom, Thumperward, TracyLinkEdnaVelmaPenny, Tsujigiri, Tubesurfer, UDScott, Uucp, Versus22, Vivaldi, Volker89, W@ntonsoup, Wasted Time R, Wayneneutron, Welsh, Wikigab2, Wwoods, Xephodark, Zeppocity, ZhaoHong, Zybergoat, 369 anonymous edits

Undeclared *Source*: http://en.wikipedia.org/w/index.php?oldid=409557896 *Contributors*: Adavidw, Afm2105, Allwham, Andland, AndrewHowse, Axem Titanium, BD2412, BabuBhatt, BagHutch, BarberFett, Bensin, Biruitorul, Bovineboy2008, CF90, Carioca, Cazhayashi, Charliefanuk, ChrisHutchins, CoolKatt number 99999, D6, Dahumorist, DatVillain83, Dcs315, DerHexer, Drovethrughosts, Dylanjbyrne, Everything counts, FMAFan1990, Fernandobouregard, FrankRizzo2006, Freshbakedpie, Fuzheado, Gil Gamesh, Hakukaji, Hansen9j, Hroo772, Iam4Lost, Illyria05, Indon, InfamousThe6, IrishTV, Irishguy, JackalsIII, Jarking, Jedispyder, Jeffq, Jmackinn, Joeran, John K, Johntex, Kane5187, Killerchopsticks, Koavf, Krazy19Karl, Madchester, Matthew, Mjpresson, Mr. Chicago, Mseyers, NaCl, Niteowlneils, ONEder Boy, Oxymoron83, Pele Merengue, Phil Boswell, Phoenix-forgotten, Phthoggos, Postcard Cathy, Ppoi307, PrawnRR, Princesskirsty, QuasyBoy, Rankersbo, Reflex Reaction, Rettetast, Reyontoyeny, Rich Farmbrough, Rlove, Rwhaun, Ryangibsonstewart, Ryulong, ST47, Sacularamacal13, Saemikneu, Sceptre, See me let go, SidP, Silent Tom, Sillywalker, Skittlesjc, Smash, Soetermans, Steve Bannos, Steve Smith, Stickguy, TAnthony, TMC1982, TTN, The wub, TheTruthiness, Tpbradbury, Tubesurfer, Undead warrior, Vivaldi, Warreed, Webbrg, 161 anonymous edits

Donnie Darko *Source*: http://en.wikipedia.org/w/index.php?oldid=409063563 *Contributors*: ***Ria777, 1mujin22, 2ndStageTurbineBlade, 2runner2, 332stupka332, 4v4l0n42, 7, A Nobody, A8UDI, AAA!, ABCDDD, AC+79 3888, ATrow, AWatts420, Aaaxlp, Aatombomb, Abdullais4u, Abhgum2, AbsoluteGleek92, Accurizer, Acetylene, Acidburn24m, Acroterion, Adam Rusbridge, AdamRusbridge, Adolphus79, Adraeus, Adrian J. Hunter, Adw2000, Aerialwombat, Aeusoes1, Afa86, Afhaalchinees, Agent Conundrum, Aka042, Alansohn, Aldini98, Ale jrb, Alex43223, Alexandre Gilbert, Alientraveller, Allenwalla, Altenmann, Amateurgynacologyst, Amchow78, Americash, Amoammo, Andrzejbanas, AndySimpson, Andycjp, Andyroo316, Angr, Angular, Animedude360, Ann Stouter, Anopheles, Antandrus, AntiVan, Anticipation of a New Lover's Arrival, The, Antonrojo, Anville, Aramgutang, Arden, Arentath8, Arite, Arjun01, ArmyOfPie, Arnesh, ArnoGourdol, AscendedMaster, Ascensionblade, AshTFrankFurter2, Ashmoo, Astavats, Asteriatic, AtaruMoroboshi, Athene cunicularia, Atmamatma, Atypicaloracle, Axl, Azucar, Backslash Forwardslash, Badwolftv, BanyanTree, Bartender371, Bbatsell, Beaux182, Belami43, Bellhalla, Belovedfreak, Benjicharlton, Bennymanarms12, Bennyp81, Betacommand, BeyondStupidity, Bfigura's puppy, Bguest, Bhall87, Bigt2259, Bigtimepeace, BillPaxton, Binh Ngo, BitterSTAR, Bjones, Bkwillwm, Blackwolf13, Blah3, Blahziin Rav, Blaximus The Great, Blotchis, BlueChainsawMan, BlueLotusLK, Bmicomp, Bob O'Bob, Bobby122, Bocker, Bonadea, BostonRed, Bovineboy2008, Branddobbe, Brandon, BrightLights, Bryan Derksen, Bsdsolomon, Bswee, Bulish Rides Again!!!, Bumphaze, Burpcycle, Byoudou, Cablebfg, Cakemix, Callmarcus, Calmer Waters, Calmypal, Caltas, Cameraman03, Cammycam, Camw, Can't sleep, clown will eat me, Cancun771, Canyouhearmenow, Capitalistroadster, Carpet345, Cassioromeda, Catgut, CattleGirl, Cburnett, Ccausey401, Cdswtchr, Celshader97, CelticJobber, Centuriono, Chantessy, CharlotteWebb, Ched Davis, Cheesy Yeast, Chris 42, Chris Bainbridge, Chris the speller, ChrisKil, Christophore, Cirruss, Claudphillips, Cleduc, Clemmy, Closedmouth, Cmh, Cnwb, Coder Dan, Coldfight, Cometstyles, Conman71, Corti, Counsell, Courcelles, Cowpepper, Cp111, Craig.lz, Crash Underride, CrazyLegsKC, Cresix, Crispinus211, Cromag, Crossmr, Cryo1, Custardninja, CyberGhostface, Cycle71, CzarTyush, D4rk0, DCEdwards1966, DJ RedSkeye, DKqwerty, DSQ, Daedalus969, Damiantgordon, Damicatz, Danny, DarkBeetle, DarkoBB07, Darkofan108, Darkride, Darrenhusted, Daryldingman, Dattebayo321, Dave420, Daveydweeb, David Gerard, Davidhorman, Davodd, Ddrphreek, DecadeMan, Delldot, Deltalima, Deor, Depressed Marvin, DerHexer, Dertt, Devanjedi, Devotchka, Dfranks078, Dgtlmoon, Diemunkiesdie, Dirk Diggler Jnr, Discospinster, Dismas, Dlabtot, Dmanning, Doc glasgow, Doczilla, Dom Kaos, DonnieDicko, Donniedarkofan2006, DoubleCross, Dr.K., DrRicebowl, DrVon2, DrZarkov, Dragon695, DragonflySixtyseven, Dragonmaster 784, Drl0618, DuckieRotten, Durova, Dvd321, Dyaa, Dylan Lake, Dyslexic agnostic, E. Fokker, EEMIV, ELF23, ESkog, Eggytoast, El aprendelenguas, Elected, Elephant Talk, Elmer Clark, Eloquence, Eluchil, Elysdir, Emeraldcityserendipity, Emmelie, EmptyPocket, Emurphy42, Endlessdan, Enemysprout, Epbr123, Epolk, Erfa, Erik, Erinsaurusrex, ErkDemon, Esperant, Esprit15d, Esurnir, Euchiasmus, Evanreyes, Everyking, Everything counts, Evmore, Exet0626, Extraordinary Machine, EyeSerene, F4k3n4m3, Falcon8765, Faradn, Fedallah, Fell Collar, Ferdinand Pienaar, Ferkelparade, Fingers-of-Pyrex, Fistful of Questions, Flapdragon, Flippy1945, Flood79, Flutefreek, Fokkie, Forestofthedead, Fram, FrankDeBunny, FrankRizzo2006, Freakofnurture, Fredrik, Freemarket, Fritz Saalfeld, Frogfusious, Fuhghettaboutit, Fullfx, Fusion, GHcool, GTJoe, Gamaliel, Garion96, Gbrading, GeneralAtrocity, Geniac, Geoff B, Ghandir, Gigor, Gilliam, Ginsengbomb, Girolamo Savonarola, Gnat, Goatasaur, Gogo Dodo, Gowen72, Gpvos, Grandmasterka, GregAsche, Gregory j, Gretchen Ross, Grieferhate, Grim Revenant, Gspr, Guy M, Gwern, Gwernol, Hadal, HaeSuse, Hamtechperson, HarmonicFeather, Hawkeye14, Heaven's Wrath, Hegowski, Henrymrx, Hibana, Hierophants heart, Hihyooka, Hirstt, Hl, Hoary, Horkana, Hotspur42, Hubcapwiki, Hugzz, Hurleyman, Husond, Hwalkeradams, Hydrogen Iodide, IAmTheCoinMan, IGeMiNix, IIIthe 13thIII, IMSoP, IRT.BMT.IND, Icestorm815, Ignus, Igoldste, Ike9898, Ilikerps, Immunize, Initiatedeye, InsaneZeroG, Intovert2438, Ircannibalcat, Isaacbanana, Isnoop, ItsTheClimb17, Itsnotadisorder, J 1982, J.delanoy, JDoorjam, JNW, Jack Merridew, Jakeformaro, Jamesriv, Jampilot, JanaBeth, Jar G., Jasabella, Jasongill, Jasonmill777, Java13690, Jaysscholar, Jbav1278, Jcrook1987, JdeJ, Je5s3r, Jeff79, Jeffthejiff, Jemerson, Jeremy Butler, Jerry FM, JesseGarrett, Jessemerriman, Jfpearce, Jiggy9205, Jim Douglas, Jodamn, JoeBaldwin, Joel medings, Joerite, Jogloran, Johandesilva, John Vandenberg, JohnABerring27A, Johnip86, Johntex, Jon186, Jonathan F, JonnyLightning, Joondan, Jorgenduncan, Josilot, Josling 7, Jpers36, Jrayk, Jredmond, Jrickclark, JuPitEer, Juancnuno, Juliancolton, JustAddPeter, Jv821, K1Bond007, KaJin, Katechapman, Katieh5584, Keilana, Keit, Kendrick7,

Kenyon, Ketans, KidArt, Kidlittle, King sarah, KingPete, Kingpin13, Kingturtle, Kintetsubuffalo, Kittycat3456789, Klawrence14, Kmalinda, Kojiro, Kollision, Konczewski, Kookyunii, Korbannc, Kornfan71, Kouvre, Koyaanis Qatsi, Kroops, Krovisser, Krystyn Dominik, Ktrip2gs, Kukini, Kuru, Kusma, LFaraone, LGagnon, Lacrimosus, Laddie64, Lamrock, Landon1980, Larry laptop, Leafyplant, LeaveSleaves, Ledguitar, Lee M, Leonardhill, Lethe, Levineps, Lewi9486, Lightmouse, LilHelpa, Lila Macintier, LinkToddMcLovinMontana, ListedRenegade, ListenerX, Lode Runner, Loganriver, Logical Defense, Lonelymiesarchie, LongLiveHendrix, Longlivefolkmusic, Loodog, Lord Informer, LordViD, Lovok, Lucashoal, LuckyDucky, Lugnuts, LukeyBoy, Lulujannings, Lumaga, Luna Santin, Lupo, Lupus Daemonicus, M fic, M4, MC10, MSJapan, Madein89, Madmaniac5, MagikGimp, Mahound, Major Danby, Manmonk, Manwe, Manwoody, Maplecrisp, Marasmusine, Marcinjeske, Marcus118, Mark henebury, Markoff Chaney, Martarius, Master Jay, MattRevell, Mboverload, Mcauburn, Mdhowe, MearsMan, Megaboz, Melchoir, Mentaka, Merbabu, Mercenary318, Merlinsorca, Merope, Metal26freak, Metrodome Distribution, Mhking, Michael Kinyon, Michaelas10, Mighty Antar, Mike Selinker, Mike Winters, MikeAllen, Mikenucklesii, Mikepanhu, Mikething, Mikinator, Milonica, Mindmatrix, Minglex, Missmarple, MisterSheik, Misterwindupbird, Modemac, Modster, Moncrief, MoogleEXE, Moondyne, Mooseofshadows, Moosikal, Morbidbunny, Mortenoesterlundjoergensen, Mr Seeks Knowledge, Mr-susans, Mr. Good, MrMoonshine, Mtat76, Mtelewicz, Mtleslie, MuscLA 1, Mygerardromance, Mygigmms, Mythi, Mytwistedworld, Mzajac, Mzyxptlk, Nadsozinc, Nashk10, Natalie Erin, NawlinWiki, Neep, Neilc, Nemo bis, Netspin, Neufusdmurder, New Jack Swing, Nick125, Nicklob, Nietzsche 2, Niffe, Night Gyr, Nihiltres, Niqua230, Noclevername, Noebse, Nofrendo, Noirceuil, Nonagonal Spider, Norm mit, Nsmith 84, Nufy8, Nymf, ONEder Boy, Ocatecir, Ohcolonel, Ohnoitsjamie, Oliviay, Omicronpersei8, Operating, Ophois, Oppugno, Orayzio, OregonD00d, Osirusr, Ours18, Oxymoron83, Ozonalayer, PDH, PET, PKtm, PTSE, Pablo X, Pakokonka, Palendrom, Palfrey, Parker!, Patrick Berry, Paul A, Paul August, Penguinbuddy, Peter G Werner, Pevernagie, Phil Bordelon, Philip Trueman, Pigganon, Piggyface, Pikawil, Pinkyfloyd417, Pipedreamergrey, Pixelface, Pladask, Pleasantville, Poineuler, Poiuyt Man, Pokercardmail, Polaroidimpulse, Polyhymnia, Pomte, Poorleno, PoprocksAndCoke, Post Tenebras Lux, Powerofjuju, Ppntori, Premeditated Chaos, Prodego, Protiek, PsychoJosh, QcRef87, QuasiAbstract, Quince, Qwerty Binary, R. fiend, RDT2, RadicalBender, Raggyrat, Rai2788, RainbowOfLight, Rapanui73, Raphaelaarchon, RattleandHum, RaviKartheek, Reason says, Redeagle688, Redeeming Light, Redraven88, Reidhoch, Reisio, Renfroe, Rettetast, ReverendG, Rhun, Rich Farmbrough, Rich257, Richard Arthur Norton (1958-), Rickterp, Rob, RobJ1981, RobertMfromLI, Robjc123, Rockerbaby, Rockerjames2, Rodasmith, Roddy stewart, Rodiger, Roger Workman, Roker, Rome Leader, Roorback, RossPatterson, Rossrs, Rpyle731, Rstinejr, Rumilofaniel, Rumpelstiltskin, Runningonbrains, Runtime, Ryulong, SHCarter, SURIV, Sadi, Salvio giuliano, Sampi, SanderK, Saraal, Saswann, Savidan, Scarian, Schwenkstar, Scooter2536, Scottberger1959, Scottryan, Scrippatori, ScrollMaker, Seaeagle04, Sean D Martin, SeanDuggan, Seed25, Ser Amantio di Nicolao, Shadowjams, Shaka, Shan246, Sharkface217, Sharpie87q, Shawn in Montreal, Shirik, Shoeofdeath, SidP, Sietse Snel, Silent reverie86, Simoes, SimonLyall, SimonP, Simpsnut14, SineWave, SirRastus, Skipe89, Skomorokh, Skumshot, Sliprockdoc, Slurms MacKenzie, Smallchick50, SmartyBoots, Smiddlemas, Smokinjose, Snake556, Snb2806, Sneakums, Solofire6, Some jerk on the Internet, Somerset219, Sonic Shadow, Soulsrocker, SouperAwesome, Soyunapuerta, Spazure, Speaker1995, Spencerk, Spiff666, Spitfire, Srleffler, Sss222, Static Universe, StaticGull, Ste5000, Stealthbreed, Steelrats, Steve, StevenDH, Strangepalefighter, StuartMurray, Sugar Bear, Sup3r4wsumd0nny, Susanna Margaret, Swainstonation, Switch32763, Sydgarrett, Syed Tirmizi, Sylosin, Synchronism, Sysy, TIGERUPPERCUT29, Tabletop, Tagishsimon, Tapir2001, Tarotcards, Tarquin, Tbhotch, Tbiegalski, Tcncv, Tdevil333, Technogreek43, Teknolyze, Tekp, Tellin, Tenshi918, Thatguyflint, Thatssoscene13, The Giant Puffin, The Inedible Bulk, The Light6, The Outcast, The Thing That Should Not Be, The Thruth, The Transhumanist, The Vector Kid, The Wookieepedian, The stuart, The wub, TheAwesomestOne, TheEasterBunny, TheMidnighters, TheOneAndOnlyX, TheOneness, TheSolomon, Thelongroad1980, Thewayforward, Thomas Richard Harrison, ThomasK, Thorenn, Thorpe, ThylekShran, Tide rolls, Tigerghost, Tim Monteath, Tim1357, Timtheassassin, Timtottman, Titoxd, Todd unt, Toddmyster, TomCat4680, Tomsequitur, Tony Sidaway, Tooboldtoocold, Toussaint, TracyLinkEdnaVelmaPenny, Transverse, Travelbird, Tregoweth, TrevorRC, Trooney3, Troy 07, Trueninja, Truthiness Jones, Ttenchantr, Turrhall, Twang, Twbi.sin, Twisturbed Tachyon, Tyler, UKER, UberMan5000, Ultimatekai, UltimatexPunch, Undead1, Unexpect, Urutapu, Useight, Uucp, V-Man737, VX-LTM, VaderRacer, Vampus, Vandalz, Vaoverland, Vary, Vassanjimenno, Vcelloho, VeiledAbyss, Veledan, Vendettax, Violetriga, Viriditas, Vkunkel, VolatileChemical, Vyxx, W3twilly, Wade's Woman, Walterk29, Ward3001, Warpflyght, Watershipper, Wayland, Wclark, Werideatdusk33, Wheelhouse, WhisperToMe, Wiki Raja, Wildhartlivie, Will dwane, Will381796, Wisemanshade, Wiz-Pro3, Wl12345678, Wolf530, Wolfdog, Woohoosong2, Wtmitchell, Wysgal, Xcissocool, Xerxes Zorlu, Xeworlebi, Xgkkp, Xhienne, Y2kcrazyjoker4, Yamamoto Ichiro, Yansa, YeshuaDavid, Yngvadottir, Yoberalf, ZICO, Zaccaz777, Zandperl, Zazaban, Zeileis, Zeppocity, Zerotonin, Ziel, Zoid62, Zotdragon, ZouBEini, Zoz, Zurishaddai, Zythe, A, 2235 anonymous edits

Dawson's Creek *Source*: http://en.wikipedia.org/w/index.php?oldid=406915783 *Contributors*: 100110100, 1dragon, 97198, ACREW, AEMoreira042281, AaB-ern, Abarax, After Midnight, Akubhai, Alama, Alan smithee, Alan16, Alessgrimal, AmadeoV, Americanhero, AndrewHowse, Andrewpmk, Andrzej07, AriGold, Arthur I Brooks, AsHlEiGh1413659, AtomicAge, Audacity, Autiger, Azertus, Azrich, Bahar101, Barkeep49, Batman tas, Bbpen, Bensin, Bhall87, Bisbis, Blurasis, Bobblewik, Bovineboy2008, Brett37, Bryan Seecrets, CAPS LOCK, CPAScott, Ca2010, Caldorwards4, CanadianLinuxUser, Cburnett, Cedars, Ceyockey, Chanlyn, Chantessy, Charles Matthews, Chocolateboy, ChrisB, Ckatz, Clapierre, Classicrockfan42, Cmcginnis, Cmdrjameson, Cnota, CobraWiki, Coffeemusiclife, Commander Keane, Crjeong, Cruz-iglesia, CurlyGirl93, Cyfal, D6, DMG413, Da monster under your bed, DanMS, Daniel C. Boyer, Danny, Dark Mage, Darth Panda, Davehi1, Daveliney, David Gerard, David Koller, Dayewalker, Dbarnes99, Dcghosts, Dejvid, Delpino, Deltabeignet, Demonslave, Dharmabum420, Diberri, Diehard2k5, Dimimimon10, Dmleach, Docu, Dougfancy101290, Dputig07, DrBat, Dugwiki, Duncharris, E-Kartoffel, EatAlbertaBeef, Ejfetters, Elcue13, EliRykellm, ElizabethTodd90, Ellimleeuk, Emersoni, Emjaybee, Epbr123, Erolos, Essjay, Esteffect, Euroboymt, Evanreyes, Eversman, Everyking, Evil Monkey, Evil silence, Exodus05, FMAFan1990, Face-2-face, Fallelsewhere, Fantastic fred, Finkefamily, Flyer22, Foucoult, Fratrep, Fudoreaper, Fuhghettaboutit, Fuzheado, Gaius Cornelius, Gareth Owen, Garing, Ghepeu, Gjd001, GoingBatty, Gracery, Graveyardkiss, Gregg02, Grusl, Guinea pig warrior, Gujuguy, Gunkarta, Gurch, HAWAIILIFE, Harro5, Hhielscher, HoodedMan, Horrorshowj, Iam4Lost, Illyria05, Inliten, Inonit, J.delanoy, JNW, JYi, Jackol, JamesBurns, JamesLucas, Jay32183, Jayron32, Jcbrazao, Jdclevenger, Jeffrey O. Gustafson, Jkelly, Jmacgrath, Jodest3, Joecasual, Joelr31, Joew2690, Joeyconnick, John Depp, Jonathan B, Joshstephen, JustAGal, K3nTjr3n6, Kajmal, Karkaputto, Kazamai, Kelly Martin, Kelson, Kevin, Khaosworks, Kidlittle, Kingboyk, KinguMalone, Koyaanis Qatsi, Kurowoofwoof111, Kusunose, Kyral, LLP, La Pizza11, Lacrimosus, Laurinavicius, Lauroroger, Lectrice007, Leonardo2505, Lightmouse, LocoBurger, Lokioak, Lordwow, LouScheffer, Luani86, Luigi.bozzo, Luk, Lupin, Lvr, MPD01605, MacDouglas, Macolly, MakeRocketGoNow, Makizushi, Maltavision, Maralia, Mark83, MarnetteD, Martarius, Marvelknight616, Matthew03, Maximus Rex, Mayamussa, MegX, Megs1502, MemeGeneScene, Mepat111, Meshal Obeidallah, Michael Hardy, Mieczyslav, Mikay, Mike Dillon, MikeJ9919, Mikeo, Milchjon, Mild Bill Hiccup, Mistycreed-01, Mmortal03, Monkeypuzzler, Montybarker, Morwen, Motownjunkman, Mrschimpf, Mrswayxd, Mundilfari, Muricio, Muxxa, Mwanner, Naddy, Namangwari, NamesCody, Nanouk, Nastja, Nboggs, Nehrams2020, Neovu79, Nestene68, Ngb, Niceguyedc, Nickfehr, Nights Not End, Nikai, Niteowlneils, Niz, Noboyo, Onetruepatriot, Opark 77, Oscar ., Otto4711, P0per, PKtm, Pagrashtak, Paranoid-andrew, PedanticallySpeaking, Pedroserafin, Pegship, Penguinsrtw, Peteforsyth, Pinkadelica, Pjär80, Preppyboy9016, Principalityofgalore, PrisonMan, Prolinesurfer, Promethean, QuasyBoy, Queer Scout, RJE42, RadicalBender, RadioFan2 (usurped), Raine r pierre, Rdsmith4, Redl@nds597198, Reetep, Reisio, Rium, Rlquall, Rlw31, Robert Merkel, Robert Moore, Rokstar841, Ronhjones, RubyOnyx, Russell29, Ryright, SDC, SaberBlaze, Sam Korn, Sampi Europa, Sectorzz9pluralzalpha, Seelie, Seth Ilys, Shaka, Shannahanbury, Shannara, Shanshu, ShortShadow, Signalhead, Sinalet, Sky83, Slanoue, Solo75244, SpigotMap, Station Agent 836, StealthyVlad, Steam5, Steampowered, Sunborn, Superm401, TAnthony, TH43, TKL, TakuyaMurata, Tassedethe, Tbsdy lives, Template namespace initialisation script, TenPoundHammer, Tharpdevenport, Thatgorgeousmidget, The Brain of Morbius, The Evil IP address, The Real One Returns, The Rogue Penguin, The undertow, TheCustomOfLife, TheDJ, TheDotGamer, Themindset, Thiseye, Thorne, Throatybeard, Tim Long, Timmay!, ToNToNi, Tobias Bergemann, TommyStardust, Tony Sidaway, Tony fanta, Tony1, TonySt, TrayCee80, Tree Biting Conspiracy, Tregoweth, Troy 07, Trusilver, TwilightFanx23, Tylerstormky, UltimatePyro, Vaoverland, Vejvančický, Ver, Victor, Vmchoff, Waggers, Wapcaplet, Warreed, Web-enthusiast, Webmok, Wendell, Westsidepb, Whiner01, Whysanitynet, Whywhenwhohow, WikiLaurent, Wwoods, XX, Xezbeth, YUL89YYZ, Yamla, YonDemon, Zundark, Zzuuzz, 844 anonymous edits

Anchorman: The Legend of Ron Burgundy *Source*: http://en.wikipedia.org/w/index.php?oldid=409560350 *Contributors*: AAA!, Aaron carass, Aarsfor, Abq7y, AbsolutDan, AbsoluteGleek92, Adrian 1001, Adufig2000, Aesinis, Alabamaalaskaarizonaarkansas, Alansohn, AlbertR, Alex43223, Alphachimp, Ametlitz, AndTheCrowdGoesWild, Andrzejbanas, Andyb73, Animum, Apterygial, Arc Lamps & Signal Flares, AriGold, Asianchick, Avengedsevenfoldacdc, Avillia, BD2412, Baa, BabuBhatt, Barneygumble, Basawala, Bblakeney, Bbx, Bencey, Benny 142, Bentley4, Bezer, Bigbadman5, Biged, Billyrageguy, Bjelleklang, Blas747, Blehfu, Bob123bob123, Bobblehead, Bovineboy2008, Bratsche, Bristow88, Bryan986, Bsadowski1, Bubbleboys, Buckner 1986, C.carish, Cabiria, Calmer Waters, Calor, Cam61589, CanadianLinuxUser, Capricorn42, CaptHayfever, Carl.bunderson, Cartoon Boy, Ceien18, CelticJobber, Chiefs1fan44, Chrellisii, Chris G, Chrisswiss83, Chriswiki, Ckatz, Claviola, Closedmouth, Cm619, CodyT3212, Collegepres, Commander Shepard, CoolKatt number 99999, Coolcaesar, Cotton, Count Ringworm, Courtkittie, Cpharding618, Cresix, Cst17, DReifGalaxyM31, DanielBeddingfield, DanielCD, Dannycali, Daquernz21, Darrenhusted, Darthgriz98, Daunrealist, DavidK93, Daviessimo, Dcheagle, Dd86, DeWaine, Decfitz2001, Defdude24, Deftonesderrick, Deltabeignet, Dennehy, Denverbroncosspata4, Devanmaher, Deviler151, Discospinster, DoctorHarris21, Donmike10, Dpodoll68, Dr. Blofeld, Drewcifer3000, DrunkenSmurf, EagleOne, Earl273A, Easchiff, Eleos, Eltoddo, Endlessdan, Engineer Bob, Ericwirtanen, Espresso Addict, Eternalfire42, Ethanwa, Evil Monkey, Extransit, FMAFan1990, Falcon9x5, Fancysun, Fernandobouregard, Finchsnows, Firsfron, Fish and karate, Flyguy649, FrankRizzo2006, Frecklefoot, FrenchIsAwesome, Fuhghettaboutit, Gabbe, Gamaliel, Geniac, Geopgeop, Gilliam, Girolamo Savonarola, Goatasaur, Gogo Dodo, GrahamHardy, Gran2, Graygrayfox, Greengecko08, Groovyn8, Guy546, Hall Monitor, Hartmde, Hayden7196, Hobartimus, Hydrargyrum, I need a name, ILovePlankton, Ian.thomson, IanManka, Ibanez RYM, Iceberg3k, Intovert2438, Irishguy, Irregulargalaxies, J.D., J.delanoy, JBK405, JMyrleFuller, Jag123, Jake Wartenberg, James086, Jauerback, JediBMar, JeezBreeze, JeffBillman, Jeffrobg, JeremyMcCracken, Jimswimmy, Jm307, Joefridayquaker, JohnM, Johnteslade, JokestrMike89, Jolivetti, Jonay81687, Jtalledo, Juansidious, Jumanji656, JustPhil, KC Panchal, Kain21, Kalmbach, Kanemileyundertaker, Karmafist, Kbdank71, Kel947, Kenneth Hardeman, Kevdo, Kevin W., King of Hearts, Kinneyboy90, KittyCollier, Klptyzm, KnowledgeOfSelf, Kollision, Konczewski, Kubigula, Kukini, Kungfuadam, Kyorosuke, Lady Aleena, Lahiru k, Lamp99, Lampsalot, Lbr123, Leathwick, LeoLark, Leroyinc, Liamskey, LilHelpa, Lockesdonkey, Logan, LordVader42, Lorian, MCTales, MER-C, MacGyverMobile, Madhava 1947, Mahjong705, MakeRocketGoNow, Mance, Mandarax, Manjesus, Manning38, Manwithbrisk, MarcK, Master Deusoma, Master Jay, Matt d84, McSly, MegX, Metao, Miabadi, Michael Greiner, Mickiscoole, Mild Bill Hiccup, Mini-macc, Miquonranger03, Miszа13, Mitico, Mjpresson, Mnotaran, Moeron, MonkeyHateClean, Morgul12, Mortdestro, Mosherjm, Mr. Absurd, Mr. Tootsie de Wootsie, Mr.bonus, Mrhobo4, Muboshgu, N5iln, Nappymonster, NawlinWiki, Nehrams2020, Nfras, Nikowoj, Nodpresion, Noirish, Normer111, NorthernThunder, Not a slave, NotACow, Nscheffey, Ocatecir, OlEnglish, Oli Filth, Omicronpersei8, Onevalefan, Ozzy1404, Panser Born, Parsonsburg, Part Deux, Patriarch, Paul August, Pax85, Peponte, Piano non troppo, Pickettc, Playahater6, Pmsyyz, Poolboy8, Popekilroy, President David Palmer, Protomanvollnut, Psantora, Public Menace, Pugno di dollari, Qwerty Binary, R'n'B, R. fiend, Radiant chains, RadioKirk, RattleandHum, Reel01, Rehevkor, Replizwank, Retired username, Rettetast, RhymeReviser, RickK, Ricky Bobby, Ricky81682, Rjwilmsi, RoMo37, RobJ1981, RobbieFal, Robchurch, Robferrer, RoyBoy, Rufous, SD6-Agent, SYLFan74, Sam15, SammoHunk, Samuel johnson, ScudLee, Shamrox, Shaneheb, Shaunthered, Shawn in Montreal, Shizane, Sidonuke, Silent Tom, SilhouetteSaloon, Slakr, SlappyMcB, Sleeper99999, Smartse, Snyden, Soapybasketball, Sochwa, Soetermans, Soupnyc807, SpaceFlight89, Sparsefarce, Spuzzdawg, Squish78, Steakbuns, SteelFan25, Stefanomione, Str8cash, StuffOfInterest, Sundevilesq, Super-Magician, SuperDude115, Surprise of the Century, TAnthony, TKD, TMC1982, TMFSG, TMan4940, TSmithengl1101, TVfanatic2K, Tapir Terrific, TashaMK, Tawker, Ted@SysAdminDay.com, Telepwn, Tell-Tale Ghost, Tempodivalse, Tenebrae, TexasDawg, Thabeesknees, Thanos6, The Gerg, The KZA, The Thing That Should Not Be, TheDoober, TheMovieBuff, ThePatman, Thebigt788, Themomofall4, Theoldgoat, Thesaluki55, Thevalaquenta, Thief12, Thomas Aquinas, Threadnecromancer, Toasty!, Tobyc75, Todd unt, Tomhinch, Tommiketimriver, Tommy2010, Tomtomb1, Treybien, Trigg travers, Trusilver, Truthiness Jones, Turgan, Twrdave, Tyhopho,

Ujeanx, Ultraviolet scissor flame, Uncle Dick, UncleFloyd, Unicorn12345, Urzadek, Uvaduck, Vegaswikian, Versus22, Vikesrule1111, Walmer 54, Wangry, Ward3001, Wavy G, WazzaMan, Web-Man, Webmgr, Whitcher, White Cat, Willfordy, Willy105, Wimt, Witchbaby, Wizardman, Woohookitty, Wrsinden, Wwwhhh, Wysprgr2005, Xezbeth, Y2kcrazyjoker4, Ylee, Ysangkok, Zanimum, Zantastik, Zcragg, Zpb52, Zundark, Zuranamee, Zzz345zzz, Δ, 1069 anonymous edits

The 40-Year-Old Virgin *Source*: http://en.wikipedia.org/w/index.php?oldid=409456301 *Contributors*: *drew, 97198, AAA!, AB, AMac2002, AN(Ger), AT3397, Acalamari, Access Denied, Accurizer, AgentKnight, Ahmad halawani, Ajhoax, Ajraddatz, Alakhriveion, Alan smithee, Alansohn, Alexius08, Alfredosolis, Andrzejbanas, Andy Marchbanks, Andy120290, AngelOfMusic, Angr, Anthony Appleyard, Architect JBF, AriGold, Arteitle, Artemisboy, Atlantabravz, Azucar, Babajobu, BabuBhatt, Badger5, Barrettmagic, Bearcat, Beautiful.wave, Beetstra, Bellhalla, Bevjpdomgem, Big Bird, Blur4760, Bobet, Bogey97, Bookofjude, Bovineboy2008, Branddobbe, Brian Kendig, Brookie, Bryan H Bell, Budtard, Bumhoolery, Burntsauce, Bzuk, CA387, Cad94, Can't sleep, clown will eat me, CardinalDan, Carinemily, Catgut, Cayla, Cbrown1023, Cburnett, Cebra, Chavando, Chester polarbear, Chris814, Cjwright79, Cliff em all 1988, CollisionCourse, Colonies Chris, ContiAWB, Craigy87, CrazyC83, CrookedAsterisk, Crumbsucker, CryptoDerk, DKqwerty, DVC12, DVC15, Daltonls, DanB DanD, DarkFireTaker, Darksauron, Darrenhusted, Dave6, David Gerard, Dburnes1, Ddomanickk, Deftonesderrick, Delta759, Deltabeignet, DethFromAbove, Dina, Discospinster, Docboxx, Doctor Sunshine, Dougie K, Download, Dp462090, DrBat, Dream out loud, Dstopping, Dukefreak1, Dwdmang, Dxco, DynSkeet, Easchiff, EdBever, El Cubano, Elephant Talk, Embryomystic, Enigmaman, Enviroboy, Erik, Esprit15d, Evergreens78, Everyking, Ferdiaob, Fernandobouregard, FlyingCowOfDoom, Footballfan190, FrankRizzo2006, Freakofnurture, Freikorp, Freshh, Froid, Fromgermany, Funnycricket, Furrykef, Fusek71, GDonato, Gamaliel, Ghosts&empties, Gmarrast, GonNeedMoWax, Gonzonoir, Grafen, GrahamHardy, Greatrobo76, Guroadrunner, Gyrorobo, HalfShadow, Henryodell, Hifrommike65, Hughezy, Hyad, Hydriotaphia, IBook of the Revolution, IanManka, Ibanez RYM, Idellateressa82, IllaZilla, Imkat, Ingolfson, Insanity Incarnate, Irishguy, Irk, IronGargoyle, ItsTheClimb17, Jake Wasdin, Janiszewski, Jason.cinema, Jaybling, Jaylaw, JesseRafe, JimDunning, Jivlain, Jkfp2004, Jmlk17, John K, John254, JohnCD, JohnnyLurg, Jon186, Jonathan Headland, Jonathan.s.kt, Jrd56, Kafziel, Kaizenyorii, Kayau, Kbdank71, Kbh3rd, Kc12286, Kchishol1970, Kenblankenship, Kevdo, Kidlittle, Kikodawgzzz, Kiowa25, Klptyzm, Koavf, Konczewski, Kotsu, Kristen Eriksen, Kross, Kuralyov, Kurzon, Kyle757, Lady Aleena, Lambstein86, Legis, Lemonlime369, Lerikal, Leroyinc, Levineps, LifeStroke420, LinkToddMcLovinMontana, Llowe2008, LoganTheGeshrat, LostOverThere, Lovepush, Ludde23, Lugnuts, Lunchscale, MStraw, Madness879, Magicallydajesus, Maher-shalal-hashbaz, Mallanox, Mankind 2k, Marcus Brute, Markus5273, Martin19, Marx01, MaryHadALamb, Mason-Haynes, MasterGupta13, Mathew5000, MatthewKeys, Maumaux, MearsMan, Melsaran, Mgard7331, MikeJ9919, Mishara, Misirlou, Mistakefix, Misterkillboy, Moncrief, Morshem, Movieman2, Mr.86, Mrmiscellanious, Mulad, Mutant, Mysekurity, NawlinWiki, Ndboy, Ndenison, NeOak, Nehrams2020, Nmatavka, NotACow, NrDg, Nytimes19992000, Nzv8fan, O process, OOODDD, Old port, Omegatron, Omicronpersei8, Onorem, Oore, Opelio, Oppugno, Oskar Sigvardsson, Oxymoron83, PJY, Patrick Berry, Pawlied, Pele Merengue, Persian Poet Gal, Phi beta, Phydend, Pickles27, Piemanmoo, Pietrow, Plasticspork, Playa 4 sho, Pleasantville, Pnkrockr, Poison the Well, PsychoFawkes, Quadell, Qutezuce, REDJASPER777, RHaworth, RPIRED, RadicalBender, RattleandHum, RazorICE, Recognizance, Remixed, Remurmur, Rentastrawberry, Rholton, Richardcavell, Richfife, Ringkichardthethird, Ripcurlking, Rjwilmsi, RobJ1981, Rock4arolla, RollschueB, RotaryAce, Rsm99833, Rtcpenguin, Rudjek, Salamurai, Saltywood, Scarian, Sceptre, Schuhpuppe, SchuminWeb, Scottanon, See me let go, Seilidair, Seinfreak37, Sgsxander, Silent Tom, Skittlesjc, Skomorokh, Skraz, Skudrafan1, SkyWalker, Smalljim, Smdo, Snakeeater93, Sohollywood, Sovereign01, Spaceflower, Spandrel, Spellcast, Squall1991, Starkiller88, Steve Bannos, Steve40yov, SteveLamacq43, Stjeanp, Stonesour025, Struway, Sturm55, Stwalkerster, Sumnjim, Sunz600, Suoerh2, TR-BT, TamahomeJenkins, Tazz20200, Tcncv, TenPoundHammer, Terrillja, Tertiary7, Tetrachloromethane, The Nut, The Prince Manifest, The Random Editor, The Stone Cutter, The stuart, The wisest man, The3seashells, TheGreatConspiracy, TheManWhoLaughs, TheMidnighters, TheTruthiness, Thelastneo, Themfromspace, Themindset, Theoneintraining, Thesevenseas, ThinkBlue, ThomasO1989, ThrowingStick, Tim!, Timotheus Canens, Tomdobb, Tomm098, TracyLinkEdnaVelmaPenny, Travelbird, Treybien, Trusilver, Tychicus, Typhoon966, Ubardak, Udonknome, Ulfer, Varlaam, Vary, Vengeful Cynic, Verbalcontract, Victor, Voldemortuet, WadeSimMiser, Waggers, Ward3001, William Graham, Williamnilly, Wknight94, X42bn6, XMarxThaSpot, Y2kcrazyjoker4, Yamalgo, Zenohockey, Zepheus, Zick0604, Zoicon5, Zzz345zzz, 711 anonymous edits

You, Me and Dupree *Source*: http://en.wikipedia.org/w/index.php?oldid=407511749 *Contributors*: *drew, 12neo12, 97198, Abe Lincoln, Acather96, Adefiniteproduct, Akelly7, Akriasas, Alphachimp, Alwayz withu2211, AnmaFinotera, AnonMoos, Aquatics, Ariel., Asarelah, BYMAstudent, Babsbabsbabs, BabuBhatt, Big Smooth, Blitz3000, Blueboy24, Boo1210, Bovineboy2008, Butros-Butros, CWenger, Canadian, Cao, Change is nice799, Cigammagicwizard, Ckimpson, Col3h, Colourblind, ConradPino, ContiAWB, Cooksey, Cosmic Latte, Crotchety Old Man, Crzycheetah, Cytang, David Gerard, Day and night332, Deathwiki, Dr. Blofeld, Dubc0724, Dutchmonkey9000, Euchiasmus, Fernandobouregard, Finlay McWalter, Foleydog, Gabbe, Gamaliel, Girolamo Savonarola, Googlewhack'd, HalJor, Hillstead, Horkana, IMLX, InfamousPrince, Inwardexposure, J.delanoy, Jabbathenut, Jeff G., Jevansen, Joliecide, Jumping cheese, Kintup, KrakatoaKatie, Kyros, LeghornB, Levineps, Llort, Lordofmodesty, Mahanga, Marychan41, Matari777, Mattlore, Mcsee, Midnight Critter, Misteror, Mpmuts, Nice poa, Not a slave, Nsaa, Omghgomg, Ommnomnomgulp, Patrick, Pop Up Ads, Q8-falcon, Quentin X, R'n'B, RDMD, RaikiriChidori, RattleandHum, Richardkselby, Riverstepstonegirl, Rogerd, Salopian, Seaphoto, Selbymayfair, ShadowyOne, Sintaku, Supernumerary, Superruss, Syxx, TKD, Tapir Terrific, The Cool Kat, This is u4399, Tide rolls, Timc, Tony Sidaway, Tregoweth, Treybien, Varlaam, VarunRajendran, Vbbdesign, Violetriga, WOSlinker, Walkiped, Wereon, Wikien2009, Yamla, Ymandd, 202 anonymous edits

Knocked Up *Source*: http://en.wikipedia.org/w/index.php?oldid=409670391 *Contributors*: 0nil0, 313phant, 97198, AAA!, AEMoreira042281, AN(Ger), Abla salama, AbsoluteGleek92, Ace Class Shadow, AdamDeanHall, Ahoerstemeier, Ajplmr, Albert109, Alegoo92, Alexfb, Alientraveller, Alpertjm, Analogue Kid, AndrewHowse, Andrzejbanas, Andy Marchbanks, Angel caboodle, Angus Lepper, Antonielly, Art10, Ashwinr, Aspirex, AxelBoldt, BandieraRossa, Bearcat, Bellhalla, Big Bird, Binx, Bladesofhalo, Bobo192, BonsaiPotato, Boris Barowski, Bremerenator, Brian Kendig, BritneySpearsAddict, Bryan H Bell, BuckwikiPDa535, BusboyRaffield, C-Woodchuck, C777, CJMylentz, CO, Canuckle, Cas510, Casull, Charmed fanatic, Chavando, Checkguy, ChesterG, Chicken Wing, Chris Bulgin, Chris the speller, Chris.bernstein, ChrisTheDude, ClarkMills, Clarkr95, Claydoolan, Cliff1911, Cnota, Colonel Activity, Cornellrockey, Coruptyd, Crumbsucker, Cuchullain, Cymbalta, Da monster under your bed, Dabilharo, DaddyPayne, Danausplexippus, DanielPenfield, Danielba894, Darrenhusted, David Gerard, Dayskidsfan, Dcs315, Deadblob93, Delicious carbuncle, Dilaudid, Disastrophe, Discospinster, Dismas, Doc Strange, Dogma343, Dolphin Jedi, Domi99, Dp76764, Dr. Blofeld, Dreadstar, Dspradau, Duhon, Easchiff, East718, Ebyabe, Echuck215, Edsully, Eggman183, Elephant Talk, Elipongo, Epbr123, Erik, Erik9, Esprit15d, Everyking, Faigl.ladislav, Fair Deal, Fantusta, Farhanhamojo, Faviang, Fdssdf, FerdinandFrog, Fernandobouregard, Ferquinteroc, Fgoetz, FightTheDarkness, FinnWiki, Flowerkiller1692, Fm90, FrankRizzo2006, Fratrep, Freakofnurture, Frederickgoetz0, Freshh, Frightwolf, Fsm83, Furrykef, Gaff, Garion96, Gecafe, Georgewilliamherbert, Gogo Dodo, Granpuff, GregorB, Guat6, GunsN'RosesFan1, H. Carver, H.M.S Me, Heywikiyouresofine, Hillman15, Hitman984, Hmains, Hmrox, Hotflboi2005, Hu Gadarn, Hullaballoo Wolfowitz, I'mMe!!, IAmTheCoinMan, IKato, Ibanez RYM, Igoldste, In Defense of the Artist, Insanity Incarnate, Iridescent, ItsTheClimb17, JNW, JTWoodsworth, JYi, Jac16888, Jack butler505, Jason.cinema, Jauerback, Jaybling, JazMc, Jcorn96, Jennavecia, Jessie4192, Jeyo9891, JimDunning, Jkfp2004, Jljordanjl@aol.com, JoeSmack, Jogers, JoshuaZ, Journalist, JulieKO, Jumpbug, Juno, Justme89, Jweiss11, Jzummak, Kbdank71, Kchishol1970, Keilana, Kgaris42, Khatru2, Kickazz, Kidlittle, Kingturtle, Kollision, Konczewski, Kusma, Kwsn, Leclaird, Leeway22, Leontios, Leroyinc, Lethe, Levineps, Lightdarkness, LilChaZz, LinkToddMcLovinMontana, Lockzeis, Lordsauran, Luna Santin, MECU, MMuzammils, Markt3, Marychan41, Matsutake, Mattarata, Matthew, Mattmcneil, Maustrauser, McNish2, Mdb1370, Meganginna, Meinterrupted, Merbabu, Mikecraig, Million Moments, Missjessica254, MisterMod, Miwunderlich, Mixtapeguru, Moncrief, Monkeytheboy, Mosquitopsu, Movie edit90, Mrbubs3, Mysekurity, NWill, NawlinWiki, Nearphotison, Nehrams2020, Nicknackrussian, Nightscream, Nuttycoconut, Nymf, OS2Warp, Omghgomg, P159700, PDRebel, Pandawful, PandoraX, Patrick, Paul Erik, Pawnkingthree, Paxsimius, Peecee1978, Pegship, Pele Merengue, PhilyG, Picaroon, Pixelface, Pleasantville, Pnkrockr, Possum, Prolog, RJASE1, RYANonWIKIPEDIA, RahadyanS, Randomjohn, RattleandHum, Razorhead, Redl@nds597198, Remurmur, RetiredWikipedian789, Rich Farmbrough, Richiekim, Rilbiz, Rito Revollto, Rje, RoadDogXVIII, Ronsparkscomedy, RoyBatty42, Rwiggum, Rx4evr, Ryan Postlethwaite, Rypcord, Ryu Kaiser, S19991002, SGGH, ST47, Sal Chiappetta, Saltywood, Sammayel, Sceptre, SeanMooney, See me let go, Seryred123, Sevenarts, Shadowjams, Sharkface217, Silent Assasin2, Silent Tom, SirLordJacob, Skittleys, SkyWalker, Smcallister, Smyd286, SnappingTurtle, Snoo52, SoWhy, Sockr44e, Sonic874, Spellcast, Spiderguy999, SpikeToronto, SteveCoppock, Steven X, Svenji, Svernon19, THF, TMC1982, Ta bu shi da yu, Tabercil, Tabletop, TaiChiChuan, Targetpuller, Tetzcatlipoca, Thaurisil, The Delivery Boy, The Hungarian, The lorax, TheFarix, TheMovieGod, Thecomedian, Thirdeyeopen33, Tinton5, Tobyfee, Tokufan, Tomm098, Tony Sidaway, TracyLinkEdnaVelmaPenny, Transcendence, Tregoweth, Treybien, Ttfreck, Tychicus, UnitedStatesian, Vagary, VatoFirme, Verbalcontract, Vivi c toro, WCityMike, WIKI-GUY-16, Wakefencer, Wakuran, Walabee95, Walkiped, Ward3001, Warlordt, Wayman975, Wbytllyw, Wbytllyw4, Weezerzero, Wesrox, Whiteguy09, Whywhenwhohow, Wiggin Tree, Wikieditor06, Wikkiegirl17, WillC, Winhunter, Wraithdart, XP1, Xedgexbikerx, Y2kcrazyjoker4, Yamla, YankeeDoodle14, ZiggyZig, Zpalmese, Zzuuzz, 1117 anonymous edits

Jay and Seth vs. The Apocalypse *Source*: http://en.wikipedia.org/w/index.php?oldid=400409613 *Contributors*: AbsoluteGleek92, Aervanath, AmazingBlueDuck, BQZip01, Bobber0001, Erik, Franamax, Girolamo Savonarola, Iridescent, Kevlar67, Kollision, Lord Pistachio, MichaelQSchmidt, MikeAllen, Mr. Chicago, PC78, Rjwilmsi, Skomorokh, Steve, SunOnMyWall, Tiggytighe08, TubularWorld, Tyrenon, Woohookitty, 22 anonymous edits

Superbad (film) *Source*: http://en.wikipedia.org/w/index.php?oldid=407705890 *Contributors*: 5minutes, A Raider Like Indiana, AK Auto, AN(Ger), AT3397, Abrech, Ace ETP, Acebloo, Acq3, Addie777, Aeronflux, Agentdemon, Aillema, Airtuna08, Airumel, Alansohn, Alex43223, Alexf, Alexluckett, All Hallow's Wraith, Alwaysthrash 09, Alyssadriana, Amphytrite, Andonic, Andrzejbanas, Andy M. Wang, Angel caboodle, Anthony Bradbury, Antiuser, Apparition11, Arevedirci, Arhsistheshoot, Art10, Arteitle, Artrush, Aruton, AshTFrankFurter2, AskFranz, Avenged Eightfold, Aximill, B, B00ge4, Badwolftv, Balthazarduju, Bananablender, Barliner, Baseballbaker23, Batman2005, Battyface, Bdburako, Bencey, Benjamintchip, Bevo74, BigHaz, Blake-, Blood sliver, Bobo192, Bongwarrior, Booyabazooka, BostonRed, Bovineboy2008, Bowlingforsoup01, Bpeps, Brabblebrex, Branddobbe, Brewcrewer, Brian The Mute, C6541, CPColin, Cajunwilson, Callmarcus, Calor, Can't sleep, clown will eat me, CanadianLinuxUser, Capitocapito, Carter9019, Cgoods, Chairboy, Chameleon684, CharlotteWebb, Chelseafc93, ChesterG, Chimichanga23, Choess, Chris Bainbridge, Chris Bulgin, Chris the speller, ChrisTheDude, Chunky Rice, Cigarette, Cinemaniac, Citymovement, Cjones132002, Clintville, Closedmouth, ClydeNut, Cmprince, Cms479, CollisionCourse, ConCompS, Coolix, Coppercat27, Courcelles, CraigFoye80, CrookedAsterisk, Cuchullain, Cwill19, D, DH85868993, DMCer, Dadude3320, Dahamsta7, Dandamanolopopper, Daniel J. Leivick, Darklilac, Darrenhusted, Davewho2, David Gerard, Davidmwhite, Delta759, DeluxNate, DerHexer, DiagonalDog, Diannaa, Dianoga, Dinosaur puppy, Discospinster, Dismas, Dominik92, Dp76764, Dr Dec, Dr.K., Dreaded Walrus, Dreadstar, Drmies, Duder999, Dustman81, Dvberm, Dysepsion, ECWAGuru, Easchiff, EdBever, EeepEeep, Effer, ElisaEXPLOSiON, Elmoeater, Enviroboy, Eparadis, Epbr123, Erik, Esrever, Evan is mclovin, Evanreyes, Fabastonmartinoneill, Faithlessthewonderboy, Falconclaw5000, Fangfufu, Faradayplank, Ferdiaob, Fernandobouregard, Finchsnows, Footballfan190, Foxmulder32, FrankRizzo2006, Frankenpuppy, Franz Richter, Freeman08, Freepsbane, FrickFrack, Friginator, Frodohair, Furrykef, GaMeRuInEr, GargoyleMT, Garion96, Gavinmcmillen, Gmarrast, Gnowxilef, GobBluthGambitDeadpool, Googleaseerch, Granpuff, Greelade, Gregfitzy, Grieferhate, Groovenstein, Gstarluxe, Gurch, Guroadrunner, Hailstone6394, HalfShadow, HarryC15, Havocrazy, Haymaker, Hellooooo!182, Hemlock Martinis, Heracles31, Hiplibrarianship, Holaboyperu, Holeinthetoad, Hoof Hearted, Horkana, HorrorMonkey, Hotdaddy, Hschmid1, Hyperman585, I Am McLovin It, I luv zelda 89, Iaxzo, Iknowyourider, Impasse, InnocuousPseudonym, Io Katai, Iridescent, IronCrow, J.delanoy, JBurn hardcore, JCO312, JForget, JNW, Jackol, Jacobtaylor1987, James Epstein, James Luftan, JamesLucas, JavaTenor, Jaybling, Jef-Infojef, Jeff G., Jefoster,

Jenni ish here, JesseRafe, Jester5x5, Jester7777, Jgera5, Jh51681, JimDunning, Jj137, Jleedev, Jmlk17, Johnmichaelfitzpatrick, Jollygreengiant305, JonasBrother1, Jonathan.s.kt, JonathanKao23, Jonny5244, Josh3580, Joshuas3521, Jovianeye, Jsagerfan, Juhachi, Jujubean55, Jusdafax, Justchill0ut, Kainaw, Kaiser matias, Kaizer13, Kane5187, Kcking69, KeasbeyMornings, Kedarbhatia, Keilana, Kennygollnick, Kicking222, Killervogel5, King of Hearts, KingMorpheus, Kingkongrasta, Klptyzm, KnowledgeOfSelf, Kollision, Kontar, Krang, Kubigula, Köbra, L Kensington, L goopy l, LN2, Lamrock, Lantay77, Latics, Lazulilasher, Lenin and McCarthy, Lepenseur09, Lerikal, Leroyinc, Levineli, Levineps, Lilac Soul, LinkToddMcLovinMontana, Londo06, Loneynig2007, Loren.wilton, Lovgun7, Ltljltlj, LukeHogg123, MCStanden, MJD86, MOOOOOPS, Madchester, Magnius, Majorly, Maniac cop, Mankytoes, Maskedunit, Master Deusoma, Mastercolto, Mattrobs, Max725, Maxis ftw, McLovin, McLovin11210, McLovin9394, Mclovinoven, Mh31092, Midnightowl, Mike Rosoft, Minimac, Mjpresson, Moncrief, Monkus2k, Motleyangel, Mrweetoes, MsDivagin, Musicforkings, Mysdaao, N5iln, NawlinWiki, Naylor07, Ncalvin, Nehrams2020, NeilN, Neilymon, Nekrogeist, Nemeses9, Nerr201, Nevermore27, Nextjj34, Nightscream, Nikkerloo, Nikzbitz, Nocarsgo, Noctibus, Nqnpipnr, NurseryRhyme, ONEder Boy, ObeyK1NGTaz, OdinReborn, Okki, Omhseoj, Onevalefan, Owsianko, Oxymoron83, Pale Autumn, ParisianBlade, Patrick, Paul August, PaulHammond2, Pele Merengue, PeteMaravich1970, Peter Fleet, Pharaoh of the Wizards, Phatom87, Phgao, PhilKnight, Philip Trueman, Physcovideos, Piano non troppo, Pixelface, Pleasantville, Pointlessname, Powerg8, PranksterTurtle, Project10509, Prolog, Pseudomonas, Punk 1441, Pygmypony, Qorzm, QuasiAbstract, Quuxplusone, Qwerty Binary, RA0808, Radiohawk, Radosław10, RainbowOfLight, Ramblinmindblues, Reallyangryrightnow, Reconsider the static, Redrocket, Reganregan, Reidhoch, Reidnf, Reiewer, Res2216firestar, Richmcrichardson, Rish10, Rjanag, RoadDogXVIII, Robertvan1, Robofish, Ronsparkscomedy, Rossgroden, Rushin97, Rusted AutoParts, Rwhollywoodfan, Rwiggum, Rypcord, Rzryr, SGGH, SMC, SQGibbon, ST47, Sager1fan, Salavat, Saltywood, SamTheButcher, Santacruzboards, Satori Son, Sayhellojana, Scanlan, Scarce, Scarian, Sceptre, Schexpir, Scottycrum1, SeanMooney, Searcher 1990, Section8pidgeon, Sephiroth BCR, Sharkface217, ShelfSkewed, Shepejps02, Shrocky2, Shunpiker, Silent Tom, Silver Edge, Simosx, Sisko199, Skier Dude, SkyWalker, SleepyheadKC, Slon02, Snowolf, SoSaysChappy, Soilwork71492, Someguy1221, Spartansjase, SpikeJones, Spinerod, Spoonyc76, Sportsgeek31, Springeragh, Stackindiem, Statalyzer, Stephen's black friend, Steven X, Stewie814, Stoner--13, Sturm55, Stwalkerster, Sully1331, Sunderland06, Surfeited, Svetovid, THF, TKD, TMC1982, TaborL, Takeaway, Tanthalas39, Tedmund, Teehe, Tempodivalse, That Asian Guy, The Hungarian, The Thing That Should Not Be, The Video Game Master, TheNewPhobia, Theflyingfrigger, Thehelpfulone, Thingg, ThinkBlue, Thomasthestudent, Thrasher6920, Thumperward, Tide rolls, Tim Long, Tiptoety, Titanosaurus, Tithonfury, Tjdodd, Tohd8BohaithuGh1, Tomdobb, Tomistomistom, Tomwissler, Tony Sidaway, Tony1, TracyLinkEdnaVelmaPenny, Tradrrboy, Trapekitty, Tregoweth, Trevor wells, Treybien, Trogga, Tslocum, Typhoon966, Uncle Dick, Uncle Milty, Useight, User789, Uucp, VernoWhitney, Versus22, Victor, Viewdrix, Vipinhari, VolatileChemical, WLU, Wack'd, WadeSimMiser, Ward3001, Watchingthevitalsigns, Wbytllyw, Werty1018, WesternRider, WhisperToMe, Wildtiger444, William Graham, Winchelsea, Wizardman, Wmcgarry, Wongm, Wutschwlllm, X!, Xavexgoem, Xihix, Y2kcrazyjoker4, Yintan, Yokes14, Yukichigai, Zchris87v, Zimbabweed, Zimzimzbob, Zookman12, Zpb52, Zzuuzz, Zzymyn, 1466 anonymous edits

The Spiderwick Chronicles (film) *Source*: http://en.wikipedia.org/w/index.php?oldid=405614658 *Contributors*: AAA!, ACSE, AN(Ger), Aarond2, Adamthompson1994, Ajcfreak, Akvarknimblus, Aldo samulo, All Hallow's Wraith, Andrzejbanas, Angel caboodle, Antonio Lopez, Astroview120mm, Beetstra, BlahBlehBlihBlohBluh, Bobeisman, Bongwarrior, Brainix, Calor, Caltas, CastAStone, Chaser, Cipkid292, Clerks, Cometstyles, Cornucopia, Courtens, CyberSkull, DarKnight80, Das Baz, DentonChrist, Depressed Marvin, Detnchris1, Detnchris14, Djbj16, Dr. Sunset's Chariot Railroad, Dynesclan, East718, Epbr123, Erik, Fdewaele, Finngall, Fram, FrankRizzo2006, Frecklefoot, GalleryofMisery, Garion96, Gordenie, Got118115147, Goth and Throbb99, Grandpafootsoldier, Greyvisitor, Guy M, GwydionM, Harryboyles, Hello, I'm a Wikipedian!, Hermione Weasley11, Hm29168, Horrorbob, Illustrious One, InfamousPrince, Irishguy, J.delanoy, JaGa, Javatyk, Jessikins, Jimd, KTC, Kachehappy, Kollision, Kune171, Limetolime, Lugnuts, M.hoeting, MARQUIS111, Materialscientist, Melaen, MikeVitale, Movingboxes, Mr. Absurd, Mr. Long Story, Mtjaws, NICHOLAS LAMINACK, Nehrams2020, Nickelodeonfan2007, Nicole.mclear, Niduzzi, Noah Salzman, Noclevername, Pase Maun, Patrick, Pegship, Pejorative.majeure, Pinkgirl1995, Pixelface, Possum, Quentin X, RJaguar3, Red-Blue-White, Redbarronalpha1, Renaissancee, Rigadoun, Rilbiz, Rjanag, Rje, Roaring Siren, Robertvan1, Roxy2k7, Rtkat3, Ryulong, Salamangkero, Salamurai, Salil.gokhale, Shoessss, SkyWalker, SorryGuy, SpOnGeFaN818, Spellcast, Spiderwickfan, SpikeJones, Spittlespat, SpongeSebastian, Spoonkymonkey, Sreejithk2000, Suckstobeabum, TMC1982, Tankerman303, The Shadow-Fighter, The Thing That Should Not Be, The Wild Falcon, TheMovieBuff, TheRealFennShysa, Theda, Thief Lord, Tiger Trek, TracyLinkEdnaVelmaPenny, TrevorX, UDScott, W Tanoto, Welsh, Whm2, Wildroot, Will-B, Wordy1, Yamla, Zasderfght, 373 anonymous edits

Horton Hears a Who! (film) *Source*: http://en.wikipedia.org/w/index.php?oldid=409478640 *Contributors*: AKR619, AWeenieMan, Abce2, Abefoulkes, Abrech, Acebloo, Advanced, Aitias, Alansohn, AlbertSM, Alex2631, Alexf, Allen4names, Allsaints23, Andromedabluesphere440, Andromine, Andrzejbanas, Andycjp, Angel caboodle, AniMate, Anticipation of a New Lover's Arrival, The, Aomd, Apple1013, ArchonMagnus, Arkyopterix, Art1991, AshTFrankFurter2, Asifsys23, Aswomekid122, Atlan, Avelinforl32, Avoided, Babyboy808, Badonkadonkhr, Bat12, Batman Fan, Bdve, Beach drifter, Bella Swan, Bender235, Benzy19, Betterthanbond, Beve, Bewareofdog, BigBang616, Bigkeyshawn, Bill bo, BirgitteSB, Blueliteway, Bobo192, Bostongal247, BoulderDrop, Bovineboy2008, Boygenius97, Braza258, Brclmu, Brianhenke, Brookie, CBFan, CWY2190, Caet, Cahk, Caloscalante1518, Calvin 1998, Cartoon Boy, Cat's Tuxedo, Catcher Block, Catgut, Cheddarjack, Christian Swenson, Christianster45, Clarince63, Closedmouth, Cnota, Conny, Coralmizu, CraigFoye80, D6, Dacman6688, DaffyDuck619, DanMat6288, Danielfolsom, Danski14, Dark Prime, Darwin-rover, Dav93Lov, DavidDCM, Davie400, Dcfreak114, DeadlyTaco, Deanb, DerHexer, Derrty2033, Discospinster, DisneyLover41, Dlwr300, Dmane1, Dmurawski, DocNox, Dougmcarthur0, Dr.Quentin X. Mathews, DrBat, Dramartistic, Drewdy, Dycedarg, Dynesclan, Edward cookie cutter, Eeeppp, Elendil's Heir, Elephant Talk, Empezardesdecero1718, EoGuy, EoinMahon, Errorlines, Esn, Eternal Pink, Eumolpo, EwanMclean2005, Fbv65edel, Frekeeehobo, Frightwolf, FriscoKnight, Frymaster, FuriousFreddy, Gabrielkat, Gail, Gary King, Genedecanter, Gnowxilef, Goa103, Gobonobo, Gogo Dodo, GoingBatty, Gojira09, GrahamHardy, Gran2, Grandpafootsoldier, Granpuff, Green Sheet, Green caterpillar, Gregfitzy, Gtr57, Guy1423, Haon 2.0, Headstrong neiva, Hectorferjr2, Hyrulian93, IJVin, Immblueversion, Iridescent, Irishguy, Irk, J.delanoy, J4musicals, JCO, JPG-GR, JacksonMiller, Jacob valliere, Jake Wartenberg, JamesBWatson, Jarrod Baniqued, Jasonbres, JayKeaton, Jayce0814, Jayron32, Jaz246, JeanColumbia, Jeremiah2man, Joltman, Joshschr, JudgeSpear, Jusdafax, JustSomeRandomGuy32, Kakofonous, Kanonkas, Karlamon, Katalaveno, Kchishol1970, King0fpenguins, Kintetsubuffalo, Kollision, Krismorel, Kubrick, Kww, LDEJRuff, Leonidas23, LilHelpa, Limetolime, Limonns, LinkToddMcLovinMontana, Lipton sale, LiteraryMaven, Madmardigan53, Magicboy666, Magioladitis, Malinaccier, Markyopp, Matanui1326, Mathew5000, Meegs, Mice never shop, MilborneOne, Milonica, MissSox, Mlaffs, MonkeeJuice, Morpose, Mouse's Ear, MovieRatIan, Movieguru2006, Movingimage, Mr. Absurd, Mr.Knox, MrBumpFan, Muerte, Mwpich, Myscrnnm, N. Harmonik, NJZombie, Nargis 2008, NawlinWiki, Ndboy, Nedloyd1970, Nehrams2020, Neorge, Nikofeelan, Nips, Noclevername, Norcaldaydreamer, NoriMori, NotNina, NrDg, Nshady16, ObsessiveJoBroDisorder, Oerjan, Oofpoot, Ortizurzaiz, Ottovonguericke, Pascal.Tesson, Patrick, Paulley, Pb12, Pegship, Phil Boswell, Philip Trueman, Phoenix1304, Phydend, Pixelface, Pizzadinosaur, Polarbear97, Powerofjuju, Psychonaut3000, Pyrrhus16, RJaguar3, RMikes, Rabidanimals, Re non verbis, Renaissancee, Reptoid333, RevWaldo, Rgoodermote, Rhindle The Red, Rockysmile11, Roth 300, Rtkat3, Ryan Holloway, Ryan the Game Master, SAkora1, Salamurai, Salvio301, Sandcastle84, SausageSandwich, Scarian, Schmiteye, SchnitzelMannGreek, Schultmc, Sesshomaru, Seussfan, Shadowagent 0, Shawisland, Shorespirit, SiameseSoul, SidP, SideshowBob99, Silent Tom, Silvlasdfj, Sjones23, SkyWalker, Smalljim, Snowman Guy, Soccerdud, Soetermans, Sorabond007, Spellmaster, SpikeJones, Spmonahan, Springnuts, SquidSK, Ste1n, Stealth500, Steven Zhang, Stfu Roy, Stwalkerster, Sugarlandfanatic, SummaBritt, Sunil060902, Swiftink, TMC1982, Tabletop, Tacrolimuses, TaerkastUA, Tango, Tb4000, Tech408, The Arachnid, The Evil Spartan, The Obfuscator, The Rogue Penguin, The Swagga, TheGoldStandard, TheRealFennShysa, TheValentineBros, TheXenocide, Thecomedian, Thewikipopo, Thingg, Tiddly Tom, Tide rolls, Tkynerd, Tnxman307, Toddst1, Tommyt, Tony Webster, Toughpigs, TracyLinkEdnaVelmaPenny, Tregoweth, TreyMarsh20, Twaz, Tylers2009, UK Liberal, Ub3rn008, UberMan5000, UnfriendlyFire, UrsaLinguaBWD, Uytku, Vchimpanzee, Versus22, Vidgmchtr, Viewdrix, Vuerqex, Wack'd, Websurfer246, WhisperToMe, WikHead, Wikibarista, Wikiboy243, Wikieditboy, Wile e2005, Winterheart, Wtooher, X3ni, Xflipypet3x, Xoxpeacexox, 1782 anonymous edits

Strange Wilderness *Source*: http://en.wikipedia.org/w/index.php?oldid=406103623 *Contributors*: All Hallow's Wraith, Andrzejbanas, Axl, B Dub550, BlueLint, Bobo192, CanadianLinuxUser, Casaaq, Casbboy, ChesterG, CraigFoye80, Double Fanucci, DoubleCross, DrugProblemm, Erik, Erroneuz1, Fordmadoxfraud, FrankRizzo2006, Goldenrowley, Hagerman, Hunterbick, Husond, InfamousPrince, Jgfan2099, John254, Jonesy702, Kap2319, Kelvin Samuel, Kintetsubuffalo, Kndy, Kramlean, Kwamikagami, Littleteddy, Mallanox, Martarius, Matt wuz heer, MikeCp76, Mrschimpf, Natesgate, Nehrams2020, NeoNorm, Okki, Onepiece226, Oofgeg, Pakaran, Pearle, Pegship, Phmovie, Pixelface, Rich Farmbrough, Rodzilla, RoyBoy, Rray, Safebreaker, Salad Days, Scetoaux, Skomorokh, Suffusion of Yellow, TheRetroGuy, Therealdavo2, Thingg, Think outside the box, TrevorX, Trogga, WaKo944, WhisperToMe, Whitejay251, Wikieditboy, Yeanold Viskersenn, 132 anonymous edits

Drillbit Taylor *Source*: http://en.wikipedia.org/w/index.php?oldid=409609577 *Contributors*: AN(Ger), AT3397, After Midnight, Andrzejbanas, Angie Y., Arcai, AshTFrankFurter2, Aurigas, Badagnani, Bandstand1102, Bark, Beemer69, Bencey, Berig, Blanchardb, Bonecrushah, Briaboru, CWii, Caiaffa, Charoog10, ChesterG, Coder Dan, ColdFusion650, DH85868993, Del91, DerHexer, Discospinster, Douglasr007, DougsTech, Dragonfly298, EZWalk, Eddie Kennedy, Endothermic, Enviroboy, Epbr123, Erik, Evilskull1992, Ewa5050, F4280, Fernandobouregard, Firsfron, Flowerpotman, For An Angel, FrankRizzo2006, Freshh, GRuban, Galactic war, Garion96, HalosLikeNooses, Hannibalking95, Happyface162, Hattiedog, Hellothere22, Horkana, Ibedagmon, J.delanoy, JBsupreme, JamesLucas, Jaybling, Jeffrey Mall, JimDunning, John of Reading, JokerZwild, Julianster, Jwein, Jweiss11, K92009, Kevdo, Koavf, Kollision, Kwsn, Kylu, LUCY1995, Lazyman713, Lemmy12, LinkToddMcLovinMontana, Lugnuts, MBD123, Madhero88, Magister Mathematicae, Mahanga, Majorclanger, Manchester15, Mannafredo, Mark272, Maxim, McSly, Merv329, Millahnna, Miquonranger03, Momo san, NO7117, Nehrams2020, Nighthawkzx, Noclevername, ObsessiveJoBroDisorder, Patrick, Pegship, Phlegm Rooster, Pixelface, Pseudomonas, Qmwpeto, Recognizance, Remytherat, Roaring Siren, RobJ1981, Robertvan1, Rogerd, Ruthless Xero, SeanB102, Shell Kinney, Signalhead, Silent Tom, SkyWalker, Soul stab, Spencerkind, Ssarti, St.daniel, Stopfigureout, Sustructu, TaerkastUA, Tffyjh, ThePhrozenPhoenix, TheValentineBros, Thebisch, Theda, ThylekShran, Tkotw12, TomEatsCake, Tozoku, TracyLinkEdnaVelmaPenny, TubularWorld, Uncle Dick, Ŭrbanchampion, Uucp, Varlaam, Walter Görlitz, Wikifried, Wisdom89, Xihix, Ylee, 338 anonymous edits

Kung Fu Panda *Source*: http://en.wikipedia.org/w/index.php?oldid=409492586 *Contributors*: 2409o0, 404notfound, 452lsskidmore16, A&ofan75, AAA!, AN(Ger), Acebloo, Acushot, Addict 2006, AdjustShift, Agentjohn1, Agus elex 2005, Ahadi12345, Ahm1993, Aidan345345, Airplaneman, Alansohn, Alientraveller, AllanGuy, Alsandro, Alshaheen15, Amberrock, And1987, Andrei Stroe, Andrejj, Andrzejbanas, Andy M. Wang, Angelo De La Paz, Angie Y., Animoviera14, Animum, AnmaFinotera, Apparition11, ArchonMagnus, Ariobarzan, Artichoker, Asaraullo05, AtheWeatherman, Atomopoly, AussieLegend, Avelinforl32, Avicennasis, Avoided, Ayrton Prost, BD2412, Baa, Badapro, Balmung0731, Banpei, BashBrannigan, Bazzargh, Becky Sayles, Beeblebrox, Bencey, Beplexor, Bernard94, Betamax the Flyer, Bibliomaniac15, BigBrother1997, BigJohnnyCool, Bjay, Blah28948, Blanchardb, Bluecatcinema, Bluemyst, Bobburson, Bobo192, Bongwarrior, BooToo2, Boombox123456, Bovineboy2008, Bradeos Graphon, Brian A Schmidt, Brianhenke, Buffysboy292818, CBFan, CCMoir, CM7Y, Cablebfg, CapitalR, Capricorn42, Carabera, Carioca, Carniolus, Cartoon Boy, Casbboy, Causa sui, Ccacsmss, Cecilvyse, Cedarpoint1994, Ceranthor, ChaosMaster16, CharlieSierra, Chasingsol, Chovain, Chrismid259, Chubaska, Cjohnson2k, ClonedPickle, Coder Dan, Cognitivelydissonant, CommanderCool1654, CoolKatt number 99999, Cooljason1, Cosmic Latte, Counsell, Craven Mongoose, Crouchbk, CrudeSword, Cubs Fan, Cyberpuke, D6, DOHC Holiday, DORC, Dabby, Dan500, Daniel rox25, Danleary25, Dann135, Dante.antonio, Darkfrog24, Darkspartan4121, Darrenhusted, Dart a00q00sdjh, DavidJohns, Dawn Bard, Dawnhosts, Debresser, Deltaz23, DepressedPer, DerechoReguerraz, Dezidor, DiogenesNY, Discospinster, Doc Dish, Doc glasgow, DocWatson42, Docu, Doczilla,

DoubleCross, Dr Demagor, Drat, Drbreznjev, Dryea, Dspark76, Duncandrake, Dynesclan, Eagc7, Easwarno1, EdGl, Eddyghazaley, Ehccheehcche, Elassint, Electronz, Elendil's Heir, Emurphy42, Enanoj1111, Enigmaaaaa, Epbr123, Epynephrin, Ergative rlt, Erik, Erik-the-red, Esn, EwanMclean2005, Excirial, Ezekiel63745, FMAFan1990, Faaaaaa, Face, FactChecker1199, Falcon9x5, Favonian, Fieldday-sunday, FinalRapture, Firestar6546, Fishhook, Flewis, Floory565, FoodleDee, Fox, FriscoKnight, Funguy06, GDallimore, GameGuy95, Gardoo03, Garret Beaumain, Gary King, Gattung, GavinTing, Geek96, Gelatart, Gfoley4, Ghmyrtle, Ghostexorcist, Gilgamesh, Gilliam, Glen, Gogo Dodo, Goodvac, Gram123, Gran2, GrandDrake, Green Sheet, Grenavitar, GroovySandwich, HDCase, HaeB, Hanaichi, Haon 2.0, Harish, Harley Quinn hyenaholic, Hasek is the best, Havelock, Hawaiian717, Herb98, Hintss, Hmrox, HomerJ Rosito, Hondel1970, Hu12, Huaiwei, Hydrogen Iodide, IAmTheCoinMan, IL7Soulhunter, IRP, Ian.thomson, Ibrahimyu, Ice Age Rlue, Ice Age lover, Idag, Idrinkfresca, Igoldste, Igor235775, Iknowshower, Iloveglynis, Immblueversion, Immunize, InfamousPrince, Inferno, Lord of Penguins, Iridescent, Isaac Rabinovitch, Ishadow21, Itzsnider, Ivirivi00, J Greb, J. Spencer, J.delanoy, JAF1970, JForget, JNW, JackalsIII, James599, Jamesontai, JanetteCruise, Jarrod Baniqued, Jason1960, JasonAQuest, Jay81go, Jaybling, Jclemens, JeanColumbia, Jeremy Butler, Jezmck, Jfire, Jingye11, Johnno613, Jojhutton, Joshschr, Jp.bc, Jpoelma13, Juanpasaenz, Juliancolton, Jwanders, Jwisser, K. Annoyomous, KHM009, KHRlue, Karin127, Kchishol1970, Keaze, Kernow, KeybladeSephi, Khalid Mahmood, Khunglongcon, Kilo-Lima, Kilrothi, Kintetsubuffalo, Kipholbeck, Kiwipat, Klow, Knowledge Incarnate, Konczewski, Kransky, Kungming2, LainEverliving, Lear's Fool, LeaveSleaves, Legohead1, Leopold Stotch, LibLord, Lightrealm, Lilsister5, Linamin, LinkToddMcLovinMontana, Ljastangs21, LlywelynII, Lots42, Louxema, LuciferBlack, Lunchscale, MBlume, MC10, Madchester, Magnius, Majorclanger, Malo, Mandarax, Manuelle Magnus, Marek69, Marshtail12, Masem, Masterofhogets, Matty, Maxis ftw, Mclanavert, Megakid2004, Megaman en m, Melly42, Menamearenick, Mendaliv, Metagraph, MetaruKoneko, Methecooldude, Mhking, Mikeypants87, Mini-Geek, Misterkillboy, Mithridates, Mmarentis, Molotron, Mongol, Mononomic, Montchav, Montgomery '39, Morio, Morpose, Mr-susans, Mr. Absurd, Mr. Soju, MrCheshire, Mriya, Msmyth, Mumble45, Mwhite148, Mygerardromance, N.Flen, Nanami Kamimura, Naruto0004, Naruto134, Nathan.tay, Navy Blue, NawlinWiki, Ndssia, Nehrams2020, Neo-Jay, Neovu79, NickW557, Nightscream, NoseNuggets, NotYouHaha, NrDg, Nsaa, NuclearWarfare, Nukleon, Nymf, ObsessiveJoBroDisorder, Ohconfucius, Ohnoitsjamie, Ohwowthisisfun, OlEnglish, Onepiece226, PMDrive1061, Papersith, Paranoid-andrew, Parent5446, Patar knight, Paulajoselynn, Paxsimius, Pearle, Pedro thy master, PericlesofAthens, Peter Pan, Pfire, Philip Trueman, Piano non troppo, Pingisawesome, Pixelface, Planninefromouterspace, Platypus222, Pomte, Pookman7497, Prem555, President Rhapsody, Proofreader77, Psychowaiter, QYV, Qconroe, Qutezuce, Quuxplusone, RC-0722, RP9, RYANonWIKIPEDIA, RainbowWerewolf, Ranpos, Ravenna1961, Rbdavis, Rdrgz93, Reaper Eternal, Recognizance, Relly Komaruzaman, RexNL, Rich Farmbrough, Richiekim, Riffic, Rjwilmsi, RoadDogXVIII, Rodimus Rhyme, Ronalm, Rossumcapek, Roth 300, Rrizqi, Rtkat3, RyanCross, SMOKELESSPOT, Salamurai, Savvyitachikun, Sb1990, SeanB102, Sebbe, Sgt. R.K. Blue, Sha-Sanio, Shalom Yechiel, Shappy, Shinyegg, Shrek976, Silver Edge, Silvlasdfj, Simba&Spirit, SimbaIsaac, Sion8, Sirius85, Sjones23, SkyWalker, Slakr, SluggoOne, Snowy150, Soetermans, Son Goharotto, SpOnGeFaN818, SpaceCaptain, Speakingsoul, Spebi, Spik3balloon, SpikeToronto, Spinc5, Statick1, Sternenmeer, Steve, Stopfigureout, Stroppolo, SummerPhD, Super-Magician, SuperFlash101, Superman666999666, Surfepegnuin79, Swcardinals3, Sylvos, TK(film), TLKSpiritFan, TREZDEL10, TarsTarkas71, Teddy.Coughlin, TenPoundHammer, Teohyc, The Cool Kat, The Hybrid, The Rogue Penguin, The Thing That Should Not Be, The Wild Falcon, TheLeopard, TheREALCableGuy, TheRealFennShysa, TheValentineBros, Thegeneralguy, Theloofa, Thomas669933, Thurpala, Tide rolls, Tiffren or Angel624, Tiger Trek, Tiggerjay, Tiptoety, TitanOne, Tlsonic214, TomCat4680, Tombomp, Tommy2010, Tony1, TracyLinkEdnaVelmaPenny, Transity, Tregoweth, Triesault, Trogga, Tsange, TurabianNights, Typhoon966, Underpants, Unregistered.coward, Useight, VanessaWang, Vernon7777777, Versus22, Vishnava, Visokor, Voidvector, Vrenator, WIKI-GUY-16, Wannger27, Wayne Slam, Websurfer246, Whaiaun, WhisperToMe, Wickethewok, WikiWikiPhil, Wikibarista, Wikitanvir, Williamhortner, Willking1979, Wine Guy, World Cinema Writer, Woseph, Wtfrog, Wtooher, Wuhwuzdat, Wyvernoid, X Runbash65 x, Xcentaur, Xyzpandaxyz, Ye Olde de la Man, Yogerty, Youal, ZZninepluralZalpha, Zain1987, Zhanzhao, Дарко Максимовић, 1773 anonymous edits

Step Brothers (film) *Source*: http://en.wikipedia.org/w/index.php?oldid=409635476 *Contributors*: A Chain Of Flowers, A More Perfect Onion, ABF, AN(Ger), AT3397, Abbywagner, AbsoluteGleek92, Abw1987, Adam McMaster, AdjustShift, Ahad Bagheri, Aitias, Alansohn, Alex43223, Alexius08, All Hallow's Wraith, AlwaysUnderTheInfluence, Ambrosia-, AnmaFinotera, Anna Frodesiak, Anneda bj, Anthonyklyza, ApprenticeFan, ArglebargleIV, Arthena, AshTFrankFurter2, Avoided, Bachrach44, Bdawg2691, Beastly21, Bennyhonna, Bensweet1, BigDunc, Blockeisu, Bobo192, Bogey97, Bongwarrior, Bovineboy2008, Brookeschneider, CL, CWenger, Capricorn42, Carr1997, Chaser, Christianster45, Christina Silverman, Cjohnson2k, Cliff1911, Clydette45, Collinf, Commando303, ConstantineChernabog, ContiAWB, Cperrott wiki, Crotchety Old Man, Cs-wolves, Cuchullain, Cunard, Cw03901ENGL1101, Cyfal, DVdm, Dabomb87, Dante.antonio, Darrenhusted, Daven200520, Daveybrown558engl1101, Deor, Dgoldwas, DiscardedDream, Djbj16, Doba1824, Doniago, Drmies, Dyolf, ESkog, Easchiff, EchetusXe, Edgar181, Epbr123, Erik, Faded, Falcon Kirtaran, Favonian, Fernandobouregard, FrankRizzo2006, Frankie0607, Funandtrvl, GG The Fly, GLaDOS, Gadfium, Gatorman6, Ghosts&empties, Gogo Dodo, Granpuff, Greatrobo76, Grieferhate, Gsmgm, Guy Harris, Happyman19, Hentaiman, Heroeswithmetaphors, HexaChord, Holdenizgolden23, Husond, Ia802, InfamousPrince, Insanity Incarnate, ItsTheClimb17, J.delanoy, JAMILAHCW, JaGa, Jagun, Jakeruby91, James1902004, Jan eissfeldt, Jason.cinema, Jhendren, Jhsounds, Jmclark911, JoeBoxer522, JohnDeere23, Johndhackensacker3d, Johnlongbond, Jordan.Nave, Jordanzed, Joshua Issac, Jovianeye, JpGrB, Jusdafax, KGasso, KMan, Kapper rocks, Katieh5584, King Cobb, Kingpin13, Klknoles, Knapman22, Kuddy, L Kensington, Lafuzion, Laughoutloud069, Leuko, Ling.Nut, Little Mountain 5, LonesomeCowboyBill, Lttljvd, MCRtheclickGH321, Maccabee341, Madhero88, Majorly, Mato, MattSutton1, MatthewGoodfan101, MattieTK, MattyFresh4, McSly, Methecooldude, Millahnna, Minnesotatwins15, Mjhorrell, Montgomery '39, Morbeen4444, Mosmof, MovieMan123, Mr pand, Mr. Chicago, Mutater, Mygerardromance, Myscrnnm, NCRcritics, Naz45228517, Nazipoo, Nehrams2020, Nick Number, Nsaa, Nymf, ObsessiveJoBroDisorder, Orderinchaos, Orphan Wiki, Otollok, Oxymoron83, Patioheater, Pax85, Phantomsteve, Phiko73, Phil3015, Philip Trueman, Piano non troppo, Poketape, Prolog, Pussyprincess, RJaguar3, Radiant chains, RaiderTarheel, RattleandHum, Rcawsey, Res2216firestar, RickRocks456, Roaring Siren, Rondolover9, Ronhjones, Rostar69, Rror, Rumiton, STEVE SURE, SVG, Scooby7292, Ser Amantio di Nicolao, Sergecross73, Shadowjams, Shamengardner, Silent Tom, Sjbw613, Sjones23, Skarebo, SkyWalker, SmartGuy28, Speedrower, Spinerod, StanislavJ, StaticGull, Steve37, Steveprutz, Stolic532, Sugarlover101, THEN WHO WAS PHONE?, TastyPoutine, Techman224, TenPoundHammer, Tenebrae, Teoryn, Terrillja, The Rogue Penguin, The Thing That Should Not Be, TheJazzDalek, TheMovieBuff, Thedoctor98, Thelilbeast, Theoneintraining, Thingg, Thirteen squared, Tomajko, Tomoso3, Tony Sidaway, Tr00st, TracyLinkEdnaVelmaPenny, Trailerspy, Tresiden, Treybien, Typhoon966, Ubergeekguy, Ukexpat, Useight, Wafulz, Wikimeelaaa, WillC, Willking1979, Yelling Bird, Yoshi032192, Youngmuz, Zacq12, Zak Hammat, Zeuslnx, 839 anonymous edits

Pineapple Express (film) *Source*: http://en.wikipedia.org/w/index.php?oldid=409503612 *Contributors*: 1337wesm, A3RO, AN(Ger), AT3397, Ace246able, Adolphus79, Aerosmithfan2012, Afs831, Airplaneman, Ajhoax, Alansohn, AlexLevyOne, Alfredapitchcock, Alientraveller, All Hallow's Wraith, AmericanGotham, Andres, Andrzejbanas, Angel caboodle, AnmaFinotera, Another Believer, Apefacethedude, Art1991, Asphaltjungle, Backslash Forwardslash, Beach drifter, Beano, Benatfleshofthestars, BethelRunner, Blanchardb, Bobo192, Boekelaar, Bongwarrior, BostonRed, Bovineboy2008, Branfeld, Bret5000, Brideshead, Bulbakuki, CL, Calor, Careful Cowboy, Casbboy, Catkilledbyagoat14, Chuunen Baka, Cjallen69, Cl ellison, Cliff smith, Closedmouth, Conman33, ContiAWB, Cperrott wiki, Crotchety Old Man, Cst17, CybDarla, CyberGhostface, Czolgolz, DJFishlips, Danteorange123, Darrenhusted, Darth Mike, David Gerard, Dbzwig, Demonuk, Deor, Discospinster, DivineAlpha, Doh286, Dreammaker182, Drmies, Dryanp, Dylan620, Dysepsion, ESkog, Ebyabe, EchetusXe, Edsully, Eggman183, Elephant Talk, Emir34, Enter Movie, Epbr123, Erik, Exquisitecorpses, Faithlessthewonderboy, Falcon9x5, Fernandobouregard, Fierce Beaver, FlamingSilmaril, FlieGerFaUstMe262, Footballfan190, Framedfigure2, FrankRizzo2006, Freshh, Frogman420, Furrycoater, Gamecheater2009, Garion96, Gavinthorp, Gimmetrow, Glacier Wolf, Golbez, Gongshow, Grandpafootsoldier, Granpuff, Grendelkhan, HAPPYNUBSAD, Harrop, Hu12, IRISHwiki15, Icarus of old, Ikip, Imasleepviking, ImperatorExercitus, Indigofire2525, InfamousPrince, Inferno, Lord of Penguins, Irishguy, IronGargoyle, J.delanoy, JForget, Jal11497, Jamesbanesmith, Jaybling, Jaylaw, Jeff Silvers, JeffWithAnF, Jheiv, Jhendren, Jmrowland, Jmundo, Johnlongbond, Jojo1234567890, Jonxwood, Josh3580, Jusdafax, Kevdo, Khigh, Kjun1 3, Klknoles, Kollision, Konczewski, Kww, L Kensington, LOT9, Lacrimosus, Lamama, Lampbane, Latics, Lear's Fool, Levineps, Lifebonzza, Loodog, Loopus9, Luke4545, MCRtheclickGH321, MLRoach, Magasin, Magicbullet5, Mahanga, Mahjong705, Mandarax, Manofthings, Marcus Brute, Mariana de El Mondongo, Markoff Chaney, Matt Deres, Matthew Francis, McGeddon, Media64, Meggogarbage, Mendaliv, Millahnna, Mitch9500, Mohrflies, Monkysjshh, Movieguru2006, Ndteegarden, Nellynel7619, NickW557, Nihiltres, Ninjawarriordex, Nn123645, NrDg, Nubiatech, OOODDD, ObsessiveJoBroDisorder, Onebravemonkey, Oroso, Orphan Wiki, Oxymoron83, P159700, ParticleMan, Pascal.Tesson, Pele Merengue, Phlegat, Powerofjuju, ProggleRock, Prolog, PsychoJosh, RainbowOfLight, RandorXeus, RescueRanger702, Rexdeaz, RoadDogXVIII, Rockguid, Ron whisky, Ronhjones, Rontrigger, Ross CJ, Rx4evr, Saltywood, Sammygee, Scooby7292, Sevenarts, Shamrox, Shandy man, ShelfSkewed, Sidonuke, Silent Tom, Sjones23, Skier Dude, Skomorokh, SkyWalker, Skyezx, Snooch123, Sohailstyle, Sonicbroom, SonyPicsEnt, Spartan, SpikeJones, StanMarsh19, Stateful, Steve, Stevedavebob, Steveprutz, Stircrazy625, Str8cash, StuartBrewer, Sugar Bear, THEN WHO WAS PHONE?, TMC1982, Tassedethe, ThaLux, TheGerm, TheRedPenOfDoom, Theburn77, Thegreat100, Themattster77, Theodork, Thevoid00, ThugginRolla, Tide rolls, Timeshifter, TomEatsCake, Tool2Die4, TracyLinkEdnaVelmaPenny, Trailerspy, Traxs7, Treybien, Triona, Trustmeimadoctor420, Tylerpaten, Versus22, Wbytllyw, Wbytllyw2, Wbytllyw3, Wbytllyw4, Whiteboy1994, Whm2, Wikieditor06, Wikifried, Wolfer68, Wyzz7, Yoitskevn, Youshouldask, Zacq12, Zealander, Zomgsupersack, Zone46, 804 anonymous edits

Zack and Miri Make a Porno *Source*: http://en.wikipedia.org/w/index.php?oldid=408074626 *Contributors*: 5150pacer, AN(Ger), Abb615, Aerosmithfan2012, Aherbert2289, Ajhoax, Alientraveller, AlphaPyro, Andrew J. MacDonald, Andy M. Wang, Angel caboodle, Artrush, BD2412, Basilrose, Bawwimp, Benatfleshofthestars, Bencey, Benshroyer, Bensullivanjp, Blackberrylaw, Blackhelmetman, Bovineboy2008, Canterbury Tail, Cherry Cotton, ChesterG, Christianster45, Cliff smith, Closedmouth, Cluebert, Comicist, Cristan, Cubs Fan, DOHC Holiday, Dale Arnett, Darelldevil775, Darrenhusted, DaveJB, Deftonesderrick, Destroyer of evil, Doc Strange, DodgerOfZion, Donald McKinney, Dp76764, Ed Fitzgerald, Erechtheus, Erik, Euryalus, Extraspeak, Faded, FallenAngelII, Fernandobouregard, Final ellipsis, Firestorm566, Foos036, Forestofthedead, FrankRizzo2006, Gdkh, Geniac, Gentgeen, Geschichte, Giants27, Hholt01, Holothurion, Horkana, Iamsuperbusie, Info845, Ironmonger117, Isadora47, Jacob Poon, JaneGrey, Jasonbres, Jaybling, Jaydec, Jbl1975, Jennica, Jgera5, Jhsounds, Joepiekarski, Joesta03, JohnnyPolo24, JpGrB, Juansidious, Kinghajj, KirbyMaster14, Kollision, Kotra, Kristiantorsten, Kuralyov, LanceHeart, Latics, Layne Phillips, LiteraryMaven, Lollp, Manofthings, MasterMapleBoy, Mfishrules, Millahnna, Mimihitam, MissAlyx, Misternunya, Mlaffs, Mopal, Motaros, Munchsack, Musicmakestheworldgoround, N5iln, NJZombie, Nehrams2020, NerdyScienceDude, New Age Retro Hippie, Newsroom hierarchies, Nicknitro6969, Nightscream, ObliQ, ObsessiveJoBroDisorder, Onetreehill02, Patrick, Pele Merengue, PhantomPatrol, Pixelface, Primus Sheck, PurrfectPeach, RafaAzevedo, Red157, Redirectorial, Remrej, Rettetast, Reuthermonkey, Richard Arthur Norton (1958-), Rikkyc, Rjwilmsi, Rlogan2, Roaring Siren, Robofish, Rtmiyake1, Rubyalmqvist, Rudowsky, Rurik16, Rwiggum, SMcCandlish, Saltywood, Sasquatch, Sawman14, Scooby7292, Searcher 1990, Secret Saturdays, Sicknessandsleep, SidP, SigKauffman, Silent Tom, Skier Dude, Skomorokh, SkyWalker, Socby19, Son of Aeolus, Soprano90, Stevenj, Supergeek Mike, Symphony Girl, The Utahraptor, The Wookieepedian, TheDefiniteArticle, TheFearow, TheRealFennShysa, TheValentineBros, Thickandy, Thief12, Tlyel37, TomCat4680, Tpbradbury, Transfinite, Treybien, Trogga, Tromaintern, Twitch1021, UJohnnyZephyr, WLU, Wadems, Wildhartlivie, Woohookitty, Y2kcrazyjoker4, YURiN, 148 anonymous edits

Fanboys (2009 film) *Source*: http://en.wikipedia.org/w/index.php?oldid=405407224 *Contributors*: 12qwert34yu, AdamDeanHall, Adultnature1989, Akumandude, Alan smithee, Alientraveller, Alphapeta, Ambartur, Anetode, Areaseven, Art1991, Asoules, Auntof6, Bencey, Bestillandknow, BlazingVen0m, Bovineboy2008, Boycool42, Callmarcus, Can't sleep, clown will eat me, CarlOnFire, Cerebellum, Cheddarjack, Chowbok, Christinahle, Cliché Online, Coruscant, CyberGhostface, Dahamsta7, DanTD, Darth Tavo, Dismas, Doctorfluffy, Dr.Quentin X. Mathews, EEMIV, EVula, Egon Eagle, Emurphy42, Ertemplin, Excirial, Faded, Fanboysmovie, Funandtrvl, Geschichte, Grandpafootsoldier, Grendy, GusF, Hairybeast92, Hanfuzzy, HidariMigi, Horkana,

Hourton Cladwell, Ikrichter, JForget, Jal1497, JasonAQuest, JediLofty, Jtalledo, JustPhil, Katana Geldar, Klow, Kollision, Krazy19Karl, Kuralyov, Lamama, LesmanaZimmer, Letatcestmoi94, Lewischuang, Lindsey8417, LinkToddMcLovinMontana, Llamarama16, Lttl pggy, Lystrodom, MagneticFlux, Manofthings, Markoff Chaney, MassvMaster, Medleystudios72, Merenta, Metallurgist, MikeWazowski, Mjrmtg, ModernTenshi04, Monkey Bounce, Mr. Comodor, Nihonjoe, NonNobisSolum, Plasticspork, Prufrocknyc, Purplellamas01, Qaqaq, Remurmur, RoadDogXVIII, RobJ1981, Rvb strongbad, S@lo, SCARECROW, Saionji1229, Salamurai, Saltywood, Sango123, Scarian, Schnack, Searcher 1990, Sha-Sanio, Shinmawa, Sin-man, Sir sigurd, Sk8erboy02, Skier Dude, Skinnyweed, SkyWalker, Snori, Starkiller88, Str8cash, Strong mouse, Supernumerary, TJ TeeJay, TX Ciclista, Tabercil, Th1rt3en, The Thing That Should Not Be, TheRealFennShysa, TheValentineBros, Timwi, Tom H12, Treybien, Trogga, Usby, Vegaswikian, Vileplume drugs, WCityMike, Warreed, Whywhenwhohow, Woohookitty, Wtmitchell, Xaraphim, Yeanold Viskersenn, ZooPro, Zotdragon, 262 anonymous edits

Monsters vs. Aliens *Source*: http://en.wikipedia.org/w/index.php?oldid=408767144 *Contributors*: 06hookerj, 1jsisdj8udefifn, 3615fun, 3DFan101, 919tswells, A More Perfect Onion, A man alone, ANGGUN, Abefoulkes, Abenev, Acebloo, AdamDeanHall, Addict 2006, Adrian 1001, Akcarver, Alabama Moon, Alansohn, AlbertSM, Aldamira, Alexcliftontrio, Alexis 23456789, Alisonken1, All Hallow's Wraith, American Eagle, Amog, And1987, Andrewpmk, Andrzejbanas, Andycjp, Angel caboodle, Angelfromladyandthetrampii, AnmaFinotera, Apollo883, Applesause454, ArielGold, Art1991, Asaraullo05, Atlantabravz, Attackoftheham, Auric, Backslash Forwardslash, Balavent, Ben-Bopper, Bencey, Bender235, Benzy19, BigBang616, Bigger digger, Bondegezou, Bovineboy2008, Brendanology, Brundi007, Buffysboy292818, Burks821, CR85747, CactusWriter, Calcagno3, Cameron Scott, CardinalDan, Cartoon Boy, Cathal Toomey, Cavatica, Cbdorsett, Cfortunato, Christianster94, Chrisyhoo99, Chuckyj1, Claimgoal, Clarisworkz, Cognitivelydissonant, ColCad4144, ContiAWB, Cooldudercks, Courcelles, Crazy4metallica, CunningWizard, Cyfal, Czolgolz, Daedalus969, Darkness2005, Darkside2000, Darrenhusted, Davehi1, David spector, Davidpar, Debresser, Demi1993, DemonRin, Depressing November, Dewey Finn, Dgabbard, Dgoldwas, Discospinster, Dogman15, Domino2097, Download, Dp76764, Drilnoth, Druffeler, Dwayne, Dwimble, Dynesclan, E-Yahpp, ETLamborghini, Egunthry, Emb021, EoGuy, Erik, Eyharburg, Falcon9x5, Fastily, Favonian, Femalesrule, Fierce Beaver, Filmview, Fourthords, Freedomlinux, FriscoKnight, Furocumarine, GRIMEBOY, Gabrielkat, Gellar55, Gggh, Giantdevilfish, Goa103, Gordonrox24, GorillaWarfare, Granpuff, Graymornings, Green Sheet, Grey ghost, Groomtech, Guineapig 456, Hailey C. Shannon, Hairybeast92, Haon 2.0, Haphestus20, Harley Quinn hyenaholic, Hertz1888, Horkana, Howard Drake, Humble user, I Am Moon, IAmTheCoinMan, ICanDrive55, Ibbn, Immblueversion, InfamousPrince, Invertzoo, Ixfd64, J. Fanning, J.delanoy, J04370859, J4lambert, JForget, JLogan, JM.Beaubourg, JMyrleFuller, Jal1497, Jamesooders, Jarrod Baniqued, Jeffreymcmanus, Jerem43, JoeLoeb, Joeisok, Johnlongbond, Johnr roberts, Juliancolton, Jusdafax, Jwhale9382, Kascnef82, Kbarends, Kchishol1970, Konczewski, Kraftlos, Ksabers, Kwiki, Kyuko, LDEJRuff, LOL, LeaveSleaves, Leoni2, Lightrealm, LilHelpa, LinkToddMcLovinMontana, LittlebutBIG, Lwiki222, Maester Seymour, Majorclanger, Majorsuave, MarcoTolo, Marek69, Mattbuck, Matty-chan, Mbarryton, Mbssbs, McSly, Mentifisto, Merlinsorca, MetaManFromTomorrow, Michaeliser, MikeWazowski, Millahnna, Mltinus, Mollymoon, Molotron, Monsterfan123, Morbeen4444, Movingimage, Mr.Grave, MrJacky, Mrfeek, Mriya, My.toa.badz, NJZombie, Nehrams2020, Nellynel7619, Neovu79, Nintendoman01, Noclevername, NoseNuggets, ONEder Boy, OliverOken123, OrangeDog, Otisjimmy1, OverlordQ, P Carn, PHDrillSergeant, PMDrive1061, Pacific Coast Highway, PancakeMistake, Pascal.Tesson, PatricKlaus, Patrij, Paul the dud, Pedro João, Phlegat, Pipedreamergrey, Pledger166, PokeHomsar, Potterfanatic247, Private Sweety, Pstink, QYV, Quentin X, Really21, Richard Barrett, Riffic, Rocket to Jupiter, Rorshacma, Rothgo, Rrburke, Rtwhiten, Rubberdude2010, Rui789, Russianname, Rutherfordjigsaw, Rwe1138, Ryanasaurus007, Sambangs, Savva0122, Sb113, Sb1990, Scoutjd, Secret Saturdays, Shawn in Montreal, Skarl the Drummer, Skeejay, Sketchmoose, Skier Dude, SkyWalker, Sleazysean, SoSaysChappy, Socby19, Some guy, Spaceghost404, Spittlespat, Srushe, StarTrek09, StarTrek10, Starcaptin, Steakbuns, Steveomania, Sturm55, Superx, Suruena, TKD, TRTX, TX55, TaerkastUA, Tailkinker, Tassedethe, Teohyc, The Rogue Penguin, The Shadow-Fighter, TheMovieBuff, TheREALCableGuy, TheValentineBros, Thechris146, Themeparkgc, Theseanweb, Thincat, ThomasVonScorpio, Thorenn, Tide rolls, Tiptoety, Toad911, TracyLinkEdnaVelmaPenny, TravisAF, Trogga, Truthiness Jones, Typhoon966, USN1977, UberMan5000, Unionhawk, Unregistered.coward, Upurbutt, VVillaPower, Vampire Snuffleupagus, Vanished user 03, Varlaam, ViperSnake151, Viscontino, Visokor, WOSlinker, Weetoddid, Wheeler0152, Wheob, Whm2, Who then was a gentleman?, WikiDjinn, Wikibarista, Wintonian, Woohookitty, Wtooher, Wyatt915, Xhienne, XxTimberlakexx, Yestyle, Zeeboo, Zillamon51, ZootyCutie, 1185 anonymous edits

Observe and Report *Source*: http://en.wikipedia.org/w/index.php?oldid=404698001 *Contributors*: Alansohn, Alxm2007, Alyeska2112, Andrzejbanas, ArcAngel, BeansTheHedgeHog, Bejnar, Benbest, BigBrightStars, Bigredone1, BillieJean2K, Blanchardb, Bobmack89x, BoosterBronze, Captain Crawdad, Ccol7280, Cheddarjack, Christianster94, Ckatz, Cknj3746, CollisionCourse, Cyster, Darrenhusted, DemonBarberTodd, Djbj16, Dkeppel, Doulos Christos, Dsavage87, Erik, Erik9, Fastily, Fierce Beaver, Fngosa, Foofbun, Forrestdfuller, FrankRizzo2006, Fuzzy510, GB fan, Gabe0463, Gaelen S., Gaia Octavia Agrippa, Galorr, Gellar55, Geni, Geoff B, Grandpafootsoldier, Greatrobo76, Hairybeast92, Hbdragon88, HexaChord, Horkana, Igby, Indianslumdog, Indydog, InfamousPrince, Info845, Intelligentsium, J.delanoy, JEN9841, Jackieboy87, Jamesbanesmith, JayExperience, Jimintheatl, JoeLoeb, Joebears1, Jojhutton, JoshuaZ, Jtran91, Jwein, Kascnef82, Katherine, Koavf, Kollision, Lankiveil, LtMuldoon, Marcus Brute, Matty-chan, Mcorco2, Michael93555, Middle 8, Millahnna, Mmb1998, Morbeen4444, Moshe Constantine Hassan Al-Silverburg, Musikxpert, Mwhite148, Mysdaao, NawlinWiki, Nnewton, Obriensg1, Observeandreport, Otisjimmy1, Pele Merengue, Piano non troppo, Pigman5, Quaxe, Redskinqueen, Reedy, Relefo, Richard Arthur Norton (1958-), Rjwilmsi, Roaring Siren, Rogercollege, Rwe1138, Rx4evr, Sarah McIntosh, Seaphoto, Searcher 1990, Silvergoat, Smond359, Snigbrook, Soprano90, SpikeJones, Spinerod, Stewie814, Stripbolt, Sunnan, Swfong, T. H. McAllister, TFX, TFunk, Tabercil, Telegraphonline, Tide rolls, Tiggytighe08, Tjwells, Tman418, Tomdobb, Traxs7, Treybien, Unicornsurprise, Varlaam, Versus22, WWGB, Willerror, Xezbeth, Yellow Hound, 303 anonymous edits

Funny People *Source*: http://en.wikipedia.org/w/index.php?oldid=409672706 *Contributors*: 7, ABarnett, AT3397, Abc518, Acebloo, Adavidb, Adultswimlaa, Alansohn, Alexanderg.13, Alexhhhh, All Hallow's Wraith, Andrzejbanas, Angel caboodle, Aquila89, Ariel ALB, AuburnPilot, Belovedfreak, Ben Stone420, Bencey, Bestperson, Bongwarrior, Boop89, Boratsagdiyev, Bovineboy2008, CJMylentz, Caltas, Carlywithcurls, Catgut, Cbrewer70, ChaosPrime, Cheat2win, Cheddarjack, Chowbok, Cliff smith, Cliff1911, ComedyLiker23, Cptnono, Crazy4metallica, Crazytonyi, Crotchety Old Man, DARTH SIDIOUS 2, DCEdwards1966, DaniRivera, Daredude10, Darrenhusted, Davidravenski, Dillard421, Doc Strange, Doctorjo5, Download, ECWAGuru, ESkog, Eckeck77, Egg Creations, Eminilyas, Emkaer, Erik, Esanchez7587, Falconclaw5000, Fastily, Fernandobouregard, FiGhT 12, Fieldday-sunday, Fierce Beaver, Francium12, FrankRizzo2006, Franz Richter, Fred Bauder, Freshh, Fvasconcellos, GG The Fly, Gaff7, Galorr, Gellar55, George415, GoingBatty, Gramophoned, Harlequin212121, Henryodell, Hiberniantears, Horkana, Hydrargyrum, IncognitoErgoSum, InfamousPrince, Iridescent, ItsTheClimb17, JRA WestyQld2, Jasonbres, Jaybling, Jeyo9891, Joebears1, Juanaguilar, Jusdafax, Kevinh456, Kidlittle, Kirachinmoku, L Kensington, Lamcph6, LeaveSleaves, LoLbox, LonerXL, Lupiomeraz, Madtv12, Magioladitis, Makeemlighter, Manhattan1626, MariAna Mimi, Martin451, Marychan41, Matty-chan, MaximumMadnessStixon, McGeddon, Millahnna, MimiBelle, Mosn1, Mr. Chicago, Mrose195, Mshashoua, Mustafa A.Hadi, NawlinWiki, Ndubzthesongs, Nehrams2020, Nightscream, Nocarsgo, Nymf, ObsessiveJoBroDisorder, PStamatiou, Peppage, Philip Trueman, Pjoef, Pops Deering, Propaniac, QuantumWake, Questatribecalled, QuiteUnusual, RadioFan, Rajah, Ratchetcomand, Raymondwinn, Regan1997, Renaissancee, Reyk, Roaring Siren, Rockmandrum, Roman888, Ronhjones, RxS, Saltywood, Salvio giuliano, Samwb123, Sdornan, Shultzc, SidP, Smith Jones, SoSaysChappy, Sofa jazz man, Solo89, Some jerk on the Internet, Sophus Bie, Speedannayya, Spencer427894, Staeiou, Staffwaterboy, Str8cash, SuperHamster, SuzyElizabeth, SylvWind, Sylvwynd, TFunk, THEN WHO WAS PHONE?, Telor, Testerman Westminster, The Gruber, The Thing That Should Not Be, Themfromspace, Thomasisgreat, Tide rolls, Tmt95, Traxs7, Trevdawg0303, Treybien, Trogga, Typhoon966, Ulric1313, Vanderdecken, WVRMad, Whisky drinker, White 720, Wii Wiki, WikHead, Wikimandia, Wikipelli, Will Beback, Wlwwybrn, Y2kcrazyjoker4, Yodalover, ZEESHAN.ca, 559 anonymous edits

Paper Heart *Source*: http://en.wikipedia.org/w/index.php?oldid=396244218 *Contributors*: Alansohn, Aleenf1, All Hallow's Wraith, Barte, Bearcat, Bencey, Billnovak, Billyseth, Bovineboy2008, CaptainComedy, Cl!ckpop, Cybercobra, Devilsalmond, Dispenser, Falcon8765, Fierce Beaver, FrankRizzo2006, Grandpafootsoldier, Interrupt feed, ItsTheClimb17, Jovianeye, Kgarr, Koavf, Llamabr, Lugnuts, OFilms, PJfixesit, Pakaran, Phantomsteve, Philkon, Sanbika, SoWhy, TFunk, Trivialist, Trogga, TwistOfCain, Utcursch, Wigfred, Xdragonxfirex, Yoshi032192, 57 anonymous edits

Family Guy *Source*: http://en.wikipedia.org/w/index.php?oldid=409549827 *Contributors*: -Midorihana-, -Ril-, 041744, 0555, 100DashSix, 12va34, 16yearold, 23skidoo, 293.xx.xxx.xx, 31stCenturyMatt, 4hands452, 5150pacer, 606582, 6z's, 711joel, 8mmfilm!, 989 RVD, A, A State Of Trance, A elalaily, A.C.E, A895, ABF, AHM, AKMask, APW, Aafm, Aaronbrick, Aathing, Abby 92, Abcdef99, Abce2, About Survival, Absurdity, Achmelvic, Acroterion, Adam Bishop, Adam4322, Adam88hirst, Adashiel, Addict 2006, Adeus666, Adrian, Adultnature, Aexcek, Affidavit4835, AgentPeppermint, Agflepsr10, Ahoerstemeier, Ahvazi, Aim Here, AirdishStraus, Airplaneman, Ajm81, Akamad, Akamp85, Akbeancounter, Alansohn, Aled D, Alex20850, Alex43223, Alexb0989, Alexshunn, Ali@gwc.org.uk, Alien343, Alison, AlistairMcMillan, Alkivar, AllFunnyNow511, Allachris, Allwham, Ally555, Alpha Shroud, Alphachimp, Alpheta, Alt, Altenmann, Alucardwolf, AlvinPing, Amgine, AmiDaniel, Aml830, Amls15flva, Ams80, AnY FOUR!, Ana 20, Anaraug, Ancient Apparition, Anclation, Andre Toulon, Andres, Andrewbecks, Andrewdt85, Andrewlane03, Andrewlp1991, Android79, Andy Marchbanks, Andy120290, Andy13121990, Andyface, Andylindsay, Andylkl, Andypandy.UK, Andythompson92, AngelGraves13, AngelHedgie, Angela, Angie Y., Angrynight, Anilocra, Annorax, Anonymous from the 21st century, Anonymous from the 21th century, Ansett, AntL, Anthonybroam, Antonio Lopez, Antonrojo, Antrophica, Anyquestions, Anythingspossibleforapossible, Aots191, Aphasia83, Apostrophe, Appelsap, Appleboy, Aquila89, Archer3, ArcticWind88, Aresef, Arjun01, ArkansasTraveler, Arkeniqiri, Armaeggeddon, Arndutcas, Arthur Holland, Artichoker, AshcroftIleum, Ashmoo, Ashnard, Ashura96, Aspensti, Asqueella, Asteriks, AtaruMoroboshi, Atemperman, Atlan, Atomic Cosmos, Atrius, Attilios, Average Earthman, Avs5221, AxG, Axelace123, AxiomShell, AzaToth, Aznkid43, Azumanga1, B Touch, B0at, B3N, BD2412, BGC, BITB, BKITU, BR9000, BSKBGM7172495, BWDuncan, BabuBhatt, Bachrach44, Backtable, Bacteria, Bada va, Badbadpatman, Badboy24, Badgernet, Bahar101, Baje Tiger, BakerBaker, BalooUrsidae, Bart133, Barticus88, Bartimaeus, Baseballdude12321, BassBone, Bastetmeow, Batfink15, Batintherain, Batman2005, Bberoth, Bdude, Bduke, Beano311, Bear300, Bearbear, Bearcat, Beausalant, Beaver39, Ben-Bopper, Ben2974, Benandorsqueaks, Bencey, Bendajamin, Benvewikilerim, Berkut, Bertcocaine, Bhadani, Bhutti, BigDan, Bigbadbyte, Bigbluefish, Bigdiego95, Bigelarkin, BiggKwell, Biggspowd, Bikeable, Bilky asko, Bill, Billbert12, Binadot, Binksternet, Biot, Bippo Ernesti, Bkell, Blaaarg, Black Falcon, Black Kat, Blah blah632, Blazingluke, Bleedingcherub, Blimpy-Buoy, Blizzy63, Bloop1, Blue387, Blue520, Bluemask, Bm superpig, Bmitchelf, Bob loblaw jr, BobLoblaw60, Bobblewik, Bobizzle, Bobo192, Boffy, Boing! said Zebedee, Bonus Onus, BoogerD, Boombox1, Bormalagurski, BostonRed, Boutitbenza 69 9, Bovineboy2008, Bovineone, Brady4mvp, Brady5412, Brainiack16, BraydenP, Brentdax, Bri123456789, Brian0918, BrianGriffin-FG, Brianga, BrickBreak, Brideshead, Brinkost, Bronks, BuBZ, Buckley002, Budd16, Budha12345, Bule kid, Bull Market, Bumblebeeman92, Bumhoolery, Burgwerworldz, BurnTheBlueSky, Bushcarrot, Bushhat27, Buttered Bread, Bydand, Bykergrove, C1k3, CASE, CBDunkerson, CBM, CIreland, CMD Beaker, CR85747, CRKingston, CWenger, CaCtUs2003, Caco134, Caitlin Rix, Caladeia, Calamity-Ace, Calbaer, Caldorwards4, Calibas, Callumthompson, Caltas, Calumbo471, Calvin 1998, Calza, CambridgeBayWeather, CameronB, Can't Nobody Step To Me, Can't sleep, clown will eat me, CanadianLinuxUser, CannedhamX, Canonblack, Canucksnhl, Cao An Min, Captain Yesterday, CaptainVindaloo, Carouselambra, Cartoon Boy, Casbboy, Cat Cave, Catapult, Catchpole, Cburnett, Cccc35, Ccradio, Cdc, Ceaser, Cedars, Centrepull, CerealBabyMilk, Chairman S., Chanting Fox, Chantoke, Chao19, Chaosdruid, Chaoshg, Charliesmith91, Cheatcode2, Chef Ketone, Chevychaser, Chicken7, Chickenmonkey, Chickpeaface, ChicosBailBonds, Chikinsawsage, Chikiroko, Chillispy, Chloemetro, Chocolateboy, Chowdit, Chris Bulgin, Chris Griffin, Chris as I am Chris, Chris the speller, ChrisRing, Chriscornwell982, Chrisg551, Chrislk02, Chrismchugh28,

Ru4sale, RubyQ, Rumbo, RunOrDie, Runningback1995, Rusl, RussellAN, Ryan Postlethwaite, RyanCahn, Ryanswingle, Ryder721, Ryulong, S.Örvarr.S, SCEhardt, SFH, SHELT0N3, SMC, SMasters, SPUI, SRCK101, SS451, SSJ Gokan, ST47, SWAdair, Saberwolf116, Sacularamacal13, Sagaciousuk, Saget53, Sajjen, Salsb, SaltyBoatr, Saltywood, SalvadorRodriguez, Salvio giuliano, Sam Hocevar, SamMichaels, Sambunn, Sampsonite5, San Saber, Sanfranfan88, Sango123, Santajack, Santimariani, Sarujo, Sashafcb, Sasuke Sarutobi, SatCam, Satchfan, SavoySison, Scapler, Scarlet Spartan, Sceptre, Scharles, SchfiftyThree, Schnauf, Schneau, Schwinnstingray1964, Scientizzle, Scohoust, Scooby7292, Scottyearl, Scyker, Seabhcan, Sean-mcquaid, Sean1290, Seanh, Seb Threemileisland, Secretsofdiffusion, Segekihei, SenorAnderson, Senordingdong, SepirothxxlodXX, Sepmix, Septemberfourth476, Serafino bueti, Seraphimblade, Seruius, Setanta747, Sethmahoney, Sfreedkin, Shadovar, Shadowlynk, Shadowy Crafter, Shadypalm88, Shakehandsman, Shanel, Shanes, Shanshu, Shappy, Shardsofmetal, Shawnnoesstuff, ShelfSkewed, Shenme, ShihoMiyano, Shinmawa, Shinmen, Shirley Ku, Shiroguma, Shoeofdeath, Shoes ferocto, Sholtar, Shortride, ShutterBugTrekker, SidP, Sighter, Silarnon, Silence, Silent52, Silent55, Sillygostly, Silver Edge, Silverhelm, Simhedges, SimonKSK, SimonLyall, Simone, Simonlebon, Simpsonary, Simpsonboy9876, Simpsonman3000, Simpsonsman18, SimsMan, Sir Nicholas de Mimsy-Porpington, SirPeebles, Sketchee, Skier Dude, SkittlzAnKomboz, Skybunny, Skydiver, Slackermagnet, Slasher600, Slayer25769, Sleeping123, Sliat 1981, Slof, Slppiper, Slusk, Smailliwsemaj, Smash, Smee, Smichae, Smijes08, Smurfy, Snake102992, Snakeman5001, Snbritishfreak, Sneakers9065, Snipingkid, Snodriftkick, Snowballreborn, Snowolf, Snowyguy10, Snpoj, SoWhy, Socby19, SofiaSoGood, Some guy, Son, Son of Kong, SonOfNothing, Song, Sonic Shadow, SonicRacer-MEC, Sonicrazy, Sonicrulez10, Sonofgoku1, Sooloo123, Sorakey899, Sottolacqua, Southpaw018, Spangineer, Sparrowman980, Spatch, Special2006, Spellcast, Speyeker, SpikeJones, Splarka, Splash, Splat5572, Spiffy, Spock2266, SpongeBrain, Spongefan, Spongesquid, Spongeyfan, Sproutviewer, Squeekyzebra, Squeemu, Sroc, Ssolbergj, Stacker, Stadler981, Stanspafford, Stardust8212, Starkiller88, Starwars404, Starwind Amada, StaticGull, Statler&Waldorf, Stattouk, Steve tutty, SteveLamacq43, Steveomania, Stevietheman, Stevsegu, Stickee, Stickeylabel, Still raining here, Stockdiver, Stranger4001, Strike Chaos, Stu42, StuartDD, StuartMurray, Stupid Corn, Stusutcliffe, Style86, Suffusion of Yellow, SunKing, SuperNick, Supercubedude, Supergeek Mike, Superking, Supersquid, Surfer154, Suruena, Svick, Sweets, Swid, Synergy, T, TAnthony, TBH, TEG24601, THEN WHO WAS PHONE?, THobern, TJ Spyke, TKK2, TMC1982, TOPSECRET99, TPIRFanSteve, TS1, TT06, TUF-KAT, TV IS GREAT!, TVArchivistUK, Tako8Yaki, Tallyho70, Talude, Tamajared, Tapests, Tapir Terrific, Tarnas, Tasc, Taw, Tbone2001, Tbone762, Tbsunday023, Tcardone05, Tdi7457, TeaDrinker, TeaganMago, Technofreak90, Ted Ted, Teethmonkey, TehBrandon, Tehhhhhh, Teiladnam, Telekan1, Telso, TenPoundHammer, Tennisdude92, Tevi, Tez99, Tezero, Tgunn2, Tgwitty, ThMadGooglr, Thadeuss, Thankyoubaby, Thardin12, That Don Guy, Thatdog, The Anome, The Cartoonist, The Future, The Gerg, The Kids Aren't Alright, The Magrathean, The Man in Question, The Moneycruncher, The Original Juggernautical, The Rogue Penguin, The Tris, The monkeyhate, The spesh man, The wub, The03era15strong, TheBlazikenMaster, TheBlueFlamingo, TheBoch, TheCustomOfLife, TheFishMan92, TheHYPO, TheKoG, TheMidnighters, TheScrivener, TheSimpsonsRocks, TheValentineBros, Thebdj, Thebigone2, Theclearestvoice, Thedoctor98, Thehelpfulone, Theleftorium, Themasterofwiki, Themeparkfanatic, Theodolite, Theresa knott, Theunknown42, Thief12, Thingg, ThinkBlue, Third, Thisis0, ThomasGeorge237, Thor2488, Thorpe, Thug3, Thumperward, Thunderlippps, TigerK 69, Tigerghost, TimBentley, Timc, Timesman626, Timkovski, Tins128, Tintero, Tiptoety, Tiswaser, Titoxd, Tmorales0410, Tobyink, Tokachu, Tokek, Tom, Tom blum, Tom harrison, Tom k&e, Tompagenet, Tomtheman5, Tony Myers, Tony Stevens, Tony1, Tonzo, Toonmon2005, Torte, Tortoiseshells, Totalaero, Trebexein, Tree Biting Conspiracy, Tregoweth, Trenchcoatjedi, Tresiden, Trevor MacInnis, TreyHarris, Treyt021, Trimz, Trivialist, Trogga, Tromatic, Trust Is All You Need, Truthy not fakie, Tspydr10, Ttenchantr, Ttony21, Tubesurfer, TusharB, Tutmosis, Tuxedo Mark, Tv's emory, Tv145033, Tvfat, Twilightfan000, Ty Cobb, Tydaj, TylerMad8, Tyson2111, Tysto, U2dude, UNHchabo, Uber Cuber, Uel, Ughface, Ukexpat, Ultimatebender, Ultrabasurero, UnDeRsCoRe, Unbreakable10000, Underfan15, UnfriendlyFire, UninvitedCompany, Unknown Dragon, Unnatural20, Unzinc, UriBudnik, Useight, VP44444, Va girl2468, Valkyrie Red, Valvin, Vanadamme, Vancouver Outlaw, Vanka5, Varlaam, Vary, VasilievVV, Vaughnstull, Vayne, Veemonkamiya, Vejvančický, Venullian, Videomixfan, Vidgmchtr, Viltharis, Violetriga, Virek, Vitriden, Vlad788, VmKid, Voldemortuet, Vonbontee, Vorador, Vrray9000@yahoo, Vrrayman1987, Vzbs34, WBardwin, WCCOfan, WJBscribe, Waddles, Wafulz, Wally, Walshicus, WalterJid, Wankofalotus, Waphle, War wizard90, Ward3001, Warteen, Wasabe3543, WashingtonPie, Watch37264, Wattlebird, Wavelength, Wayward, Webbrg, Webichen, Websterkntz7, Websterwebfoot, Websurfer246, Weedar, Weijew, Wellesradio, Wellspring, Wellsywuzhere13, Werdna, Werdnak84, Wesman1023, Wezzo, Whavercroft, Wheeler0152, Whimemsz, Whomp, Whotookthatguy, Whouk, WikHead, Wiki alf, WikiMarcus, WikiSatch, Wikibarista, Wikibofh, Wikipedical, Wikipeterproject, Wikisplasher, Wikiwiki67, WildFan48, Wildhartlivie, Will2k, WilliamBrown, Williamnilly, Wilybadger, Windemere Wally, Windowsbeak, Wirbelwind, Witwicky555, Wknight94, Wolfkeeper, Woofygoodbird, Woohookitty, Workaphobia, Wossi, Wren5x, Wsdw34534, Wsultzbach, X 0, X201, XD375, Xaosflux, Xavier J, Xcentaur, Xezbeth, Xiahou, Xihix, Xp54321, Xtreambar, XuperUber, Xyzzyva, Y2kcrazyjoker4, Yamamoto Ichiro, Yamla, Yangro, Yankeesrj12, Yankovicfan, Yayadam, Year 2144, Yesopenilno, Yeti Hunter, Ylee, Yoasif, Yoink23, Yossarian, Yotimbob, Youngamerican, Z-d, Z.E.R.O., ZZninepluralZalpha, Zachary, Zack Shadow, Zafiroblue05, Zagahock, Zanarky, Zandperl, Zapper258, ZeLonewolf, Zelphics, Zenohockey, Zeromaru, Zeromega, Zeus, Zewill, Zhang Liang, Zidane4028, Zimbabweed, Ziola1039, Zoddy, Zoe, Zoicon5, Zone46, Zuejay, Zythe, Zzuuzz, Zzyzx11, Zzzzeta, 3172 anonymous edits

Homer the Whopper *Source*: http://en.wikipedia.org/w/index.php?oldid=407557505 *Contributors*: 09curranm, A, Chard513, Comixbear, Commandr Cody, Ctjf83, Cubs197, Debresser, Dylanfromthenorth, EoGuy, Francisco97, GM11, Gran2, Hack-Man, ILOVELOL32, Itsmadoublet, Joe59108, Joshua Scott, JustPhil, Lugnuts, Martarius, Mecingfence, MeekSaffron, Mike R, Minpinlovingperson, Music2611, NewYorkCity101, Nickrewindfan2, Pedro thy master, Quirky215, Rhino131, SPKirsch, Scorpion0422, Scorpion0422's PC Account, Sergey82-276, SoWhy, SuperFlash101, TAnthony, Talix, TheFarix, TheSimpsonsRocks, Theleftorium, TnAdct1, TuesdayTV, Turian, Weedle McHairybug, XuxiRawe22, 69 anonymous edits

The Green Hornet (2011 film) *Source*: http://en.wikipedia.org/w/index.php?oldid=409672943 *Contributors*: -5-, 95j, AbsoluteGleek92, Akerans, Alshaheen15, Andrzejbanas, Areaseven, Art1991, Artoasis, Benatfleshofthestars, Bencey, BillyBatty, Bladesfan96, Booksurle, Bovineboy2008, Brambleclawx, Brittany Ka, Chuck369, Darkenmal, Diggypop5, Dusti, Dutchmonkey9000, DynasticAnthony, Eekerz, Erik, EsonLinji, Facetoface333, Fear Itself, Fram, FrankRizzo2006, Freshh, Funandtrvl, GrahamHardy, Guppylover5, Halls4521, HarryC15, Hchanggt, HrZ, Hullaballoo Wolfowitz, InfamousPrince, Invisiboy42293, J Greb, JAR88, Jayunderscorezero, Jdrew1516, Jedi94, Johncharlesfreelance, Johnlongbond, JonathanDP81, Jvcdude, KConWiki, Klow, Lacon432, Leszek Jańczuk, Lg16spears, LilHelpa, MASLEGOMan, Makeemlighter, Martarius, Matt FJ, Miceagol, Mike Rosoft, Millahnna, Mjrmtg, Multivariable, NBbeauty, NJZombie, Nightscream, Nihonjoe, Num1dgen, OMGimgettinblackops2day, OldWestDoc, Philip Trueman, Rdunn, Rich Farmbrough, SGM-Slayer, SQGibbon, SkeeterVT, Skier Dude, Slasher-fun, Slipperyweasel, Soangry, Sreejithk2000, Steam5, TaerkastUA, Takemetothemalltongith, TazDev00, Tbrittreid, Teemeah, Telecomtom, Tenebrae, The News Hound, TheRealFennShysa, Theburn77, Themoodyblue, Time keeper 10, Tinman44, Tredmen88, Treybien, Trivialist, Turian, Versedi, Waltshep, WesleyDodds, Wildroot, Willgee, William hittle, Yobol, YokoIrl, Yworo, Zzyzx11, Тунгелов, 319 anonymous edits

Paul (film) *Source*: http://en.wikipedia.org/w/index.php?oldid=409185140 *Contributors*: AmericanMovieBuff, Bob Castle, Bovineboy2008, Ccacsmss, Crimsonvipor, DepressedPer, Djbj16, Donald McKinney, E. Ripley, Erik, Floydgeo, FrankRizzo2006, Friparvus, Gabrasca, Geoff B, GroovyandPears, JForget, Jedd the Jedi, JoeLoeb, Klow, Kuralyov, MER-C, Martarius, Materialscientist, Mpejko, NBbeauty, Prolog, Quentin X, Reaper Eternal, RoadTrain, Sandhritha, Shaunthered, ShelfSkewed, Silent Tom, Sreejithk2000, SummerPhD, Svick, The Giant Puffin, TheFeds, Thegreat100, Treybien, Trogga, Yoshiboy998, Себульба, 120 anonymous edits

Kung Fu Panda 2 *Source*: http://en.wikipedia.org/w/index.php?oldid=409553535 *Contributors*: A&ofan75, Addict 2006, Airplaneman, Alshaheen15, Angie Y., Anon e Mouse Jr., Asian.piano.dude, Bencey, BetoCG, Bfern8788, Boing! said Zebedee, Bold Clone, Bovineboy2008, Califajo002, Ceauntay59, Cerebral11, Chao200, Cineplex, Cirt, Clocks22, Courcelles, Dale Arnett, Derild4921, Discospinster, Donlammers, Exrain, Exxolon, FMAFan1990, Fernando2343, Fnlayson, Forteblast, Freshh, GD 6041, Ged UK, Ghostexorcist, Glane23, Gordan3194, Green Sheet, Gregshack, Hadinho, HelloAnnyong, Homey104, Inmblueversion, InfamousPrince, J Greb, Jadolfo, Jagged 85, Jhenderson777, Kakorot84, Kchishol1970, Kedadi, Kidmann, Konczewski, L Kensington, Laqbn, LilHelpa, Logan, Majorclanger, Mayaralp, McDoobAU93, Mhking, MikeAllen, Mingwei.Samuel, Miyagawa, NBbeauty, Noclador, Nymf, Paul Erik, Pedro thy master, Philip Trueman, Reavus, RugratsFan2, Secret Saturdays, Shadow Carrot, Shadowjams, Sjö, SkyWalker, Soetermans, Spidey104, SpikeJones, SpongeSebastian, Stroppolo, TarsTarkas19, Tbhotch, ThaddeusB, The Editor 155, The Movie King!, The Rogue Penguin, TheIblisTrigger, TheValentineBros, Tide rolls, Timotheus Canens, Tlsonic214, Tyevco10, Uncle Dick, Upgrader1, Vilnisr, Wayne Slam, Yankeeman237, IradeninKuvveti, 627 anonymous edits

Live With It *Source*: http://en.wikipedia.org/w/index.php?oldid=380754347 *Contributors*: 97198, Bencey, Bonadea, Bovineboy2008, Donmike10, GroovyandPears, Joaquin008, LtMuldoon, Matt Heard, Mohkalb, OOODDD, Socerizard, Surv1v4l1st, The Editor 155, Wool Mintons, 18 anonymous edits

Image Sources, Licenses and Contributors

File:SethRogen 7 2007.JPG *Source*: http://en.wikipedia.org/w/index.php?title=File:SethRogen_7_2007.JPG *License*: GNU Free Documentation License *Contributors*: Original uploader was Philkon at en.wikipedia

Image:Tambor and Rogen at Comic-Con.jpg *Source*: http://en.wikipedia.org/w/index.php?title=File:Tambor_and_Rogen_at_Comic-Con.jpg *License*: Creative Commons Attribution-Sharealike 2.0 *Contributors*: Ronald Woan

File:Freaks and Geeks.jpg *Source*: http://en.wikipedia.org/w/index.php?title=File:Freaks_and_Geeks.jpg *License*: unknown *Contributors*: Drovethrughosts, Iam4Lost

File:Undeclared intertitle.jpg *Source*: http://en.wikipedia.org/w/index.php?title=File:Undeclared_intertitle.jpg *License*: unknown *Contributors*: Drovethrughosts

File:Undeclared DVD.jpg *Source*: http://en.wikipedia.org/w/index.php?title=File:Undeclared_DVD.jpg *License*: unknown *Contributors*: Drovethrughosts, Iam4Lost

File:Donnie Darko poster.jpg *Source*: http://en.wikipedia.org/w/index.php?title=File:Donnie_Darko_poster.jpg *License*: unknown *Contributors*: Anakin101, Braghis, Byoudou, Chilifix, Dfranks078, Fastily, Haseo9999, Kollision, M4, Nehrams2020, Quentin X, Richard Arthur Norton (1958-), Sfan00 IMG, Skier Dude, Stezton, TheDJ, 5 anonymous edits

File:Dawsons creek credits.jpg *Source*: http://en.wikipedia.org/w/index.php?title=File:Dawsons_creek_credits.jpg *License*: unknown *Contributors*: Noboyo, Preppyboy9016

File:Dawson-katie.jpg *Source*: http://en.wikipedia.org/w/index.php?title=File:Dawson-katie.jpg *License*: unknown *Contributors*: Esteffect, Noboyo, Stan Shebs

File:Flag of Albania.svg *Source*: http://en.wikipedia.org/w/index.php?title=File:Flag_of_Albania.svg *License*: Public Domain *Contributors*: User:Dbenbenn

File:Flag of Australia.svg *Source*: http://en.wikipedia.org/w/index.php?title=File:Flag_of_Australia.svg *License*: Public Domain *Contributors*: Ian Fieggen

File:Flag of Austria.svg *Source*: http://en.wikipedia.org/w/index.php?title=File:Flag_of_Austria.svg *License*: Public Domain *Contributors*: User:SKopp

File:Flag of Belgium (civil).svg *Source*: http://en.wikipedia.org/w/index.php?title=File:Flag_of_Belgium_(civil).svg *License*: Public Domain *Contributors*: Bean49, David Descamps, Dbenbenn, Denelson83, Fry1989, Howcome, Ms2ger, Nightstallion, Oreo Priest, Rocket000, Sir Iain, ThomasPusch, Warddr, Zscout370, 4 anonymous edits

File:Flag of Brazil.svg *Source*: http://en.wikipedia.org/w/index.php?title=File:Flag_of_Brazil.svg *License*: Public Domain *Contributors*: Brazilian Government

File:Flag of Bulgaria.svg *Source*: http://en.wikipedia.org/w/index.php?title=File:Flag_of_Bulgaria.svg *License*: Public Domain *Contributors*: Avala, Denelson83, Fry1989, Homo lupus, Ikonact, Kallerna, Klemen Kocjancic, Martyr, Mattes, Neq00, Pumbaa80, SKopp, Scroch, Serjio-pt, Spacebirdy, Srtxg, Ultratomio, Vonvon, Zscout370, 9 anonymous edits

File:Flag of Canada.svg *Source*: http://en.wikipedia.org/w/index.php?title=File:Flag_of_Canada.svg *License*: Public Domain *Contributors*: User:E Pluribus Anthony, User:Mzajac

File:Flag of Chile.svg *Source*: http://en.wikipedia.org/w/index.php?title=File:Flag_of_Chile.svg *License*: Public Domain *Contributors*: User:SKopp

File:Flag of Croatia.svg *Source*: http://en.wikipedia.org/w/index.php?title=File:Flag_of_Croatia.svg *License*: Public Domain *Contributors*: AnyFile, Argo Navis, Denelson83, Denniss, Dijxtra, Klemen Kocjancic, Kseferovic, Minestrone, Multichill, Neoneo13, Nightstallion, O, PatríciaR, Platonides, R-41, Rainman, Reisio, Rocket000, Suradnik13, Zicera, ZooFari, Zscout370, 5 anonymous edits

File:Flag of Cuba.svg *Source*: http://en.wikipedia.org/w/index.php?title=File:Flag_of_Cuba.svg *License*: Public Domain *Contributors*: see below

File:Flag of the Czech Republic.svg *Source*: http://en.wikipedia.org/w/index.php?title=File:Flag_of_the_Czech_Republic.svg *License*: Public Domain *Contributors*: special commission (of code): SVG version by cs:-xfi-. Colors according to Appendix No. 3 of czech legal Act 3/1993. cs:Zirland.

File:Flag of Denmark.svg *Source*: http://en.wikipedia.org/w/index.php?title=File:Flag_of_Denmark.svg *License*: Public Domain *Contributors*: User:Madden

File:Flag of France.svg *Source*: http://en.wikipedia.org/w/index.php?title=File:Flag_of_France.svg *License*: Public Domain *Contributors*: User:SKopp, User:SKopp, User:SKopp, User:SKopp, User:SKopp, User:SKopp

File:Flag of Germany.svg *Source*: http://en.wikipedia.org/w/index.php?title=File:Flag_of_Germany.svg *License*: Public Domain *Contributors*: User:Madden, User:Pumbaa80, User:SKopp

File:Flag of Greece.svg *Source*: http://en.wikipedia.org/w/index.php?title=File:Flag_of_Greece.svg *License*: Public Domain *Contributors*: (of code) (talk)

File:Flag of Hungary.svg *Source*: http://en.wikipedia.org/w/index.php?title=File:Flag_of_Hungary.svg *License*: Public Domain *Contributors*: User:SKopp

File:Flag of India.svg *Source*: http://en.wikipedia.org/w/index.php?title=File:Flag_of_India.svg *License*: Public Domain *Contributors*: User:SKopp

File:Flag of Indonesia.svg *Source*: http://en.wikipedia.org/w/index.php?title=File:Flag_of_Indonesia.svg *License*: Public Domain *Contributors*: User:Gabbe, User:SKopp

File:Flag of Ireland.svg *Source*: http://en.wikipedia.org/w/index.php?title=File:Flag_of_Ireland.svg *License*: Public Domain *Contributors*: User:SKopp

File:Flag of Israel.svg *Source*: http://en.wikipedia.org/w/index.php?title=File:Flag_of_Israel.svg *License*: Public Domain *Contributors*: AnonMoos, Bastique, Bobika, Brown spite, Captain Zizi, Cerveaugenie, Drork, Etams, Fred J, Fry1989, Geagea, Himasaram, Homo lupus, Humus sapiens, Klemen Kocjancic, Kookaburra, Luispihormiguero, Madden, Neq00, NielsF, Nightstallion, Oren neu dag, Patstuart, PeeJay2K3, Pumbaa80, Ramiy, Reisio, SKopp, Technion, Typhix, Valentinian, Yellow up, Zscout370, 31 anonymous edits

File:Flag of Italy.svg *Source*: http://en.wikipedia.org/w/index.php?title=File:Flag_of_Italy.svg *License*: Public Domain *Contributors*: see below

File:Flag of Lithuania.svg *Source*: http://en.wikipedia.org/w/index.php?title=File:Flag_of_Lithuania.svg *License*: Public Domain *Contributors*: User:SKopp

File:Flag of Malaysia.svg *Source*: http://en.wikipedia.org/w/index.php?title=File:Flag_of_Malaysia.svg *License*: Public Domain *Contributors*: User:SKopp

File:Flag of Malta.svg *Source*: http://en.wikipedia.org/w/index.php?title=File:Flag_of_Malta.svg *License*: Public Domain *Contributors*: Fry1989, Gabbe, Homo lupus, Klemen Kocjancic, Liftarn, Mattes, Nightstallion, Peeperman, Pumbaa80, Ratatosk, Zscout370, 2 anonymous edits

File:Flag of Mexico.svg *Source*: http://en.wikipedia.org/w/index.php?title=File:Flag_of_Mexico.svg *License*: Public Domain *Contributors*: User:AlexCovarrubias

File:Flag of the Netherlands.svg *Source*: http://en.wikipedia.org/w/index.php?title=File:Flag_of_the_Netherlands.svg *License*: Public Domain *Contributors*: User:Zscout370

File:Flag of New Zealand.svg *Source*: http://en.wikipedia.org/w/index.php?title=File:Flag_of_New_Zealand.svg *License*: Public Domain *Contributors*: Adambro, Arria Belli, Bawolff, Bjankuloski06en, ButterStick, Denelson83, Donk, Duduziq, EugeneZelenko, Fred J, Fry1989, Hugh Jass, Ibagli, Jusjih, Klemen Kocjancic, Mamndassan, Mattes, Nightstallion, O, Peeperman, Poromiami, Reisio, Rfc1394, Shizhao, Tabasco, Transparent Blue, Väsk, Xufanc, Zscout370, 35 anonymous edits

File:Flag of Norway.svg *Source*: http://en.wikipedia.org/w/index.php?title=File:Flag_of_Norway.svg *License*: Public Domain *Contributors*: User:Dbenbenn

File:Flag of Panama.svg *Source*: http://en.wikipedia.org/w/index.php?title=File:Flag_of_Panama.svg *License*: Public Domain *Contributors*: -xfi-, Addicted04, Duduziq, Fadi the philologer, Fry1989, Klemen Kocjancic, Liftarn, Mattes, Nightstallion, Ninane, Pumbaa80, Reisio, Rfc1394, Thomas81, ThomasPusch, Zscout370, Фёдор Гусляров, 17 anonymous edits

File:Flag of Peru.svg *Source*: http://en.wikipedia.org/w/index.php?title=File:Flag_of_Peru.svg *License*: Public Domain *Contributors*: User:Dbenbenn

File:Flag of the Philippines.svg *Source*: http://en.wikipedia.org/w/index.php?title=File:Flag_of_the_Philippines.svg *License*: Public Domain *Contributors*: Aira Cutamora

File:Flag of Poland.svg *Source*: http://en.wikipedia.org/w/index.php?title=File:Flag_of_Poland.svg *License*: Public Domain *Contributors*: User:Mareklug, User:Wanted

File:Flag of Portugal.svg *Source*: http://en.wikipedia.org/w/index.php?title=File:Flag_of_Portugal.svg *License*: Public Domain *Contributors*: User:Nightstallion

File:Flag of Romania.svg *Source*: http://en.wikipedia.org/w/index.php?title=File:Flag_of_Romania.svg *License*: Public Domain *Contributors*: User:AdiJapan

File:Flag of Saudi Arabia.svg *Source*: http://en.wikipedia.org/w/index.php?title=File:Flag_of_Saudi_Arabia.svg *License*: Public Domain *Contributors*: Unknown

File:Flag of Serbia.svg *Source*: http://en.wikipedia.org/w/index.php?title=File:Flag_of_Serbia.svg *License*: Public Domain *Contributors*: ABF, Avala, B1mbo, Denelson83, EDUCA33E, Fry1989, Herbythyme, Homo lupus, Imbris, Mormegil, Nightstallion, Nikola Smolenski, Nuno Gabriel Cabral, Odder, R-41, Rainman, Rokerismoravee, Sasa Stefanovic, Siebrand, ThomasPusch, Túrelio, Zscout370, 7 anonymous edits

File:Flag of South Korea.svg *Source*: http://en.wikipedia.org/w/index.php?title=File:Flag_of_South_Korea.svg *License*: Public Domain *Contributors*: Various

File:Flag of Spain.svg *Source*: http://en.wikipedia.org/w/index.php?title=File:Flag_of_Spain.svg *License*: Public Domain *Contributors*: Pedro A. Gracia Fajardo, escudo de Manual de Imagen Institucional de la Administración General del Estado

File:Flag of Sri Lanka.svg *Source*: http://en.wikipedia.org/w/index.php?title=File:Flag_of_Sri_Lanka.svg *License*: Public Domain *Contributors*: Zscout370

File:Flag of Switzerland.svg *Source*: http://en.wikipedia.org/w/index.php?title=File:Flag_of_Switzerland.svg *License*: Public Domain *Contributors*: User:-xfi-, User:Marc Mongenet, User:Zscout370

File:Flag of Thailand.svg *Source*: http://en.wikipedia.org/w/index.php?title=File:Flag_of_Thailand.svg *License*: Public Domain *Contributors*: Andy Dingley, Chaddy, Duduziq, Emerentia, Fry1989, Gabbe, Gurch, Homo lupus, Juiced lemon, Klemen Kocjancic, Mattes, Neq00, Paul 012, Rugby471, Sahapon-krit hellokitty, TOR, Teetaweepo, Xiengyod, Zscout370, Δ, 23 anonymous edits

File:Flag of Turkey.svg *Source*: http://en.wikipedia.org/w/index.php?title=File:Flag_of_Turkey.svg *License*: Public Domain *Contributors*: User:Dbenbenn

File:Flag of Ukraine.svg *Source*: http://en.wikipedia.org/w/index.php?title=File:Flag_of_Ukraine.svg *License*: Public Domain *Contributors*: User:Jon Harald Søby, User:Zscout370

File:Flag of the United Kingdom.svg *Source*: http://en.wikipedia.org/w/index.php?title=File:Flag_of_the_United_Kingdom.svg *License*: Public Domain *Contributors*: User:Zscout370

License

Printed in Great Britain
by Amazon.co.uk, Ltd.,
Marston Gate.